Building Equitable Access to Knowledge Through Open Access Repositories

Nikos Koutras
University of Antwerp, Belgium

A volume in the Advances in Library and Information Science (ALIS) Book Series

Published in the United States of America by
IGI Global
Information Science Reference (an imprint of IGI Global)
701 E. Chocolate Avenue
Hershey PA, USA 17033
Tel: 717-533-8845
Fax: 717-533-8661
E-mail: cust@igi-global.com
Web site: http://www.igi-global.com

Library of Congress Cataloging-in-Publication Data

Names: Koutras, Nikos, 1983- author.
Title: Building equitable access to knowledge through open access repositories / by Nikos Koutras.
Description: Hershey, PA : Information Science Reference, [2020] | Includes bibliographical references and index. | Summary: "This book argues that open access repositories have the potential to provide an equilibrium among the interests of authors, publishers, and users of scientific publications and online published works"-- Provided by publisher.
Identifiers: LCCN 2019025546 (print) | LCCN 2019025547 (ebook) | ISBN 9781799811312 (hardcover) | ISBN 9781799811329 (paperback) | ISBN 9781799811336 (ebook)
Subjects: LCSH: Open access publishing. | Open access publishing--European Union countries. | Institutional repositories. | Institutional repositories--European Union countries. | Copyright--Electronic information resources.
Classification: LCC Z286.O63 .K68 2020 (print) | LCC Z286.O63 (ebook) | DDC 070.5/7973--dc23
LC record available at https://lccn.loc.gov/2019025546
LC ebook record available at https://lccn.loc.gov/2019025547
This book is published in the IGI Global book series Advances in Library and Information Science (ALIS) (ISSN: 2326-4136; eISSN: 2326-4144)

British Cataloguing in Publication Data
A Cataloguing in Publication record for this book is available from the British Library.

Advances in Library and Information Science (ALIS) Book Series

ISSN:2326-4136
EISSN:2326-4144

Editor-in-Chief: Alfonso Ippolito, Sapienza University-Rome, Italy & Carlo Inglese, Sapienza University-Rome, Italy

MISSION

The **Advances in Library and Information Science (ALIS) Book Series** is comprised of high quality, research-oriented publications on the continuing developments and trends affecting the public, school, and academic fields, as well as specialized libraries and librarians globally. These discussions on professional and organizational considerations in library and information resource development and management assist in showcasing the latest methodologies and tools in the field.

The **ALIS Book Series** aims to expand the body of library science literature by covering a wide range of topics affecting the profession and field at large. The series also seeks to provide readers with an essential resource for uncovering the latest research in library and information science management, development, and technologies.

COVERAGE

- Library Budgets in Times of Recession
- Partnerships in Library Communities
- E-Books in Libraries
- Cases on Library Management
- Digital Literacy
- Free Online Resources
- Knowledge Management Learning (Course) Management Software
- Gaming in Libraries
- Academic Libraries in the Digital Age
- Blogging in Libraries

IGI Global is currently accepting manuscripts for publication within this series. To submit a proposal for a volume in this series, please contact our Acquisition Editors at Acquisitions@igi-global.com or visit: http://www.igi-global.com/publish/.

The Advances in Library and Information Science (ALIS) Book Series (ISSN 2326-4136) is published by IGI Global, 701 E. Chocolate Avenue, Hershey, PA 17033-1240, USA, www.igi-global.com. This series is composed of titles available for purchase individually; each title is edited to be contextually exclusive from any other title within the series. For pricing and ordering information please visit http://www.igi-global.com/book-series/advances-library-information-science/73002. Postmaster: Send all address changes to above address.

Titles in this Series

For a list of additional titles in this series, please visit:
https://www.igi-global.com/book-series/advances-library-information-science/73002

Critical Approaches to Information Retrieval Research
Muhammad Sarfraz (Kuwait University, Kuwait)
Information Science Reference • ©2020 • 400pp • H/C (ISBN: 9781799810216) • US $195.00

Handbook of Research on Digital Devices for Inclusivity and Engagement in Libraries
Adeyinka Tella (University of Ilorin, Nigeria)
Information Science Reference • ©2020 • 491pp • H/C (ISBN: 9781522590347) • US $265.00

Research Data Access and Management in Modern Libraries
Raj Kumar Bhardwaj (University of Delhi, India) and Paul Banks (The Royal Society of Medicine, UK)
Information Science Reference • ©2019 • 418pp • H/C (ISBN: 9781522584377) • US $195.00

Handbook of Research on Transdisciplinary Knowledge Generation
Victor X. Wang (Liberty University, USA)
Information Science Reference • ©2019 • 475pp • H/C (ISBN: 9781522595311) • US $285.00

Social Media for Communication and Instruction in Academic Libraries
Jennifer Joe (University of Toledo, USA) and Elisabeth Knight (Western Kentucky University, USA)
Information Science Reference • ©2019 • 319pp • H/C (ISBN: 9781522580973) • US $195.00

Enhancing the Role of ICT in Doctoral Research Processes
Kwong Nui Sim (Victoria University of Wellington, New Zealand)
Information Science Reference • ©2019 • 278pp • H/C (ISBN: 9781522570653) • US $185.00

Social Research Methodology and New Techniques in Analysis, Interpretation, and Writing
M. Rezaul Islam (University of Dhaka, Bangladesh & University of Malaya, Malaysia)
Information Science Reference • ©2019 • 320pp • H/C (ISBN: 9781522578970) • US $195.00

For an entire list of titles in this series, please visit:
https://www.igi-global.com/book-series/advances-library-information-science/73002

IGI Global
DISSEMINATOR OF KNOWLEDGE

701 East Chocolate Avenue, Hershey, PA 17033, USA
Tel: 717-533-8845 x100 • Fax: 717-533-8661
E-Mail: cust@igi-global.com • www.igi-global.com

Table of Contents

Foreword

This is an optimistic book. It is optimistic about open access to knowledge when there does not appear to be that much to be optimistic about. Monopoly and cartelism in publishing has always been a problem, the British Publishers Traditional Market Agreement of 1947 that was used by US and UK publishers to formalize their division of global markets being one prominent example. One of the promises of the digital age was that it would free us from copyright's private monopolies. Knowledge, represented electronically, could be moved around the globe at the speed of electrons. As the cost of technologies to move electrons came down, hopes rose for a truly universal freedom of access to knowledge. The words of the Budapest Open Access Initiative of 2002 spoke of a possible 'world-wide electronic distribution of the peer-reviewed journal literature and completely free and unrestricted access to it by all scientists, scholars, teachers, students, and other curious minds'.

In 2015 Larivière, Haustein, Mongeon published a paper under the title of 'The Oligopoly of Academic Publishers in the Digital Era'. Drawing on a dataset of around 44.5 million journals indexed in the period 1973-2013 they were able to show how four private publishers - Reed-Elsevier, Wiley-Blackwell, Springer, and Taylor & Francis - had in this period increased their capacity to extract monopoly rents from academic publishing. This period more than any other accelerated the transformation of academic publishing as an activity of learned societies into one dominated by multinational conglomerates and private capital.

These conglomerates have been able to use digital technologies to lower their own costs while using copyright to extract supranormal profits from the academic market. Of course, there is no academic market in any conventional sense of the word. Overwhelming, the costs of the discovery of new knowledge in university settings continue to be met by public tax dollars. The incentives for the production of new knowledge come not from its sale, but rather from a combination of the intrinsic excitement of the discovery process, peer recognition, promotion, wider community acknowledgement and an increase in reputational capital. And yet we live in a world where most academics upon having made a contribution to knowledge send it as a free stream of electrons to a publishing conglomerate which, through copyright law, will generally gain exclusive control or ownership of it and price it for various markets such as the library market, a single purchase by a member of the public, the anthology market, the translation market etc. It is hard to think of another extractive industry that enjoys this combination of free inputs and monopoly pricing power.

So, how does Nikos Koutras approach what is a profound problem, profound because a world that allows publicly-generated knowledge to be privately taxed restricts the freedom of many individuals to use knowledge. He explores how the use of a specific mechanism, the open access repository (OAR), might help advance the bigger goal of open access to knowledge. Before I read Nikos Koutras' work I had not thought much about the role of the OAR. I suspect that I am not alone in this. Among other things, Nikos Koutras carried out surveys in Greek Universities showing that some academics had only a vague understanding of OARs. One of the great strengths of this volume is its fine-grained investigation of how OARs actually work in specific national settings.

For me, the most important contribution of this book is the positive story it has to tell about the potential of OARs to contribute to the global public good ideal of knowledge. I had tended to think of OARs as isolated islands of limited access. But the picture that emerges from Nikos Koutras' work is much more organic and networked than I had realized. OARs have grown in number. Importantly, there is an association in the form of the Confederation of Open Access Repositories that is helping to build a network of OARs. Every social movement, every industry in our world has to have a collective networked agency through which to fight for the technical standards it needs to prosper.

So, on my reading of Nikos Koutras' work, OARs form one potentially hugely important strand of a possible response to the oligopoly structure of today's academic publishing market. In the end I think universities will have to form a monopsony network to contest the private monopoly power of today's academic publishing conglomerates. Public monopsony must counter private monopoly capital. Well run OARs could do much, as Nikos Koutras shows, to improve public access to knowledge. They could form part of a longer term strategy in which universities through their presses and disciplinary networks built an intellectual commons that shadowed the world of proprietary licensing packages, reducing the dependency of universities upon these packages. A monopsony university network might, under creative entrepreneurial leadership, aim to buy out the Elseviers of this world. Access to knowledge is too important to the future of citizens everywhere to be left in the hands of monopoly capitalists. OARs could be one of the building blocks of a very different kind of the future. We can thank Nikos Koutras for revealing how they can be much more than isolated islands.

Peter Drahos
European University Institute, Italy

Preface

In modern times a response to rapid technological evolution and relevant issues of intellectual protection that emerge is open access which constitutes a collection of possible conditions and solutions (for instance, those offered from Creative Commons licenses) under which the creator can protect his or her work and deliver free of charge reproduction of copyright works (Ayris, 2007). Identifying the attempts of trade companies that invest crucial resources in deploying new technology should not claim to neglect benefits of whole society. Hence, open access could be a tool of enhancement for copyright regime as social prosperity should be enabled since the benefits of society should have pros over specific material interests.

CHALLENGES TO BE TACKLED

- Intellectual property rights are a significant part of the regulatory environment appropriate to support economic development in the digital age. Illustrations of growth as regards production are strongly related to investments in information technology advances (posts in Facebook, 'tweets' in Tweeter, creating and uploading videos in YouTube and so forth) (Anderson, 2004).
- Furthermore, intellectual property rights correlate with the extent to which such technology-driven goods and services are disseminated throughout the economy. Thus, by granting property rights in the fruits of innovative and creative endeavors has long been policy instrument of choice to accomplish these objectives.
- Information technology developments determine a basic contributor to economic growth

Given this, open access practice could play a crucial role in the context of information technology progress. Therefore, it should be considered as an instrument towards dissemination of information resources which are distinguished by exclusive ownership. This book pursues to give a comprehensive approach to the concept of open access practice, its foundations and current status. In addition, it anticipates answering questions relevant with current implementation process and examples from Europe as well as Greece. The book argues that open access repositories have a potential to provide an equilibrium among the interests of authors, publishers and users of scientific publications and online published works.

The book is organized into six chapters. A brief description of each of the chapters follows:

CHAPTER 1

The first chapter is divided into six parts. The first part sets up the background context which is going to be discussed in following chapters. In part two, the basic argument and associated research questions are articulated. In part three, there is consideration of the theoretical background. In part four, a brief analysis of regulatory models for open access repositories is undertaken. In part five, a preliminary literature review and justifications for and against open access practice are addressed. The last part discusses about the research methodology applied.

CHAPTER 2

In order to understand the significance of open access repositories it is necessary to know the context of the debate. Therefore, it is required to trace the historical development of the concept of copyright as a property right (Atkinson & Fitzgerald, 2014). The continued relevance of the rationales for copyright interests, both philosophical and pragmatic, will be assessed in the contemporary times of digital publishing. It will then canvas the reasons or explanations for the rise of the concept of open access practice and includes a brief analysis of the effect of online revolution on the conventional publishing methods.

CHAPTER 3

In the light of previous discussion in this chapter there is examination of open access practice as an instrument of social justice and social cohesion towards the enhancement of copyright regime. The discussion in this chapter relies on two basic justifications (i.e. philosophical and pragmatic justification that argues about equal opportunities for information access). Habermas' ideas explain how genuine consensus can be achieved in modern complex societies, but the core requirement is that everybody is equally able to participate in creating consensus in civil society. It is this requirement of equality of participation that links back to the kind of equality that should be pre-supposed in theories of justice (Habermas, 2015). As argued above Rawls' theory of distributive justice helps me to create a theoretical foundation for my argument that a cohesive society requires involvement of well-informed citizens or in other words, active citizens (Rawls, 2009). It is in this respect that access to knowledge is an important resource and it should be available to all.

Open access repositories are one form of resource that can function as a contemporary response in the digital age. Therefore, they should be integrated in the current copyright regulations. They can thus help increase access opportunities equally as well as offer protection in creative content that the traditional copyright law is increasingly unable to do. Additionally, this chapter provides the theoretical framework about the interplay of open access with public policy objectives that could lead to better social cohesion.

CHAPTER 4

In this chapter the objective is to analyze the design and assumptions underlying thc open access framework in the European Union (Ayris, 2007). Based on this information follows analysis of the strengths and shortcomings of the European regulations in relation to open access, sharing information and protection of intellectual property among European member states. This helps to examine strategies that aim to foster open access of scientific data and ask whether, and how these policies are monitored and enforced.

Recently, 2015, the press release by the European Commission stresses the significance of access to online content and outlines its vision to modernize European copyright regulations (European Commission, 2015). Based on this press release the overarching objective of the European Commission regarding intellectual protection is to modify copyright rules to fit the digital age, accordingly. Additionally, this press release shows that the European Commission outlines its vision of a modern European copyright framework. This political preview can be translated into legislative proposals and policy initiatives in the future, considering all inputs from several public consultations. Overall, the European Commission wants to make sure that Europeans can access a wide legal offer of content, while ensuring that authors and other rights holders are better protected and remunerated. The key sectors of education, culture, research and innovation will also benefit from a more modern and European framework. It follows that open access practice should be integrated to forthcoming European Directives about intellectual property law.

Examination of open access growth in Europe determines how crucial is the role of open access repositories to disseminate information and improve European citizens' assets (European Research Council, 2006). Moreover, such examination clarifies that the relevant regime for the governance of open access repositories is also important. In the European context, open access practice can demonstrate an important factor for trade, improvement of negotiations in industry and exchange of information resources that potentially can lead towards development, innovation and new knowledge. Thus, gradually collaboration among European countries emerge. Such collaboration can facilitate the access to information resources via European agreements, policies and initiatives addressed in this chapter.

CHAPTER 5

This chapter examines the relevant governance framework for open access repositories in Greece as European case study distinguished by bilateral agreements where open access and sharing of information should form crucial components (Georgiou & Papadatou, 2010). Early work by Crow suggested that institutional repositories could be seen as contributing factors in 'a new disaggregated model' of scholarly publishing, one that may help to weaken the monopolistic power of the traditional academic journal system over scholarly communication. Through developing and maintaining 'institutionally defined', 'scholarly', 'cumulative and perpetual', and 'open and interoperable' repositories, institutions can increase their visibility and prestige by centralizing the intellectual work of their members, thus enabling researchers to find relevant materials more easily.

CHAPTER 6

The last chapter discusses about international perspectives and expectations for open access from the view of modern publishing enterprise in the context of the globalizing world. There is also discussion about whether open access practice can be embraced and not only tolerated by public or private institutions. Because of the rapid growth of internet, our needs for distributing information and communicating have shifted dramatically. Open access determines one of the distinctive manifestations of modern technological developments primarily for publishing and therefore its aspects were examined. The chapter argues that open access publishing is one of the effective outcomes that stems from the concept of open access which is originated from the continuous technological developments and the new digital platforms. Thus, it is realized that current copyright regimes should be reformed, and consequently printing policies implemented from commercial publishers ought to change appropriately. To sum up, the previous statement clarifies that there is need for coexistence of copyright laws and open access in the light of publishing procedure, effectively.

REFERENCES

Atkinson, B., & Fitzgerald, B. (2014). *A Short History of Copyright: The Genie of Information*. Springer Science & Business Media. doi:10.1007/978-3-319-02075-4

Ayris, P. (2007, August 9). Embedding Open Access into the European Landscape – the Contribution of LIBER. *LIBER Quarterly*, *17*(2). doi:10.18352/lq.7876

European Commission. (2015). *Towards a Modern, More European Copyright Framework*. Retrieved from http://ec.europa.eu/newsroom/dae/document.cfm?action=display&doc_id=12526

European Research Council. (2006). *ERC Scientific Council Statement on Open Access*. Retrieved from https://erc.europa.eu/sites/default/files/press_release/files/erc_scc_statement_2006_open_access_0.pdf

Georgiou, P., & Papadatou, F. (2010). Open Access in Greece. *Open Access in Southern European Countries*, 39–62. Retrieved from http://www.researchgate.net/post/Open_Access_in_Southern_European_Countries

Habermas, J. (2015). *Between Facts and Norms: Contributions to a Discourse Theory of Law and Democracy*. John Wiley & Sons.

Rawls, J. (2009). *A Theory of Justice*. Harvard University Press.

Chapter 1
Introduction:
The Background of Discussion

ABSTRACT

This chapter is divided into seven parts. In part one, the background context of the thesis is discussed briefly. In the following part, the thesis argument and research questions are articulated. There is examination of the theoretical background in part three. Part four briefly analyses regulatory models for OARs. In part five, a preliminary literature review and justifications for and against OA practices are addressed. Part six determines the methodology applied and the last part explains the thesis plan.

INTRODUCTION

Continuous technological growth is one of the defining features of present times, and it gives rise to new situations in publishing. Because of the rapid growth of the Internet, our modes of and needs for distributing information and communicating have shifted dramatically. The example of five open access principles released in September 2017 by the Association of European Research Libraries (Ligue des Bibliotheques Europeennes de Recherche [LIBER]; Ayris, 2007, 2011) concerning negotiations with publishers can be considered as an agreement with potentials to balance open access and copyright. According to these principles, research libraries are encouraged to make the move from paying for information access to organizing the publishing costs for their researchers. In addition, this example highlights the change of

DOI: 10.4018/978-1-7998-1131-2.ch001

policy that should be applied on behalf of libraries to enhance information distribution. Such a change could be achieved via open access (OA). One of the distinctive manifestations of technological developments OA primarily for digital publishing and distribution of such published works. However, the relatively wider access to online published works and the related ease of replicating the original creations come into conflict with the copyright protection regimes.

In such a context, a critical question that needs to be addressed is whether open access repositories (OARs) can work as a mechanism to enhance current copyright regulations. It will be argued in this thesis that OARs can provide an equilibrium among the interests of authors, publishers, and users of online published works.

The following chapter contains seven parts. In part one, the background context of the thesis is discussed briefly. In part two, the central argument and associated research questions are articulated. In part three, there is consideration of the theoretical background. In part four, a brief analysis of regulatory models for OARs will be undertaken. In part five, a preliminary literature review and justifications for and against OA practices are addressed. Part six is the methodology section, and the last part explains the plan of the thesis.

BACKGROUND

The OARs are digital document servers with archived information resources that usually operate in the context of higher education or research institutions in which scientific and scholarly information is deposited and made accessible worldwide and free of charge. Documents made publicly available via a repository are frequently also formally published by a publisher; for example, in a journal or edited volume or as a monograph. In contrast to publishing a work in an OA journal, for example, open content licenses are of secondary importance when a work is deposited in an OAR. This is because scholars and scientists who self-archive their work in a repository, which is also known as green open access publishing (OAP), have, in addition to formal publication, often transferred exclusive rights of use in the published work to the publisher and are not, therefore, entitled to make it available under an open content license.

The overarching objective for OARs is to provide OA to the institution's research output. In addition, the OARs are now run by a great number of research universities and research institutions (Haug et al., 2013; Mathelier et al., 2014, Bloom, Ganley, & Winkler, 2014; Lasko, 2014). This fact indicates that they are gradually gaining ground in the scientific and research communities Ebrahim, 2017). For example, universities that host an OAR can deposit any research papers that are required to be freely available. In turn, this provides online in a free-to-view mode a substantive part of the research produced in universities. The contents of OARs are indexed by WWW search engines (e.g., Google and Google Scholar). Therefore, OARs can help to maximise the visibility and impact of research outputs.

There are a few issues still to be resolved concerning OARS in relation to institutional repositories, though the associated advantages are clear. The OARs have the potential to improve the dissemination of scientific information. They can reduce access restrictions to content inherent in the subscription-based commercial publishing regime. To sum up, it is beneficial to make scholarly content openly available in a timely way to those who are interested in using a Web search engine, and the potential benefits of this are profound.

This thesis argues for a beneficial governance framework for OARs that balances the interests of publishers and the users of content. There are several pragmatic and philosophical reasons for arguing this. The nature of publishing has changed since the Internet age and the digital revolution. This technological evolution brings new circumstances, such as digital platforms and online databases related to both social media and academia. For instance, e-databases in all academic disciplines and YouTube, Facebook and Twitter (see also Burgess & Green 2013; Dwyer, Hiltz, & Passerini, 2007; and Saakaky, Okazaki, Matsuo, 2010). In particular, social media platforms offer incentives that make it easy to become creators or authors. Therefore, it can be stated that intangible aspects such as thoughts, innovations, and intellectual creation, in general, bring dissimilar classes of content (such as digital archives). As a result, it can be stated that intellectual creation is undergoing a revolution in conjunction with new types of publishing resources and, thus, data can be more easily shared and disseminated nowadays. Moreover, the current copyright regime is beset by practical difficulties regarding the intellectual protection of online data. Hence, the ongoing technological evolution bombards the framework of copyright laws. It is for these reasons that there is an urgent need to consider how copyright regimes can be enhanced so that they can offer better intellectual protection in accord with the necessities of the digital age. At the same time, it is important that everyone can participate in the so-called knowledge revolution. Therefore, it is argued that social justice and social inclusion can be enhanced by making equitable access to knowledge available to all globally.

In recognition of the fact that creative endeavours should be supported and encouraged, it is necessary that OA should coexist with copyright regimes and constitute a productive way to preserve online data, as well as to share and disseminate information of digital resources. (Regarding Open Access, see also Suber, 2012).

THE CENTRAL ARGUMENT AND ISSUES TO BE EXAMINED

The central argument of this thesis is:

OARs can be an effective instrument of OA with the potential to balance author, publisher, and user interests concerning online published works.

To substantiate this argument, a number of related issues should be addressed and can be formulated as sub-questions. In particular:

1. To what extent does an examination of the history of the concept of private property help explain the emergence of intellectual property (IP)? A brief history of copyright, its growth and the phenomenon of OA will link the developments. To examine the relevance of these historical developments, the sub-research questions of this chapter will focus on the philosophical developments regarding the emergence of the concept of private property. It will allow me to examine when, why, and how copyright law first appeared. How did copyright as a concept change into the law of copyright? Put another way, how was it transformed into a legal concept? What was its role and significance? That is, it gave expression to the liberal notion of the subject as the possessor of rights, including property rights in things produced. What are the main economic justifications in relation to the role of IP rights? What relevant changes have taken place with the digital revolution? That is, anyone can publish online, there are difficulties in enforcing copyright rights

in the digital age, and so on. What are the explanations for the rise of OA and its implications for copyright law and rights?

2. Why is OA significant? What are the philosophical and pragmatic justifications for OA? Can OA operate as a tool to achieve greater social justice in society by facilitating more efficient and widespread dissemination of knowledge? To address these questions, a number of related issues will be addressed: What is the importance of social justice and relevant theories in the context? How can they be associated with OA practices? What is its importance in designing a governance framework? What are the arguments for the connections between OA and social justice—including the argument that it can facilitate greater social cohesion?
3. To what extent is the present governance framework of OARs in the European Union able to provide a model law for other nations to follow? To address this issue, the thesis will consider the design and assumptions underlying the European OA regime. Further questions are: What are the strengths and shortcomings of the European regulations in relation to OA, sharing information, and protection of IP among European Member States? This question will be answered by focusing on: What are the foundations of the European copyright framework? What are the European directives that show the importance of copyright protection? What is the current state of information accessibility among European Member States? Is there a European public policy in relation to the use and sharing of information through OARs? What are the European regulations that constitute the European Research Area (ERA)? This analysis will help me conclude that the governance framework of OARs in the European Union can better balance the interests of copyright owners and end users within the European continent.
4. A comparison of the Greek OA model and its efficacy in comparison with the European governance framework will help address the issue of whether and how the design of national and international regulations mutually influences each other. This will lead to an assessment of whether the Greek framework should be reformed to keep pace with continuous technological evolution and define more strictly the concept of OA for beneficial dissemination and spread of information. Therefore, several further issues that need to be answered are: (a) When and how was the concept of OA introduced in Greece? (b) What were the scholarly

discussions around the introduction of OARs in Greece? (c) Should the current framework of copyright protection in Greece be enhanced?

5. Can commercial publishers be expected to adopt OA practices? What are the arguments to encourage, or even compel, contemporary commercial publishers to integrate OA and OARs as part of their publishing policy to facilitate academic scholarly communication and the pursuit of knowledge? To answer this question, the sub-issues to be considered are: What are the influences of the publishing industry from the interrelation of globalisation with the Internet? Should the commercial publishers modify their publishing policies to integrate OA? Can OARs play the role of intermediator to balance commercial publisher and academic community interests?

Based on the analysis of the above issues, it will be argued that OARs can form a significant OA tool with a potential to both enhance copyright frameworks and further support the access to knowledge by wider sections of the global society. The thesis will culminate in recommendations to improve the regulatory framework of current copyright regimes. It will be proposed that the OARs should incorporate the "just" green standard of access, which in turn can improve the balance between copyright owners' and end users' interests.

In the following section, the connections between the issues identified will be elaborated.

THE THEORETICAL FRAMEWORK

A variety of different theoretical frameworks for the governance of IP law, including copyright law, have been developed by a diverse set of scholars. In this thesis, these frameworks will be analysed and integrated to construct an overarching theoretical rationale for the governance of OARs and their creation and operation supported through appropriate regulatory regimes. It is argued that access to information is a component of creating just societies and that copyright regimes can be modified without unduly burdening the publishers or authors. These reforms recognise the changes brought about by online publishing and aim to make OA to knowledge a reality for people globally. In this way, the human rights of everyone are advanced. It follows that an appropriate standard of OA has to be formulated.

To substantiate the claim that OA is important for a fair global society, the argumentation relies on a number of theoretical assumptions: (a) OA is important, as it constitutes wider access to knowledge; (b) since knowledge is power, a fair society should make access to knowledge widely available; thus, OA can be one means of creating social justice at a global scale. In addition, there are (c) practical reasons for supporting OA, but they must address (d) the opposition to OA in the name of protecting copyright interests.

The following specific theoretical issues will be examined in detail to set the context for the following substantive chapters.

Implications of the Digital Age: Towards Copyright Modification

The computer revolution has altered the practical landscape of copyright protection (Forman & Pufall, 2013). The digitization of copyrighted works has dramatically increased the efficiency of unauthorized copying (Feki, Kawsar, Boussard, & Trappeniers, 2013). Infringers can produce thousands of perfect copies of copyrighted works at little cost (Balganesh, 2013). The emergence and rapid proliferation of the Internet have compounded the issue extremely (Hampton, Livio, & Sessions Goulet, 2010). The Internet allows copyrighted material to be distributed instantaneously and globally (Gubbi, Buyya, Marusic, & Palaniswami, 2013). Copyright owners have attempted to combat these threats in numerous ways (Marshall & Frith, 2013). They have sued the providers and users of online file-sharing networks (McCourt & Burkart, 2003). And they have developed technological barriers to unauthorized copying (Nissenbaum, 2011). Indeed, technological developments are raising issues for copyright law related to digital storage and transmission of works. There is a variety of aspects to these technologies that have implications for copyright law as (a) the ease of reproduction; (b) the ease of dissemination; and (c) the ease of storage. These implications of the digital age justify that modification of the copyright law should be considered. Therefore, OA and its means (e.g., OARs) can be considered as additional support to enhance the framework of copyright protection in the digital age.

Access to Knowledge

There are theoretical arguments that interpret reasons as to why OA should be promoted. First, the notion of OA is a pillar of knowledge as it offers access to information, which, in turn, helps construct knowledge. In this context, access to information is a crucial factor for the knowledge economies of the future and fortified if, inter alia, OARs are given a fair chance of both development and of survival. The information revolution has given the best chance it will obtain for the enlargement of information accessibility. OARs can be a means to safeguard human rights for the future of developing and developed countries.

There are many advocates who argue that everyone has the right to knowledge. What is more, they also state that "[T]he call for change is being echoed by the academic community, which is asking for greater OA and the removal of economic barriers to science" (Demaio, Dorch, & Herch, 2012, para. 20). In "The Open Access to Knowledge (OAK) Law Project Report No. 1," the authors state that OA is fundamental for knowledge, and specifically that:

[T]he Report calls upon Australian research and funding institutions to consider their commitment to open access and articulate in clear policies and copyright management frameworks. The Report details a methodology for cataloguing and better understanding publishers' attitudes towards open access. (Fitzgerald et al., 2006, p. ii)

Therefore, it is evident that access to knowledge is a founding principle of any open society. New technologies bring new opportunities for knowledge creation and distribution, and OA is part of these types of shifts that stem from technological evolution.

Researchers are restricted from accessing available databases freely as publishers hold copyright over most published work. As indicated above, the discussion incorporates several issues that are interconnected and need to be addressed. First, the issue of the existence of copyright law and its historical development needs to be addressed. Finding answers to questions regarding when, why, and how copyright law first appeared will provide the necessary background context to the issue of assessing the desirability of

OARs. Is there a connection between the invention of the printing press and the development of the concept of copyright? What, if any, links can be drawn between the power of commercial interests of publishers, the governance elite, and copyright laws?

In light of the growth of the Internet and the profound shift regarding how information is shared, it is relevant to ask if the new regimes, such as OARs, constitute the way forward. With the arrival of digital publishing, there is a possibility that research works could be published online and without the help of commercial publishers. Otherwise, the research and higher education institutions bear the very high costs of accessing subscription journals. This is not an ideal solution, as will be argued later. Therefore, it is useful to explore how OA can be made feasible for both the creative content makers and the publishers. This is essential if "knowledge is power" is to be made possible.

Knowledge Is Power

Theoretical arguments about the nexus of knowledge and power are well known; in this regard, the work of Foucault and Habermas will form the basis for substantiating the claim that a just social world requires access to knowledge by everyone. Moreover, Habermas argues that the current vision of law achieves social integration, channelling political participation, and subordinating power to democratic purposes. Therefore, by relying on the philosophical views of these two thinkers, an argument justifying OA will be developed, as it offers the power of knowledge and can be used as an instrument for social justice to broaden social cohesion globally.

Social justice considerations require information be available to as many people as possible. Sharing of these benefits can be conducive to creating a more cohesive society. For this reason, the concepts of public policy, social cohesion, and social justice will be analysed in relation to the desirability of sharing information, while also protecting the interests of creators of content. It is well established that public policy can be considered a social phenomenon and, therefore, can be analysed under three different aspects: as a principle, as a procedure, and as a relation. Accordingly, public policy is crucial to simultaneously developing OARs as a form of social justice and enhancing social cohesion.

Therefore, the connections between necessary public policy and social justice to broaden social cohesion should be examined. It is already widely acknowledged that information accessibility is imperative, while the current copyright regimes afford overly broad protection in terms of the duration, works, and uses covered. Hence, the analysis needs to apply a theoretical framework to develop a standard concerning the balance of stakeholder interests based on a different type of license designation.

Practical Reasons Why Open Access Can Be Effective

Moreover, there are practical reasons why OA can be effective. David Proser, an eminent scholar, in his paper, "Institutional Repositories and Open Access: The Future of Scholarly Communication," argues that OA can provide a future for scholarly communication. He claims that "[w]e currently have an aggregated system for scholarly publishing whereby the journal fulfils four different and specific functions in one package." These functions are registration, certification (peer review), awareness (communications), and archiving. They have currently been packaged together in an aggregated system, but new technologies, notably the Internet, offer incentives for unlocking that system and devising new methods in which we can fulfil those functions.

In addition, it is argued that OARs can fulfil such functions as (a) there are national repositories among European Member States and in Greece; (b) they contain a great variety of materials, including pre-prints, working papers, published articles and student dissertations; (c) they are cumulative and perpetual and hence act as an archive; and (d) most significantly, they are interoperable, interactive and distinguished by OA. That means that different search machines are able to view the content of the OARs so that it is available to everyone who has Internet access and is seeking information. Additionally, a notable illustration concerning this issue is that the American Association for the Advancement of Science (AAAS) and others are reluctant to fully embrace OA and maximise the impact of publicly funded research. Hence, it can be considered missed opportunities for the world's largest general scientific society to lead the way in increasing access to information throughout the world (Tennant, 2014).

However, it is also a fact that the commercial publishers are trying to maintain their market share, and in doing so, they are adopting the language of OARs. Therefore, it is necessary to analyse how OA policy is used in different settings; for instance, by commercial publishers (such as BRILL and Wiley), by creative agents or even by developers of free software (such as ORACLE, Eclipse and Cnet) versus commercial companies like Microsoft and Apple. This analysis will allow me to develop a desirable model of OARs.

This theoretical frame will be relied upon to investigate the norms and forms endorsed as part of governmental policies regarding an effective governance framework for the OARs. The W3C Internet Group Note claims that:

[G]overnments have been striving since the late 1990s to find better ways to connect with their constituents via the Web. By putting government information online, and making it easily findable, readily available, accessible, understandable, and usable people can now interact with their government in ways never before imagined. (Alonso et al., n.d.)

This is an example of how governmental policies to adopt OA that allows wide distribution and sharing of information can work as an effective governance tool.

Another significant aspect of the theoretical framework concerns the current printing methods in conjunction with information sharing and dissemination. The theoretical issue is whether a suitable standard for OA can be devised. In this field, the well-known document is the Finch report (Finch, 2012, 2013). According to this report, several different channels for communicating research results are going to remain crucial for the next few years. A policy direction in the UK towards the support for gold OAP is recommended in this report. In the gold OA model, publishers receive their revenues from authors rather than readers, and so research articles become freely accessible to everyone immediately upon publication. Conversely, green OA means that scholars publish in copyrighted journals but retain the possibility of also publishing in an OA model (self-archiving, for example). The report suggests further extensions to current licensing arrangements in higher education, health and other sectors; improvements to the infrastructure of repositories; and support for the moves by publishers to provide access to the great majority of journals in public libraries. These recommendations will be assessed in view of the above theoretical framework, and a possible regulatory regime should emerge from the analysis.

Oppositions to Open Access

However, there also exist several arguments against OA, which include the following: (a) OA can be considered infringement of IP rights, (b) commercial profits and publication expenses, and (c) the fact that OA discourages further investments in technology. A discussion of these objections will enable me to further support the theoretical issue of the significance of OA.

Open Access as Constituting Infringement of IP Rights

It is evident that access to information of online databases may be considered as infringement of copyright, and the well-known Napster case is discussed to illustrate this fact (Merriden, 2001). In early 1999, Shawn Fanning, who was only 18 at the time, started developing a notion as he talked with friends concerning the obstacles to find the kind of MP3 files they were interested in. He thought that there should be a method to create a program that could combine three key functions in one. In addition, these functions included a search engine, file sharing and an Internet Relay Chat (IRC), which was a means of finding and chatting with other MP3 users while online. Fanning spent several months creating the code that would become the utility later know as Napster. Thus, Napster became a non-profit online music information trading program that became especially popular among college students who had access to high-speed Internet connections.

In April 2000, the heavy metal rock band Metallica sued the online music trading website of Napster for copyright infringement. Several universities were also named in this suit. Metallica argued that these universities violated Metallica's music copyrights by permitting their students to have free access via Napster and to trade songs illegally using university servers. Besides, a number of universities banned Napster prior to April 2000 out of concerns about potential copyright infringement and/or because traffic on the Internet was slowing down university servers. Yale University, which was named in the suit, instantly blocked student access to Napster. Further, Metallica argued that Napster facilitated illegal use of digital audio devices, which the group alleged was a violation of the Racketeering Influenced and Corrupt Organizations (RICO) Act, 18 U.S.C.§ 1961.

As a result, Napster responded that the fair use Act allows owners of compact discs to use them as they wish. Therefore, if an owner of the disc decides to copy into a computer file, he or she should be allowed to do so. If this file happens to be accessible on the Internet, then others can also access or download it without being guilty of a crime. Napster further stated that since it made no profit off the trades, it owed no money in royalties. The Ninth Circuit held that Napster's operation constituted copyright infringement (Molteni & Ordanini, 2003; Leyshon, Webb, French, Thrift, & Crewe, 2005).

This opposition to OA compels an urgent consideration of the issue of what comprises the appropriate reform of the current copyright regimes that can embrace the concept of OA.

Open Access as Inimical to Commercial Profits and Publication Expenses

Like everything in life, OA has disadvantages. One disadvantage of paramount importance concerns the reduction of publishers' benefits and publication costs. Since the end user does not have to pay to read an OA article, there should be someone that has to pay for relevant expenses concerning publication. In contemporary OA models, it is usually the author's responsibility to cover such costs. However, in times of austerity and funding cuts, this can discourage researchers from adopting OA. For instance, the global pricing consultancy Simon–Kucher & Partners say that it is difficult for everybody to continue enjoying free OA materials from the long-term perspective. Based on their recent survey, they suggest that in the next three years as much as 90% of online content will find itself behind a paywall (Lepitak, 2013).

In addition, a renowned scholar in this area, Willinsky, in his book, *The Access Principle: The Case for Open Access to Research and Scholarship*, traces the genesis of the OA movement in scholarly publishing since 2003. He claims that there were also significant shifts in relation to modern publishing enterprises since 2004. In particular, he argues that:

[T]he major corporate publishers of academic journals . . . had to blink in the midst of all the attention being paid to 'free' journals and access to knowledge . . . In May 2004, Reed Elsevier, the largest of them . . . changed its policies on its authors' rights. (Willinsky, 2009)

In accordance with the new policy framework, the authors of articles published in Elsevier journals are granted the right to post their own version (which is not Elsevier's published version) of the final manuscript in an OA e-print archive at their institution. Hence, the implications of this policy shift were significant for Elsevier authors and made clear that they were instantly in a position to give OA to all of the material published in Elsevier's journals.

Another significant policy shift was indicated in the practices of a major scholarly publisher, Springer Verlag. In June 2004, Springer already permitted its authors to post their versions of published articles in e-print archives, but it went on to introduce Springer Open Choice and was titled, "Your research. Your choice" (Springer, 2004). Authors of articles accepted for publication in a Springer journal can choose, for a fee of 3000 euros, to make their articles "freely available for anyone to read, download, or print," as Springer's website puts it. The shift of the printing press industry is towards embracing OA and not just tolerating it; therefore, such literature will be identified and considered in the last chapter.

Open Access Discourages Investments in Technology

Critics argue that OA does not allow for sufficient investment in technology. Part of the reason for publishers generating profits is to ensure that investment for new product development can take place—in the digital era this has proved more crucial than before, with the high costs of developing online services. This kind of investment is not only beneficial to end users, but also provides a platform through which publishers can compete with one another. The April 2004 Wellcome Report stated that:

[A]n appropriate and conservative estimate of the charge per article necessary for "author pays" journals thus lies in the range $500–$2500, that is first-copy costs plus other fixed costs and an element to cover the variable cost of running the distribution system. A contribution for overheads and profit will need to be added to this figure. Most journals are likely to fall nearer to the middle of the range than the extremes and their total costs including overhead and profit will be well below $2500, as evidenced by the average Blackwell revenue figure quoted above of $2000. It is technically feasible to add all sorts of bells and whistles to the electronic version of an article and increase costs by so doing, or to keep the open-access element of the system spartan and therefore relatively cheap, but these items are not the primary elements of cost. The primary elements, as with subscription journals, are essentially first-copy costs. (Wellcome Trust, 2004)

However, while the report's authors have allowed for costs of peer review, production, and administration as well as profit, no mention of investment in online systems and service development has been made.

Competition in the scientific publishing world has previously been constrained to a certain extent because highly renowned journals are not substitutable. However, in recent years publishers and other interested parties have invested significantly to develop services such as Thomson's Web of Knowledge or Elsevier's Scopus, which allow access to content from a range of publishers through a single point—it seems likely that, since many readers are unaware of the publishers of the journals they use, capturing the end user in this way rather than through individual journal titles will be an important guarantor of long-term business success. The concern here with regard to OA is that if, as expected, OA services are not as profitable as traditional activities, then less investment will be made in these systems and the publishers' ability to compete will be affected; ultimately, end users will suffer as services stagnate and price rises continue. Capacity for innovation is particularly important in this information age. Eventually, and as a follow-up of the preceding analysis, it is logical to recognise that OA carries negative aspects, although OA is part of ongoing technological growth. Thus, an appropriate regulatory framework that can offer effective solutions for further investments in technology will be proposed. It follows reasonings concerning a comparison of selected OA regimes which will be useful for the thesis argument.

Comparing Regulatory Models for OARs

Comparison is an essential tool of analysis. It sharpens the power of description and plays a crucial role concerning the formulation of concepts by bringing into focus suggestive similarities and contrasts among cases. In addition, comparison is inherent in all science, including the social sciences, where comparative research has historically played an important role in their growth as scientific disciplines (Lor, 2011).

Comparative research is the act of comparing two or more things with a view to explore something about one or all of the things being compared. What is more, this technique often uses multiple disciplines in one study. When it comes to method, the majority agreement is that there is no methodology peculiar to comparative research. Thus, it is evident that a multidisciplinary approach is beneficial for the flexibility it offers (Kennet, 2004). However, the

European and Greek governance frameworks have been chosen to compare but not in a technically rigorous sense. This is because the book aim is limited to illustrating how the international regulations of the European Union have influenced the shape of domestic Greek law in this area.

Regarding the European OA governance framework, the design and assumptions underlying the OA regime in Europe are going to be analysed. Based on this information, an analysis of the strengths and shortcomings of the European regulations in relation to OA, sharing information and protection of IP among European Member States will also be presented. For instance, an analysis of the report produced for the European Commission Directorate General Research and Innovation examining policies and strategies towards OA of scientific data in the ERA from 2000 onwards will yield relevant ideas. This helps me examine strategies that aim to foster OA of scientific data and ask whether and how these policies are monitored and enforced (Aurore, Caruso, & Archambault, 2013).

The European Union has enacted significant policies and laws to address the issue of OA and protection of IPRs. Despite this transnational aspect that can be adopted regarding the information access, we should focus on and examine the perspectives incorporated in the European regulations, decisions, press conferences, initiatives and programs, and the European infrastructure as a whole.

The question that will be addressed here is how EU laws claim to balance the competing interests between copyright holders and end users either within public or private sectors better. Answers to these issues will be based on the analysis of the research projects and initiatives that stem from the European Seventh Research Framework Program (FP7).

For example, there is a specific European recommendation that illustrates this fact. This recommendation, plus the sixth paragraph, provide a clarification about the significance of policies on OA to scientific research. It is claimed that these policies should apply to all research that receives public funds. Moreover, it is mentioned that such policies are expected to improve conditions for conducting research and in terms of the time spent searching for and accessing information (European Commission, 2012).

In accordance with the 2000 Lisbon Summit, the European Commission adopted the triangle of knowledge, which consists of education, research and innovation (European Commission, 2000; for further details concerning this issue, see Maassen & Stensaker, 2012). These terms have this particular sequence, and their main import stems from the production, sharing, and dissemination of information. Therefore, information is the instrument leading to educational outcomes, which lead to research and then to innovation. Hence, OARs play a key role here. As a result, they represent a major gateway to knowledge.

The Internet sector is now big enough to exert an influence on the entire economy. The public sector must lead, not trail, in the take-up of new technologies. It must establish the legal framework for the private sector to flourish and exploit technology to bring more efficient delivery of public services. Therefore, the European Council emphasised that the transmission of the information is crucial to future growth, and by introducing the eEurope initiative continues to be a major policy objective initiator since 2001. As part of the Lisbon strategy of paramount importance, eEurope's objectives are to accelerate the development of the information resources in Europe and to ensure their potential is available and accessible to everybody—that is, to all Member States, all regions, and all citizens.

An additional European issue is the initiative adopted by the European Commission since 2005. It is called "i2010—A European information society for growth and employment" (Commission of the European Communities, 2005). Under this framework, the European Union aims to ensure that it fully benefits from the changes the information revolution is bringing. Thus, it is one more step to promote the availability and accessibility of information resources within European infrastructure. Hitherto, it aimed to coordinate the actions undertaken by the European Member States to facilitate digital convergence and to respond to the challenges associated with information sharing and dissemination. Specifically, its first objective was to establish a Single European Information Space (SEIS) offering affordable and secure high-bandwidth communications, rich and diverse content and digital services.

This book will analyse the design and assumptions underlying the European OA regime. Based on this information, an analysis of the strengths and shortcomings of the European regulations in relation to OA, sharing information and protection of IP among European Member States will also be made. For instance, an analysis of the report produced for the European Commission Directorate General Research and Innovation that examines policies and strategies towards OA of scientific data in the ERA from 2000 onwards will yield relevant ideas. This helps me examine strategies that aim to foster OA of scientific data and to ask whether and how these policies are monitored and enforced. This provides the necessary information to move to the next issue, which is to examine the copyright regime in Greece.

The great variety of OA definitions shows that this concept can have more than one meaning. The original three formal definitions of OA are the Budapest (Chan et al., 2002), Bethesda (Suber et al., 2002), and Berlin (Harnad, 2005) definitions; they are usually referred to as a consolidated BBB definition (Suber, 2007). Yet, there are proponents who highlight that OA is free online access to peer-reviewed research. (This is how Harnad defines this term in his address to the European Rectors' meeting on OA that took place at the University of Liege 4 October 2007.) However, Greek researchers do not have this privilege currently, since access to peer-reviewed research is provided mainly within subscriptions to databases and journals. Initiatives to provide OA have so far focused on providing online access to theses and dissertations, with some success (see Chantavaridou, 2009).

In regard to OARs in Greece, it is significant to mention that the Greek educational system is provided at no expense to Greek citizens. From pre-primary school to the higher educational levels (such as universities), Greek people are not obliged to pay tuition fees, unless they choose not to attend public schools or universities. A few years ago, it would have been impossible for the administrator of a library to carry on initiatives such as the creation of a digital library that would provide free access to the full text of documents written by faculty members or students, but now that it is possible to do so the issue is whether the law permits it. The wider issue is whether the law should permit or enable such sharing to happen (Makridou, Araka, & Koutras, 2012).

Therefore, the Greek OA model and its efficacy in comparison with the European governance framework will be examined. Additionally, the impact of European actions, regulations, and directives as well as programs and initiatives of the FP7 will be clarified for the purposes of assessing the Greek OA model. This requires an assessment of whether the Greek framework should be reformed to keep pace with continuous technological evolution and define more strictly the concept of OA for beneficial dissemination and spread of information. An examination of the Greek OA governance framework and its efficacy in comparison with the European governance framework will be undertaken. This discussion will consider the impact of European actions, regulations, and directives, as well as programs and initiatives of the FP7 for the Greek OA model as a case study. This leads to an assessment as to whether the Greek framework should be reformed to keep pace with continuous technological evolution and define more strictly the concept of OA for beneficial dissemination and spread of information.

In conclusion, and as a follow-up from this analysis, the final issue to be examined is the future expectations for OA from the view of modern publishing enterprises (such as Elsevier, Wiley, Taylor and Francis Company, IEEE and Oxford University Press) in the context of a globalising world. Therefore, contemporary publishing companies could make a difference, and not only could they tolerate OA, but they can also embrace it in the context of a globalising world. Moreover, because of the interconnection between globalisation and the Internet, there are major implications for how the publishing industry will be modified in the foreseeable future. This change may be technology-driven, but there is a place for intellectual debate about appropriate regulation of the field. This requires an examination of commercial and moral claims of the authors or creators and the conventional publishers' vis-à-vis those of the end users, both nationally and internationally. This analysis will enable me to make an argument about the importance of OA as an appropriate governance mechanism for both protection and distribution of information in the international arena. This analysis develops the argument that, in a globalised world, justice and social cohesion requires commercial multinational corporations (MNCs) to act responsibly and ethically. Most of the big publishing houses are MNCs; if OARs are to be relevant, then such publishing houses will have to embrace the concept. It may be asked why they would do so. The concept of corporate social responsibility will be applied in this respect. Hence, it is logical and feasible for publishing MNCs to modify their business practices and adopt the concept of OARs.

This thesis aims to propose an appropriate agreement called the "just" green agreement, which can be integrated into copyright law policymaking. This agreement is designed to create policies for depositing the online published works in OARs, which will be able to balance the interests of authors, publishers, and users. This book aims to substantiate the claim that current copyright frameworks can be enhanced with the adoption of the "just" green agreement, at both international and local levels. This, in turn, helps me argue that OA can be a "friend" or "colleague" and not a "foe" regarding copyright regulations.

LITERATURE REVIEW

The following literature review will mainly focus on the writings that resonate with the reasons why OARs are examined as one way of broadening access to information. OARs may be institutionally based, enhancing the visibility and impact of the institution or they may be centralised, subject-based collections for example the economics repository RePEc (Research Papers in Economics) or the physics repository, arXiv (Xia, 2008). It is also argued that libraries and other bodies can create local copies and OARs of the resources available to them. Libraries can, by working together, make repositories of open access literature and in this way, guarantee continued access to these scholarly publications into the distant future (Corrado, 2005).

In many countries, there is a push to have publicly funded research available via open access. It is OA, which has driven the creation of repositories, especially institutional repositories. There is also an impetus to make learning objects more accessible, shareable, and reusable (Richardson & Wolski, 2012). An example of reasons that enabled me to decide to examine OARs as a means to increase access to information comes from the case study of Asia and OARs in agricultural sciences. The first repository started working in 2004 at the Indian Institute of Science, Bangalore. After that, efforts are being made to make agricultural research publicly available globally. Particularly, the first OAR for agricultural sciences was initiated in 2008. In 2009, another important move in this regard was the establishment of OAR in agricultural sciences with the help of International Crops Research Institute for the Semi-Arid Tropics (ICRISAT; Kumar Roy, Chandra Biswas, & Parthasarathi, 2016).

There exists ample literature discussing various aspects of OARs and their potential towards the further distribution of information (Clobridge & Clobridge, 2014; Creaser et al., 2010; Ghosh & Kumar Das, 2007). Furthermore, international perspectives show that OARs' role is gaining ground in discussions about access to information resources (Chan, 2004; Lynch & Lippincott, 2005; Roy, Biswas, & Mukhopadhyay, 2012; Vierkant, 2013). It is argued that the concept of OARs is determined as a means to increase the visibility of research outcomes (Abrizah, & K, 2017; Lee-Hwa, Abrizah, & Noorhidawati, 2013). Other scholars argue that OARs aim to support access to information resources, to increase information distribution, and encourage scholarly communication (Bhat, 2010; Karaesony, 2013; Wacha & Wisner, 2011). Another aspect worthy of mention stems from the benefits of information dissemination offered via self-archiving in OARs hosted by libraries (Mamtora, Yang, & Singh, 2015; Priyanto, 2015; Sabha, Sumaira, & Amin, 2013). However, there is no specific literature on the precise research question to be examined in this thesis concerning agreements about depositing works in OARs that can work as a mechanism to balance the interests of authors, publishers, and users of online published works. Hence, the following review seeks to review the literature in the general field and identify the gaps in the literature in a number of related areas and find a way of synthesising the available knowledge to form the basis for the argumentation. In doing so, the discussion is divided as follows.

First, the relevant literature on the theoretical issues is considered, and it highlights why OA is important, including (a) OA is a means of access to knowledge, (b) the knowledge–power nexus and thus the importance of OA for access to knowledge, and (c) practical reasons according to which OA can be effective. There is also consideration regarding whether OA is problematic and further examination of the literature related to the issues so far as it (a) is considered to infringe IPRs, (b) restricts commercial profits, and (c) discourages investments in technology.

Why Open Access Is Important

Access to Knowledge

The literature reflects that developing countries should pursue to train national policymakers and institutions involved in copyright law designation with a special focus on the importance of limitations and exceptions (Okediji, 2017). In turn, training skills acquired potentially ensure that the copyright framework could benefit economy and encourage protection, use, and information distribution (Papadopoulou, 2010). At the international level, technical assistance programs of institutions such as the World Intellectual Property Organization (WIPO) should incorporate training and education with respect to the value and importance of copyright limitations and exceptions.

While penalties for intellectual property infringement are compulsory pursuant to the Trade-Related Aspects of Intellectual Property Rights (TRIPS) Agreement, a penalty for a copyright owner who violates a limitation or exception is not indicated. It is argued that several courts have recognized a doctrine of "copyright misuse," where a copyright owner who abuses the copyright privilege is precluded from enforcing the copyright until the abusive conduct has been stopped (Hartzog, 2003). It is extremely important to recognize that the existing limitations and exceptions recognized by the Berne Convention and implemented in national copyright regulations are not sufficient to deal efficiently with the development needs introduced by copyrighted works.(Ricketson & Ginsburg, 2006) While the existing limitations and exceptions in the Berne Convention do extend to educational uses, a close examination of these exceptions shows that they apply primarily to the use of copyrighted works by instructors and teachers (Hugenholtz & Okediji, 2009). Thus, this exception and limitation is of very limited value for supplying the local market with sufficient numbers of affordable copies for students and the public. In other words, current copyright exceptions and limitations do not provide adequate access to information regarding information needs in the digital age.

There are proponents who argue that everyone has the right to knowledge. What is more, they also state that "[T]he call for change is being echoed by the academic community, which is asking for greater open access and the removal of economic barriers to science" (Demaio et al., 2012). Fitzgerald, who is the prominent scholar in this area, claims that the Internet and associated digital technologies provide us with an enormous potential to access and build information and knowledge networks (see also Fitzgerald, 2005. p. 2; and Atkinson & Fitzgerald, 2014, p. 121-128). Moreover, he argues that "[i] nformation and knowledge can be communicated in an instant across the globe, cheaply and with good quality, by even the most basic Internet user." However, Fitzgerald states that:

Copyright law which takes definition from international conventions and is similar in most countries provides that you cannot reproduce or communicate copyright material without the permission of the copyright owner subject to exceptions for fair use/dealing, private use and educational use.

It is widely accepted in the literature that there is a need to amend the current copyright regime to make it relevant to changing practices and expectations as to the dissemination of information. More specifically, there is an acknowledgement that regulations should aim to make intellectual protection sustainable and safeguard the interests of all stakeholders. In another context, Fitzgerald claims that "[i]n the midst of this 'information revolution' one message has floated to the surface seamless access to knowledge has become a key driver of social, economic and cultural development" (for further information, see Fitzgerald, 2007; and Fitzgerald, Coates, & Lewis, 2007). Following this statement, the right to information is significant concerning the development of knowledge. Article 19(2) of the International Covenant on Civil and Political Rights (ICCPR) holds that freedom of expression includes the right to information and states:

[E]veryone shall have the right to freedom of expression; this right shall include freedom to seek, receive and impart information and ideas of all kinds, regardless of frontiers, either orally, in writing or in print, in the form of art, or through any other media of his choice. (ICCPR Article 9(1) United Nations, 1966)

Additionally, the Freedom of Information Act (2002) has been replaced by the Right to Information Act (2005) which determines an action by the Indian government to set out the practical framework concerning the right to information for citizens (Roberts, 2010).

Scholars also argue that governments can place certain restrictions on these rights, though only if it is required. This has long been understood to cover access to government information, such as rights covered by the Freedom of Information Act in the US. But increasingly some are starting to include access to knowledge, particularly regarding the Internet. The rationale of open access empowers Internet phenomena such as Wikipedia and Creative Commons. This rationale also clarifies another justification that stands behind academic sharing, such as the OpenCourseWare Consortium (Downes, 2007). This is the general thinking behind a right to information that encompasses a right to knowledge and instruments to gain that knowledge. In addition, this view describes the reasoning of organizations, such as UNESCO, to encourage OA policies (e.g., its joint statement COAR–UNESCO on OA examined in the last chapter).

Another aspect that should be considered in the context of copyright amendments required to broaden access to information resources is the international IP treaty, the Marrakesh Treaty (Hua, 2014). This treaty facilitates access to published works for persons with special abilities (e.g., people with no vision), visually impaired or otherwise printed disabled. Its rationale helps me argue that works as an international legal basis from the rights-holder's perspective and encourages WIPO member countries to establish a network for the cross-border exchange of accessible format of copies of work (Caso & Giovanella, 2014). Additionally, the provisions of this treaty highlight the importance of the right to knowledge which should be offered equally. Therefore, it is necessary to develop further arguments about how precisely such access to knowledge can be achieved while simultaneously protecting the interests of producers of knowledge.

There is no specific literature that combines the above issues, but the available literature on separate issues (not yet identified) will be synthesised to develop the argument in this thesis. Moreover, there are advocates who argue that everyone has the right to knowledge. They state that "[T]he call for change is being echoed by the academic community, which is asking for greater open access and the removal of economic barriers to science" (Demaio, Dorch, & Herch, 2012, para. 20). In another work titled *The Open Access to Knowledge (OAK) Law Project Report No. 1*, the authors state that OA is fundamental for knowledge and specifically that "[T]he Report calls upon Australian research and funding institutions to consider their commitment to open access . . . The Report details a methodology for cataloguing and better understanding of publishers' attitudes towards open access" (Fitzgerald et al., 2006, p.ii). Therefore, it is evident that access to knowledge is a founding principle of any open society.

In conclusion, new technologies bring new opportunities for knowledge and innovation; thus, OA is part of this type of shift stemming from technological evolution. In addition, Drahos, a notable scholar in the field, argues that in the modern world, IP rules and IP generated using those rules are globally pervasive phenomena. Moreover, he claims that two significant multilateral agreements on IP were negotiated among some states: the Berne Convention for the Protection of Literary and Artistic Work (1886) and the Paris Convention for the Protection of Industrial Property (1883). In present times, WIPO administers some 23 treaties on IP. Therefore, Drahos is alluding to a greater debate on the role of modern copyright regimes and information accessibility to the freedom of design over property rights issue, which is of paramount significance to countries. By focusing on the matter, the literature appears to argue that it is possible to enhance the contemporary IP framework. Drahos specifically makes this argument in a working paper, as he observes that "[d]esign freedom over property rights matters. It matters to the kinds of exchanges that can take place and therefore to the structure of markets and long-run economic growth," further noting that "[g]roups must have the capacity to change the rules of property in order to adapt the use of resources to new contexts." This scientific approach illustrates the importance of balancing the competing interests of copyright holders and end users, as they can be observed as two different groups, or stakeholders. The examination of this theoretical issue will help me address the abilities offered to different groups after a reform of current copyright regimes in order to change property regulations to use and reuse resources.

Knowledge Is Power

The relevant literature consists of major texts on Foucault and Habermas. Concerning Foucault, the discussion relies on the chapter authored by Joseph Rouse in *The Cambridge Companion to Foucault* (2005), Stephen Ball's work, *Foucault and Education: Disciplines and Knowledge* (2013), and Foucault's work, *The Archeology of Knowledge* (2012). For the discussion on Harbermas' ideas, the major texts that will be used include Lincoln Dalhberg's article, "The Habermasian Public Sphere: Taking Difference Seriously?" (2005); Eriksen and Weigard's *Understanding Habermas: Communicating Action and Deliberative Democracy* (2004); and the book chapter by Douglas Kellner, "Habermas, the Public Sphere, and Democracy" (2014).

Practical Reasons Why Open Access Can Work

There are facts that prove OA as an effective means of greater access to knowledge. In the OA literature, these facts are relevant to alternative forms of licensing and its efficacy. For example, Creative Commons is a non-profit organisation in the United States (US), devoted to expanding the range of creative works available for others to build upon legally and to share. The organisation has released several copyright licenses, known as Creative Commons licenses, free of charge to the public. These licenses allow creators to communicate which rights they reserve and which rights they waive for the benefit of the recipients or other creators. Lessig, one of the founders of Creative Commons, is a prominent scholar in this field; he considers that Creative Commons licenses tend to be a dominant and increasingly restrictive permission culture. He also describes this as "[a] culture in which creators get to create only with the permission of the powerful, or of creator from the past" (see Lessig, 2005). Additionally, Lessig maintains that the current culture is dominated by traditional content distributors, in order to maintain and strengthen their monopolies over cultural creations such as popular music and popular movies. Creative Commons can provide alternatives to these restrictions. As a result of his critique, it may be asked if and how this type of licensing can be incorporated within the current copyright regime. Moreover, what are the specific reforms that should be made in relation to current copyright regimes? No specific literature exists on these issues; hence, there will be a discussion about critiques on commercial OARs combined with perspectives about OARs as a viable model of regulation.

For example, there are two international organizations for forming and regulating OARs and address matters related to their functionality: The Confederation of Open Access Repositories (COAR) and the Registry of Open Access Repositories Mandates and Policies (ROARMAP). OARs can be considered as a significant infrastructure component supporting the growing number of open access policies and laws, the majority of which recommend or require the deposit of articles into an OAR. Thus, these organizations indicate that the desirability of OARs is gaining ground as they have been implemented around the world and are now widespread across all regions.

Why Open Access Is Considered Problematic

Infringement of IPRs

It is argued that access to data released online can be considered copyright infringement (Weitzner et al., 2008). A significant concern for the proponents of the OA model concerns online creation that can be attached to digital platforms and whether it is possible to capture associated value through IP licensing. The example of Napster shows possible implications on copyright frameworks when there is sharing of online information. However, note that Suber argues that OA for science does not work as a Napster (Suber, 2003). Another fact that indicates why OA is problematic is in relation to the new licensing system of Creative Commons, which is examined in Chapter Six. This licensing system relies on OA, and whenever such a license is applied, the author or creator gives permission for use and distribution of the work. However, there are issues when the work is freely available for non-commercial use when it is possible for it to be used for commercial purposes and the Creative Commons license cannot be revoked (Billieux & Van der Linden, 2012). These oppositions to OA practice lead me to question which proposal has the potential to improve current copyright regimes to embrace the concept of OA.

Implications on Commercial Publishing

OA practices are said to create many disadvantages for commercial publishing related to academic scholarly works (considered in Chapter Six). One of them is about the reduction of publishers' benefits as the OA practice gains further ground in publishing and "urges" publishers to modify their publishing policies.

In other words, in the long term, publishers should integrate OA practice as part of their publishing policy. Moreover, it is argued that publishers and publishers' organisations usually claim that the proliferation of OA would set in motion changes in the publishing regime, which would seriously undermine the current peer review system (Björk & Solomon, 2012). The literature does not sufficiently integrate the advantages of OA relative to the disadvantages. It follows argumentation concerning making OA acceptable to commercial publishers. These implications lead me to question what practices must be integrated by commercial publishers to secure their profits while supporting improvements in the pursuit of knowledge.

Open Access Discourages Investments in Technology

The extant literature on this topic explores the negative aspects rather than developing arguments for supporting OA as advantageous to commercial interests. For example, the April 2004 Wellcome Report found that an appropriate and conservative estimate of the charge per article necessary for "author pays" journals lies in the range of $500–$2,500, with these costs varying depending on the type of journal. However, while the report's authors allowed for costs of peer review, production, and administration and for-profit, no mention of investment in online systems and service development was made. Critics argue that OA does not allow for sufficient investment in technology. Part of the reason for publishers generating profits is to ensure investment in new product development can take place—in the digital era, this has proved more crucial than before, with the high costs of developing online services. This kind of investment is not only beneficial to end users, but also provides a platform through which publishers can compete with one another. Competition in the scientific publishing world has previously been constrained to an extent because highly renowned journals are not substitutable. However, publishers and other interested parties have invested significantly in recent years to develop services such as Thomson's Web of Knowledge or Elsevier's Scopus, which allow access through a single point to content from a range of publishers. It seems likely that since many readers are unaware of the publishers of the journals they use, capturing the end user in this way, rather than through individual journal titles, will be an important guarantor of long-term business success. The concern here with regard to OA is that if, as expected, OA services are not as profitable as traditional activities, then less investment will be made in these systems and the publishers' ability to compete will be affected; it is possible for the users of online published works to suffer as services stagnate and prices continue to rise (Crawford, 2012). The capacity for innovation is particularly important in this information age, whereas the literature does not investigate how to support the capacity for innovation. Market demands from the academic and scientific communities are changing and developing alongside the growth of the Internet, and journal publishers are adapting their views of how journal article content fits into the information spectrum. There are now examples of publishers offering more than just the journal content or bypassing the publication of research results as articles, while instead providing citable references within a database. However, there is little published scholarly analysis of these changing practices. It is one of the issues that is going to be examined, linking the commercial aspects of OAP with the need for appropriate protection of copyright interests.

METHODOLOGY

The Latin noun *doctrina* means instruction, knowledge or learning. It is argued that the doctrine in question is distinguished by legal concepts and principles of cases, statutes and regulations. Mann defines the doctrine as a mix of diverse laws, norms, principles and values that can be either binding or non-binding (Mann, 2015). The conducted research in the context of this book relies on this methodology, as international, local mandates and relevant norms that stem from these regulations will be considered. In this context of examination, national regulations of Greece will also be considered for the development of the argument of this book.

In addition, doctrinal research has been highlighted as the basic category that encompasses any form of purely legal analysis, including what the law is now and whether there are indications as to how the law might be evolving (Watkins & Burton, 2013). This methodology is appropriate as it analyses how OARs can be a mechanism to enhance international and local copyright regimes (e.g., in European and Greek contexts, respectively). The doctrinal research is applied to examine what the previous copyright law was and what the current copyright law is, to identify whether there are any specific issues about whether the copyright law might evolve in light of the emergence of OARs.

Another aspect of doctrinal research applied in this book concerns the examination of the copyright frameworks in Europe and Greece as written bodies of principles that can be discerned and analysed using legal sources. In this respect, specific European directives that are part of soft law and establish the European copyright framework will be considered. This examination will help me argue that OARs and relevant governance are gradually gaining ground through European soft law that introduces a set of principles to be implemented by the European countries. Then, it follows examination of particular Greek Copyright Act and Greek Constitution provisions (i.e., articles). The doctrinal analysis will assist in developing the argument that there are obvious influences of European soft regulation on how domestic Greek law develops.

It is argued that interdisciplinary research has become a frequently used methodology (Klein, 2008). The methodology in this book will also include this research method, as old and modern philosophical theories on the concepts of property, IP, consensus and social justice are examined. In this respect, literature of the humanities is significant and applied (Repko, 2008; Van Noorden, 2015). In addition, this methodology will encompass the concept of social cohesion that is engaged and, therefore, relies on literature from the social sciences and develop arguments drawing upon their significance for understanding the role of legal regulation and social justice (Monahan & Walker, 2014).

More specifically, there will be analysis of the history of property as a concept, the transition from property in goods to property in ideas and rights, the historical growth of copyright as a property right and copyright's emergence as a modern "trait" that should be included in the governance of copyright framework. Such interdisciplinary knowledge will help me to argue about the importance and role of OA in conjunction with public policy and regulations that should be designated towards social justice and social cohesion.

THE PLAN OF THE BOOK

There is growing recognition that OARs provide an opportunity for equal access to everybody; they can improve the pursuit of knowledge and further enhance academic scholarly communication. However, there is a compelling need to create regulatory frameworks that can enhance copyright regimes and balance copyright owner and end user interests. To address the central research question, the thesis contains six chapters, five of which have been published in scholarly refereed journals listed on the Australian Research Council's *Excellence in Research* list.

This chapter is introductory and the central research objectives, the book argument, literature review and methodology, and establishes how the argumentation will be developed.

The second chapter of the thesis is titled "From Property Rights to Copyrights: A Philosophical and Scientific Approach." A short part of it has already been published in a peer-reviewed journal (Koutras, n.d.). The chapter is based on the premise that to understand the significance of OARs it is necessary to know the context of the debate. Therefore, it is necessary to trace the historical development of the concept of private property and trace the emergence of copyright as a property right. The continued relevance of the rationales for copyright interests, both philosophical and pragmatic, will be assessed in the contemporary context of digital publishing. It will then canvas the reasons or explanations for the rise of the concept of OA and its significance in the digital society.

The third chapter is titled "The Green Open Access: Significant Scientific Considerations in the Light of Public Policy and Access to Knowledge." A short part of it has been published in the peer-reviewed *Seattle Journal for Social Justice* (Koutras, 2016). In this chapter, two main justifications are presented. One philosophical and one pragmatic in nature, regarding the implementation of OA. The philosophical justification relies on Foucault's views about power and knowledge; based on this rationale, it is argued that knowledge is power and that it is necessary in the digital age for everyone to have access to knowledge. The pragmatic justification relies on cases showing that it is impractical to enforce copyright in the traditional sense in the present digital age, and OA can be of help in this regard (Blakeney, 2012). As OARs constitute the contemporary mainstream regarding sharing and dissemination of information resources, it is important to examine the theoretical arguments about the desirability of OARs in the digital age to develop them as a form of social justice and to strengthen social cohesion. This chapter develops theoretical arguments for using public policy as a means of social justice and cohesion, and for conceptualising OARs as facilitating social justice and cohesion. In conclusion, the public policy objective is crucial to developing OARs as a form of social justice while simultaneously enhancing social cohesion.

The fourth chapter is titled "Open Access in Practice: The European Union's Regulation of OARs." A short part of it has been published in the peer-reviewed *Intellectual Property Quarterly* (Koutras, in press). In this chapter, there is discussion about the design and assumptions underlying the European Union's OA regime. Based on this information, it follows an analysis of the strengths and shortcomings of the European regulations in relation to OA, sharing information and protection of IP among European Member States. For instance, an analysis of the report produced for the European Commission Directorate General Research and Innovation, which examines policies and strategies towards OA of scientific data in the ERA from 2000 onwards, will yield relevant ideas. This will help me examine strategies that aim to foster OA of scientific data and ask whether, and how, these policies are monitored and enforced.

The fifth chapter is titled "Examining the Governance Framework of OARs in Greece as a European Case Study." Part of it has been published in the peer-reviewed *Intellectual Property Quarterly*. This chapter examines the Greek OA model and its efficacy in comparison with the European governance framework. Additionally, this chapter will clarify the impact of European actions, regulations and directives, as well as programs and initiatives of FP7 for the Greek OA model, and will serve as a case study. This will lead to an assessment of whether the Greek copyright framework should be reformed to keep pace with continuous technological evolution and define more strictly the concept of OA for the beneficial dissemination and spread of information. Given this, the existing Greek Copyright Act is going to be assessed; this assessment will enable me to question whether OA is possible and desirable in Greece and how the existing Greek Copyright Act can incorporate the concept of OA. Building on the understanding of the assessment of governance framework of OARs in Greece, the thesis will further examine the research topic about the implications of OA on the process of publishing. To consider the publishers' contrary perspective, their responses to OA will be examined in the following chapter.

The sixth chapter is titled "The Evolving Role of Commercial Publishers and the Future of Online Access Repositories." A part of it has been published in the peer-reviewed *University of Western Australia Law Review*. This chapter will enable me to make an argument about the importance of OA as an appropriate governance mechanism for both protection and distribution of information in the international arena. This analysis builds on the earlier discussion in chapter three and develops the argument that social cohesion requires the widest possible access to knowledge in the contemporary times of digital revolution. Most of the big commercial publishing houses should act responsibly and ethically to align with corporate social responsibility (CSR) for the public good; if OARs are to be relevant, such publishing houses will have to embrace the concept.

Therefore, by examining the concepts of OA as a means of creating wider access to knowledge and recommending that OARs should become the basic component in the publishing practices of public institutions as well as commercial publishers, the thesis seeks to contribute to the literature in the field of open science and its significance in creating a just global society. It addresses the governance framework of copyright laws by recommending integration of OARs with copyright interests of all stakeholders to improve access to knowledge by greater numbers of people.

REFERENCES

Abrizah, A., A, N., & K, K. (2017). Global visibility of Asian universities' Open Access institutional repositories. *Malaysian Journal of Library and Information Science*, *15*(3), 53–73.

Ali Feki, M., Kawsar, F., Boussard, M., & Trappeniers, L. (2013). The Internet of Things. *The Next Technological Revolution.*, *26*(February), 24–25. doi:10.1109/MC.2013.63

Alonso, J. (n.d.). *Improving access to government through better use of the web*. Retrieved from http://www.epractice.eu

Atkinson, B., & Fitzgerald, B. (2014). Access and networking. In *A Short History of Copyright*. Retrieved from http://link.springer.com

Aurore, N., Caruso, J., & Archambault, E. (2013). *Open data access policies and strategies in the European research area and beyond*. Retrieved from http://www.science-metrix.com

Bailey, C. W. Jr. (2007). Open access and libraries. *Collection Management*, *32*(3–4), 351–383. doi:10.1300/J105v32n03_07

Balganesh, S. (2013). Copyright Infringement Markets Essay. *Columbia Law Review*, *113*(8), 2277–2332.

Ball, S. J. (2013). *Foucault and Education: Disciplines and Knowledge*. Routledge. doi:10.4324/9780203092781

Bhat, M. H. (2010). Open Access Repositories. *RE:view*, 356.

Billieux, J., & Van der Linden, M. (2012). Problematic use of the Internet and self-regulation: A review of the initial studies. *The Open Addiction Journal, 5*(1), 24–29. doi:10.2174/1874941001205010024

Björk, B.-C., & Solomon, D. (2012). Open access versus subscription journals: A comparison of scientific impact. *BMC Medicine, 10*(1), 73. doi:10.1186/1741-7015-10-73 PMID:22805105

Blakeney, M. (2012). *Intellectual property enforcement: A commentary on the Anti-Counterfeiting Trade Agreement (ACTA)*. Edward Elgar Publishing. doi:10.4337/9781781006009

Bloom, T., Ganley, E., & Winker, M. (2014). Data access for the open access literature: PLoS's data policy. *PLoS Biology, 12*(2), e1001797. doi:10.1371/journal.pbio.1001797

Bovaird, T., Löffler, E., & Loeffler, E. (2004). *Public Management and Governance*. Routledge. doi:10.4324/9780203884096

Buchanan, G., & Masoodian, M. (2008). Digital Libraries: Universal and Ubiquitous Access to Information. In *11th International Conference on Asian Digital Libraries, ICADL 2008, Bali, Indonesia, December 2-5, 2008, Proceedings*. Springer Science & Business Media. 10.1007/978-3-540-89533-6

Burgess, J., & Green, J. (2013). *YouTube: Online video and participatory culture*. John Wiley & Sons.

Caso, R., & Giovanella, F. (Eds.). (2014). *Balancing Copyright Law in the Digital Age: Comparative Perspectives* (2015 edition). Springer.

Chan, L. (2004). Supporting and Enhancing Scholarship in the Digital Age: The Role of Open Access Institutional Repository. *Canadian Journal of Communication, 29*(3). doi:10.22230/cjc.2004v29n3a1455

Chantavaridou, E. (2009). Open access and institutional repositories in Greece: Progress so far. *OCLC Systems & Services, 25*(1), 47–59. doi:10.1108/10650750910931922

Clobridge, C., & Clobridge, A. (2014). All About Open Access Repositories: The Other Side of Open Access. *Online Searcher, 38*(5), 38–41.

Commission of the European Communities. (2005). *Communication from the Commission to the Council, the European Parliament, the European Economic and Social Committee and the Committee of the Regions: "i2010—A European Information Society for Growth and Employment."* SEC (2005) 717.

Corrado, E. M. (2005). The Importance of Open Access, Open Source, and Open Standards for Libraries. *Issues in Science and Technology Librarianship*, (42). Retrieved from http://www.istl.org/05-spring/article2.html

Crawford, W. (2012). *Open access: What you need to know now*. American Library Association.

Creaser, C., Fry, J., Greenwood, H., Oppenheim, C., Probets, S., Spezi, V., & White, S. (2010). Authors' Awareness and Attitudes Toward Open Access Repositories. *New Review of Academic Librarianship, 16*(sup1), 145–161. doi:10.1080/13614533.2010.518851

Dahlberg, L. (2005). The Habermasian public sphere: Taking difference seriously? *Theory and Society, 34*(2), 111–136. doi:10.100711186-005-0155-z

Demaio, A., Dorch, B., & Herch, F. (2012). *Open access: Everyone has the right to knowledge*. Retrieved December 14, 2014, from The Conversation website: http://theconversation.com/open-access-everyone-has-the-right-to-knowledge-10342

Depoorter, B. (2009). Technology and Uncertainty: The Shaping Effect on Copyright Law. *University of Pennsylvania Law Review, 157*(6), 1831.

Downes, S. (2007). *Places to Go*. Sakai: Innovate.

Dwyer, C., Hiltz, S. R., & Passerini, K. (2007). Trust and privacy concern within social networking sites: A comparison of Facebook and MySpace. In *Proceedings of the Thirteenth Americas Conference on Information Systems* (pp. 339–351). Retrieved from https://aisel.aisnet.org/amcis2007/339/

Ebrahim, N. A. (2017). *Improving research visibility part 4: Open access repositories*. doi:10.6084/m9.figshare.5010749.v1

Eriksen, E. O., & Weigard, J. (2004). *Understanding Habermas: Communicating Action and Deliberative Democracy*. London: Bloomsbury Academic.

European Commission. (2012). Commission Recommendation of 17 July 2012 on Access to and Preservations of Scientific Information. *Official Journal of the European Communities*, (L 167), 39–43. Retrieved from http://eur-lex.europa.eu/legal-content/EN/TXT/PDF/?uri=CELEX:32012H0417&rid=1

European Council. (2000). Employment, economic reform and social cohesion: A strategic goal for the next decade. In *Lisbon European Council 23 and 24 March 2000: Presidency conclusions*. Retrieved from http://www.europarl.europa.eu/summits/lis1_en.htm

Finch, J. (2012). *Accessibility, sustainability, excellence: How to expand access to research publications*. Report of the Working Group on Expanding Access to Published Research Findings. Retrieved from http://www.researchinfonet.org

Finch, J. (2013). Accessibility, sustainability, excellence: The UK approach to open access. *Information Services & Use*, *33*(1), 11–18. doi:10.3233/ISU-130687

Fitzgerald, B. (2005). *The Creative Commons model of open content licensing*. Retrieved from http://eprints.qut.edu.au

Fitzgerald, B. (2007). *Open content licensing (OCL) for open educational resources*. Retrieved from http://www.oecd.org

Fitzgerald, B. F. (2006). *Open Access to Knowledge (OAK) law project report no. 1: Creating a legal framework for copyright management of open access within the Australian academic and research sector*. Retrieved from http://eprints.qut.edu.au/6099/

Fitzgerald, B. F., Coates, J. M., & Lewis, S. M. (2007). *Open content licensing: Cultivating the Creative Commons*. Sydney University Press. Retrieved from http://eprints.qut.edu.au

Forman, G., & Pufall, P. B. (2013). *Constructivism in the Computer Age*. First. doi:10.4324/9780203771242

Foucault, M. (2012). *The archaeology of knowledge*. Knopf Doubleday Publishing Group.

Friesike, S., Widenmayer, B., Gassmann, O., & Schildhauer, T. (2015). Opening science: Towards an agenda of open science in academia and industry. *The Journal of Technology Transfer, 40*(4), 581–601. doi:10.100710961-014-9375-6

Ghosh, S. B., & Kumar Das, A. (2007). Open Access and Institutional Repositories — A Developing Country Perspective: A case study of India. *IFLA Journal, 33*(3), 229–250. doi:10.1177/0340035207083304

Ginsburg, J. C., & Ricketson, S. (2006). Inducers and Authorisers: A Comparison of the US Supreme Court's Grokster Decision and the Australian Federal Court's Kazaa Ruling. *Media & Arts Law Review, 11*(1). Retrieved from https://papers.ssrn.com/abstract=888928

Gubbi, J., Buyya, R., Marusic, S., & Palaniswami, M. (2013). Internet of Things (IoT): A vision, architectural elements, and future directions. *Future Generation Computer Systems, 29*(7), 1645–1660. doi:10.1016/j.future.2013.01.010

Hampton, K. N., Livio, O., & Sessions Goulet, L. (2010). The Social Life of Wireless Urban Spaces: Internet Use, Social Networks, and the Public Realm. *Journal of Communication, 60*(4), 701–722. doi:10.1111/j.1460-2466.2010.01510.x

Harnad, D. (2005). The implementation of the Berlin Declaration on Open Access. *D-Lib Magazine, 11*(3). doi:10.1045/march2005-harnad

Hartzog, N. (2003). Gaining Momentum: A Review of Recent Developments Surrounding the Expansion of the Copyright Misuse Doctrine and Analylsis of the Doctrine in Its Current Form. *Michigan Telecommunications and Technology Law Review, 10*, 373–406.

Haug, K., Salek, R. M., Conesa, P., Hastings, J., de Matos, P., Rijnbeek, M., ... Steinbeck, C. (2013). MetaboLights—An open-access general-purpose repository for metabolomics studies and associated meta-data. *Nucleic Acids Research, 41*(D1), D781–D786. doi:10.1093/nar/gks1004 PMID:23109552

Hua, J. (2014). Reconstruction of copyright limitations and exceptions in the digital network age: Importation of legal flexibility and certainty. *International Journal of Technology Policy and Law, 1*(4), 363. doi:10.1504/IJTPL.2014.061637

Hugenholtz, P. B., & Okediji, R. L. (2009). *Contours of an International Instrument on Limitations and Exceptions: Global Intellectual Property and Developing Countr*. doi:10.1093/acprof:oso/9780195342109.003.0020

Journal, A. (2002). *Abstracting Knowledge Formation: A Report on Academia and Publishing (Part Three: The University and Global Restructuring: The Scholars Meet the Market)* (Critical Essay). Retrieved from https://books.apple.com/fr/book/abstracting-knowledge-formation-report-on-academia/id526086447

Karaesony, G. (2013). HUNOR: The Collaboration of Hungarian Open Access Repositories. *Procedia: Social and Behavioral Sciences*, *73*, 57–61. doi:10.1016/j.sbspro.2013.02.019

Kellner, D. (2014). Habermas, the Public Sphere, and Democracy. In D. Boros & J. M. Glass (Eds.), *Re-Imagining Public Space* (pp. 19–43)., doi:10.1057/9781137373311_2

Kennett, P. (2004). *A handbook of comparative social policy*. Edward Elgar Publishing.

Klein, J. T. (2008). Evaluation of interdisciplinary and transdisciplinary research: A literature review. *American Journal of Preventive Medicine*, *35*(2supplement), S116–S123. doi:10.1016/j.amepre.2008.05.010 PMID:18619391

Koutras, N. (2016). Open access as a means for social justice in the context of cultural diversity in Europe. *Seattle Journal for Social Justice*, *15*(1). Retrieved from http://digitalcommons.law.seattleu.edu/sjsj/vol15/iss1/10

Koutras, N. (2016). History of copyright, growth and conceptual analysis: Copyright protection and the emergence of open access. *Intellectual Property Quarterly*, (2), 135-150.

Koutras, N. (2018). The copyright law framework and its interaction with open access repositories in Europe. *Publishing Research Quarterly Journal*, *34*(1), 32-53.

Kumar Roy, B., Chandra Biswas, S., & Parthasarathi, M. (2016). Status of Open Access Institutional Digital Repositories in Agricultural Sciences: A Case Study of Asia. *Library Philosophy and Practice (e-Journal), 1329*. Retrieved from http://digitalcommons.unl.edu/cgi/viewcontent.cgi?article=3615&context=libphilprac

Laakso, M. (2014). Green open access policies of scholarly journal publishers: A study of what, when, and where self-archiving is allowed. *Scientometrics*, *99*(2), 475–494. doi:10.100711192-013-1205-3

Lepitak, S. (2013). 90% of Online content to be held behind paywalls in three years media company survey suggests. *The Drum*. Retrieved from http://www.thedrum.com

Leslie Chan et al. (2002). *Budapest Open Access Initiative*. Retrieved from http://www.opensocietyfoundations.org

Lessig, L. (2005). *Free culture: The nature and future of creativity*. Penguin Books.

Levine, H., & Zahradnik, A. G. (2012). Online media, market orientation, and financial performance in nonprofits. *Journal of Nonprofit & Public Sector Marketing*, *24*(1), 26–42. doi:10.1080/10495142.2012.652908

Leyshon, A., Webb, P., French, S., Thrift, N., & Crewe, L. (2005). On the reproduction of the musical economy after the Internet. *Media Culture & Society*, *27*(2), 177–209. doi:10.1177/0163443705050468

Lor, P. J. (2019). *International and Comparative Librarianship: Concepts and Methods for Global Studies*. Walter de Gruyter GmbH & Co KG. doi:10.1515/9783110267990

Lynch, C. A., & Lippincott, J. K. (2005). Institutional Repository Deployment in the United States as of Early 2005. *D-Lib Magazine*, *11*(09). doi:10.1045eptember2005-lynch

Maassen, P., & Stensaker, B. (2011). The knowledge triangle, European higher education policy logics and policy implications. *Higher Education*, *61*(6), 757–769. doi:10.100710734-010-9360-4

Makridou, E., Araka, I., & Koutras, N. (2012). Open educational resources and freedom of teaching in college education in Greece: Rivals or fellows? In *Proceedings of the 5th International Conference of Information Law and Ethics* (p. 605). NB Production.

Mamtora, J., Yang, T., & Singh, D. (2015). Open access repositories in the Asia–Oceania region: Experiences and guidelines from three academic institutions. *IFLA Journal, 41*(2), 162–176. doi:10.1177/0340035215582219

Mann, T. (Ed.). (2015). *Australian Law Dictionary* (2nd ed.). Oxford University Press.

Marshall, L., & Frith, S. (2013). *Music and Copyright*. Second. doi:10.4324/9780203036105

Mathelier, A., Zhao, X., Zhang, A. W., Parcy, F., Worsley-Hunt, R., Arenillas, D. J., ... Wasserman, W. W. (2014). JASPAR 2014: An extensively expanded and updated open-access database of transcription factor binding profiles. *Nucleic Acids Research, 42*(D1), D142–D147. doi:10.1093/nar/gkt997 PMID:24194598

McCourt, T., & Burkart, P. (2003). When Creators, Corporations and Consumers Collide: Napster and the Development of On-line Music Distribution. *Media Culture & Society, 25*(3), 333–350. doi:10.1177/01634437030250030003

Merriden, T. (2001). *Irresistible forces: The business legacy of Napster and the growth of the underground Internet* (1st ed.). Capstone.

Molteni, L., & Ordanini, A. (2003). Consumption patterns, digital technology and music downloading. *Long Range Planning, 36*(4), 389–406. doi:10.1016/S0024-6301(03)00073-6

Monahan, J., & Walker, W. (2014). *Social science in law* (8th ed.). Foundation Press.

Nissenbaum, H. (2011). A Contextual Approach to Privacy Online. *Daedalus, 140*(4), 32–48. doi:10.1162/DAED_a_00113

Okediji, R. L. (Ed.). (2017). *Copyright Law in an Age of Limitations and Exceptions*. Cambridge, UK: Cambridge University Press. doi:10.1017/9781316450901

Papadopoulou, M. D. (2010). *Copyright limitations and exceptions in an e-education environment*. Retrieved from http://go.galegroup.com.simsrad.net.ocs.mq.edu.au/ps/i.do?ty=as&v=2.1&u=macquarie&it=DIourl&s=RELEVANCE&p=LT&qt=SN~2042-115X~~TI~%22Copyright%20limitations%20and%20exceptions%22~~VO~1~~IU~2&lm=DA~120100000&sw=w

Priyanto, I. (2015). *Readiness of Indonesian academic libraries for open access and open access repositories implementation: A study on Indonesian open access repositories*. Retrieved from https://digital.library.unt.edu/ark:/67531/metadc804888/

Repko, A. F. (2008). Interdisciplinary research: Process and theory. *Sage (Atlanta, Ga.).*

Richardson, J., & Wolski, M. (2012). The importance of Repositories in Supporting the Learning Lifecycle. *ICERI 2012*, 2602–2608. Retrieved from https://research-repository.griffith.edu.au/bitstream/handle/10072/48263/80937_1.pdf;sequence=1

Ricketson, S., & Ginsburg, J. (2006). *International Copyright and Neighbouring Rights: The Berne Convention and Beyond Two volume set* (2nd ed.). Oxford, UK: Oxford University Press.

Roberts, A. (2010). A Great and Revolutionary Law? The First Four Years of India's Right to Information Act. *Public Administration Review*, *70*(6), 925–933. doi:10.1111/j.1540-6210.2010.02224.x

Rouse, J. (2005). Power/knowledge. In *The Cambridge companion to Foucault* (p. 95). Cambridge University Press. doi:10.1017/CCOL0521840821.005

Rousseau, J.-J. (2012). *Rousseau: The Basic Political Writings: Discourse on the Sciences and the Arts, Discourse on the Origin of Inequality, Discourse on Political Economy, On the Social Contract, The State of War*. Hackett Publishing.

Roy, B., Biswas, S. C., & Mukhopadhyay, P. (2012). Open Access Repositories in Asia: From SAARC to Asian Tigers. *Library Philosophy and Practice (e-Journal)*. Retrieved from http://digitalcommons.unl.edu/libphilprac/808

Sabha, A., Sumaira, J., & Amin, I. (2013). *Status of Open access Repositories: A Global perspective*. Academic Press.

Sakaky, T., Okazaki, M., & Matsuo, Y. (2010). Earthquake shakes Twitter users: Real-time event detection by social sensors. *Proceedings of the 19th International Conference on World Wide Web*, 851–860. http://doi.acm.org/10.1145/1772690.1772777

Springer. (2004). *Open choice: Your research. Your choice.* Retrieved from http://www.springer.com

Suber, P. (2002). *Bethesda statement on open access publishing.* Retrieved from http://dash.harvard.edu

Suber, P. (2003). Not Napster for science. *SPARC, 66*. Retrieved from https://dash.harvard.edu/handle/1/4455490

Suber, P. (2007). *Gratis and libre open access.* Retrieved from http://dash.harvard.edu/handle/1/4322580

Suber, P. (2012). *Open access.* MIT Press. doi:10.7551/mitpress/9286.001.0001

Tan, L.-H., Abrizah, A., & Noorhidawati, A. (2013). Availability and visibility of open access digital repositories in ASEAN countries. *Information Development*, *29*(3), 274–285. doi:10.1177/0266666912466754

Tennant, J. (2014). Top scientific publisher chooses not to advance open access. *The Conversation.* Retrieved from http://theconversation.com

Trust, W. (2004). *Costs and business models in scientific research publishing: A report commissioned by the Wellcome Trust.* Retrieved from https://wellcome.ac.uk/sites/default/files/wtd003184_0.pdf

United Nations. (1966). *International Covenant on Civil and Political Rights.* Retrieved from http://www.ohchr.org/Documents/ProfessionalInterest/ccpr.pdf

Van Noorden, R. (2013). Open access: The true cost of science publishing. *NATNews*, *495*(7442), 426. doi:10.1038/495426a PMID:23538808

Vierkant, P. (2013). 2012 Census of Open Access Repositories in Germany: Turning Perceived Knowledge Into Sound Understanding. *D-Lib Magazine*, *19*(11/12). doi:10.1045/november2013-vierkant

Vitale, D. (2006). Between deliberative and participatory democracy: A contribution on Habermas. *Philosophy and Social Criticism*, *32*(6), 739–766. doi:10.1177/0191453706064022

Wacha, M., & Wisner, M. (2011). Measuring Value in Open Access Repositories. *The Serials Librarian*, *61*(3–4), 377–388. doi:10.1080/0361526X.2011.580423

Wang, S. (2017). The cloud, online piracy and global copyright governance. *International Journal of Cultural Studies*, *20*(3), 270–286. doi:10.1177/1367877916628239

Watkins, D., & Burton, M. (2013). *Research Methods in law*. Routledge. doi:10.4324/9780203489352

Weitzner, D. J., Abelson, H., Berners-Lee, T., Feigenbaum, J., Hendler, J., & Sussman, G. J. (2008). Information accountability. *Communications of the ACM*, *51*(6), 82–87. doi:10.1145/1349026.1349043

Willinsky, J. (2009). *The access principle: The case for open access to research and scholarship* (1st ed.). MIT Press.

Xia, J. (2008). A Comparison of Subject and Institutional Repositories in Self-archiving Practices. *Journal of Academic Librarianship*, *34*(6), 489–495. doi:10.1016/j.acalib.2008.09.016

Chapter 2
The Copyright:
History, Growth and Conceptual Analysis

ABSTRACT

It makes sense to discuss the history of copyright before open access. This chapter will establish the background for context. In order to understand the significance of open access repositories, it would be reasonable to be aware of the relevant debate. Therefore, it is necessary to trace the historical development of the concept of copyright as a property right. The continued relevance of the rationales for copyright interests, both philosophical and pragmatic, will be assessed in the contemporary times of digital publishing.

INTRODUCTION

As explained in the introduction, this chapter is based on the premise that to understand the significance of open access repositories, it is necessary to know the context of the debate. Therefore, it is necessary to trace the historical development of the concept of copyright as a property right. The continued relevance of the rationales for copyright interests, both philosophical and pragmatic, will be assessed against the contemporary times of digital publishing. Additionally, the reasons for the rise of open access practice and the impact of the online revolution on conventional publishing methods will be considered.

DOI: 10.4018/978-1-7998-1131-2.ch002

The discussion in this chapter is about the proper equilibrium between self-interest and social good. In other words, there is a need to find an appropriate means to balance individuals' interests and the common will. Thus, the concept of property that interrelates justice (Plato), private ownership (Aristotle), labour (Locke), growth of personality (Hegel) and a bundle of rights that constitute legal relations (Hohfeld) will be considered. It is evident from the literature that the core notion of property as a concept and its subject matter stems from Aristotle's ideas, which are about private property that leads to evolution, production and personal growth. It could be argued that the concept of property has evolved from Plato's joint ownership theory to full liberal ownership theory and moved in the direction set by Aristotle. Following Aristotle, all philosophers similarly describe the concept of private property.

However, Plato's concept of property for communal use helps me argue that it is a potentially more desirable model in the context of open access philosophy. The origins of the notion of property lie in his philosophy; in accordance with his ideas, the concept of property was introduced as joint ownership in terms of social justice and, moreover, as a beneficial tool to support the growth of the whole republic—the ideal republic. He argues that there should not be private property and, therefore, property under the umbrella of joint ownership forms the appropriate factor for peace and justice. Aristotle, although a student of Plato, focuses on a more individualistic aspect; he contends that private property is more effective and will lead to improvement. It is obvious that he denies his teacher's (Plato's) rationale about joint ownership by signaling that such extreme unification is against the diversity of personal identity and against the benefit that everyone gathers through market exchange.

This leads to a discussion of Locke's philosophy, as he extends the aspect of private property ownership by combining it with work. Locke claims that whatever work is produced by an individual becomes his/her property. This idea justifies the connection between ownership and creation. Specifically, in his work titled *Second Treatise on Government* (Locke, 2016), Locke proposes an explanation of by what right an individual can claim to own one part of the world when, according to the Bible, God gave the world to human beings in common. Locke argues that individuals own themselves and thus their own labour. At this point, the connection between Aristotle's and Locke's logic is evident. Locke and Aristotle agree that the issue of private property is one of many intricacies. However, Locke contends a more individualistic rationale for property ownership than Aristotle.

Further on, according to Hegel's views, the concept of property is used to comprehend it as a phase in the development of humankind and the growth of individual personality; thus, he extends the appropriate environment or surroundings of private property following Aristotle's and Locke's logic or reasoning. This chronological order could be an effective flow of thinking that enables me to propose justifications for the emergence of OA as additional support to current copyright regimes.

From Aristotle's philosophy to modern times there are differences regarding traits of property and its ownership, as, one by one, philosophers added new features to their theories. Plato's basic argument about joint ownership was neglected. However, Plato's philosophy on property will enable me to draw on his notions about communal property or joint ownership and its significance within OA. The argumentation in this book relies on Plato's logic, partly because later philosophers also subliminally support his ideas regarding communal use of property, as they highlight several unique aspects of community.

The OA practice supports the wider distribution of information resources. In modern times, when information and communication technologies are undergoing a revolution, it is imperative to go back to Plato's concept and argue that open access could be considered as an instrument with benefits for wider dissemination of information resources. Hence, the discussion sets the background to connect the emergence of copyright protection with developments in the concept of property. The same connections can justify the development of open access in contemporary times; for instance, balancing individual rights with the social good. Thus, justifications follow based on which the concept of private property was introduced and how the idea of private property in land and goods was extended to creative efforts. In the last part of the chapter, the concept of open access is introduced in terms of an appropriate shift of existing copyright protection in the digital age, which leads to the distribution of information and information accessibility. This chapter considers an effective way to balance individuals' interests and the common will.

In the following discussion, part one deals with the conceptualisation of property based on Plato's and Aristotle's views about property. This discussion will trace the transition from public or communal property (Plato's perspective) to the understanding of property as an individual ownership right and the change in the understanding of private property that helps personal developments (Aristotle's perspective). This helps to associate basic features of previous philosophers with modern philosophers about the concept of property. The argument will be further developed in part two with a discussion that relies on modern philosophers' ideas (e.g., Locke and Hegel) about property as they further develop the connection between ownership and the input of labour to create property.

THE CONCEPT OF PROPERTY: FIRST INTRODUCTION

Plato's Notions of Property

Plato's ideas about property were related to his ideas about family, society and the republic. They also contain the origins of notions of patents. His ideas are explained below. In the period around 500 B.C. in Ancient Greece, some form of patent rights was recognised. For example, in the Greek city of Sybaris, patents were granted regarding the creation of unique culinary dishes (Rich, 2010). Encouragement was held out to those who may discover new refinements in luxury; relevant profits emerging from such endeavours were secured to the inventor by a patent for the period of one year (W. Smith, 2010). Thus, this kind of protection for one year illustrates that creative endeavours were encouraged in a manner that protected the whole market from monopolies. At the same time, one or more persons could enjoy an economic advantage in relation to their creative efforts. In this context, Plato's ideas are plausible to describe an ideal republic in which only philosophers ought to keep private property in terms of justice (Kahn, 1998). For the rest, he suggests that there should be joint ownership (Kochin, 2002). The shape of Plato's ideal republic requires justice as its main purpose (Rosen, 2005).

Another relevant aspect that stems from Plato's ideas concerns wealth in conjunction with private property. Plato contends that there should be no legacy or private property and thus, no nepotism that brings negative influences into society (Corlett, 2005). The abolishment of wealth leads directly to the decay of the traditional family; therefore, children should not acknowledge their parents and vice-versa. However, it could be considered as not efficient to interconnect legacy and private property, as it is not only something tangible that can be considered as legacy or private property, especially in our days. As the above example about protection for creators of culinary dishes shows, such protection of creative efforts was an extension of Plato's original idea of private property in goods to property in creative endeavours. This was achieved through the shape of patent protection. Therefore, Plato's insights should be introduced at this point (Kaizer, 2010; Press, 1988; Riegel, 2011; Silver, 2003); an intellectual creation can be legacy for the public domain and the entire society.

Plato contends that owning private property leads to greed and lust. He claims that children should be taken from their biological parents and redistributed by the state to other parents; that is how he supported his arguments concerning private property and the right to "own" a child (Zuckert, 2009). In other words, Plato does not believe in private property as such; he believes that, eventually, no one should own anything, except for the philosophers (Zoller, 2007). Therefore, some scholars call Plato a proto-socialist or a proto-communist. In response, it can be said that this view of property was applied by Plato only to the guardian class and the auxiliaries for the purpose of focusing their attention on the ever-important matter of the state. It should not under-emphasise the fact that it is the first time that someone initiated a discussion about the importance of private property, its content and how it was going to be used, as well as to explicate the main purposes for someone owning property (Press, 1996).

Plato's ideas about private property are fundamentally affiliated with the concept of family and particularly with children, as he argues that having a child leads to greed and lust. However, as children become adults and consequently active members of society, Plato's views about private property are not ultimately productive and are less humanitarian. Plato influenced his student, Aristotle, just as Socrates influenced Plato. However, each man's influence eventually moved in different directions. Plato believes that concepts such as property have a universal form—an ideal form—that led to his idealistic philosophy and ideal republic. Conversely, Aristotle believes that universal forms are not appropriately connected to each other, and thus, each instance of an object has to be examined itself. In the light of these logics, Plato is more interested in justifying communism of the elites based on joint ownership, whereas Aristotle is more interested in justifying a political order based on private property from an individual aspect—something that is relevant for me and leads me to examine Aristotle's views for the concept of property.

Aristotle's Philosophy and His Concept of Property

Aristotle's views are particularly crucial because the entire structure of his thought had a great and even dominant influence on the economic and social thought of the Western world. Although Aristotle, in the Greek tradition, scorns moneymaking and is scarcely a partisan of laissez-faire, he sets forth a trenchant argument in favour of private property (Brady, 2010; Calkins & Werhane, 1998). Perhaps influenced by the private property arguments of another Greek philosopher, Democritus, Aristotle delivers a cogent attack on the concept of communism among the ruling class, as called for by Plato (Brunschwig, 2003; Nolan, 2011; Spiegel, 1991). He denounces Plato's goal of the perfect unity of the state through communism by pointing out that such extreme unity runs against the diversity of mankind and against the reciprocal advantage that everyone reaps through market exchange (Bloom, 1991; Mayhew, 1997).

As Plato's student, Aristotle continues his teacher's work regarding the issue of private property, but from the exact opposite point of view (Parel & Flanagan, 2006). After repeatedly rejecting Plato's ideal state as a dream that will never happen, he develops a stand in favour of private property (Gill & Pellegrin, 2009). He believes that owning private property is necessary to the stability of the state, especially if everyone has a moderate and sufficient amount. Aristotle delivers a point-by-point contrast of private versus communal property (Ostrom & Hess, 2007).

First, private property is more highly productive and will, therefore, lead to progress. According to Aristotle's view, goods owned in common by many people will receive little attention, since people will mainly consult their own self-interest (Ash, 2000; Besson & Martí, 2006; De Dreu & Nauta, 2009; Maitland, 2002; Rocha & Ghoshal, 2006). In contrast, people will devote the greatest interest and care to their own property. Aristotle connects creation and production with progress, and this connection provides a justification for the need to extend Plato's idea of private property in goods to creative endeavours.

Second, Aristotle responds to one of Plato's arguments for property: that it is conducive to social peace as no one will be envious, or try to grab the property, of another. Aristotle argues that property will lead to continuing and intense conflict, as each will complain that he has worked harder and obtained less than others who have done little and taken more from the common store. Further, Aristotle declares that not all crimes or revolutions are powered by economic motives. As Aristotle trenchantly puts it, "men do not become tyrants in order that they may not suffer cold" (Aristotle, 2004). Aristotle's statements make it evident that in his view, creators have to be rewarded and protected as regards their work and contribution to the whole society. In light of this rationale, it is imperative to create an appropriate form of property to protect intellectual creations. Plato's concept of property has distinct negative aspects, and it easily causes injustice and conflict regarding creators' profits (Hoppe, 2004). Thus, Aristotle's arguments help to justify the need to transform Plato's idea of property and expand it from property in goods to also include property in creative efforts.

Aristotle provides a third argument against Plato's concept of property. He says that private property is plainly embedded in man's essence. His admiration of personality or individuality, money and property are interconnected with a natural love of exclusive ownership. Fourth, Aristotle specifies that private property has existed always and everywhere (Rothbard, 2009). To enforce communal property on society would be to disregard the record of human experience and to leap into the new and untried. Abolishing private property would probably create more problems than it would solve. Eventually, Aristotle weaves together his economic and moral theories by providing the brilliant insight that only private property furnishes people with the opportunity to act morally; for example, to practice the virtues of welfare and charity. The compulsion of communal property would destroy that opportunity. To sum up, in accordance with Aristotle, the concept of private property constitutes a means of wealth, production and justice and thus should be protected. While Aristotle is critical of moneymaking, he still opposes any limitation on an individual's accumulation of private property. Instead, in his view, education should teach people voluntarily to curb their rampant desires and thus lead them to limit their own accumulation of wealth. Despite his cogent defence of private property and opposition to coerced limits on wealth, the aristocrat, Aristotle, is fully as scornful of labour and trade as his predecessors.

Aristotle created great trouble for the future by morally condemning the lending of money and decrying the charging of interest as unnatural (Kraut & Skultety, 2005; Staveren, 2013). Since money cannot be used directly and is employed only to facilitate exchanges, it is "barren" and cannot itself increase wealth. Therefore, the charging of interest, which Aristotle thought to imply a direct productivity of money, was strongly condemned as contrary to nature.

Yet the classical philosophy of Aristotle was, in due time, followed by the development of liberal philosophy. Locke was one of the foremost liberal thinkers of his time, and his ideas on property inform our contemporary understandings. Therefore, Aristotle's concept of private property in the context of Locke's ideas regarding property. It is instructive that when Locke's political theory was first published in 1689, the impressive authority of Aristotle stood ready to defeat it. When it was confirmed that the renowned author of An Essay Concerning Human Understanding had also written the anonymously published Two Treatises of Government, Locke was broadly taken to show a distinctive kind of political theory based on individual rights and social contract; this type of account of politics has in many ways rested on Aristotle.

THE INTRODUCTION OF PRIVATE PROPERTY: FROM LANDS AND GOODS TO CREATIVE EFFORTS

Locke's Philosophy on Property

An analysis of Locke's philosophy will help me highlight the importance of work in relation to property ownership. As an initial issue, it should be noted that both Locke and Aristotle acknowledge the issue of private property is one with numerous intricacies. Though both philosophers sketch disparate interpretations on how land should be distributed among human beings, Locke puts forward a more individualistic notion of property ownership than Aristotle. Specifically, in his Second Treatise on Government (Locke, 2013), Locke pursues an answer to the question: by what right can an individual claim to own one part of the world when, according to the Bible, God gave the world to human beings in common? In this work, Locke argues that individuals own themselves and thus their own labour. Accordingly, he argues that individual property rights are natural rights. It is evident that this idea is similar to Aristotle's, which did not support Plato's idea concerning joint ownership.

Following this argument, it is plausible that when an individual works and the outcome of this work is the creation of tangible objects, those objects become his property. Political philosopher Robert Nozick calls this idea the Lockean proviso. Further, according to Locke, the labourer has to hold a natural property right in the resource itself as the exclusive ownership was immediately appropriate for production. In addition, within the connection of right on property with production, Locke clarifies that, in accordance with his philosophy, the concept of property illustrates exclusive rights on tangible abstracts and especially creative endeavours, as he interconnects ownership with production.

Aristotle and Locke disagree on many other issues concerning property ownership, including acquisition, maintenance and divine intervention. Nevertheless, there are indeed several issues regarding property rights where these two philosophers converge, specifically on the issue of equity.

Locke's theory on property can be examined as an expansion of Aristotle's main argument regarding private property. Locke argues that individuals can acquire full property rights over moveable and non-moveable parts of earth in a state of nature. The terms *moveable* and *non-moveable* are, in other words, tangible and intangible abstracts comprising notions, ideas, innovations, thoughts and, in general, intellectual creations. Regarding Locke and his contribution to theories of property, he expands Aristotle's concept by stating that everyone owns a property, and to this, nobody else has any right on that property. Admittedly, Aristotle argues something that Locke would not, as Aristotle states that those with private property should share it. However, it is also the case that Locke revised Aristotle's ideas about sharing and argues that one should only acquire as much property as is appropriate; he or she should not gather in an endless manner. Hence, Locke is Aristotle's successor concerning the development of the concept of property and offers the original point for justifications for moving from private property in goods to property in creative endeavours. Following Locke's philosophy on property comes Hegel's theory. It can also be considered a further successor, as Hegel developed these ideas regarding property and made them into a natural right. Hegel's philosophy of property is discussed in the section below.

Hegel's Philosophy of Property

There are several approaches and different definitions of property from a philosophical perspective; regardless of these differences, the element common to the concept of property is that it is treated as a means rather than an end. In most theories of property, it is regarded as a means to the good life—as a term for gaining freedom or as a term for the recognition of human being (May, 2013; Radin, 1993; Resnik, 2003). Hegel follows Locke's rationale regarding the relationship between individual and property; he argues that property is the embodiment of personality. Further, his view can be seen as extending Locke's notions regarding private property, as in claiming that property is the embodiment of personality, he transforms it into a natural right.

Simultaneously, he argues that the basis of individual rights lies in property. Property is not merely material acquisition, as it is central to an individual's assertion of identity and personality, and thus Hegel follows the same logic as Locke. What is more, Hegel says that property comprises both material and non-material aspects—in other words, tangible and intangible abstracts. Since Aristotle introduced private ownership as an aspect of self-interest, it encouraged philosophers like Locke and Hegel to develop this issue further and argue that property rights are natural rights and embodiments for personal growth, respectively. Suffice to say, individuals' notions and self-interests are inherently distinguished from intellectual creation. From this mutual philosophical consideration, Intellectual creation should be secured and protected as an additional instrument that accomplishes the move from property in goods to personal creations.

According to Hegel, property is an expression of *we* and the location/room/space where an individual can claim rights and state that "this is mine"—a claim that others respect (Knowles, 1983; Salter, 1987; Busch, 2008; Chitty, 2013). The system of private property establishes individuality via contract and exchange. Based on this point, Hegel justifies the inevitable links among property, growth of personality and profits that stem from the aspect of self-interest. The contract demonstrates ownership through institutionalised patterns of mutual respect for individual rights and commitments. Economic life governed by the free exchange of goods is based on an institutionalised notion of the individual as having some claim to recognition as a right-bearing person. If an exchange market is to operate effectively, economic actors have to identify universal standards by which a person can claim to own property. Established patterns of mutual recognition in the modern economic sphere are embodied in economic actors and depict a common will (Hollingsworth & Boyer, 1997; Knill & Lehmkuhl, 2002; Nicolaidis & Shaffer, 2005; Zhang, Shan, Chen, & Gao, 2007; Shan, Gong, & McOwan, 2009).

As a result, the individual has no social traits and thus, no reference to the social environment. This means that individuals have no private or personal life with features to be integrated into society, such as marriage, family, or children, thus no social reference (Honneth, 2010). Therefore, rights demonstrated by Hegel's idea for private property are abstract rights and engage individuals as universal subjects without specific features (Hegel, 1991/2016; Cropanzano,

Byrne, Bobocel, & Rupp, 2001). In addition, morality is called by Hegel the system of mutual recognition and abstract right. Hegel tries to merge various features of his philosophy and social views into a general declaration about the nature of modernity (Hegel, 2015). He traces a contemporary conception of individuality and of the individual as the agent of rights to modern social, economic and political institutions. To Hegel, morality is the subjective part of the mutual social commitments that are politically institutionalised in contracts and economic markets. Therefore, individuals experience mutual commitments as a moral obligation to respect abstract rights as ideals or a vision of good based on mutual recognition of abstract rights.

From the perspective of freedom and in accordance with Hegel's philosophy where emphasis is placed on human needs, property is the first component of freedom and, therefore, is in itself a substantive end. Following this notion, Hegel highlights that if possession, as power over things, is simply pursued to satisfy self-interest, then possession is the means of satisfying these sorts of needs. However, according to Hegel, human needs satisfaction is the aspect of mediation regarding recognition of the subject as a free agent. In this manner, power over things appears as a means for the growth of individual personality. Therefore, this justification represents the importance of an effective interconnection among self-interest, property and personal progress or individual advancement.

Accordingly, Hegel claims that property is the manifestation of the individual's effort to deploy his or her powers and come to self-consciousness by the appropriation of his or her environment (Schroeder, 2005). Consequently, Hegel's task is not to provide a justification for property, but rather to comprehend and understand it as a phase in the production of the human mind. It is also the case that any effort to justify property in the context of Plato's ideas regarding joint ownership will not be suitable for Hegel, as he ignores the role that property plays in the growth of self-awareness among individuals. So long as property is the manifestation of one's will, it is appropriate to make clear that the substantial relationship between the willing subject and what should be individual's property is a procedure which should be relied on self-determination. Intellectual property demonstrates individuals' thoughts, ideas, notions, and ways of thinking, and thus it is necessary to clarify that the individual participates in a process where notions or thoughts develop in accordance with the individual's subliminal willingness. Hence, Hegel's ideas regarding comprehension of property can be considered a phase in the process of human mind production.

From the above discussion, it is evident that Plato, Aristotle, Locke, and Hegel have developed the concept of property from communal property to individual ownership. Simultaneously, the justifications for ownership have expanded the concept of property from physical to intellectual goods. Thus, the concept of private property as a natural right gradually lends itself to the growth of notions regarding the elements of such a right.

The Bundle Theory

Regardless of Hegel's justification of property as a natural right, it remains the case that philosophers have to elaborate on what it means to have a natural right to property. The most notable writer in this regard is Wesley Hohfeld. His theory comprises eight legal relations (Hohfeld, 1913/ 2017), and his views further develop and clarify the meaning of property as a right. In the following discussion, Hohfeld's ideas regarding a right to property are explained, as they inform the bundle theory, which is a legacy of legal realism (H. E. Smith, 2011). Its origins lie in the late 19th- and early 20th-century analytical jurisprudence (Merrill & Smith, 2011). Hohfeld seeks to break down into clear and unambiguous parts what people loosely called rights. Thus, an entitlement might be proper or claim entitlement. It can also be a legitimate entitlement to insist that someone else do or avoid some action with an equivalent duty in that person.

According to bundle theory, there is no unified concept of private property that lends to its comprehension either as a natural right or as intellectual creation in the context of the law. On the contrary, the law gives particular people's rights to tangible objects (Kameas et al., 2003; R. Epstein, 2004; Madison, 2005). Moreover, the property that someone holds in any granted occasion is simply the sum total of specific rights that law gives to him or her in that state. In particular, these rights are metaphorically termed *sticks,* and the property that a person holds is the particular bundle of sticks law grants to them in the given situation. Therefore, it is obvious that law reforms the subject matter of property rights by adding or removing specific sticks from the bundle.

What is more, Hohfeld argues that rights in the context of law can be broken down into their constituent element blocks. More complex legal rights are built with these element blocks. He calls these basic rights *jural relations* (legal relations). In addition, Hohfeld outlines eight legal relations, two of which are significant for the conceptualisation of property: power and immunity.

Hohfeld's analysis demonstrates that property is not as simple a notion as it may first appear. Instead, property is a particular pack of determinate types of Hohfeldian legal relations (Nyquist, 2002). In accordance with Hohfeld's logic, property can be conceptually analysed into particular rights that law gives to the Aristotelian individual. In fact, there is always a subliminal link between Aristotle's and Hohfeld's notions about the importance of a person or individual. What is more, this justification also highlights the importance of personal growth and further social benefits for Plato's republic or the state.

Hence, since the case of property emerged, philosophers have elaborated on personal development on a long-term basis. Despite the long history of property as a concept and as a topic of philosophical consideration, more recently the right to property has come to play a crucial role in discussions within multiple disciplines outside the law and has shown that its content is complex (Yu, 2007). This fact is additional justification for Hohfeld's views in accordance with the concept of property, which is built in more complex rights and legal relations.

Accordingly, this theory does not construct a new normative notion but is more analytical and descriptive in its emphasis. This does not deny the fact that this theory developed in light of a long-lasting and critical philosophical debate regarding legal rights and legal liberties (Johnson, 2007; Breakey, 2012). Based on its rationale, the state should choose appropriate rights to grant in terms of rewarding someone in any given circumstance; that bundle of sticks forms the property that an individual possesses.

Hohfeld's theory makes it obvious that the concept of property is complex and, moreover, it does not contain characteristics relevant to private property to delineate private ownership as one of its features. Therefore, Hohfeld's views justify the position that there is no connection of property to private ownership, and from that fact, the inevitability of joint ownership emerges. Thus, Hohfeld's views, in conjunction with Plato's philosophy regarding communal use of property, seem to provide a plausible argument that can justify the philosophy of open access to creative efforts. That is, the proprietary interests of copyright holders can arguably be shared more widely in the era of the digital revolution. However, contemporary times are also characterised by economic aspects and profits that are associated with and come from creative efforts, respectively (Riahi-Belkaoui, 2003; Cantwell & Santangelo, 2001; Kujansivu & Lonnqvist, 2007; S. Harrison & Sullivan, 2000). The following subsection examines economic justifications for why the concept of property has been extended to intellectual endeavours and efforts.

The Extension of Property to Intellectual Efforts: Justifications

An important form of property in contemporary society is intellectual property, which refers to original expressions of thought and new applications of ideas (Lemley, 2004). The efforts to recognise and protect intellectual property and the relevant markets in such intellectual property have developed considerably over the course of this century. If anything, the effects of ongoing information technology advancements point to the influence of intellectual creations and the corresponding desire to protect the economic and intellectual aspects of the same (Kumar, 2003; Yang & Maskus, 2009). Thus, in many ways, intellectual property is justified as a kind of property. The following discussion is not meant to be an exhaustive analysis of all the relevant issues in this regard. Under this technological growth and progress, another aspect of property that should be considered is related to actual profits, as the concept of creation can be associated to such profits (Ritter, 2005; Arezzo, 2007).

A notable scholar in the area of intellectual property theories is Robert Merges, who claims that property does have a future. In addition, he states that if property demonstrates proper respect both for individual proprietors and social needs, it can contribute beneficially to a well-organised socio-political framework (Merges, 2011). As long as modern society's profitable resources come to be intangible, this capacity will gradually be served by the crucial part of property called IP (Mgbeoji, 2012). Accordingly, Merges clearly sets out the basic features of a workable justification of intellectual property; according to him, these elements are: (a) properties' creative labour in accordance with creative work is recognised and rewarded with true legitimate rights, hence work from hourly wages is converted into a freestanding economic asset whenever possible; (b) grant of real rights, though not absolute rights, and within this element the creator's contribution is acknowledged by granting intellectual property rights, but society's contribution to creative work is also acknowledged; and (c) accommodation of consumers' and users' necessities by facilitating and encouraging cost-effective and easy intellectual property permission and licensing tools, combined with plain methods that allow binding dedication of rights to the public benefit. This last element of Merge's justification for intellectual property lends support to the book argument and works as an additional justification for the model of open access.

In the contemporary discourse of intellectual property, the economic aspects of intellectual property outweigh all other considerations. Therefore, it is imperative that the economic justifications of intellectual property should be addressed. This analysis could provide an additional factor in determining reasons for which the notion of property may be extended to creative endeavours. In addition, it would provide further support to the book argument regarding the designation for the appropriate framework for OARs.

Not surprisingly, economists explore ways of efficiently allocating scarce resources to unlimited wants, and they realise that intellectual property rights are a plausible way of dealing with scarcity in an efficient manner (Pugatch, 2004, 2006). Another significant justification is that of utilitarianism; proponents argue that technological inventions are utilitarian works and, therefore, the principal economic theory applied is about utilitarianism. Moreover, utilitarian theorists generally endorse the creation of intellectual property rights as an appropriate instrument to foster innovation (Menell, 2007a, 2007b). Hence, it is acknowledged that freedom of expression and creation and dissemination of information—and its protection—ought to coexist to support effective outcomes, such as innovation. Nevertheless, this justification illustrates the importance of creators' rights and a recognition that such efforts enhance social evolution; thus, creative efforts should be protected and shared (Landry, Amara, & Lamari, 2002; Lane, Pumain, Leeuw, & West, 2009; Guastello, 2013).

However, a great number of authors who have pursued economic analyses of intellectual property have relied on the Kaldor–Hicks criterion that advises lawmakers to select a system of regulations that maximises aggregate welfare measured by end users' ability and willingness to pay for the goods and services in relation to information. Thus, three different economic justifications dominate the literature. First, incentive theory is the most common; it claims that the optimal doctrine is the one that maximises the difference between (a) the current discounted value to end users of the intellectual products whose creation is induced by holding out to creators and inventors the carrot of monopoly power, and (b) the ensemble detriments generated by such a system of incentives. In uneven terms, this theory urges governmental lawmakers to establish or further develop intellectual property protection when doing so would help end users by stimulating creative efforts more than it would hurt them by constricting their access to intellectual products or raising their taxes.

Second is the economic justification, which is based on patent regimes that reduce rental dissemination. Accordingly, its objective is to eliminate or reduce the tendency of intellectual property rights to advance duplicative or uncoordinated inventive activity. Economic waste of this sort can occur at three stages in the inventive process. Thirdly, it is indispensable to realise that copyright and patent systems play crucial roles in letting potential producers of intellectual products know what end users want; hence, they channel productive outcomes in directions most likely to enhance end users' welfare. Based on this rationale, sales and licenses will ensure that goods get into the hands of people who need them and can pay for them. Only under specific circumstances in which transaction costs would prevent such voluntary exchanges should the holders of intellectual property rights be denied total scrutiny in relation to the uses of their works. This also brings into focus the necessity of public policy as an imperative concerning the governance of OARs of educational material, as discussed later in the book.

This overview of the economic rationales of intellectual property rights needs to be related to the wider issue of whether the products of creative efforts can even be characterised as property. At this point, it is logical for me to ask how the concept of property ownership has informed the development of notions of intellectual property. Intellectual property refers to the rights associated with the expression of an idea or other abstract objects (Bouchoux, 2012). In other words, intellectual property indicates goods created from our mind. Well-known types of intellectual property rights comprise patents, trademarks and copyrights. In general, intellectual property law supports exclusive rights to the appropriator over the use of intellectual property and its aforementioned goods. The notion of intellectual property rights was originally created to protect inventors and scientists, aiming to protect creative procedures and benefit society simultaneously. However, by amplifying the shield of protection, this concept caused the opposite result. A few alternative initiatives to protect intellectual property with less emphasis on trade emerged in the early nineties as a response to the progressively high level of capitalisation of intellectual property rights.

THE HISTORICAL GROWTH OF COPYRIGHT AS PROPERTY RIGHT

This part examines development of copyright as property right. By presenting copyright's historical evolution, follows consideration of the stages that copyright passed through, from being considered property of goods to property of creative endeavours with legal protection. There is also a connection between Renaissance developments with the creation of the printing press. Scientific explanation about whether these resulted in the necessity for conceptualising intellectual property and then protecting it through laws. Additionally, the Renaissance period was distinguished by a great revolution regarding intellectual creations and, therefore, the concept of legitimate protection from relevant works emerged. Because of this revolution, printing press industries started growing. In conformity with the argumentation in this book, this growth will lend further support to the claim that it is necessary to reform the concept of copyright to property right.

The following discussion is divided into six parts. In the first part follows discussion about the importance of the Renaissance and the rapid growth of intellectual creations, which indicated the end of medievalism and the beginning of the new age that would eventually introduce the law and economy of copyright. In the second part, there is also discussion about printing and publishing in Europe during the 15th century were two advances that illustrate a stage in the growth of copyright. In the third part, the Speyer's monopoly is considered (Witcombe, 2004; Geiger, 2012), which was introduced in Venice, and the English printing culture as two issues that stand out in the Renaissance period. The fourth part analyses the Statute of Anne, the first official copyright regime; it signifies the first introduction of an intellectual protection regime that translates the concept of copyright into property right. The fifth part examines the significance of the Berne Convention as an international agreement governing copyright. In the last part, the significance of the TRIPS Agreement administered by the World Trade Organization (WTO) is considered. The TRIPS Agreement introduced intellectual property law into the international trading system for the first time and remains the most comprehensive international agreement on intellectual property (Correa, 2000; Abbott, 2002; Matthews, 2003; Deere, 2009). It will provide the background for the discussion in subsequent chapters.

Renaissance Period

In the midst of the 14th century, the Black Death was one of the most devastating pandemics in human history, resulting in the death of one-third of the population when the plague swept through Europe (Dols, 1977; Raoult et al., 2000; Ziegler, 2013). Every institution of the medieval world was disconcerted, setting peasants free from feudal commitments (Bean, 1989; Brown, 1974; Canning, 2014; Forgeng & Singman, 1999; Oakley, 1999; Stein, 1985). It was almost a century after the eruption of the Black Death when innovation in printing processes appeared, which more than any other event pointed to the end of medievalism and played a crucial role in the growth of the Renaissance. Moreover, it was the sign for the beginning of the new age that would finally introduce the law and economy of copyright (Bowker, 2012; Landes & Posner, 2009).

In 1439, Johannes Gutenberg, a German blacksmith, goldsmith, publisher and printer, introduced printing to Europe (Eisenstein, 2005; Kostylo, 2010). His invention was a mechanical moveable type of printing, which shifted society as a whole and illustrates why it is regarded as the most crucial event of the modern period (Briggs & Burke, 2010; McLuhan, Gordon, Lamberti, & Scheffel-Dunand, 2011; Reed, 2011). Notions, considerations and discussions stimulated minds across Europe, and a trend of publishing arose. The literate people of any class could publish pamphlets and even books in their own language (Suhr, 2012). It is worth noting that the first books printed in Europe were block books, with each page cut from a single block of wood, and usually, these books were produced in two colours (Buringh & Van Zanden, 2009; Chartier, 1994). Additionally, the procedure of cutting letters into the wood was labour-intensive, and so books had only a small number of pages (Febvre & Martin, 1997).

As years passed by, another German goldsmith, Johannes Gutenberg, invented a more convenient process of printing by creating punches and casting styles of letters that permitted book printing within a more effective moveable form. Imitations of Gutenberg's printing press spread rapidly through Europe and by the end of the century publishing industries all over Europe printed prolifically. The first printed European creation in moveable form is a papal indulgence of 1454 that was created in Mainz (Gillespie & Powell, 2014). In the 1460s, German printers established workshops in Venice, Rome and

Basel, which were under German dominance at the time (Benedict, 2007). Installing workshops for printing books was a costly enterprise as it required appropriate instruments and technology.

The following subsection examines the main features of intellectual protection in the Renaissance period, in contrast with after the Renaissance period, to prove that its content gradually changed.

The Contrast of Contents

Obviously, the Renaissance period has affected European intellectual life and, therefore, appropriate surroundings arose in which new attitudes regarding ownership, authorship and intellectual production were deployed. The necessity for intellectual protection did not stem from the intangible aspect of intangible objects, such as ideas, but from the very tangible world of craftsmanship and mechanical inventions (Sennett, 2008; Senseney, 2011; Womack, Jones, & Roos, 2008).

Therefore, trends at that time were associated with growth, but in different "clothes" compared with after the Renaissance period. This comparison highlights the process of how copyright transformed into a property right. The contemporary world is distinguished by the continuous technological developments that comprise the basic feature of modern times (Givoni, 2006; Landes, 2003). The Renaissance period's primary characteristic was the growing amount of intellectual creations in the many perspectives mentioned above and, consequently, monopolies, relevant privileges and the necessity of creators' protections that gradually emerged. In contemporary times, creators have sought to protect their online creations by using several digital licenses (US7310729 B2, 2007; Liu, Safavi-Naini, & Sheppard, 2003; Rosset, Filippin, & Westphall, 2005).

Moreover, the Renaissance period was characterised by a growth of interest in classical learning and values, the decline of feudal regimes, development of commerce and the application of inventions with effective potential, such as paper and printing. Therefore, if someone had the willingness to publish, the printing process was required, but there was no specific regime of intellectual protection to be applied for his publication afterwards. Throughout the Renaissance, creators had need of protection regarding their creations, but there was no particular redress or legitimate regime for intellectual protection.

From this point on, the Statute of Monopolies (1623) is considered, which clarifies how monopolies are a crucial element in the relationship between governments and publishers by excluding creators' roles and rights. This statute was an Act of the English Parliament and was the first statutory expression of English patent law (Pottage & Sherman, 2010). Chris Dent argues that the Statute of Monopolies was a crucial marker in the history of patents, with ongoing importance (Raoult et al., 2000). Further, it is worth noting that the monarch issued the patents involved to grant monopolies over specific enterprises to skilled individuals with new techniques. However, earlier English patent law was based on custom and common law, not on a statute (Durham, 2013; MacLeod, 2002). Moreover, the Crown granted patents as a form of economic protection to ensure high industrial production; it was in response to this state of affairs that this statute emerged.

The issue was that these patents were the Crown's "presents" or gifts, with no judicial review, oversight or consideration; consequently, no actual law developed around patents (Nachbar, 2005). This practice came from guilds—groups who were manipulated by the Crown and in turn held monopolies over specific industries (S. Epstein, 1991; Kieser, 1989; Richardson, 2004). Unlike the context of the current copyright and patent system where privileges stem from creations, in the earlier period privileges were accepted as gifts from those who were ruling and were for the exclusive benefit of those who had governmental connections. Accordingly, Kostylo claims that "[I]n contrast to modern copyright and patent, early privileges were conceived as a form of municipal favour (gratiae) and an exception to the law (priva lex) rather than the recognition of the author's inherent rights" (Kostylo, 2008). In addition, she points out that these privileges took various shapes, such as exclusive monopolies granting the creators the right to take advantage of their work or engage in other productive activity, and printing privileges bestowing publishers or authors with exclusive rights to print and sell a work. Hence, both privileges were granted in terms of manipulation rather than as the acknowledgement of the creator's production and affiliated intellectual property rights. Moreover, these types of privileges would later be determined as patents for inventions and proto-copyrights, respectively (Bottomley, 2014).

Thus, in the context of legitimacy, printing privileges and grants for automated inventions were practically identical. Further, according to Karjala, if patents are in the current century to be restricted to tangible objects and their operation by industrial procedures, it is to become progressively irrelevant as we steadily approach an information-as-product economy (Karjala, 2002; Long, 2004; Walterscheid, 1999). Considering that the history of patents initiates not with inventions but with royal grants of industrial monopolies in the Renaissance period, such as those granted by the English Crown, the origin of the idea that intellectual property is a legal right is significant. Advocates claim that this radical change from monopoly privilege to legal property emerged solely in response to institutional and economic demands (Mossoff, 2006). This history is relevant, as the concepts of copyright and patent were not very distinct.

Going back to Kostylo's argument regarding the lack of differentiation between copyright and patents, there are at least two explanations: legal and cultural. In legal terms, primary printing privileges for mechanical inventions had not produced a separate bureaucratic framework and continued to rely on the same system of discretionary privileges. In cultural terms, this convergence could be analysed by explaining the way in which the content of copyright protection developed, targeting first the tangible abstracts of printing technology before it expanded to the protection of intangible abstracts (Elias & Stim, 2004). A notable effort that shows the first attempt to differentiate these concepts was the 1710 enactment of the Statute of Anne, which introduced a legitimate framework for intellectual protection (Bradford, 2015). In the following section examines the significance of such a framework concerning the first official regime of copyright law.

Early Printing and Publishing in Europe

Early printers were also publishers for themselves, but by the 16th century, there was a considerable increase of printers. However, other individuals, who undertook the majority of costs and commercial risks, financially supported them (Pasley, 2002; Pettegree, 2010). Many title pages of books from that time claim at the bottom that the work was printed "by *xxx* for *yyy*" (publisher or bookseller of the book). Occasionally, the publisher or bookseller was responsible for covering the costs for part of the supplies and equipment in the print shop and usually was sharing the income from the print run with the printer (Curran & Seaton, 2009; Fyfe, 2006; Goff, 2011). It is worth mentioning that several books were published under the auspices of a significant patron, such as the Pope, a monarch or a wealthy cardinal, which shows that the financial issue regarding the printing process was of paramount importance. For example, Aldus Manutius was an Italian humanist who became a printer and publisher when he founded the Aldine Press at Venice (Barker, 1992). He made significant contributions to the enterprise of publishing, including inventing the italic form, the use of the modern semicolon, the contemporary appearance of the comma, and introducing inexpensive books in small formats. Additionally, and in relation to the costs of the printing process, it should be mentioned that Aldus Manutius issued various books with papal financial support (Martin, 1995). According to Sider, most printing projects were meant to make a profit, but not necessarily constantly regardless of total costs.

Moreover, many early printers had serious difficulties publishing, as printing was a capital-intensive and highly competitive business (Costas, 2012; Milward & Saul, 2013; Sider, 2007). It is to be expected that the publishers wanted to secure their investment and gains. Therefore, before printing a particular text, the printer would request permission from governments for an exclusive monopoly on printing that text. It is not surprising that privileges, monopolies and relevant revenues associated with intellectual creations and relevant efforts arose (Gresser, 2013; Idris, 2003; Maskus, 2000; Romer, 2002). However, it is obvious that the author's role was not so important in relation to the management of his works and potentials agreements with publishers. Indeed, in the hierarchy of interests in the context of trade, the authors' role was set at the bottom of importance, and the bilateral agreements between the publishers and the rulers highlight the emerging disadvantage of the author's role. According to Kretschmer, the rhetoric of author's rights has been broadly pushed by third parties (i.e., investors in creativity, rather than creators), who also turn out to be the chief beneficiaries of the extended protection. Moreover, he argues that ever since the beginning the printing press environment has been extremely blurred, still showing traces of feudal features (Kretschmer, 2000; Kretschmer, Bently, & Deazley, 2010). In early times, the creators were mostly men and therefore the pronoun *he* is applied to address them.

The following section presents an analysis of the relationship between Speyer, the publisher, and the Venetian Government that granted exclusive privileges for printing in Venice. This is relevant to support the argumentation that the concept of copyright developed from the exclusive privilege of printing rather than from a desire to protect the author's creation.

Speyer's Monopoly and the English Printing Culture

During the 15th century, the home of first printing privileges was Venice. The very first publicly claimed copyright was decided by the rulers of Venice on 18 September 1469, a short time after the German Master Johannes of Speyer opened a printing shop there and started printing with the support of the rulers of the Venetian Republic. This was the earliest European initiative where Speyer was granted an exclusive monopoly on printing in Venetian territories. Johannes Speyer was indeed bestowed with much more than merely a right to copy. He was given a five-year monopoly to print. In contemporary terms, this was a formal paradigm "infant" industry protection (Grossman & Horn, 1987; Head, 1994; Shafaeddin, 2000). The practice of granting exclusive privileges to print in a particular city, to print a particular text or to print a particular category of texts spread instantly from Venice throughout the Italian states, and from there to France and England (Hesse, 2002).

Even though this monopoly has been addressed as the first acknowledged patent, developing a long tradition of granting printing privileges in Europe, Speyer's monopoly does not seem to be something new or outstanding in the economic life and legal tradition of Venice. This can be explained with the help of the fact that Venetians may not have been the first to introduce printing into Italy, though they rapidly determined the significance of this new craft (Kostylo, 2012). Thenceforth, in the 13th century, the Venetian people led Europe in their endeavours by granting monopoly rights to immigrants who brought new skills and qualifications to the city.

Certainly, during the 15th and 16th centuries, the Venetian Government received over a thousand applications from specialists in diverse areas, including from the makers of soap, gunpowder, saltpetre and glass, tanners, miners and civil engineers (Weatherford, 2009). These applications cover every possible subject, from machines and tools for draining the marshes to poisons and windmills. Significantly, this new craft of printing flourished outside the guild structure and, consequently, in the absence of any administrative framework controlling and supervising this sort of commerce. As for the guilds, the rest of society usually judged these institutions as "rivals" of the public good and not as laudable patterns for organising society on corporate lines (Beinin, 2001; Lucassen, Moor, & Zanden, 2008). It is evident that printing and publishing commerce was not organised into a closed form until

1549. Hence, for the first 80 years of printing in Venice, relevant privileges continued to be granted occasionally and on an ad hoc basis. In this manner, the distinction between commercial monopolies and proto-copyrights did not exist in early modern Venice.

To sum up, it can be stated that the practice of granting industrial privileges in early modern Italy constituted a crucial field in which new ways and methods arose concerning authorship and property. These developments formed the social and philosophical vocabulary of intellectual property that foreshadowed its legal outline and adjustment as part of copyright tradition in the longer term. At this point, the discussion turns to England, a country with a long history concerning copyright and its growth. As England was also influenced by the rapid growth of intellectual creations in the Renaissance period, it acquired a well-established literary and print culture.

In the 16th century, the society of England was affiliated with Aristotle's views regarding property and the significance of individual evolution, and thus, society was individualistic (Mun, 2008). Second, England has a long history of literary and printing culture in which the concept of authorship could have been constructed. In addition, and as mentioned before, it is well known that printing had a revolutionary influence in Europe. England adopted the moveable sort of printing press from Germany during the Renaissance and instantly improved its publishing industry (Harrison & Matthew, 2004). Third, in terms of copyright protection, England has the longest legal tradition of copyright protection, and it was the first country to demonstrate a common law tradition of authors' rights (Barron, 2006).

The Statute of Anne, 1710

Ronan Deazley claims that there were no less than 13 failed efforts between 1695 and 1704 to accord a framework of statutory regulation for printing (Deazley, 2004). Eventually, the Worshipful Company of Stationers and Newspaper Makers, usually known as the Stationer's Company (Rose, 2010), agreed to the Statute of Anne, which was enacted in the spring of 1710. Accordingly, there are advocates who argue that the passing of the Statute of Anne in 1710 is the seminal moment in copyright history (Geller, 2000; Hughes, 2009; Rose, 1995). It is evident that, for the first time, regulations identified an author's—not the bookseller's—right to administer the reproduction of books. Further, the author's copyright as the exclusive right to administer the reproduction of books, according to the Statute of Anne, lasted for 14 years since publication and could be renewed by the author for an additional seven years (Bently, Suthersanen, & Torremans, 2010). By acknowledging the author's right to property in books and other printed material, the Statute of Anne set the foundation for the contemporary structure of copyright law.

Atkinson and Fitzgerald (2014, p. 25) claim, "[T]he Act also resolved long-standing antagonism between publishers and parliamentarians, many of whom wanted to drive a dagger through the heart of the booksellers' monopoly." The Statute of Anne was an agreement that stemmed from the publishers' willingness to regulate a chaotic market and politicians' willingness to strike at monopoly. Additionally, it is necessary to mention that the regulations, which were affiliated with the Statute of Anne, could not be described as friendly to booksellers. However, the most important transformation brought about by this Statute is in relation to what it does not legislate. It makes no provision whatsoever for the state arrangement of what could or could not be published (E. Lee, 2007). Additionally, the Statute of Anne argues about liberties that offending printers and booksellers have taken with authors and owners of intellectual creations who have realised that their books, inventions or writings were printed without their acquiescence. Deazley claims that:

[T]he basic plank of the Statute of Anne was then, and remains, a social quid pro quo. To encourage 'learned men to compose and write useful books' the State would provide a guaranteed, if finite, right to print and reprint those works. (Deazley, 2006, pp. 13–14).

With the Statute of Anne, a critical opportunity or bargain emerged involving authors, booksellers and the public. Deazley's statement correctly reflects the significance of the Statute of Anne as the first attempt at an effective equilibrium among the stakeholders of intellectual property.

The scope of licensing under this statute was to regulate what might be said in print to control the publishers in the interests of good order. The primary aim of the Statute of Anne was to inspire further study and speech and to empower debates in the public sphere. Therefore, by entrusting the copyright of a printed work in the creator or author rather than publisher or bookseller the author is responsible for publishing and reproduction of his/her book; thus, the Statute reformulates the concept of copyright as a property right. That is, copyright, rather than being an advantage, benefit or gift to authors, is the natural consequence that stems from their intellectual creativity. Hence, the Statute grants a legal framework to the public sphere, supporting a regime in which authors are invited to bring their intellectual creations or writings into the public forum. The rationale is that these are the creations that stem from their authority, their learning and their considerations.

The old regime of licensing that strengthened the Stationer's Company was an opportunity for mutually beneficial discussions between the booksellers and the state. Accordingly, there are proponents who claim that the Statute of Anne offered a triple-path opportunity among creators, authors, booksellers and the reading community (Deazley, 2008; Rose, 2009).

Specifically, authors were granted legal recognition and definite monopoly rights, and booksellers were granted the chance to purchase and take advantage of these monopoly rights and the reading community was certain that after the end of the restricted term of protection the works would become free and open to everyone. By designating limitations, the Statute of Anne produced the literary commons, which is now known as public domain, and offered more social aspects in conjunction with intellectual creations (Boyle, 2003; Fennell, 2010; Goldberg et al., 2006; Morris & Shin, 2002; Patterson, 2000). In other words, authors and booksellers began to enjoy mutual benefits.

From Privilege to Berne Convention

As a cumulative consequence of the invention of the printing press by Gutenberg in 1436 and in conjunction with Speyer's monopoly and the Statute of Anne, the amount of publishing and copying worldwide developed considerably (Wallerstein, 2011). Before the emergence of the printing press, booksellers used to copy authors' manuscripts by hand (Mayer, 2004; Rouse & Rouse, 2000). After the introduction of printing, booksellers were able to copy authors' manuscripts at a much faster rate. Therefore, profits from the sale of books accommodated booksellers in respect of recovering the costs for authors' manuscripts and the process of printing.

Because of the ease of printing, printing presses led to piracy; there were "pirate" booksellers who copied books already published by the lawful booksellers. In addition, these pirate booksellers could sell copied books at lower prices. This was because they were able to avoid paying for authors' manuscripts (Everton, 2005, 2005; Johns, 2010; Slauter, 2013). It is reasonable to expect that neither the lawful booksellers nor the authors had any legal recourse against these pirate booksellers. And it is obvious that from this point on the necessity of protection of the interests of the authors and publishers emerged. This necessity first emanated from the booksellers, whose economic interest was endangered by the pirate booksellers. The booksellers successfully lobbied their respective sovereigns for protection in the form of an exclusive right, better known as a privilege (Yamada, 2012). The privilege granted legitimate booksellers the exclusive right to print and sell specific authors' manuscripts for a limited time.

The government bestowed upon the printer a limited monopoly. The sovereigns also benefited from this arrangement, because they could decide which booksellers would receive a privilege and which manuscripts were suitable for printing (Biagioli & Galison, 2014). The sovereign censored manuscripts that it believed would threaten the public order (Birn, 2005; Castillo, 2009; Müller, 2003). The use of these privileges came to an end about two hundred years after they were introduced (Shao, 2011). There are threefold reasons or justifications for their demise: (a) Printers began to abuse their monopoly power, thereby angering their sovereigns in the process. In England, for instance, such abuses were one factor in the House of Commons' refusal to renew privileges (O'Brien & Bosc, 2009). (b) As governments matured, the need for censorship diminished. (c) The authors argued more actively for the protection of their own rights (Karolides, Bald, & Sova, 2011).

The new system of protection that filled the vacuum left by the privilege system was a statutory form of protection that focused, for the first time, on the rights of the authors (Ricketson & Ginsburg, 2006). With the Statute of Anne, the first statutory copyright for the protection of authors spread throughout Europe and the US. However, a great number of authors' works crossed national boundaries and, as authors were unprotected in foreign countries, pirates easily targeted their literary works (Bold, 2011). The authors from different countries acted to force governments to protect their works under an international system and not just via domestic regimes (Ederington, 2001). As the magnitude of piracy extended, the scope of relevant activity regarding copyright protection from an international perspective also developed. More countries pursued the aim to settle copyright relations based on a treaty (Dinwoodie, 2007; Jackson, 2000).

Material reciprocity was the core concept of the first international copyright treaties (Curzon, 1989; Elliott & Bayard, 1994; Fehr & Gächter, 2000; Gintis, 2005). In accordance with this concept, country one would grant country two's authors the same protection as country two would grant country one's authors (Yu, 2004). However, this regime was ineffective and complicated

(Cammaerts, 2011), and a number of countries maintained piracy as the focal theme of their international copyright relations. They declined to sign any treaties, or if they did sign such treaties, they failed to abide by the terms.

The first attempt for the protection of foreign authors via the national treatment regime came from the decree of 1852 (Gutu, 2014). According to this treatment, country one grants authors from country two the same protection that country one grants its own authors. Thus, a national treatment framework is much easier to manage than a reciprocity framework, as courts need only interpret their own domestic copyright law (Leaffer, 2010). Therefore, any advances in domestic authors' rights in country one would automatically accrue to authors from country two.

Following the decree of 1852, a trend arose in Europe for better international protection of the authors' rights. The extension of copyright protection demonstrated additional support to authors' rights. As authors' rights triggered even more attention in domestic legislation, authors became an effective political group. Since the beginning of the movement, in the context of international copyright protection, two explicit principles competed for supremacy. First, the non-discrimination principle of domestic treatment preserves the probity of national regulations and ensures that foreign authors will be homogenised with local authors. Second, multilateral patterns ensure international consistency and thus increase the distribution of works of authorship globally.

In 1858, the first international Congress of Authors and Artists met in Brussels; the work of this group laid the groundwork for the drafting and signing of the Berne Convention (Ginsburg, 2000). In addition, the decisions issued by the Congress impelled the gradual elimination of formalities, national treatment and domestic regulations. Thus, in accordance with the first draft of the Berne Convention, national forms were to work in cooperation with international forms, but the latter were to be applied via domestic regulations. Although the convention did not achieve every goal outlined at the first Congress in 1858, it illustrated the taking of a great step regarding international copyright protection. And despite the diverging views expressed from the participating countries, the last draft of the Berne Convention (1886) laid the groundwork for later developments concerning the universality of an appropriate international copyright regime, which was introduced in earlier drafts. Therefore, the adoption by members of the WTO of the TRIPS Agreement further extended the Berne Convention's minimum standards to countries beyond the Berne Union. Therefore, the TRIPS Agreement is addressed in the following subsection.

From Berne Convention to TRIPS Agreement

The broadly differing patterns of protection and enforcement of IP rights, as well as the absence of a universal regime of regulations and disciplines to deal with the international trade in products, became a critical trend in the international trade relations (Harris, 2004). Eventually, the TRIPS Agreement was negotiated. It comprised an integral part of the multilateral trade negotiations under the Uruguay Round of the General Agreement on Tariffs and Trade (GATT; McCalman, 2005). It covers copyright and related rights (i.e., the rights of performers, producers of sound recordings and broadcasting organisations); trademarks, including service marks; geographical indications, including appellations of origin; industrial designs; patents, including the protection of new varieties of plants; the layout designs of integrated circuits; and undisclosed information, including trade secrets and test data.

A significant trait of the TRIPS Agreement concerns the extension of the multilateral GATT dispute settlement as an appropriate regime for IP protection. This permits the application of trade approvals by comprising, for instance, the suspension of concessions or other obligations (Babovic & Wasan, 2011; Di Vita, 2013).

Sell and Prakash argue that, while the TRIPS Agreement represents the first comprehensive and enforceable global agreement on IP rights, it has been the subject of much criticism since its inception (Sell & Prakash, 2004). The standard argument in support of TRIPS arises from the recognition of the modern importance of the knowledge economy and private IP as a crucial element of international commerce (Bossche, 2008; Hoekman & Kostecki, 2009; Narlikar, Daunton, & Stern, 2012). According to Matthews, disputes regarding IP protection constitute significant non-tariff obstacles to commerce; thus, TRIPS is a consequence of the necessity for a robust multilateral scheme to substitute what was an ineffective patchwork of pre-existing intellectual property conventions (Matthews, 2004, 2005, 2006). For the first time since GATT was launched in 1947, the Uruguay round of multilateral trade negotiations comprised an effort to harmonise international IP rights protection. By the end of these negotiations, participating states signed the TRIPS Agreement to regulate and protect trade-related aspects of intellectual property rights (May, 2013). Additionally, the TRIPS Agreement brought intellectual property into the trade regime overseen by the WTO and put in place a global minimum standard of intellectual protection that WTO members must follow. This covers copyrights, trademarks, industrial designs, geographical indications, patents, integrated circuit designs, trade secrets and anti-competitive contract restrictions. Suffice to say, by globalising intellectual property rights via the TRIPS Agreement obstacles to trade were overcome.

Various wider benefits to society are said to accrue from the imposition of temporary monopolies and other limitations that result from private intellectual property rights (Goldstein, Rivers, & Tomz, 2007; D. Lee, 2004). By instituting legal protection, the disclosure of new knowledge and creativity is encouraged, and the significant costs associated with the creative process (such as with research and development) can be recouped, and remuneration earned. Innovation is thus both rewarded and further promoted. The scope and reliability offered by a global intellectual property rights regime should not only stimulate domestic innovation, but the security offered to developed world patent holders and others can also encourage foreign direct investment, technology transfer and licensing, and the diffusion of knowledge to the developing world (Matthews, 2003).

What is more, the TRIPS Agreement represents a significant advance from previous agreements regarding IP rights in terms of monitoring, enforcement and dispute settlement capabilities. In addition, a TRIPS Council reviews domestic legislation and application of the accord. Therefore, its supporters see the TRIPS Agreement as representing an enforceable global regime of IP protection that plays an essential role in the contemporary global information society. The rewarding and encouraging of innovation spurs economic growth and enables technological evolution.

Since the TRIPS Agreement came into force, it has received a growing level of criticism from developing countries, academics and non-governmental organisations. Some of this criticism is against the WTO as a whole, but many advocates also regard the TRIPS Agreement as ineffectual policy. The TRIPS Agreement's wealth concentration effects (moving money from people in developing countries to copyright and patent owners in developed countries) and its imposition of artificial scarcity on the citizens of countries that would otherwise have had weaker IP laws are common bases for such criticisms. For example, Drahos claims that:

[I]t was an accepted part of international commercial morality that states would design domestic intellectual property law to suit their own economic circumstances. States made sure that existing international intellectual property agreements gave them plenty of latitude to do so. (Drahos & Braithwaite, 2002, p. 38; Klein, 2009)

Further, Archibugi and Filippetti contend that the importance of TRIPS in the process of generation and diffusion of knowledge and innovation has been overestimated by both their supporters and their detractors (Archibugi & Filippetti, 2010). Claude Henry and Joseph E. Stiglitz state that the modern intellectual property global framework may impede both innovation and distribution and suggest reforms to empower the global dissemination of innovation and sustainable deployment (Henry & Stiglitz, 2010). In this book, the concept of open access is justified as a means of widening access to knowledge; the next part introduces the issues that will be developed further in the following chapters.

THE CONCEPT OF OPEN ACCESS AS A MEANS OF ENHANCEMENT FOR COPYRIGHT PROTECTION IN THE DIGITAL AGE

It is evident from the discussion in the preceding sections that scholars have been communicating thoughts, considerations, claims, research outcomes and examinations of these throughout the ages in a diversity of forms. For instance, lectures, discussions, essays, manuscripts, monographs, articles and books are among the most common ways of sharing intellectual ideas or scholarship. With the coming of the Enlightenment, the first scholarly periodicals, Philosophical Transactions of the Royal Society of London and Journal des Scavans, appeared in 1665 from leading learned societies (Weber, 2005).

Since that time, scholarly articles became a principal form for beneficial scholarly communication (Bergstrom, 2007; Tenopir, King, Edwards, & Wu, 2009). Learned societies took authority and responsibility for editing and publishing scholarly journals during their early years (Hopkins, 2011). This trend continues; various contemporary scholarly societies publish some of the leading journals in a variety of science areas. However, after World War Two, government investment in Western Europe and the US in the field of scientific research increased the numbers of scholarly researchers who could communicate with their fellows. Simultaneously, the learned societies were slow to adapt to this instant flow of investment and the representatives of the printing press industry entered the area in growing numbers to provide new titles in a variety of scientific areas.

The growing literature obligated subscribers of scholarly journals, such as academic libraries, government agencies, industrial research centres and individuals, to obtain access to scholarly data (Boyd & Crawford, 2012). However, the affiliated expenses with such access began to increase with the rise of electronic publication (Lyon, 2013; Turner, 2010). In addition, journal publishers were forced to produce their content in two different forms: the hard copy journal and the electronic or digital version, hosted on a digital network. As prices of scholarly journals surpassed costs, worries regarding maintenance of affordable access to this sort of literature began to amplify. What is more, the development of the Internet and specifically the World Wide Web (WWW) introduced new terms, challenges and circumstances regarding scholarly communication. Therefore, the printing press initiated to be attached to a digital or online platform to follow up with the Internet, which in turn offers a contemporary way to publish.

Regardless of the emergence of the Internet that promised the possibility of extending access to the scholarly literature via cost-effective ways, for-profit publishers instead of non-profit scholarly societies inhabit scholarly publishing to the greater extent, and they have increasingly consolidated their economic power. By using their collective power over pricing, for-profit publishers firmly developed journal subscription prices, obligating academic libraries and other subscribers to struggle to benefit from their patrons' desire for access to up-to-date research.

A renowned author in the field of open access, Michael Carroll, argues that born out of frustrations over foregone opportunities to grow Internet diffusion of scholarly research and ever-rising journal prices, academic librarians, autodidacts and some academic leaders unified to initiate open access (Carroll, 2006). Accordingly, Carroll argues that the principal goal of open access is quite simple, as within open access scholarly literature and relevant resources information is freely available on the public Internet for end users and researchers of all kinds (Carroll, 2013).

Open access is a useful innovation, even if there are minor obstacles regarding the online availability of information that end users could enjoy while using scholarly journal articles. However, more significantly, copyright protection issues emerged, and these should be considered. In this context, advocates argue that there are two ways scholars can make their articles accessible and protect copyright at the same time. They can do so either by publishing via the "gold road" of open access, in which publications are freely available online to the public, or by publishing via the "green road" of open access in a subscription-access journal, in which the author should self-archive an e-print of his/her work in an online OAR (Harnad, 2007). Once an article is freely accessible within either method, it is indexed by search engines and is immediately locatable and retrievable by anyone with Internet access (Cramond, 2011).

Taking everything into account, the concept of open access is a response to current technological developments in conjunction with creative efforts that should be formulated and attached to modern copyright laws, appropriately.

CONCLUSION

In this chapter there is discussion about the historical development of the concept of copyright as property right and the transition from property in goods to property of ideas; The main argument of the book relies on old and modern philosophies about property.

To understand the significance of OARs, it is necessary to know the context of the debate. In modern times, a response to rapid technological evolution and relevant issues of intellectual protection is open access, which constitutes a collection of possible conditions and solutions (for instance, those offered from Creative Commons licenses) under which the creator can protect his or her work and deliver free reproductions of copyright works (Willinsky, 2003). Considering the efforts of trade companies to develop new technologies for publishing should not neglect social benefits. Hence, open access could be a tool of enhancement for copyright regimes, as social prosperity should be enabled since the benefits of society should have pros over specific material interests.

Intellectual property rights are a significant part of the regulatory environment appropriate to support economic development in the digital age (Maskus & Reichman, 2005). Current illustrations of growth regarding production are strongly related to investments in information and technology advances (posts on Facebook, "tweets" on Twitter, creating and uploading videos on YouTube and so forth) and correlate with the extent to which such technology-driven goods and services are disseminated throughout the economy (Organisation for Economic Co-operation and Development, 2001). Thus, granting property rights in the fruits of innovative and creative endeavours has long been the policy instrument of choice to accomplish these objectives (Boudreau, 2007; Fairclough, 2002; Gangopadhyay & Mondal, 2012). All in all, by highlighting inform as a basic contributor to economic growth it demonstrates that open access, as one of its significant parts, should be considered a tool that supports the dissemination of information resources that are distinguished by exclusive ownership. Therefore, within the following chapter, the concept of open access will be examined as part of additional support for the main argument.

In the following chapter, the continued relevance of the rationales for copyright interests, both philosophical and pragmatic, will be assessed in the contemporary context of digital publishing. It will then canvas the reasons and explanations for the rise of the concept of open access, including an analysis of the effect of the online revolution on conventional publishing methods.

REFERENCES

Abbott, F. (2002). *The Doha Declaration on the TRIPS Agreement and Public Health: Lighting a Dark Corner at the WTO*. Rochester, NY: Social Science Research Network. Retrieved from http://papers.ssrn.com/abstract=1493725

Archibugi, D., & Filippetti, A. (2010). The globalisation of intellectual property rights: Four learned lessons and four theses. *Global Policy*, *1*(2), 137–149. doi:10.1111/j.1758-5899.2010.00019.x

Arezzo, E. (2007). Struggling around the natural divide: The protection of tangible and intangible indigenous property. *Cardozo Arts & Entertainment Law Journal*, *25*, 367.

Aristotle. (2004). *Politics*. Digireads.com Publishing.

Ash, C. (2000). Social-Self-Interest. *Annals of Public and Cooperative Economics*, *71*(2), 261–284. doi:10.1111/1467-8292.00142

Atkinson, B., & Fitzgerald, B. (2014). The nineteenth century: Liberty and literary property. In *A short history of copyright* (pp. 37–43). Springer International Publishing. doi:10.1007/978-3-319-02075-4_5

Babovic, S., & Wasan, K. M. (2011). Impact of the trade-related aspects of intellectual property rights (TRIPS) agreement on India as a supplier of generic antiretrovirals. *Journal of Pharmaceutical Sciences*, *100*(3), 816–821. doi:10.1002/jps.22326 PMID:20740678

Barker, N. (1992). *Aldus Manutius and the development of Greek script & type in the fifteenth century*. Fordham Univ Press.

Barron, A. (2006). Copyright. *Theory, Culture & Society, 23*(2–3), 278–282. doi:10.1177/026327640602300237

Bean, J. (1989). *From lord to patron: Lordship in late medieval England.* Manchester University Press.

Beinin, J. (2001). *Workers and peasants in the modern Middle East.* Cambridge University Press. doi:10.1017/CBO9780511612800

Bently, L., Suthersanen, U., & Torremans, P. (Eds.). (2010). Global copyright: Three hundred years since the Statute of Anne, from 1709 to cyberspace (1st ed.). Cheltenham, UK: Edward Elgar Pub.

Bergstrom, C. (2007). Eigenfactor: Measuring the value and prestige of scholarly journals. *College & Research Libraries News, 68*(5), 314–316. doi:10.5860/crln.68.5.7804

Besson, S., & Martí, J. L. (2006). *Deliberative democracy and its discontents.* Ashgate Publishing, Ltd.

Biagioli, M., & Galison, P. (2014). *Scientific authorship: Credit and intellectual property in science.* Routledge. doi:10.4324/9780203954270

Birn, R. (2005). Book censorship in eighteenth-century: France and Rousseau's response. In *History of Ideas; Travel Writing; History of the Book; Enlightenment and Antiquity.* Academic Press.

Bloom, A. D. (1991). *The Republic of Plato.* Basic Books.

Bold, C. (2011). *The Oxford history of popular print culture.* Oxford University Press. doi:10.1093/acprof:osobl/9780199234066.001.0001

Bottomley, S. (2014). *The British patent system during the Industrial Revolution 1700–1852: From privilege to property.* Cambridge, UK: Cambridge University Press.

Bouchoux, D. E. (2012). *Intellectual property: The law of trademarks, copyrights, patents, and trade secrets.* Cengage Learning.

Boudreau, K. J. (2007). *Does opening a platform stimulate innovation? The effect on systemic and modular innovations (SSRN Scholarly Paper No. ID 913402).* Rochester, NY: Social Science Research Network. Retrieved from http://papers.ssrn.com/abstract=913402

Bowker, R. (2012). *Copyright: Its history and its law*. Retrieved from http://www.gutenberg.org/ebooks/39502#download

Boyd, D., & Crawford, K. (2012). Critical questions for big data. *Information Communication and Society*, *15*(5), 662–679. doi:10.1080/1369118X.2012.678878

Boyle, J. (2003). The second enclosure movement and the construction of the public domain. *Law and Contemporary Problems*, *66*(1/2), 33–74.

Bradford, L. (2015). *Inventing patents: A story of legal and technical transfer*. Rochester, NY: Social Science Research Network. Retrieved from http://papers.ssrn.com/abstract=2566162

Brady, E. (2010). Aristotle, Adam Smith and the Virtue of Propriety. *Journal of Scottish Philosophy*, *8*(1), 79–89. doi:10.3366/E1479665109000529

Breakey, H. (2012). Property concepts. *Internet encyclopedia of philosophy*. Retrieved from http://www.iep.utm.edu/prop-con/

Briggs, A., & Burke, P. (2010). Social history of the media: From Gutenberg to the Internet. *Polity*.

Brown, E. (1974). The tyranny of a construct: Feudalism and historians of medieval Europe. *The American Historical Review*, *79*(4), 1063–1088. doi:10.2307/1869563

Brunschwig, J. (2003). *A guide to Greek thought: Major figures and trends*. Harvard University Press.

Buringh, E., & Van Zanden, J. L. (2009). Charting the "rise of the West": Manuscripts and Printed books in Europe, a long-term perspective from the sixth through eighteenth centuries. *The Journal of Economic History*, *69*(02), 409–445. doi:10.1017/S0022050709000837

Busch, H.-C. S. (2008). Personal respect, private property, and market economy: What critical theory can learn from Hegel. *Ethical Theory and Moral Practice*, *11*(5), 573–586. doi:10.100710677-008-9118-6

Calkins, M. J., & Werhane, P. H. (1998). Adam Smith, Aristotle, and the virtues of commerce. *The Journal of Value Inquiry*, *32*(1), 43–60. doi:10.1023/A:1004273132568

Cammaerts, B. (2011). The hegemonic copyright-regime vs. the sharing copyright users of music? *Media Culture & Society*, *33*(3), 491–502. doi:10.1177/0163443711398764

Canning, J. (2014). *A history of medieval political thought: 300–1450*. Routledge. doi:10.4324/9781315020617

Cantwell, J., & Santangelo, G. D. (2001). Capitalism, profits and innovation in the new techno-economic paradigm. In P. D. D. C. Mueller & P. D. U. Cantner (Eds.), *Capitalism and democracy in the 21st century* (pp. 137–163). Physica-Verlag HD. doi:10.1007/978-3-662-11287-8_8

Carroll, M. W. (2006). The movement for open access on law. *Lewis & Clark Law Review*, *10*, 741.

Carroll, M. W. (2013). Creative Commons and the openness of open access. *The New England Journal of Medicine*, *368*(9), 789–791. doi:10.1056/NEJMp1300040 PMID:23445090

Castillo, A. (2009). *GRIN-banned books: Censorship in eighteenth-century England*. Retrieved from http://www.grin.com/en/e-book/156569/banned-books-censorship-in-eighteenth-century-england

Chartier, R. (1994). *The order of books: Readers, authors, and libraries in Europe between the fourteenth and eighteenth centuries*. Stanford University Press.

Chitty, A. (2013). Recognition and property in Hegel and the early Marx. *Ethical Theory and Moral Practice*, *16*(4), 685–697. doi:10.100710677-013-9408-5

Corlett, J. A. (2005). *Interpreting Plato's dialogues* (Vol. 47). Parmenides Pub.

Correa, C. (2000). *Intellectual property rights, the WTO and developing countries: The TRIPS Agreement and policy options*. Zed Books.

Costas, B. R. (2012). *Print culture and peripheries in early modern Europe: A contribution to the history of printing and the book trade in small European and Spanish cities*. BRILL.

Cramond, S. (2011). *Explainer: Open access vs traditional academic journal publishers*. Retrieved June 2, 2017, from http://theconversation.com/explainer-open-access-vs-traditional-academic-journal-publishers-2511

Cropanzano, R., Byrne, Z. S., Bobocel, D. R., & Rupp, D. E. (2001). Self-enhancement biases, laboratory experiments, George Wilhelm Friedrich Hegel, and the increasingly crowded world of organizational justice. *Journal of Vocational Behavior, 58*(2), 260–272. doi:10.1006/jvbe.2001.1798

Curran, J., & Seaton, J. (2009). *Power without responsibility: Press, broadcasting and the Internet in Britain*. Routledge. doi:10.4324/9780203871409

Curzon, V. (1989). Non-discrimination and the rise of "material" reciprocity. *World Economy, 12*(4), 481–500. doi:10.1111/j.1467-9701.1989.tb00473.x

De Dreu, C., & Nauta, A. (2009). Self-interest and other-orientation in organizational behavior: Implications for job performance, prosocial behavior, and personal initiative. *The Journal of Applied Psychology, 94*(4), 913–926. doi:10.1037/a0014494 PMID:19594234

Deazley, R. (2004). *On the origin of the right to copy: Charting the movement of copyright law in eighteenth century Britain*. Portland, OR: Hart Publishing.

Deazley, R. (2006). *Rethinking copyright: History, theory, language*. Edward Elgar Publishing. doi:10.4337/9781847201621

Deazley, R. (2008). *Commentary on the Statute of Anne 1710*. Retrieved from www.copyrighthistory.org

Deere, C. (2009). *The implementation game: the TRIPS Agreement and the global politics of intellectual property reform in developing countries*. Oxford, UK: Oxford University Press.

den Bossche, P. V. (2008). *The law and policy of the World Trade Organization: Text, cases and materials*. Cambridge University Press. doi:10.1017/CBO9780511818394

Di Vita, G. (2013). The TRIPS Agreement and technological innovation. *Journal of Policy Modeling, 35*(6), 964–977. doi:10.1016/j.jpolmod.2013.02.001

Dinwoodie, G. (2007). *Copyright lawmaking authority: An (inter)nationalist perspective on the treaty clause*. Rochester, NY: Social Science Research Network. Retrieved from http://papers.ssrn.com/abstract=1001268

Dols, M. (1977). *The Black Death in the Middle East*. Princeton, NJ: Princepton Legacy Library Press.

Drahos, P., & Braithwaite, J. (2002). *Information feudalism: Who owns the knowledge economy?* Earthscan.

Durham, A. L. (2013). *Patent law essentials: A concise guide* (4th ed.). Santa Barbara, CA: Praeger.

Ederington, J. (2001). International coordination of trade and domestic policies. *The American Economic Review, 91*(5), 1580–1593. doi:10.1257/aer.91.5.1580

Eisenstein, E. (2005). *The printing revolution in early modern Europe*. Cambridge University Press. doi:10.1017/CBO9780511819230

Elias, S., & Stim, R. (2004). *Patent, copyright & trademark* (7th ed.). Nolo.

Elliott, K., & Bayard, T. (1994). *Reciprocity and retaliation in U.S. trade policy*. Peterson Institute for International Economics. Retrieved from https://ideas.repec.org/b/iie/ppress/78.html

Epstein, R. (2004). *Liberty versus property? Cracks in the foundations of copyright law*. Rochester, NY: Social Science Research Network. Retrieved from http://papers.ssrn.com/abstract=529943 doi:10.2139srn.529943

Epstein, S. (1991). *Wage labor and guilds in medieval Europe*. UNC Press Books.

Everton, M. (2005). "The would-be-author and the real bookseller": Thomas Paine and eighteenth-century printing ethics. *Early American Literature, 40*(1), 79–110. doi:10.1353/eal.2005.0018

Fairclough, J. (2002). *Rethinking construction innovation and research—A review of the government's R&D policies and practices*. DTI Press.

Febvre, L., & Martin, H.-J. (1997). *The coming of the book: The impact of printing 1450–1800*. Verso.

Fehr, E., & Gächter, S. (2000). Fairness and Retaliation: The Economics of Reciprocity. *The Journal of Economic Perspectives, 14*(3), 159–181. doi:10.1257/jep.14.3.159

Fennell, L. (2010). *Commons, anticommons, semicommons*. Rochester, NY: Social Science Research Network. Retrieved from http://papers.ssrn.com/abstract=1348267

Forgeng, J. L., & Singman, J. L. (1999). *Daily life in medieval Europe*. Greenwood Publishing Group.

Fyfe, A. (2006). Information revolution: William Chambers, the publishing pioneer. *Endeavour, 30*(4), 120–125. doi:10.1016/j.endeavour.2006.11.001 PMID:17112590

Gangopadhyay, K., & Mondal, D. (2012). Does stronger protection of intellectual property stimulate innovation? *Economics Letters, 116*(1), 80–82. doi:10.1016/j.econlet.2012.01.006

Geiger, C. (2012). *Criminal enforcement of intellectual property: A handbook of contemporary research.* Edward Elgar Publishing. doi:10.4337/9781781005149

Geller, P. (2000). Copyright history and the future: What's culture got to do with it. *Journal of the Copyright Society of the U.S.A., 47*, 209.

Gill, M. L., & Pellegrin, P. (2009). *A companion to ancient philosophy.* John Wiley & Sons.

Gillespie, V., & Powell, S. (2014). *A companion to the early printed book in Britain, 1476–1558.* Boydell & Brewer Ltd.

Ginsburg, J. C. (2000). *International copyright: From a "bundle" of national copyright laws to a supranational code? (SSRN Scholarly Paper No. ID 222508).* Rochester, NY: Social Science Research Network. Retrieved from http://papers.ssrn.com/abstract=222508

Gintis, H. (2005). *Moral sentiments and material interests: The foundations of cooperation in economic life.* MIT Press. doi:10.7551/mitpress/4771.001.0001

Givoni, M. (2006). Development and impact of the modern high-speed train: A Review. *Transport Reviews, 26*(5), 593–611. doi:10.1080/01441640600589319

Goff, N. (2011). Direct-response bookselling: How it died, why it is alive again, and why it will become even more important in the future. *Publishing Research Quarterly, 27*(3), 259–267. doi:10.100712109-011-9219-2

Goldberg, L., Johnson, J., Eber, H., Hogan, R., Ashton, M. C., Cloninger, C. R., & Gough, H. G. (2006). The international personality item pool and the future of public-domain personality measures. *Journal of Research in Personality, 40*(1), 84–96. doi:10.1016/j.jrp.2005.08.007

Goldstein, J., Rivers, D., & Tomz, M. (2007). Institutions in international relations: Understanding the effects of the GATT and the WTO on world trade. *International Organization, 61*(01), 37–67. doi:10.1017/S0020818307070014

Gordon, M., & Raciborski, N. (2007). *US7310729 B2*. Retrieved from http://www.google.com/patents/US7310729

Gresser, E. (2013). *U.S. share of world intellectual property revenue—39 percent*. Retrieved April 16, 2015, from http://www.progressive-economy.org/trade_facts/u-s-share-of-world-intellectual-property-revenue-39-percent/

Grossman, G., & Horn, H. (1987). *Infant-industry protection reconsidered: The case of informational barriers to entry* (Working Paper No. 2159). National Bureau of Economic Research. Retrieved from http://www.nber.org/papers/w2159

Guastello, S. J. (2013). *Chaos, catastrophe, and human affairs: Applications of nonlinear dynamics to work, organizations, and social evolution*. Psychology Press. doi:10.4324/9780203773895

Gutu, G. (2014). Interpretative dimensions on object of public property. *Contemporary Legal Institutions*, *6*(1), 163–167.

Harnad, S. (2007). The green road to open access: A leveraged transition. In *The Culture of Periodicals from the Perspective of the Electronic Age* (pp. 99–105). L'Harmattan. Retrieved from https://eprints.soton.ac.uk/263309/

Harris, D. (2004). TRIPS' Rebound: An historical analysis of how the TRIPS Agreement can ricochet back against the United States. *Northwestern Journal of International Law & Business*, *25*(1), 99–164.

Harrison, B. H., & Matthew, H. C. G. (2004). The Oxford dictionary of national biography: In association with the British Academy: From the earliest times to the year 2000 (British Academy, Ed.). Oxford, UK: Oxford University Press.

Harrison, S., & Sullivan, P. H. Sr. (2000). Profiting from intellectual capital: Learning from leading companies. *Journal of Intellectual Capital*, *1*(1), 33–46. doi:10.1108/14691930010324124

Head, K. (1994). Infant industry protection in the steel rail industry. *Journal of International Economics*, *37*(3–4), 141–165. doi:10.1016/0022-1996(94)90043-4

Hegel, G. W. F. (1991). Hegel: Elements of the philosophy of right (A. W. Wood, Ed.; H. B. Nisbet, Trans.). Cambridge, UK: Cambridge University Press.

Hegel, G. W. F. (2015). *The philosophy of right* (A. White, Trans.). Hackett Publishing.

Henry, C., & Stiglitz, J. (2010). Intellectual property, dissemination of innovation and sustainable development. *Global Policy*, *1*(3), 237–251. doi:10.1111/j.1758-5899.2010.00048.x

Hesse, C. (2002). The rise of intellectual property, 700 B.C.–A.D. 2000: An idea in the balance. *Daedalus*, *131*(2), 26–45.

Hoekman, B., & Kostecki, M. (2009). *The political economy of the world trading system*. Oxford University Press.

Hohfeld, W. N. (1913). Some fundamental legal conceptions as applied in judicial reasoning. *The Yale Law Journal*. Retrieved from http://archive.org/details/jstor-785533

Hohfeld, W. N. (2008). Fundamental legal conceptions. *Nottingham Law Journal*, *17*, 39.

Hollingsworth, J. R., & Boyer, R. (1997). *Contemporary capitalism: The embeddedness of institutions*. Cambridge University Press. doi:10.1017/CBO9781139174701

Honneth, A. (2010). *The pathologies of individual freedom: Hegel's social theory*. Princeton University Press.

Hopkins, J. (2011). The role of learned societies in knowledge exchange and dissemination: The case of the Regional Studies Association, 1965–2005. *History of Education*, *40*(2), 255–271. doi:10.1080/0046760X.2010.518161

Hoppe, H.-H. (2004, October 11). *The ethics and economics of private property*. Retrieved April 10, 2015, from http://mises.org/library/ethics-and-economics-private-property

Hughes, J. (2009). *A short history of intellectual property in relation to copyright*. Rochester, NY: Social Science Research Network. Retrieved from http://papers.ssrn.com/abstract=1432860

Idris, K. (2003). *Intellectual property: A power tool for economic growth*. WIPO.

Jackson, J. (2000). *The jurisprudence of GATT and the WTO: Insights on treaty law and economic relations*. Cambridge University Press.

Johns, A. (2010). *Piracy: The intellectual property wars from Gutenberg to Gates*. University of Chicago Press.

Johnson, D. R. (2007). Reflections on the bundle of rights. *Vermont Law Review*, *32*, 247.

Kahn, C. H. (1998). *Plato and the Socratic dialogue: The philosophical use of a literary form*. Cambridge University Press.

Kaizer, H. (2010). *Plato and Frankfurt: Two theories of the relations between love and living well* (Honors thesis). Retrieved from http://digitalcommons.bucknell.edu/honors_theses/76

Kameas, A., Bellis, S., Mavrommati, I., Delaney, K., Colley, M., & Pounds-Cornish, A. (2003). An architecture that treats everyday objects as communicating tangible components. In *Proceedings of the First IEEE International Conference on Pervasive Computing and Communications, 2003. [PerCom 2003]* (pp. 115–122). IEEE. 10.1109/PERCOM.2003.1192733

Karjala, D. (2002). Distinguishing patent and copyright subject matter. *Connecticut Law Review*, *35*, 439.

Karolides, N., Bald, M., & Sova, D. (2011). *120 banned books: Censorship histories of world literature* (2nd ed.). New York, NY: Checkmark Books.

Kieser, A. (1989). Organizational, institutional, and societal evolution: Medieval craft guilds and the genesis of formal organizations. *Administrative Science Quarterly*, *34*(4), 540–564. doi:10.2307/2393566

Klein, D. (2009). *The strategic management of intellectual capital*. Routledge. doi:10.4324/9780080517926

Knill, C., & Lehmkuhl, D. (2002). Private actors and the state: Internationalization and changing patterns of governance. *Governance: An International Journal of Policy, Administration and Institutions*, *15*(1), 41–63. doi:10.1111/1468-0491.00179

Knowles, D. (1983). Hegel on property and personality. *The Philosophical Quarterly*, *33*(130), 45–62. doi:10.2307/2219203

Kochin, M. S. (2002). *Gender and rhetoric in Plato's political thought*. Cambridge University Press.

Kostylo, J. (2008). *Commentary on Johannes of Speyer's Venetian monopoly* (1469). Retrieved April 17, 2015, from http://www.copyrighthistory.org/

Kostylo, J. (2010). *From gunpowder to print: The common origins of copyright and patent*. Retrieved from http://books.openedition.org/obp/1062

Kostylo, J. (2012). Sinking and shrinking city: Cosmopolitanism, historical memory and social change in Venice. In *Post-cosmopolitan Cities: Explorations of Urban Coexistence* (pp. 170–193). Berghahn Books.

Kraut, R., & Skultety, S. (2005). *Aristotle's Politics: Critical essays*. Rowman & Littlefield.

Kretschmer, M. (2000). Intellectual property in music: A historical analysis of rhetoric and institutional practices. *Studies in Cultures, Organizations and Societies*, *6*(2), 197–223. doi:10.1080/10245280008523547

Kretschmer, M., Bently, L., & Deazley, R. (2010). The history of copyright history: Notes from an emerging discipline. In *Privilege and property: Essays on the history of copyright* (pp. 1–20). Cambridge: Open Book Publishers. Retrieved from http://www.openbookpublishers.com/reader/26

Kujansivu, P., & Lonnqvist, A. (2007). How do investments in intellectual capital create profits? *International Journal of Learning and Intellectual Capital*, *4*(3), 256–275. doi:10.1504/IJLIC.2007.015610

Kumar, N. (2003). Intellectual property rights, technology and economic development: Experiences of Asian countries. *Economic and Political Weekly*, *38*(3), 209–226.

Landes, D. (2003). *The unbound Prometheus: Technological change and industrial development in western Europe from 1750 to the present*. Cambridge University Press. doi:10.1017/CBO9780511819957

Landes, W. M., & Posner, R. A. (2009). *The economic structure of intellectual property law*. Harvard University Press.

Landry, R., Amara, N., & Lamari, M. (2002). Does social capital determine innovation? To what extent? *Technological Forecasting and Social Change*, *69*(7), 681–701. doi:10.1016/S0040-1625(01)00170-6

Lane, D., Pumain, D., Leeuw, S. E. d., & West, G. (2009). *Complexity perspectives in innovation and social change*. Springer Science & Business Media. doi:10.1007/978-1-4020-9663-1

Leaffer, M. (2010). *Understanding copyright law*. LexisNexis.

Lee, D. (2004). Understanding the WTO dispute settlement process. In *Trade Politics*. Psychology Press. doi:10.4324/NOE0415310178.ch8

Lee, E. (2007). *Freedom of the press 2.0.* Rochester, NY: Social Science Research Network. doi:10.2139srn.1008877

Lemley, M. A. (2004). Property, intellectual property, and free riding. *Texas Law Review*, *83*, 1031.

Liu, Q., Safavi-Naini, R., & Sheppard, N. P. (2003). Digital rights management for content distribution. In *Proceedings of the Australasian Information Security Workshop Conference on ACSW Frontiers 2003, 21* (pp. 49–58). Darlinghurst, Australia: Australian Computer Society, Inc. Retrieved from http://dl.acm.org/citation.cfm?id=827987.827994

Locke, J. (2013). *Two treatises of government.* CreateSpace Independent Publishing Platform.

Locke, J. (2016). *Second treatise of government and a letter concerning toleration.* Oxford University Press.

Long, C. (2004). Information costs in patent and copyright. *Virginia Law Review*, *90*(2), 465–549. doi:10.2307/3202440

Lucassen, J., Moor, T. D., & van Zanden, J. L. (2008). *The return of the guilds.* Cambridge University Press.

Lyon, D. (2013). *The electronic eye: The rise of surveillance society—Computers and social control in context.* John Wiley & Sons.

MacLeod, C. (2002). *Inventing the Industrial Revolution: The English patent system, 1660–1800.* Cambridge University Press.

Madison, M. J. (2005). *Law as design: Objects, concepts and digital things.* Rochester, NY: Social Science Research Network. Retrieved from http://papers.ssrn.com/abstract=709121

Maitland, I. (2002). The human face of self-interest. *Journal of Business Ethics*, *38*(1–2), 3–17. doi:10.1023/A:1015716928549

Martin, H.-J. (1995). *The history and power of writing.* University of Chicago Press.

Maskus, K. (2000). *Intellectual property rights in the global economy.* Peterson Institute.

Maskus, K. E., & Reichman, J. H. (2005). *International public goods and transfer of technology under a globalized intellectual property regime*. Cambridge University Press. doi:10.1017/CBO9780511494529

Matthews, D. (2003). *Globalising intellectual property rights: The TRIPS Agreement*. Routledge.

Matthews, D. (2004). WTO decision on implementation of paragraph 6 of the Doha Declaration on the TRIPS Agreement and public health: A solution to the access to essential medicines problem? *Journal of International Economic Law*, *7*(1), 73–107. doi:10.1093/jiel/7.1.73

Matthews, D. (2005). *TRIPS flexibilities and access to medicines in developing countries: The problem with technical assistance and free trade agreements*. Retrieved from http://qmro.qmul.ac.uk/jspui/handle/123456789/183

Matthews, D. (2006). *From the August 30, 2003 WTO decision to the December 6, 2005 agreement on an amendment to TRIPS: Improving access to medicines in developing countries?* Retrieved from http://qmro.qmul.ac.uk/jspui/handle/123456789/2124

May, C. (2013). *The global political economy of intellectual property rights: The new enclosures?* Routledge. doi:10.4324/9781315011233

Mayer, L. (2004). *Worlds made flesh: Chronicle histories and medieval manuscript culture*. Routledge. doi:10.4324/9780203500880

Mayhew, R. (1997). *Aristotle's criticism of Plato's Republic*. Rowman & Littlefield Publishers.

McCalman, P. (2005). Who enjoys "TRIPs" abroad? An empirical analysis of intellectual property rights in the Uruguay Round. *The Canadian Journal of Economics. Revue Canadienne d'Economique*, *38*(2), 574–603. doi:10.1111/j.0008-4085.2005.00293.x

McLuhan, M., Gordon, W. T., Lamberti, E., & Scheffel-Dunand, D. (2011). *The Gutenberg galaxy: The making of typographic man*. University of Toronto Press.

Menell, P. S. (2007a). *Intellectual property and the property rights movement*. Rochester, NY: Social Science Research Network. Retrieved from http://papers.ssrn.com/abstract=1000061

Menell, P. S. (2007b). *The property rights movement's embrace of intellectual property: True love or doomed relationship? (SSRN Scholarly Paper No. ID 965083)*. Rochester, NY: Social Science Research Network. Retrieved from http://papers.ssrn.com/abstract=965083

Merges, R. P. (2011). *Justifying intellectual property*. Harvard University Press. doi:10.4159/harvard.9780674061125

Merrill, T. W., & Smith, H. E. (2011). *Making Coasean property more Coasean*. Rochester, NY: Social Science Research Network. Retrieved from http://papers.ssrn.com/abstract=1758846 doi:10.1086/661946

Mgbeoji, I. (2012). Justifying intellectual property. *Osgoode Hall Law Journal*, *50*, 291–1071.

Milward, A., & Saul, B. (2013). The economic development of continental *Europe* 1780–1870. Routledge.

Morris, S., & Shin, H. S. (2002). Social value of public information. *The American Economic Review*, *92*(5), 1521–1534. doi:10.1257/000282802762024610

Mossoff, A. (2006). Rethinking the development of patents: An intellectual history, 1550–1800. *The Hastings Law Journal*, *52*, 1255.

Müller, B. (2003). Censorship and cultural regulation: Mapping the territory. *Critical Studies*, *22*(1), 1–31.

Mun, S.-H. (2008). *Culture-related aspects of intellectual property rights: A cross-cultural analysis of copyright*. ProQuest.

Nachbar, T. (2005). Monopoly, mercantilism, and the politics of regulation. *Virginia Law Review*, *91*(6), 1313–1379.

Narlikar, A., Daunton, M., & Stern, R. M. (2012). *The Oxford handbook on the World Trade Organization*. Oxford University Press.

Nicolaidis, K., & Shaffer, G. (2005). Transnational mutual recognition regimes: Governance without global government. *Law and Contemporary Problems*, *68*(3/4), 263–317.

Nolan, L. (2011). *Primary and secondary qualities: The historical and ongoing debate*. Oxford University Press. doi:10.1093/acprof:oso/9780199556151.001.0001

Nyquist, C. (2002). Teaching Wesley Hohfeld's theory of legal relations. *Journal of Legal Education*, *52*(1/2), 238–257.

O'Brien, A., & Bosc, M. (Eds.). (2009). *House of Commons procedure and practice* (2nd ed.). Ottawa, Canada: Yvon Blais.

Oakley, F. (1999). *Politics and eternity: Studies in the history of medieval and early modern political thought.* BRILL.

Organisation for Economic Co-operation and Development. (2001). *The new economy: Beyond the hype. Paris: Organisation for Economic Co-operation and Development.* Retrieved from http://www.oecd-ilibrary.org/content/book/9789264033856-en

Ostrom, E., & Hess, C. (2007). *Private and common property rights (SSRN Scholarly Paper No. ID 1936062).* Rochester, NY: Social Science Research Network. Retrieved from http://papers.ssrn.com/abstract=1936062

Parel, A., & Flanagan, T. (2006). *Theories of property: Aristotle to the present.* Wilfrid Laurier Univ. Press.

Pasley, J. (2002). *The tyranny of printers: Newspaper politics in the early American republic.* University of Virginia Press.

Patterson, R. (2000). Understanding the copyright clause. *Journal of the Copyright Society of the U.S.A., 47*, 365.

Pettegree, A. (2010). *The book in the Renaissance.* New Haven, CT: Yale University Press.

Pottage, A., & Sherman, B. (2010). *Figures of invention: A history of modern patent law. Oxford, England.* New York: Oxford University Press. doi:10.1093/acprof:osobl/9780199595631.001.0001

Press, G. A. (1988). Rethinking Plato and Platonism [Review]. *Journal of the History of Philosophy*, *26*(2), 311–312. doi:10.1353/hph.1988.0024

Press, G. A., & Press, G. A. G. A. (1996). Methods of interpreting Plato and his dialogues [Review]. *Journal of the History of Philosophy*, *34*(1), 135–136. doi:10.1353/hph.1996.0005

Pugatch, M. P. (2004). *The international political economy of intellectual property rights.* Edward Elgar Publishing. doi:10.4337/9781845420741

Pugatch, M. P. (2006). *The intellectual property debate: Perspectives from law, economics and political economy*. Edward Elgar Publishing. doi:10.4337/9781847201782

Radin, M. J. (1993). *Reinterpreting property*. University of Chicago Press.

Raoult, D., Aboudharam, G., Crubézy, E., Larrouy, G., Ludes, B., & Drancourt, M. (2000). Molecular identification by "suicide PCR" of Yersinia pestis as the agent of medieval Black Death. *Proceedings of the National Academy of Sciences of the United States of America*, *97*(23), 12800–12803. doi:10.1073/pnas.220225197 PMID:11058154

Reed, C. (2011). *Gutenberg in Shanghai: Chinese print capitalism, 1876–1937*. UBC Press.

Resnik, D. (2003). A pluralistic account of intellectual property. *Journal of Business Ethics*, *46*(4), 319–335. doi:10.1023/A:1025631902384

Riahi-Belkaoui, A. (2003). Intellectual capital and firm performance of US multinational firms: A study of the resource-based and stakeholder views. *Journal of Intellectual Capital*, *4*(2), 215–226. doi:10.1108/14691930310472839

Rich, A. (2010). *A dictionary of Roman and Greek antiquities*. Nabu Press.

Richardson, G. (2004). Guilds, laws, and markets for manufactured merchandise in late-medieval England. *Explorations in Economic History*, *41*(1), 1–25. doi:10.1016/S0014-4983(03)00045-7

Ricketson, S., & Ginsburg, J. (2006). *International copyright and neighbouring rights: The Berne Convention and beyond* (2nd ed.). Oxford, UK: Oxford University Press.

Riegel, N. (2011). *Beauty, to Kalon, and its relation to the good in the works of Plato*. University of Toronto. Retrieved from http://www.synergiescanada.org/theses/otu/29848

Ritter, C. (2005). *Refusal to deal and essential facilities: Does intellectual property require special deference compared to tangible property?* Rochester, NY: Social Science Research Network. Retrieved from http://papers.ssrn.com/abstract=726683

Rocha, H. O., & Ghoshal, S. (2006). Beyond self-interest revisited. *Journal of Management Studies*, *43*(3), 585–619. doi:10.1111/j.1467-6486.2006.00603.x

Romer, P. (2002). When should we use intellectual property rights? *The American Economic Review*, *92*(2), 213–216. doi:10.1257/000282802320189276

Rose, M. (1995). *Authors and owners: The invention of copyright*. Harvard University Press.

Rose, M. (2009). Public sphere and the emergence of copyright: Areopagitica, the Stationers' Company, and the Statute of Anne. *Tulane Journal of Technology and Intellectual Property*, *12*, 123.

Rose, M. (2010). The public sphere and the emergence of copyright: Areopagitica, the Stationers' Company, and the Statute of Anne. In *Privilege and Property: Essays on the History of Copyright* (pp. 67–88). Cambridge, UK: Open Book Publishers. doi:10.2307/j.ctt5vjt9v.7

Rosen, S. (2005). *Plato's Republic: A study*. Yale University Press.

Rosset, V., Filippin, C., & Westphall, C. (2005). A DRM architecture to distribute and protect digital contents using digital licenses. *Advanced industrial conference on telecommunications: service assurance with partial and intermittent resources conference*, 422–427. 10.1109/AICT.2005.5

Rothbard, M. N. (2009). *Aristotle on private property and money*. Retrieved October 3, 2014, from http://mises.org/daily/3902/Aristotle-on-Private-Property-and-Money

Rouse, R., & Rouse, M. (2000). *Manuscripts and their makers: Commercial book producers in medieval Paris, 1200–1500*. Harvey Miller Press.

Salter, M. (1987). Justifying private property rights: A message from Hegel's jurisprudential writings. *Legal Studies*, *7*(3), 245–262. doi:10.1111/j.1748-121X.1987.tb00365.x

Schroeder, J. L. (2005). Unnatural rights: Hegel and intellectual property. *University of Miami Law Review*, *60*, 453.

Sell, S., & Prakash, A. (2004). Using ideas strategically: The contest between business and NGO networks in intellectual property rights. *International Studies Quarterly*, *48*(1), 143–175. doi:10.1111/j.0020-8833.2004.00295.x

Sennett, R. (2008). *The craftsman*. Yale University Press.

Senseney, J. (2011). *The art of building in the classical world: Vision, craftsmanship, and linear perspective in Greek and Roman architecture*. Cambridge University Press. doi:10.1017/CBO9780511976711

Shafaeddin, M. (2000). *What did Frederick list actually say? Some clarifications on the infant industry argument* (UNCTAD Discussion Paper No. 149). United Nations Conference on Trade and Development. Retrieved from https://ideas.repec.org/p/unc/dispap/149.html

Shan, C., Gong, S., & McOwan, P. W. (2009). Facial expression recognition based on local binary patterns: A comprehensive study. *Image and Vision Computing*, *27*(6), 803–816. doi:10.1016/j.imavis.2008.08.005

Shao, K. (2011). Monopoly or reward: The origin of copyright and authorship in England, France and China and a new criticism of intellectual property. *Hong Kong Law Journal*, *41*, 731.

Sider, S. (2007). *Handbook to life in Renaissance Europe*. Oxford University Press.

Silver, C. (2003). *Critical essays dealing with the philosophy of Plato on the good life—The Platonic philosophy on the good life*. Retrieved April 9, 2015, from http://ancienthistory.about.com/library/bl/uc_bakaoukas4b2.htm

Slauter, W. (2013). Upright piracy: Understanding the lack of copyright for journalism in eighteenth-century Britain. *Book History*, *16*(1), 34–61. doi:10.1353/bh.2013.0011

Smith, H. E. (2011). Property is not just a bundle of rights. *Econ Journal Watch*, *8*(3), 279–291.

Smith, W. (2010). *A concise dictionary of Greek and Roman antiquities*. London: Nabu Press.

Spiegel, H. W. (1991). *The growth of economic thought*. Duke University Press.

Stein, B. (1985). Politics, peasants and the deconstruction of feudalism in medieval India. *The Journal of Peasant Studies*, *12*(2–3), 54–86. doi:10.1080/03066158508438265

Suhr, C. (2012). Publishing for the masses: Early modern English witchcraft pamphlets. *Neuphilologische Mitteilungen*, *113*(1), 118–121.

Tenopir, C., King, D. W., Edwards, S., & Wu, L. (2009). Electronic journals and changes in scholarly article seeking and reading patterns. *Aslib Proceedings*, *61*(1), 5–32. doi:10.1108/00012530910932267

Turner, F. (2010). *From counterculture to cyberculture: Stewart Brand, the Whole Earth Network, and the rise of digital utopianism*. University of Chicago Press.

van Staveren, I. (2013). *The values of economics: An Aristotelian perspective*. Routledge. doi:10.4324/9780203122396

Wallerstein, I. (2011). *The modern world—System I: Capitalist agriculture and the origins of the European world—Economy in the sixteenth century, with a new prologue*. University of California Press.

Walterscheid, E. C. (1999). Defining the patent and copyright term: Term limits and the intellectual property clause. *Journal of Intellectual Property Law*, *7*, 315.

Weatherford, J. (2009). *The history of money*. Crown Publishing Group.

Weber, D. J. (2005). *Bárbaros: Spaniards and their savages in the Age of Enlightenment*. Yale University Press.

Willinsky, J. (2003). The nine flavours of open access scholarly publishing. *Journal of Postgraduate Medicine*, *49*(3), 263. PMID:14597793

Witcombe, C. L. C. E. (2004). *Copyright in the Renaissance: Prints and the privilegio in sixteenth-century Venice and Rome*. BRILL.

Womack, J., Jones, D., & Roos, D. (2008). *The machine that changed the world*. Simon and Schuster.

Yamada, S. (2012). *"Pirate" PUBLISHING: The battle over perpetual copyright in eighteenth-century Britain*. Shoji Yamada.

Yang, L., & Maskus, K. E. (2009). Intellectual property rights, technology transfer and exports in developing countries. *Journal of Development Economics*, *90*(2), 231–236. doi:10.1016/j.jdeveco.2008.11.003

Yu, P. K. (2004). Currents and crosscurrents in the international intellectual property regime. *Loyola of Los Angeles Law Review*, *38*, 323.

Yu, P. K. (2007). *International enclosure, the regime complex, and intellectual property schizophrenia*. Rochester, NY: Social Science Research Network. Retrieved from http://papers.ssrn.com/abstract=1007054

Zhang, W., Shan, S., Chen, X., & Gao, W. (2007). Local Gabor binary patterns based on mutual information for face recognition. *International Journal of Image and Graphics*, *7*(4), 777–793. doi:10.1142/S021946780700291X

Ziegler, P. (2013). *The Black Death*. Faber & Faber.

Zoller, C. (2007). Interpreting Plato's dialogues [Review]. *Journal of the History of Philosophy*, *45*(3), 486–487. doi:10.1353/hph.2007.0073

Zuckert, C. H. (2009). *Plato's philosophers: The coherence of the dialogues* (1st ed.). Chicago: University of Chicago Press. doi:10.7208/chicago/9780226993386.001.0001

Chapter 3
The Green Open Access:
Significant Scientific Considerations in the Light of Public Policy and Access to Knowledge

ABSTRACT

This chapter considers green open access (e.g., OARs). OARs constitute a contemporary response regarding the dissemination of information. Thus, it is important to examine theoretical arguments about the desirability of OARs in the digital age. The chapter argues that OARs could be seen as a form of social justice towards strengthening social cohesion in modern societies. The argument relies on the concept of public policy as one means of achieving social justice. The discussion about OARs aligns with public policy, and social justice considerations should be examined. Additionally, the chapter demonstrates that public policy should concentrate on social cohesion, whereas open access could be considered as an instrument towards social cohesion. The chapter is divided into three broad topics. First, two main justifications for access to knowledge are addressed: (1) the philosophical justification, based on the concept that knowledge is power, and it is significant that everyone has access to knowledge; and (2) the pragmatic justification that it is impractical to enforce copyright in the traditional sense in this digital age. Second, the concept of social justice and relevant theories are considered. Third, theories concerning connections between public policy and social justice towards social cohesion are examined.

DOI: 10.4018/978-1-7998-1131-2.ch003

INTRODUCTION

In this chapter, it is argued that unfettered access to information and knowledge is important to create a just global society. Access to knowledge through OARs can be understood as a related dimension of this concept. OARs are an efficient mechanism to enable interaction of technical developments with copyright laws to disseminate information legitimately. Scholars argue that knowledge is power and, therefore, OA can determine an appropriate pathway to power (Elden & Crampton, 2012). Thus, current copyright laws and policies should be examined, and such examination would lead to a rigorous theoretical argument about the desirability of OARs in the digital age. OA can also be understood as a form of social justice, which can strengthen social cohesion in modern societies. Public participation can ensure that just policies are enacted and, therefore, the creation of public spaces for consensus formation is necessary (Boeder, 2005; Rawls, 2009). This argument will be developed by relying on the concept of public policy that constitutes a means of achieving social cohesion, as good governance requires that people participate in policy formation.

The chapter deals with three broad, interrelated matters. In the first part, an examination of justifications for OA (as a means of access to knowledge) is undertaken. There is discussion about two main justifications for access to knowledge: (a) the philosophical justification that knowledge is power and for that reason it is important that everyone has access to knowledge, and (b) the pragmatic justification that recognises that in this digital age it is impractical to enforce copyright in the traditional sense. The first justification in the first section relies on Foucault's views about the relation between power and knowledge, wherein he argues that knowledge is power. The second section addresses the pragmatic issue and uses examples that highlight the impracticability of copyright enforcement, which necessitates reform of the copyright regime. Both justifications for greater access to knowledge are, in turn, arguments for access to information resources like the OARs.

The second matter follows from the above. That is, access to knowledge is necessary to create a just society. For enabling a socially just society, an assessment of social justice theories is required. Thus, in the second part of the chapter, there is a focus on the concept of social justice; the argument in this chapter relies on Rawls' theory of justice, which attempts to solve the issue of distributive justice. Rawls' views help to point out the importance of the appropriate form for social justice and the crucial role of distributive justice in society. In the context of this book, justice requires that OA should be integrated with copyright laws. Integration here does not necessarily require changing copyright standards but does require adopting licensing policies, improving government initiatives, and so on. Therefore, OARs are one way of making access to knowledge available in a fair manner. However, for OARs to exist in this manner, appropriate public policy should be formulated (Birkland, 2014; Cairney, 2012; Richards & Martin, 2002). Hence, a related issue to be examined is about whether social justice and public policy are interrelated. Thus, social cohesion could be enhanced by just public policy, and in that sense, OARs could be one means of creating a cohesive society, both nationally and globally.

Therefore, the third part of this chapter examines the issue of generating social consensus for making appropriate public policies. In this regard, Jean-Jacques Rousseau's views about the social contract need to be combined with Habermas' theory. That is, the consensus of social contract cannot be assumed, but must be generated in modern societies (Hillier, 2003). In this part, an examination of Habermas' views will help create a theoretical foundation for the argument that a cohesive society requires the involvement of well-informed participants or civil society in creating consensus. However, Habermas' ideas about the public sphere need to be adapted to current circumstances in view of the digital age after the emergence of the Internet. Therefore, in the digital age, the public sphere in Habermas' terms is constituted, to a significant extent, through the Internet. This is where everyone is or should be able to create, share, disseminate and freely discuss ideas. In this way, the Internet is a crucial component for the construction of social consensus. Such consensus will enable the construction of appropriate policies of OARs.

Each one of the matters listed above is a field of study in its own right. Of necessity, there is a capacity to engage in an in-depth analysis of all the relevant issues. The main effort is directed at synthesising ideas across these diverse areas of knowledge to support the concept of OARs as an essential aspect of the knowledge management systems in contemporary digital societies.

JUSTIFICATIONS FOR OPEN ACCESS

Philosophical Justification: Knowledge Is Power

The concepts of knowledge and power have a long association. Plato argues that human attitude flows from three basic sources: desire, emotion and knowledge (Crombie, 2012). The well-known proverb, "*ipsa scientia potestas est*," meaning "knowledge itself is power," was coined by Sir Francis Bacon (Bacon, 2008, 2013). It is also admitted that the concept of knowledge constitutes an important factor that helps people achieve great results (Black, 2015). Consequently, the more knowledge a person gains, the more powerful he/she becomes. Kofi Annan similarly argues that knowledge is power, information is liberating, and education is the premise of progress in every society and every family (Stromquist, 2002). Hence, well-educated people can be part of a well-developed society. Given this, Foucault's understanding of knowledge as power plays a significant role in the discussion of this part, and for that reason, an explanation of Foucault's argument follows.

This section aims to offer a philosophical justification about knowledge as a form of power, which helps me argue that when there is access to information resources, there is also access to knowledge. Foucault's ideas are applied in two ways, and two related points need to be made in this regard. In agreement with Foucault, what constitutes knowledge is itself an aspect of power. That is, disciplinary conventions play a crucial role in determining what counts as authoritative knowledge. Thus, universities and scholarly journals play an important role in establishing the benchmarks of authoritative knowledge in any discipline. Access to information is a pathway to access to knowledge and OARs are, therefore, an important mechanism of making such access widespread. Secondly, since not all information can be considered reliable, the OARs can function as sources of reliable information and knowledge.

Foucault's works extend the consideration of the concept of power from sociology to all the areas of the social sciences (Taylor, 2000). He also argues that knowledge and power are mutually formed. For this, he introduces the concept of *discursive formations*, meaning that discourse is more than just language and more than just things that reflect reality. Foucault's ideas regarding the concepts of power and knowledge and the concept of discursive formations are interlinked. Below, a brief introduction to Foucault serves as a context for the following discussion of his ideas.

His books constitute a vehicle to show the various factors that interact and collide in his analysis regarding social shifts and their impacts. As a philosopher and observer of human relations, his work concentrates on dominant genealogical and archaeological knowledge systems and practices, tracking them through different historical fields. In other words, he explains in a novel manner the nature of power in a society. In conceptualising power as connected to discourse, he is challenging the prevailing orthodoxy that sees power as exercised in a top-down manner and that mostly referred to state power. According to Foucault's understanding, power is everywhere and not only in the sovereign. Moreover, power is constituted but is also constitutive. We are the agents of power but are also constituted by it. Thus, it follows that it is a dynamic process. Foucault clearly drafts a dynamic of power, and he also suggests a related dynamic interpretation of knowledge.

Foucault had been writing about the history of knowledge long before he ever had concerns about the concept of power. The issue that interested Foucault is the epistemic context within which bodies of knowledge compiled within disciplinary investigations at various times became intelligible and authoritative. He argues that specific investigations are shaped by various concepts and clarifications, by which of those clarifications count as "serious," by who is authorised to speak seriously and by what procedures are appropriate in terms of assessing the credibility of those clarifications that are taken seriously (Gutting, 1989, 2005). In *The Archaeology of Knowledge*, Foucault calls these historically located areas of knowledge *discursive formations* (Foucault, 2012).

Foucault further argues that knowledge is a form of power (Rowley & Hartley, 2008). In particular, he states that "[K]nowledge linked to power, not only assumes the authority of the truth but has the power to make itself true. All knowledge, once applied in the real world, has effects, and in that sense, at least, becomes true" (Foucault, 1995, p. 27). More importantly, he emphasises that knowledge is not pre-existing but is a result of discourse. He states that "[t]here is no power relation without the correlative constitution of a field of knowledge, nor any knowledge that does not presuppose and constitute at the same time, power relations" (Foucault, 1995, p. 27).

According to Foucault, power does not only exclude but also repress, censor, mask and conceal (Gaventa & Cornwall, 2013; Townley, 1993). He writes that power "reaches into the very grain of individuals, touches their bodies and inserts itself into their actions and attitudes, their discourses, learning processes and everyday lives" (Foucault, 1980). In making this argument,

Foucault is challenging the conventional understanding of power. He argues that the most important component for the concept of power lies in the effect that power has on entire networks, practices, and the world around us, and how our attitude can be affected, not power itself. For Foucault, the concepts of knowledge and power are inevitably associated.

If it was accepted that in contemporary societies knowledge dissemination primarily happens through the digital media, it follows that access to knowledge must be a significant means of accessing and exercising power. Therefore, access to information resources leads to access to knowledge, and such access can happen through OARs in the digital age. Not only do OARs provide access to the process of knowledge, but they also give users the opportunity to exercise such power. This helps me to argue that there should be equal opportunities to access information for everybody, and OARs can also play a dynamic role in knowledge acquirement. However, in this context, a further issue that remains to be examined is what constitutes authoritative knowledge because of the operation of power.

Simply having access to information resources does not produce authoritative knowledge or some will to hierarchy in the abstract (Davis-Floyd & Sargent, 1996; Lewis, Rodgers, & Woolcock, 2008). What interested Foucault is the epistemic context within which knowledge became authoritative. For any field of study, several knowledge frameworks exist, some of which, by consensus, are more important than others, either because they explain the state of the world better in terms of efficacy or because they are associated with a stronger power base (and usually both; Jordan, 2014). Thus, authoritative knowledge is a way of organising power relations for an effective social agreement. For example, an agreement among universities regarding the policy to be implemented in terms of OARs and efficient ways of information dissemination would formulate the norms for managing digital publications. This is particularly relevant in the digital age where anyone can publish on the Internet. There is no way of judging the quality of the knowledge produced. In the original or traditional publishing model for academic works, editors performed the gatekeeping role. This is no longer the case with digital publishing, and the issue is whether we still need standards for judging the quality of any scholarly work and who should perform this task. This book argues that the OARs can perform the function of gatekeeping and of making the works available widely.

To sum up, Foucault's views provide a philosophical justification to argue that knowledge is power. Moving on to the next issue, a pragmatic aspect for wider access to information exists and is discussed below.

Pragmatic Justifications for Open Access

The pragmatic argument for greater access to information and knowledge is related to the difficulties of enforcing copyright protections in the changed circumstance of digital publications. The problems in enforcing conventional conceptions of copyright are threefold. The first issue concerns the ambit of intellectual property law, namely that intellectual property is an intangible and what constitutes an infringement of intellectual property rights is invariably a matter of interpretation. The second issue concerns managing information resources because of the great speed of information transmission and exchange of copyrighted works in the digital age. The last issue is interrelated with the concept of digital publishing and relevant concerns with copying.

The first issue is that what constitutes copyright itself is difficult to ascertain. The framework of US copyright law is relevant to this issue and helps me illustrate the difficulties in the enforcement of intellectual property rights. Whether any practice infringes the copyright of the creator is always subject to legal interpretation, which can authoritatively come only from the courts. As a result, the complexity of the law and the associated expenses for artists or creative content creators concerning the enforcement of the rights that copyright laws grant them operate as real impediments (Ginsburg, 2009). The official purpose of US copyright law is claimed to be to motivate artistic production and to afford the full ability to copy, reproduce, and gain value from creative work for the general public good (Ginsburg, 2004). However, in effect, it is very difficult for the authors to know whether their rights have been infringed and how to enforce their entitlements under the law. This difficulty is, in turn, exacerbated by the modern ways to distribute copyrighted works.

The second issue for discussion is related to the digital ways and speed of distribution of content. Liu argues that copyrighted works are increasingly disseminated in digital form through the Internet. Consequently, the copyright owner's right to limit copying is under challenge with the ease of copying made possible by the digital revolution (Liu, 2000). However, Liu goes on to argue that copyright law should acknowledge the unrestricted right to access digital copies in one's possession and a more restricted right to transfer such copies to others. Houle argues that it is hard to determine what makes a great song or great sound. In addition, he argues that several record creators and authors believe they are not breaching another's rights if they use a small part of a copyrighted work (Houle, 1991). Thus, copying practices are not significantly aligned with the copyright regime framework and its provisions, globally. These statements illustrate that the ease of replication does not mean that it is always lawful to disseminate copyrighted works. There are different perspectives regarding how much copying should be permissible. The issue is compounded by the lack of uniform legal regulation across various jurisdictions and is discussed next. Among other options, it is increasingly being suggested that copyright laws ought to be relaxed.

Two examples from Germany and China illustrate some of the difficulties of enforcing copyright laws. A study on behalf of the German Federal Association of the Music Producing Industry shows that the number of illegal music album downloads in Germany increased in 2011 by about 35% when compared with 2010. At the same time, a new philosophy regarding the pros and cons of contemporary German copyright laws has arisen, and suggestions have been made that the copyright laws should be relaxed. Eckhard Höffner, a German economic historian, argues that Germany's rapid technological expansion and superiority by the late 1800s and at the turn of the 19th century was due directly to Germany's relaxed copyright laws (Thadeusz, 2010).

A report of the Australian Law Reform Commission (ALRC) regarding recommendations to relax copyright laws is also relevant here (Australian Law Reform Commission, 2014). In this report, the ALRC recommends that Australian copyright laws should be relaxed and modernised to allow more people to use copyright material without acquiring permission from the rights holders. The Commission was asked by the Federal Government to consider whether present copyright exceptions were adequate and appropriate in the digital era. The Australian report contains 30 recommendations to relax copyright laws, but it does not recommend allowing piracy of copyrighted material. Another relevant example in this context stems from the Dutch legislature's efforts to relax its copyright laws. Its approach is to provide additional protection for fair use of copyrighted material (Hugenholtz & Senftleben, 2012). Current fair use exceptions in the European Union are strictly defined and not subject to interpretation by the courts (as they are in the US; Burk & Cohen, 2007). Hence, the Dutch stance on relaxed copyright protections shows the increasing reticence of individual governments to go along with restrictive copyright legislation like the Anti-Counterfeiting Trade Agreement (ACTA) treaty.

So far, Germany, Poland, the Czech Republic and Slovakia have stopped their ACTA ratification process. It is expected that the Netherlands will not abide by the European Commission to reach a compromise on the treaty. It seems that the Netherlands will proceed with its own legislation (Chesal,

2012). These examples help me to suggest that if copyright laws' overarching objective is to serve the public good better, they should be as flexible and fluid as possible. A possible option in this regard is that legal regulation of exchange and transfer of digital information should be clearly regulated.

China demonstrates another difficulty in the enforcement of copyright. It is the sheer scale of piracy that characterises the business structure in China. Wang et al. argue that businesses, especially those engaged with manufacturing and information distribution, are sensitive to piracy (Wang & Zhu, 2003). The previous business model focused on payments for the use of copyright material via reproduction and distribution is becoming something akin to the Maginot Line, which was bypassed by the dawn of the Internet (Hughes, 2006). The immediate problem is that the people and organisations that have spent hundreds of years to establish a business model in the industry with the reliance on copyright—that is, copyright pays for the reproduction of its content—now do not have any protection (Dobusch & Schüßler, 2014). Copyright laws were initially designed to compensate the creator of content for the time and effort they had spent in developing their ideas and products by giving them protection against unauthorised reproduction of their works. However, with the arrival of digital technology and the Internet, it is now relatively easy to reproduce and communicate ideas and content. Consequently, the ways of protecting creative works through copyright laws have become inadequate in the digital age.

At this moment, the protection model in the copyright law of China is faced with new challenges (Younting, 2014). The key protection in the current copyright law of China, similar to most other countries, is focused on the right of reproduction and the right of distribution. Technology growth makes reproduction simpler, so that anyone could reproduce and distribute what they have on the Internet (Leyshon, Webb, French, Thrift, & Crewe, 2005). When almost everyone breaches the current copyright law, the question is whether the law is of any use. Further, serious online copyright infringement in China also puts some large companies like Microsoft into a difficult position (Nolan, 2005; Shen, 2005). Thatcher argues that although China's growth as a burgeoning market economy is ensconced within a socialist political system, it encounters a dilemma in becoming a fully-fledged actor in the copyright field. During the last decades, China has made important steps regarding the construction of a system to administer and enforce copyright (Thatcher, 2008). However, such implementation has left much to be desired and shows to some extent a cultural tolerance for applications opposed to nourishing wide respect for copyright. Therefore, in contemporary times, the copyright holder may have legal interests, but it is becoming more and more difficult to enforce them.

The digital revolution has made access to information (and knowledge) very easy, but at the same time, the creator of content has some interest in protecting their investment of time and effort through copyright protection. The balancing of these considerations of easy access and need to ensure conditions that encourage creativity requires a response. In the following section, a brief discussion of the concept of social justice is provided to argue that open access is necessary for creating a fair global society. In later chapters, arguments in support of the rights of the authors and publishers are considered.

THE CONCEPT OF SOCIAL JUSTICE

Social justice requires consideration of theories of justice. These, in turn, are mostly about distributive justice. In this regard, one of the most discussed theories is that of Rawls. This discussion will help us claim that suitable institutions and policies are integral to good governance. The concept of social justice necessarily involves government, policy, and institutions in terms of distribution (Sen, 2000). In the modern context, social justice is typically considered equivalent to distributive justice (Agyeman, 2003). The terms *justice* and *social justice* are generally understood to be synonymous and interchangeable in both common discourse and the language used within international relations. The concept of social justice is implied in many international legal texts, such as the Universal Declaration of Human Rights. Felice argues that the importance of social justice can be observed through this Declaration (Felice, 1996; Puybaret, 2008). He argues that the Universal Declaration of Human Rights determines the significance of collective human rights. Additionally, he claims that the Declaration constitutes an instrument to examine the evolution and development of human rights concepts in international contexts. Thus, the Declaration helps me argue that social justice should be considered a vital part of national and global social infrastructures.

Moreover, social justice is the virtue that guides us in creating institutions that provide access to what is beneficial for the person on an individual basis and in association with others. Thus, social justice imposes a personal responsibility to work with others to design and continually improve our institutions as the means for personal and social development.

JOHN RAWLS' THEORY OF JUSTICE

A brief analysis of the structure of John Rawls' theory will set the context for extending it to the issue of access to knowledge. Rawls' theory of social justice is commonly referred to as justice as fairness. Rawls set out to draft a theory of social justice that would answer two questions. What principles are most necessary to a democratic society once we view it as a just system of social cooperation between citizens considered free and equal? Which principles are most suitable for a democratic society that not only professes but wants to take seriously the stance that citizens are free and equal, and tries to realise that notion in its main institutions? According to Rawls, social justice is about satisfying the protection of equal access to liberties, rights, and opportunities, and taking care of the least benefited members of society. Thus, whether something is just or unjust depends on whether it promotes or hinders equality of access to civil liberties, human rights, and opportunities for healthy and fulfilling lives, and whether it allocates a fair share of benefits to the least benefited members of society.

In the same way as Hobbes, Rawls' ideas of social justice are developed around the notion of a social contract (Boucher & Kelly, 2003). The central issue, as with Rousseau, is how to explain that free or autonomous individuals voluntarily agree to curtail their freedom in the form of a social contract to form political authority. Rawls posits that rational and free people will agree to play by the rules under fair conditions, and ensuring that everyone plays by the rules is necessary to assure social justice. Further, public support is critical to the acceptance of the rules of the game (John Rawls, 2001). These rules or principles specify the basic rights and duties to be assigned by the main political and social institutions, and they also regulate the division of benefits arising from social cooperation and allot the burdens necessary to sustain it.

In this way, Rawls' theory, being a part of the liberal political tradition, provides a framework for the legal use of political power to curtail individual autonomy. He constructs justice as fairness based on interpretations of liberal notions that citizens are free and equal. Accordingly, the guiding views of justice as fairness are expressed through the two principles of justice, as mentioned above. These principles can be described as follows (Wenar, 2013): according to the first principle, in a liberal society each person has the same inalienable claim to a fully adequate scheme of equal basic liberties; the second principle states that social and economic inequalities are to satisfy specific conditions (Rawls, 2009). Further, the basic elements for the first principle are of paramount importance with regard to the equal basic rights and liberties and additional components that make it distinctive.

Rawls' second principle consists of two components. The first component is about the fair equality of opportunity, and it requires equality in terms of education and economic chances for individuals or citizens with the same skills or talents and intention to use them, regardless of their economic background. The second component highlights the importance of difference that confers the dissemination of wealth and income. This component requires that social institutions be arranged so that any inequalities of wealth and income work beneficially for those who are worst off. It also requires that economic inequalities be to everyone's benefit, and particularly to the greatest benefit of the least advantaged. Moreover, he explains that these principles follow a four-phase procedure for implementation. The first is the adoption of the principles of justice to regulate a society. The second phase is the constitutional convention, which sets forth the institutions and basic processes of governance. The third phase is the legislative stage, where just laws are enacted. Finally, the fourth phase is the application of the regulations by those who govern/rule, the interpretation of the constitution and laws by the judiciary, and the following of the rules by citizens in the conditions required by justice as fairness.

For Rawls, the first principle deals with the right to equality. That means fair dissemination of each of the capacities needed to be normal and contributing members of society over a complete life. According to his first principle, freedom of speech and assembly, private property and freedom from arbitrary norms of arrest and seizure are specified as the basic necessities. The second principle deals with the conditions for any inequality that may be part of or produced from the social structure. This second principle stipulates that inequality is just only if it serves the public good. He also claims that to be just, advantaged positions within an unequal system should be equally accessible to all members of that system.

Rawls' rationales for the two principles can be interpreted as an argument that opportunities to gain wealth should be part of every individual's advantage. Freeman argues that within Rawls' first principle, democratic equality provides formal assurance to individuals. In other words, this formal assurance secures equal basic liberties to people. Freeman further argues that these principles guarantee individuals that their needs as free and equal citizens are fulfilled (Freeman, 2003). Fulfilment here means equal support in terms of basic or overarching goods, such as basic liberties and opportunity. Freeman explains that citizens have two primary abilities or competences, both rational and reasonable. On the one hand, such rationality is apparent in their capacity to work on, to decide and to reconsider their life goals. On the other, citizens are reasonable, as they have the capacity to understand the concept of justice; that means that in ordinary social situations, they can judge things and act accordingly. Freeman's interpretation of Rawls' opinion on egalitarianism helps me to extend these ideas to the issue at hand—that is, open access and intellectual property rights of the authors. First, it is reasonable to expect everyone can agree that the creative content creators should benefit from their intellectual endeavour. Second, consumers should have equal opportunities to access the knowledge thus created.

Aligned with Rawls' argument, David and Foray argue that knowledge has been a crucial component of economic development and an important cause of the gradual rise of social wealth since time immemorial. They argue that the ability to produce new ideas and knowledge has always served well the wealth in a society (Carlaw, Oxley, Walker, Thorns, & Nuth, 2006; David & Foray, 2002). Mueller also argues that knowledge is considered a significant component in terms of economic development (Mueller, 2006). She argues that human resources, labour and knowledge constitute such development. What is more, knowledge can be transformed into products and processes; therefore, it can be part of commercialisation. The ability to produce, identify and exploit knowledge depends on the existing knowledge stock and the absorptive capacity of actors, such as employees at firms and researchers at universities and research institutions. This statement enables the argument that the current stock of information gathered by universities and research institutions might not be disseminated to its full extent; hence, better knowledge flows should occur, and ways for further dissemination of information are needed. Today, open access is a form of essential resource, and it is reasonable to expect that equal access to information would be fair (Buchanan, Masoodian, & Cunningham, 2008; Grüttemeier & Mahon, 2003). It further supports the argument that open access could be a significant means for social justice that gives opportunities to everybody. Scholars also argue that a significant area of inequality that should be considered in terms of dissemination of goods, opportunities, and rights is that of access to knowledge (Darling-Hammond, 1995; Eeckhout & Jovanovic, 2002).

Another aspect of Rawls' theory is that any procedure or outcome should be consistent with social justice. Any procedure or outcome is inconsistent with social justice if it interferes with an individual's claim to equal liberties

(Feinberg, 2014). The device of a veil of ignorance thus helps justify why any of us would be interested in creating fair and just rules. It follows that public policy ensuring the participation of all citizens is likely to enable the formulation of fair and just rules. Furlong and Kerwin argue that citizens' interest groups are one of the most important policymaking venues in rulemaking (Furlong & Kerwin, 2005). In other words, participatory democracy could be one mechanism that leads towards a society with fairer and just institutions.

However, the possibility of participation in rule formation and public policy formulation, in turn, depends upon people having the capacity for meaningful participation. Moreover, social justice is not possible without strong and coherent redistributive policies conceived and introduced by public agencies (United Nations, 2006). Therefore, institutions such as universities should play a crucial role as actors in the context of social justice. They could offer equal opportunities for access to information through OARs. The following brief discussion of the concept of participatory democracy is designed to explain its significance to the conditions that would enable the formation of appropriate public policy and fairer regulations.

SOCIAL COHESION REQUIRES PUBLIC POLICY THAT CREATES SOCIAL JUSTICE

The Importance of Public Policy and Participatory Democracy

This section argues about whether fairer regulations may be made through appropriate public policy. It requires that informed citizens ought to be able to participate in the formulation of appropriate public policy (Pateman, 2012). Thus, participatory democracy could be considered a significant innovation in democracy (Cabannes, 2004). Moreover, public policy—in both aspects of its processes and substantive content—requires that people have a voice in its formation (Fischer, 2003). An obvious aspect of public policy is that access to information is critical for enabling citizens to exercise their voice, to effectively monitor government and hold the government to account, and to enter into an informed dialogue about decisions that affect their lives. Moreover, citizens can improve their living standards and better their lives when they have access to knowledge (Calland & Bentley, 2013).

The following discussion examines different understandings of public policy sets the context for the argument that participatory democracy is a suitable device for citizens to engage in the processes of forming policies. There are several definitions of public policy, and they highlight relevant theoretical debates. The concept of social justice in the broader sense is about the links between citizens, institutions, and governments. Strong public policy should solve problems efficiently, serve justice, support governmental institutions and governmental policies, and encourage active citizenship (Hill & Varone, 2014). Thus, the ideal objective of public policy is of direct relevance to social infrastructure and consequently, active citizenship (Bishop & Davis, 2002; O'Faircheallaigh, 2010; Rowe & Frewer, 2000). Public policy and governance are thus interrelated, as both require fairness, and that means adhering to principles of social justice.

For example, Edwards notes that the challenge for governments is to find ways to engage others in the policymaking process and to make citizens' participation fundamental (Bovaird, Löffler, & Loeffler, 2004). The issue of citizens' participation is part of a large debate among scholars. Such participation provides an opportunity to influence public decisions and has long been a component of the democratic decision-making process (Grabow, Hilliker, & Moskal, 2006). Public administration is progressively concerned with placing the citizen at the core of policymakers' decisions. Not only is citizens' participation crucial to the scope of public policy and long-term efforts (Dunn, 2003; Evans, 2011; Hesmondhalgh, 2005; Kahan & Braman, 2005), but it can also be an additional instrument for efficient governance (Goldin & Reinert, 2012).

There is extensive literature on participatory democracy and not every scholar has the same understanding of the concept. For instance, Brown argues that participatory democracy is direct democracy in the sense that all citizens are actively involved in all important decisions. The concept commonly refers to movements, such as the civil rights movement or the women's suffrage movement, that gather a group of people who democratically make decisions about the direction of the group' (Brown, 2010). Generally, it is a concept that points to political consideration regarding improving collective decision-making (Besson & Martí, 2006). It emphasises the right of everyone to participate and considers it important that everybody subjected to a collective decision has the opportunity to participate in consequential deliberation about that decision (Hendriks, 2006).

Pateman argues that participatory democracy is often treated as a normative argument concerned with aspirations (Pateman, 2012). It follows that participatory democracy establishes an ideal, and so do OARs, but both are desirable aspirations. This book aims to build and construct an argument that justifies OARs as the foundation of creating a participatory democracy of well-informed citizens. Citizens can influence public policy by being involved in the processes of policy formation. This leads me to the next relevant issue: how to create social consensus within participatory democracy. For this reason, the next part of the argument will develop rationales for engaging people in creating fairer regulations; by implication, and more specifically, this would help in the creation of regulations regarding OARs. The following discussion relies on Habermas' ideas about creating genuine consensus in contemporary complex societies.

Habermas and Consensus Formation

This is the last part of the argument of the chapter, and it is about the creation of social consensus. It is widely accepted that Rousseau's social contract theory only partially conceptualises the idea of social cohesion (H. Mansfield, 2008; H. C. Mansfield, 2014; Rousseau, 2012). This forms the basis for them to form regulations that would be effective in terms of protecting liberty (Mutz, 2006). Richard Margerum similarly argues that the process of social participation constitutes an interactive process of consensus building. He further declares that it is also a transformative instrument for social change (Margerum, 2002). Thus, the concepts of social interaction and consensus are affiliated with citizens' participation and arguably associated with the possibility of creating better social infrastructure (Stott & Drury, 2004).

On the opposite side to Rousseau's ideas about the social contract is Habermas, who argues that such views constitute an uncritical, non-deliberative general will (Dahlberg, 2005; Habermas & Rehg, 2001). He further claims that Rousseau relies on an apolitical version of contemporary 18th-century concepts of 'public opinion' towards strengthening democracy. In addition, Habermas describes Rousseau as using the prefix 'public' to highlight the people's presence during the election process, rather than to amplify the openness of their opinions (Putterman, 2010). Therefore, the openness of opinions is a way to share and disseminate various ideas, and the widest possible access to information would help in the relevant opinions. Following this statement, the first thing to be considered is that sharing and exchange of information are crucial for the formation of the general will, which, in turn, is for the public good. Further, the main aim of Habermas' views about deliberative democracy is to provide a normative account of legitimate law (Baynes, 2015). Deliberative democracy is dependent on the discursive space in a civil society, where individuals gather to discuss important issues freely and come to a consensus on them.

Habermas argues for more participatory democracy, which will lead to the completion of the Enlightenment project of rationality. It is widely accepted that Habermas has sought to produce a variety of tools for this task, such as empowerment through communicative rationality to enhance the democratic process. His conception of deliberative democracy, drawn from the amalgamation of a liberal focus on justice and a republican perception of negotiations and self-understanding, aims to improve the practice of democracy (Dryzek, 2005). Vitale argues that deliberative democracy has established a crucial role in the discussion about deepening democratic practices in complex modern societies. Admitting that individuals are the basic actors in the political procedure, social concerns, and political deliberation introduces a powerful view of participation that has not been properly clarified. Further, she claims that Habermas' philosophical contribution and notion highlights the importance of democratic practice (Vitale, 2006). However, she questions the Habermasian conception of democracy, specifically its lack of concern with social and economic justice and its failure to illustrate concrete procedures for institutionalising democratic practices. Thus, she introduces her own conception about the concept of participatory democracy and concentrates on social and economic inequalities. She concludes that a Habermasian focus on deliberation combined with a concern for social and economic justice can enhance democratic practice.

Habermas develops the argument that in a civil society (as the sphere between political and personal spheres), conditions of genuine participation by everyone can and should be created. It is important to emphasise that Habermas aims for rational and empirical consensus formation, and he assumes that most of the existing procedures of consensus formation are only empirical (Mendieta, 2002). A brief overview of Habermas' theory regarding the public sphere is necessary to appreciate how various parts of his argument fit together and help us comprehend how consensus can be formed and become effective in terms of individuals' active participation.

To Habermas, the public sphere is a composite concept constituted by three main elements. These three elements are called *institutional criteria* and constitute preconditions for the emergence of the public sphere (Kellner,

2014). In his work, The Structural Transformation of the Public Sphere, Habermas describes these elements and develops the concept of the public sphere (Johnson, 2006). He explains that one component of it is the social sphere. Thus, the public and private spheres constitute our life. The public sphere can be understood as including the political sphere, where political decisions regarding being a citizen are relevant. The private sphere is divided into civil society and personal spheres. The personal sphere is where emotions and relationships of affection govern our behaviour. It is in civil society that we come together with relative strangers and have to find ways of operating in an efficient manner. Market relationships are private in the sense that they are not public or political sphere activities. Yet they are not personal relationships that we have with persons in our emotional and affective life. Habermas wants to refine the concept of private market relations and explains that in civil society, we come together in various capacities, not only as market actors. Thus, clubs, the press, the market of culture products, social concerns and circumstances "in town" are various layers of civil society associations (Calhoun, 1992; Crossley & Roberts, 2004).

Habermas considers that, ideally, civil society is the proper area of social life where the dissemination and exchange of information, statements and views regarding common concerns or goods occur, eventually shaping public opinion. Consequently, it affects the conduct of the political system and those who rule or govern. Marshal agrees with these claims—that public opinion formed collectively is not only a mediator between society and state but is also the source of ideas required to affirm and guide the affairs of state (Johnson, 2006). Significantly, for Habermas mere coming together and forming opinions is not enough. His main ideas emphasise the conditions in which true or un-coerced discourse can develop. To Habermas, the core element of discourse stems from communication among people (Eriksen & Weigard, 2004). Thus, Habermas' theory of communicative action relies on the notion that what happens in a society eventually depends on the capacity of those who govern to comprehend and cooperate efficiently with social groups to improve social wealth. To conceptualise social cooperation, Habermas highlights the rational and cognitive character of such cooperation by presuming that good reasons could be given to justify social needs in the face of criticism. Thus, the theory of communicative action is aligned to an account of such justification, which Habermas calls the *reflective form* of communicative action required as a fundamental component for the civil society (Habermas, 2015).

Scholars argue that Habermas' interests in political theory and rationality come together in his theory for discourse ethics in civil society. Cohen and Arato argue that Habermas also discusses whether his highly idealised, multi-dimensional theory has real institutional purchase in contemporary societies (Cohen & Arato, 1994; Ekman & Amnå, 2012; Flyvbjerg, 1998). In this context, argumentation appears in the form of public discussion and debate over practical questions that encompass governmental bodies. Hence, the challenge is to consider whether an idealised form of practical discussion connects with real institutional contexts of decision-making (Chambers, 2009). At this point, this issue is also relevant in charting a possible pathway from theoretical discussion to legal policy decision-making. There is extensive literature and discussion on this topic. The Danish example of consensus conferences and scenario workshops reflects the importance of establishing an actual dialogue with citizens about a common concern (Andersen & Jæger, 1999; Glöckner & Betsch, 2008). In addition, this example illustrates that such dialogue provides incentives for people to come together meaningfully. More specifically, in consensus conferences, citizens are the leaders, and thus, they are responsible for the panel that sets up topics for discussion. In scenario workshops, a group of citizens interacts with other social actors to exchange information, experience and knowledge and to develop a draft for action. Both forms help me to argue that if there is a framework for discussion among citizens, experts, and policymakers, then new knowledge will emerge, and consensus will be achieved more efficiently.

Such a framework can be provided from several means of communication and information sharing. To Habermas, means such as newspapers, magazines, radio, and television are the media of the public sphere that can help the discussion and free sharing of information about common concerns. In modern times, we can also include the Internet as part of this media (Brants, 2005). Habermas' concepts of the public sphere and social space could be adapted in the current circumstances of the digital age. It can be argued that the modern *public sphere* and relevant *social space* are available on the Internet. As mentioned above, the Internet is the platform where users can freely have discussions, consider several issues, create content and share, disseminate, and exchange information through a variety of platforms, such as social networks. Hence, the Internet could form a substantial part of the construction for social consensus. Other thinkers support this idea. For instance, Dahlgren says that the best example of the contemporary public sphere in the digital age that promotes free speech, discussions, and agreements by creating an online social space is the Internet (Dahlgren, 2005).

Habermas is primarily arguing that in modern societies, we do not participate in a meaningful way in the matters of governance and forming collective opinions. That is why sharing and information exchange can play a meaningful role in the creation of consensus; its fundamental component should be the ability for everyone to participate in such creation. Equality of participation determines the kind of equality that should be pre-supposed in theories of justice. A cohesive society requires the involvement of active citizens. Hence, access to information that leads to knowledge is a significant resource, and it should be available to all.

As mentioned above, contemporary societies are quite complex, and more effective ways of creating consensus are required. The basic reason for such a lack of genuine consensus is the shrinking of civil society; modern societies are made up of individuals who do not come together in any meaningful way. If genuine consensus could be created, it would create a community out of the isolated individuals. Today, there is an information revolution going on where we are surrounded by ideas, terms, and concepts such as *knowledge society*, *information society*, and *big data*. Arguably, access to these novel information resources could play a vital role in modern societies and their structures. This is where dissemination and exchange of information could have a significant role in consensus creation. In other words, access to information can be the instrument that helps the creation of consensus in contemporary times.

For example, instead of simply voting for an issue and the majority getting their way, a consensus formed after due deliberation provides a better way to resolve problems among people or to form relevant policy. A possible example of this could be the process established through the TRIPS Agreement, which offers solutions in terms of trading. The TRIPS Agreement determines the most comprehensive and influential international accord concerning intellectual property rights (IPRs). It brings IP rules into the framework of the WTO, obliging its members to meet minimum required standards of IP protection and enforcement. Consequently, this has required great shifts in some local regulations, particularly in developing countries (Correa, 2007; Kur, 2011). Moreover, under the umbrella of a deliberative consensus, all views, concerns, and ideas are considered and lead to the creation of consensus. By listening closely to each other, a group of people with common interests, concerns or issues to solve aim to come up with recommendations that can work for everyone.

Another recent example concerning the structure of communication and the creation of consensus through Internet channels is the so-called Arab Spring. The Arab Spring movement illustrates the creation of public opinion through online channels (Gimmler, 2001; Lee, 2000; Stepanova, 2011). Protests during the Arab Spring of 2011 through social media networks played a crucial role in terms of instant disintegration of at least two regimes—those of Tunisia and Egypt. At the same time, such protests contributed to sociopolitical mobilisation in Bahrain and Syria (Eltantawy & Wiest, 2011). Contemporary technologies and social media had little to do with the underlying sociopolitical and socioeconomic factors behind the protest movement. However, the crisis occurred sooner rather than later, due to the initial mobilising impacts of modern technologies and social media networks. The protests were spurred to action by a Facebook campaign run by the opposition, the April 6 Youth Movement, which generated tens of thousands of positive responses to the call to rally against government policies.

The Arab Spring movement thus shows how people can come together in a meaningful way. It demonstrates how the Internet-based media represents an avenue for consensus formation with great potential. Regardless of the fact the Arab Spring did not result in great changes, it is still true that the Internet can be a tool that has the potential to unite people for the generation of a common will and public good. The modern public sphere, offered through the Internet, establishes an efficient way to be an active citizen in contemporary societies. It follows that if there are equal opportunities to access online information resources, that can help all citizens to be well equipped or well educated. To sum up, the April 6 Youth Movement helps me to argue that when people can share and exchange information (in this case, through the social network of Facebook), they come together and work together.

CONCLUSION

This chapter started by proposing that three interrelated ideas or matters need to be discussed. In the first part, it was demonstrated that open access to knowledge is necessary for philosophical as well as pragmatic reasons. Foucault's ideas helped me establish that access to knowledge is essential for a global society. Further, Foucault's ideas helped argue that knowledge assets can be gathered when there are equal information access opportunities. Therefore, access to information can lead to knowledge and consequently, to people's empowerment.

It follows consideration about whether access to knowledge is necessary to create a fair society. Assessing social justice theories will help us argue about a socially just society. Such an argument should be built upon Rawls' theory of justice, which in turn points out the significance of appropriate forms for social justice. In the context of this book, justice requires that OA should be integrated with copyright laws. Hence, OARs are one way of making access to knowledge available in a fair manner. However, for OARs to exist in this manner, appropriate public policy should be formulated. Therefore, a related issue for the argument is to examine how social justice and public policy are interrelated. It follows that social cohesion is ameliorated by just public policy. It follows that OARs can be a tool towards the creation of a cohesive society.

The last issues examined concern the process of generating social consensus for making appropriate public policies. In this regard, Jean-Jacques Rousseau's views about the social contract with Habermas' views on the public sphere were combined and adapted in modern circumstances in light of the emergence of the Internet. This helped us produce a theoretical foundation in order to argue that a cohesive society requires the involvement of well-informed participants or civil society in creating consensus. That is, the consensus of the social contract cannot be assumed but must be generated in modern societies. Therefore, such consensus could be enabled through the development of appropriate policies for OARs.

In conclusion, Habermas' ideas explain how genuine consensus can be achieved in modern complex societies, but the core requirement is that everybody is equally able to participate in creating consensus in civil society. It is this requirement of equality of participation that links back to the kind of equality that should be pre-supposed in theories of justice. As argued above, Rawls' theory of distributive justice helps us to create a theoretical foundation that a cohesive society requires the involvement of well-informed citizens, or, in other words, active citizens. It is in this respect that access to knowledge is an important resource, and it should be available to all.

OAP and OARs are forms of resources that can function as a contemporary response in the digital age. Therefore, they should be integrated into current copyright regulations. They can thus help increase equal access opportunities and offer protection of creative content that traditional copyright laws are increasingly unable to offer. This chapter has provided the theoretical framework for the interplay of open access with public policy objectives that could lead to better social cohesion. In the following chapter, the primary aim is to analyse the design and assumptions underlying the open access policy framework in the European Union. Based on this information, it follows an analysis of the strengths and shortcomings of the European regulations in relation to open access, sharing information and protection of intellectual property among European Member States. This will help us examine strategies that aim to foster open access to scientific information and ask whether, and how, these policies are monitored and enforced.

REFERENCES

Agyeman, J. (2003). *Just sustainabilities: Development in an unequal world.* MIT Press.

Andersen, I.-E., & Jæger, B. (1999). Scenario workshops and consensus conferences: Towards more democratic decision-making. *Science & Public Policy, 26*(5), 331–340. doi:10.3152/147154399781782301

Australian Law Reform Commission. (2014). *Copyright and the Digital Economy (Copyright and the Digital Economy No. 122).* Retrieved from http://www.alrc.gov.au/publications/copyright-report-122

Bacon, F. (2008). *Francis Bacon: The major works* (B. Vickers, Ed.). New York: Oxford University Press.

Bacon, F. (2013). *Complete works of Francis Bacon.* Minerva Classics.

Baynes, K. (2015). *Habermas.* Routledge. doi:10.4324/9781315696423

Besson, S., & Martí, J. L. (2006). *Deliberative democracy and its discontents.* Ashgate Publishing, Ltd.

Birkland, T. A. (2014). *An introduction to the policy process: Theories, concepts and models of public policy making.* Routledge. doi:10.4324/9781315706399

Bishop, P., & Davis, G. (2002). Mapping public participation in policy choices. *Australian Journal of Public Administration, 61*(1), 14–29. doi:10.1111/1467-8500.00255

Black, J. (2015). *The power of knowledge: How information and technology made the modern world.* New Haven, CT: Yale University Press.

Boeder, P. (2005). Habermas' heritage: The future of the public sphere in the network society. *First Monday, 10*(9). doi:10.5210/fm.v10i9.1280

Boucher, D., & Kelly, P. (Eds.). (2003). *The social contract from Hobbes to Rawls*. Routledge. doi:10.4324/9780203392928

Bovaird, T., Löffler, E., & Loeffler, E. (2004). *Public Management and Governance*. Routledge. doi:10.4324/9780203884096

Brants, K. (2005). Guest editor's introduction: The Internet and the public sphere. *Political Communication*, *22*(2), 143–146. doi:10.1080/10584600590933133

Brown, J. (2010). *What is participatory democracy? It means you get involved*. Retrieved January 14, 2016, from http://www.glasgowdailytimes.com/opinion/what-is-participatory-democracy-it-means-you-get-involved/article_d0e062df-de30-502e-94bd-7cfdf00a5130.html

Buchanan, G., Masoodian, M., & Cunningham, S. J. (2008). *Digital libraries: Universal and ubiquitous access to information*. Springer Science & Business Media. doi:10.1007/978-3-540-89533-6

Burk, D. L., & Cohen, J. E. (2007). *Fair use infrastructure for copyright management systems (SSRN Scholarly Paper No. ID 1007079)*. Rochester, NY: Social Science Research Network. Retrieved from https://papers.ssrn.com/abstract=1007079

Cabannes, Y. (2004). Participatory budgeting: A significant contribution to participatory democracy. *Environment and Urbanization*, *16*(1), 27–46. doi:10.1630/095624704323026133

Cairney, P. (2012). *Understanding public policy: theories and issues*. New York: Palgrave Macmillan. doi:10.1007/978-0-230-35699-3

Calhoun, C. J. (1992). *Habermas and the public sphere*. MIT Press.

Calland, R., & Bentley, K. A. (2013). *The impact and effectiveness of transparency and accountability initiatives: Freedom of information (SSRN Scholarly Paper No. ID 2305479)*. Rochester, NY: Social Science Research Network. Retrieved from http://papers.ssrn.com/abstract=2305479

Carlaw, K., Oxley, L., Walker, P., Thorns, D., & Nuth, M. (2006). Beyond the hype: Intellectual property and the knowledge society/knowledge economy. *Journal of Economic Surveys*, *20*(4), 633–690. doi:10.1111/j.1467-6419.2006.00262.x

Chambers, S. (2009). Rhetoric and the public sphere: Has deliberative democracy abandoned mass democracy? *Political Theory*, *37*(3), 323–350. doi:10.1177/0090591709332336

Chesal, R. (2012). *Loosen up copyright law, says Dutch government*. Retrieved December 13, 2016, from https://www.rnw.org/archive/loosen-copyright-law-says-dutch-government

Cohen, J. L., & Arato, A. (1994). *Civil society and political theory*. MIT Press.

Correa, C. (2007). *Trade related aspects of intellectual property rights: A commentary on the TRIPS Agreement*. Oxford University Press. doi:10.1093/law/9780199271283.001.0001

Crombie, I. M. (2012). *An examination of Plato's doctrines, Volume 2: Plato on knowledge and reality*. Routledge.

Crossley, N., & Roberts, J. M. (2004). *After Habermas: New perspectives on the public sphere*. Sociological Review Monograph. Retrieved from https://philpapers.org/rec/HABAHN

Dahlberg, L. (2005). The Habermasian public sphere: Taking difference seriously? *Theory and Society*, *34*(2), 111–136. doi:10.100711186-005-0155-z

Dahlgren, P. (2005). The Internet, public spheres, and political communication: Dispersion and deliberation. *Political Communication*, *22*(2), 147–162. doi:10.1080/10584600590933160

Darling-Hammond, L. (1995). *Inequality and access to knowledge*. Retrieved from http://eric.ed.gov/?id=ED382721

David, P. A., & Foray, D. (2002). An introduction to the economy of the knowledge society. *International Social Science Journal*, *54*(171), 9–23. doi:10.1111/1468-2451.00355

Davis-Floyd, R., & Sargent, C. (1996). The social production of authoritative knowledge in pregnancy and childbirth. *Medical Anthropology Quarterly*, *10*(2), 111–120. doi:10.1525/maq.1996.10.2.02a00010 PMID:8744079

Dobusch, L., & Schüßler, E. (2014). Copyright reform and business model innovation: Regulatory propaganda at German music industry conferences. *Technological Forecasting and Social Change*, *83*, 24–39. doi:10.1016/j.techfore.2013.01.009

Dryzek, J. S. (2005). Deliberative democracy in divided societies alternatives to Agonism and Analgesia. *Political Theory*, *33*(2), 218–242. doi:10.1177/0090591704268372

Dunn, W. (2003). *Public policy analysis: An introduction* (3rd ed.). Prentice Hall.

Eeckhout, J., & Jovanovic, B. (2002). Knowledge spillovers and inequality. *The American Economic Review*, *92*(5), 1290–1307. doi:10.1257/000282802762024511

Ekman, J., & Amnå, E. (2012). Political participation and civic engagement: Towards a new typology. *Human Affairs*, *22*(3), 283–300. doi:10.247813374-012-0024-1

Elden, P. S., & Crampton, D. J. W. (2012). *Space, knowledge and power: Foucault and geography*. Ashgate Publishing, Ltd.

Eltantawy, N., & Wiest, J. B. (2011). The Arab Spring: Social media in the Egyptian revolution: Reconsidering resource mobilization theory. *International Journal of Communication*, *5*(0), 18.

Eriksen, E. O., & Weigard, J. (2004). *Understanding Habermas: Communicating action and deliberative democracy*. London: Bloomsbury Academic.

Evans, S. J. (2011). *Public policy issues research trends*. New York: Nova Science Publishers, Inc.

Feinberg, J. (2014). *Rights, justice, and the bounds of liberty: Essays in social philosophy*. Princeton University Press.

Felice, W. F. (1996). *Taking suffering seriously: The importance of collective human rights*. SUNY Press.

Fischer, F. (2003). *Reframing public policy: Discursive politics and deliberative practices*. Oxford: Oxford University Press. doi:10.1093/0199 24264X.001.0001

Flyvbjerg, B. (1998). *Habermas and Foucault: Thinkers for civil society? (SSRN Scholarly Paper No. ID 2237923)*. Rochester, NY: Social Science Research Network. Retrieved from http://papers.ssrn.com/abstract=2237923

Foucault, M. (1980). Two lectures. In C. Gordon (Ed.), *Power/knowledge: Selected interviews and other writings, 1972–1977* (1st American ed.; pp. 78–108). New York: Vintage.

Foucault, M. (1995). *Discipline & punish: The birth of the prison* (2nd ed.). (A. Sheridan, Trans.). New York: Vintage Books.

Foucault, M. (2012). *The archaeology of knowledge*. Knopf Doubleday Publishing Group.

Freeman, S. R. (2003). *The Cambridge companion to Rawls*. Cambridge University Press.

Furlong, S. R., & Kerwin, C. M. (2005). Interest group participation in rule making: A decade of change. *Journal of Public Administration: Research and Theory*, *15*(3), 353–370. doi:10.1093/jopart/mui022

Gaventa, J., & Cornwall, A. (2013). Power and knowledge. In *The SAGE handbook of action research: participative inquiry and practice* (pp. 172–189). SAGE.

Gimmler, A. (2001). Deliberative democracy, the public sphere and the Internet. *Philosophy and Social Criticism*, *27*(4), 21–39. doi:10.1177/019145370102700402

Ginsburg, J. C. (2004). The right to claim authorship in U.S. copyright and trademarks law. *Houston Law Review*, *41*, 263.

Ginsburg, J. C. (2009). The U.S. experience with mandatory copyright formalities: A love/hate relationship. *Columbia Journal of Law and the Arts*, *33*, 311.

Glöckner, A., & Betsch, T. (2008). *Modeling option and strategy choices with connectionist networks: Towards an integrative model of automatic and deliberate decision making (SSRN Scholarly Paper No. ID 1090866)*. Rochester, NY: Social Science Research Network. Retrieved from https://papers.ssrn.com/abstract=1090866

Goldin, I., & Reinert, K. (2012). *Globalization for development: Meeting new challenges*. Oxford University Press.

Grabow, S., Hilliker, M., & Moskal, J. (2006). *Comprehensive planning and citizen participation*. University of Wisconsin: Extension Service.

Grüttemeier, H., & Mahon, B. (2003). Open access to scientific and technical information: State of the art and future trends. In *ICSTI/INIST/INSERM Seminar, 23–24 January 2003, Paris, France*. IOS Press.

Gutting, G. (1989). *Michel Foucault's archaeology of scientific reason: Science and the history of reason*. Cambridge University Press. doi:10.1017/CBO9781139172141

Gutting, G. (2005). *The Cambridge companion to Foucault*. Cambridge University Press. doi:10.1017/CCOL0521840821

Habermas, J. (2015). *The theory of communicative action: Reason and the rationalization of society* (1st ed., Vol. 1). Polity.

Habermas, J., & Rehg, W. (2001). Constitutional democracy: A paradoxical union of contradictory principles? *Political Theory*, *29*(6), 766–781. doi:10.1177/0090591701029006002

Hendriks, C. M. (2006). Integrated deliberation: Reconciling civil society's dual role in deliberative democracy. *Political Studies*, *54*(3), 486–508. doi:10.1111/j.1467-9248.2006.00612.x

Hesmondhalgh, D. (2005). Media and cultural policy as public policy: The case of the British Labour government. *International Journal of Cultural Policy*, *11*(1), 95–109. doi:10.1080/10286630500067861

Hill, M., & Varone, F. (2014). *The public policy process*. Routledge. doi:10.4324/9781315832937

Hillier, J. (2003). Agonizing over consensus: Why Habermasian ideals cannot be 'real.'. *Planning Theory*, *2*(1), 37–59. doi:10.1177/1473095203002001005

Houle, J. R. (1991). Digital audio sampling, copyright law and the American music industry: Piracy or just a bad rap. *Loyola Law Review*, *37*, 879.

Hugenholtz, P. B., & Senftleben, M. (2012). *Fair use in Europe: In search of flexibilities (SSRN Scholarly Paper No. ID 2013239)*. Rochester, NY: Social Science Research Network. Retrieved from https://papers.ssrn.com/abstract=2013239

Hughes, J. M. (2006). *To the Maginot Line*. Harvard University Press.

Johnson, P. (2006). *Habermas: Rescuing the public sphere*. Routledge. doi:10.4324/9780203020166

Jordan, B. (2014). Technology and social interaction: Notes on the achievement of authoritative knowledge in complex settings. *Talent Development and Excellence*, *6*(1), 95–132.

Kahan, D. M., & Braman, D. (2005). *Cultural cognition and public policy (SSRN Scholarly Paper)*. Rochester, NY: Social Science Research Network. Retrieved from http://papers.ssrn.com/abstract=746508

Kellner, D. (2014). Habermas, the public sphere, and democracy. In D. Boros & J. M. Glass (Eds.), *Re-imagining public space* (pp. 19–43). Palgrave Macmillan, US. doi:10.1057/9781137373311_2

Kur, A. (2011). *Intellectual property rights in a fair world trade system: Proposals for reform of TRIPS*. Edward Elgar Publishing. doi:10.4337/9781849809580

Lee, J. (2000). Knowledge management: The intellectual revolution. *IIE Solutions*, *32*(10), 34–34.

Lewis, D., Rodgers, D., & Woolcock, M. (2008). The fiction of development: Literary representation as a source of authoritative knowledge. *The Journal of Development Studies*, *44*(2), 198–216. doi:10.1080/00220380701789828

Leyshon, A., Webb, P., French, S., Thrift, N., & Crewe, L. (2005). On the reproduction of the musical economy after the Internet. *Media Culture & Society*, *27*(2), 177–209. doi:10.1177/0163443705050468

Liu, J. P. (2000). Owning digital copies: Copyright law and the incidents of copy ownership. *William and Mary Law Review*, *42*, 1245.

Mansfield, H. (2008). *Why is political philosophy important?* Retrieved October 25, 2015, from http://bigthink.com/videos/why-is-political-philosophy-important

Mansfield, H. C. (2014). *A student's guide to political philosophy*. Open Road Media.

Margerum, R. D. (2002). Collaborative planning building consensus and building a distinct model for practice. *Journal of Planning Education and Research*, *21*(3), 237–253. doi:10.1177/0739456X0202100302

Mendieta, E. (2002). *The adventures of transcendental philosophy: Karl-Otto Apel's semiotics and discourse ethics*. Rowman & Littlefield.

Mueller, P. (2006). Exploring the knowledge filter: How entrepreneurship and university–industry relationships drive economic growth. *Research Policy, 35*(10), 1499–1508. doi:10.1016/j.respol.2006.09.023

Mutz, D. C. (2006). *Hearing the other side: Deliberative versus participatory democracy*. Cambridge University Press. doi:10.1017/CBO9780511617201

Nolan, M. E. (2005). Search for original expression: Fan fiction and the fair use defense. *Southern Illinois University Law Journal. Southern Illinois University at Carbondale. School of Law, 30*, 533.

O'Faircheallaigh, C. (2010). Public participation and environmental impact assessment: Purposes, implications, and lessons for public policy making. *Environmental Impact Assessment Review, 30*(1), 19–27. doi:10.1016/j.eiar.2009.05.001

Pateman, C. (2012). Participatory democracy revisited. *Perspectives on Politics, 10*(01), 7–19. doi:10.1017/S1537592711004877

Putterman, E. (2010). *Rousseau, law and the sovereignty of the people*. Cambridge University Press. doi:10.1017/CBO9780511776861

Puybaret, E. (2008). *Universal declaration of human rights*. United Nations Publications.

Rawls, J. (2001). *Justice as fairness: A restatement (E. Kelly* (M. Cambridge, Ed.). London: Belknap Press.

Rawls, J. (2009). *A theory of justice*. Harvard University Press.

Richards, D., & Martin, S. (2002). *Governance and public policy in the United Kingdom*. Oxford University Press.

Rousseau, J.-J. (2012). *Rousseau: The Basic Political Writings: Discourse on the Sciences and the Arts, Discourse on the Origin of Inequality, Discourse on Political Economy, On the Social Contract, The State of War*. Hackett Publishing.

Rowe, G., & Frewer, L. J. (2000). Public participation methods: A framework for evaluation. *Science, Technology & Human Values, 25*(1), 3–29. doi:10.1177/016224390002500101

Rowley, J., & Hartley, R. J. (2008). *Organizing knowledge: An introduction to managing access to information*. Ashgate Publishing, Ltd.

Sen, A. (2000). Social justice and the distribution of income. In *Handbook of income distribution* (Vol. 1, pp. 59–85). Elsevier. doi:10.1016/S1574-0056(00)80004-4

Shen, X. (2005). A dilemma for developing countries in intellectual property strategy? Lessons from a case study of software piracy and Microsoft in China. *Science & Public Policy*, *32*(3), 187–198. doi:10.3152/147154305781779533

Stepanova, E. (2011). *The role of information communication technologies in the "Arab Spring"* (Eurasia Policy Memo No. 159; p. 6). Retrieved from http://www.ponarseurasia.com/sites/default/files/policy-memos-pdf/pepm_159.pdf

Stott, C., & Drury, J. (2004). The importance of social structure and social interaction in stereotype consensus and content: Is the whole greater than the sum of its parts? *European Journal of Social Psychology*, *34*(1), 11–23. doi:10.1002/ejsp.183

Stromquist, N. P. (2002). *Education in a globalized world: The connectivity of economic power, technology, and knowledge*. Rowman & Littlefield Publishers.

Taylor, M. (2000). Communities in the lead: Power, organisational capacity and social capital. *Urban Studies (Edinburgh, Scotland)*, *37*(5–6), 1019–1035. doi:10.1080/00420980050011217

Thadeusz, F. (2010). *No copyright law: The real reason for Germany's industrial expansion?* Retrieved August 30, 2016, from http://www.spiegel.de/international/zeitgeist/no-copyright-law-the-real-reason-for-germany-s-industrial-expansion-a-710976.html

Thatcher, S. G. (2008). China's copyright dilemma. *Learned Publishing*, *21*(4), 278–284. doi:10.1087/095315108X356707

Townley, B. (1993). Foucault, power/knowledge, and its relevance for human resource management. *Academy of Management Review*, *18*(3), 518–545. doi:10.5465/amr.1993.9309035149

United Nations. (2006). *Social justice in an open world: The role of the united nations*. Retrieved from http://www.un.org/esa/socdev/documents/ifsd/SocialJustice.pdf

Vitale, D. (2006). Between deliberative and participatory democracy: A contribution on Habermas. *Philosophy and Social Criticism*, *32*(6), 739–766. doi:10.1177/0191453706064022

Wang, S., & Zhu, J. J. H. (2003). Mapping film piracy in China. *Theory, Culture & Society*, *20*(4), 97–125. doi:10.1177/02632764030204007

Wenar, L. (2013). John Rawls. In E. N. Zalta (Ed.), *The Stanford encyclopedia of philosophy* (Winter 2013). Retrieved from http://plato.stanford.edu/archives/win2013/entries/rawls/

Younting, Y. (2014). *What are the difficulties in the online copyright enforcement in China?* Retrieved August 30, 2016, from http://www.chinaiplawyer.com/difficulties-online-copyright-enforcement-china/

Chapter 4
Open Access in Practice:
The European Union's Regulation of OARs

ABSTRACT

The basic scope of the European Union is the political and economic unification through harmonisation of European Member States' national regulations and associated frameworks. Should the European Union aim to harmonise and unify these national regulations, it is only reasonable to do so through copyright-specific policy provisions implemented by the European countries. The European copyright regime could potentially facilitate open access practice, should this practice be tailored to policy-making actors regarding the European copyright law framework. This chapter examines efforts and initiatives made by the European institutions (e.g., European Commission, European Parliament) in order to construct a coherent copyright framework for the European Union Members.

INTRODUCTION

The previous chapters argue that public policy objectives of a fair and just society require greater access to knowledge by an ever-broadening cross-section of the global society. This raises the issue of creating a balance between the competing interests of copyright owners and end users. OARs are a response to new realities that stem from technological growth regarding the

DOI: 10.4018/978-1-7998-1131-2.ch004

production and dissemination of information (Castells, 2002). Accessibility to information resources has become a modern necessity that needs to be met to share the wealth of European society equitably (Héritier, 2003). Therefore, this chapter will analyse the efforts made by the European Union to create a regulatory framework. Scholars argue that the European directives, which will be examined below, establish the European copyright framework (Majone & Baake, 1996; Wallace, Pollack, & Young, 2015).

Scholars assert that an important factor for economic integration in Europe is the concept of information (Goodwin & Spittle, 2002). Given the fact that the "information society" is a critical element of modern Europe, it is acknowledged that information resources play a crucial role in the context of economic integration and the design of future research policy in Europe. For instance, the European Commission in 2011 conducted a consultation on the future of such policy, which led to the production of new foundations for the upcoming Eighth Framework program for research (FP8), renamed Common Strategic Framework for Research and Innovation funding (CSFRI) and presented under the Horizon 2020 program (Granieri & Renda, 2012). This will be discussed later in the chapter.

The design and assumptions underlying the modern framework of open access in Europe can be discerned by an examination of the directives that are the foundation of the European copyright regime. Based on this information, an analysis follows of the strengths and shortcomings of the European directives in relation to intellectual property, copyright protection and related rights, sharing information and open access among European Member States that constitute the modern European copyright regime. Examination of the governance framework regarding the OARs in the European Union helps us argue that it can be an instrument to balance the interests of copyright owner and end user interests. Furthermore, it will set the background and help to contextualise the implementation of open access in Greece in the following chapter as a pertinent European case study.

The European directives will be studied as a contemporary example of how copyright and digital revolution have adapted to create new possibilities, including that of OARs. The open access practice in the European context was introduced through the program titled Horizon 2020, which focuses on research and aims to foster information accessibility based on open access. The example of open access to research can be used to show whether an information society can facilitate new ways of thinking and furthering access to information resources. In conclusion, mandates, statements and projects relating to open access adopted from European institutions will also be addressed to present pragmatic justifications for open access.

The basic scope of the European Union is unification and harmonisation of all European Member States' national laws (Antezana, 2003). Since the European Union aims to harmonise and unify national laws, it is only reasonable that it provides specific copyright policy that could be implemented by the European countries. Such policy, found in the directives, is examined below. In addition, these directives provide legal provisions in relation to open access and dissemination of information within the European continent (European Commission, 2007, 2014; European Communities, 2001; European Parliament, 2013; European Parliament & European Council, 2009; Giannopoulou, 2012). An analysis and explanation of the rationales for the governance framework of OARs in the European Union will help identify the standard that others may wish to follow.

The following chapter is divided into four parts. The first part considers the European copyright regime and illustrates its historical growth during and since the process of European integration, which is the overarching objective for Europe. Part two presents an analysis of specific directives of the European Union, which are the foundations of the current European copyright regime. Part three contains a discussion of the significant regulations of Horizon 2020 (European Commission, 2013). This European regulation is the first to introduce ways for open access to be applied through research projects and/ or initiatives funded from the Horizon 2020 program. The last part examines perspectives on the advocacy of OARs in the European context.

THE EUROPEAN COPYRIGHT REGIME

From the Treaty of Rome (January 1958) to the Maastricht Treaty (November 1993), Europe moved gradually towards achieving one of its overarching objectives: economic integration. Therefore, it is relevant to examine the impact of developing explicit governance structures at the European level, which lead to integration. The directives examined below show that their objective is the harmonisation among national or local regimes for intellectual protection in Europe. Hence, copyrighted goods (e.g., books, music, films, and software) and services (e.g., services offering access to these goods) will move freely within the internal market, which constitutes a substantial part of European integration. This section illustrates the impact of Europeanisation on local structures of the Member States (Cowles, Caporaso, & Risse-Kappen, 2001).

History of European Integration

Moussis argues that the course of the multinational integration process in Europe is established by three currents that converge at certain points and empower this integration: (a) the growing number of participants, (b) the ongoing increase of their aims during stages of the integration progress and (c) the constant increase of their activities by the development of common policies.

It is worth recapitulating the main facts concerning these major trends of European integration (Moussis, 2014). The process of European integration initiated in 1951 among six countries as a customs union regarding the resources of coal and steel (i.e., Belgium, France, West Germany, Italy, the Netherlands and Luxembourg). At the time, the union was based on the European Coal and Steel Community (ECSC) Treaty, and it was named as such. The ECSC Treaty introduced the principle of supranationalism. In general terms, supranationalism formed the rationale for European integration and led towards the founding of the current European Union (Tsebelis & Garrett, 2001). In 1958, the ECSC countries extended the ambit of the union's operation to other sectors of their economies. Hence, another treaty was signed, entitled the European Economic Community (ECC) Treaty (Craig & Búrca, 2011; Kohler-Koch & Eising, 1999). In 1973, three countries joined the ECC; the ECC had already decided upon intergovernmental collaboration within a common trade area, the boundaries of which were aligned with the borders of the Member States (Jones, 2003). Since 1992, the European common market gradually emerged; it had 12 Member States bonded with the Single European Act (European Parliament, 1987). Moreover, the Member States signed the Treaty of Maastricht, which lead towards the next stage for European integration (Chalmers, Davies, & Monti, 2010). In 1995, another three countries joined the union, and in 1997 the 15 Member States decided to unify or integrate the fields of freedom, security, and justice, based on the Treaty of Amsterdam. In 2007, European integration was extensive; a further 12 new Member States joined the European "family" based on the Lisbon Treaty (Davies, 2014).

The process of European integration has followed a steady evolution; it mainly aims to create a convergence of the economies of the European Member States (Button & Pentecost, 1995; Cuadrado-Roura, 2001; Whitley & Kristensen, 1996). It was anticipated that this convergence would lead to a political union (Hix & Høyland, 2011; Sabel & Zeitlin, 2010). It should be mentioned that in December 1991, during the Maastricht process, the European Member States decided to start elaborating details of such convergence, and thus, as an overarching aim, the Economic and Monetary Union (EMU) was adopted. Therefore, the Maastricht process clarified that single or mutual monetary policy and harmonisation of regional economic policies should be adopted to achieve social cohesion (de la Porte, Pochet, & Room, 2001). In addition, in 2002, the Maastricht process was accomplished with the circulation of the Euro currency. At the time, European Member States initiated considerations for coordinating in the context of non-economic policies. The European Union has now become a global actor that plays a crucial role in the international arena (Bretherton & Vogler, 1999; Lucarelli & Fioramonti, 2009). Thus, the European Member States reached the threshold for an ever-closer political integration (Cowles et al., 2001; Dinan, 2010).

The above developments show that policies pursuing common targets and serving common interests form the foundations of the European integration process. European citizens' supreme interests are the certainty for peace among European neighbours and ongoing improvement of their social welfare (Abrahamson, 2005; Taylor-Gooby, 2004). The policies of the European Union serve those interests efficiently (Manners & Whitman, 2000). The next subsection examines one of these common policies based on the specific directives regarding copyright protection and associated issues.

The Role of the Copyright Regime in European Integration

The discussion in this section explains the importance of the copyright regime to European integration. Given the fact that the European Union operates in the context of other international conventions and agreements, it follows that its copyright protection role should be compatible with other international instruments. Therefore, the interplay between specific international agreements with the European copyright regime and its regulations will be considered. The European directives examined in this chapter reflect the European countries' obligations under these international agreements.

The Berne Convention for the Protection of Literary and Artistic Works (1886) represents the first attempt on behalf of European countries to protect authors' rights over their literary and artistic creations. As the years passed, new technological advances in the technology for the transmission of speech sounds (phonograms) and information (radio and television) emerged (Tschmuck, 2012). Thus, new necessities also emerged in terms of copyright protection (Marriott, 2009). In 1994, the WTO introduced the TRIPS Agreement. Its overarching objective was to diminish obstacles regarding international trade, consider the need to promote effective protection of IP rights and ensure that measures to enforce IP rights do not themselves become impediments to legitimate trade. The TRIPS Agreement illustrates a tight connection between the WTO and the WIPO. In 1996, the WIPO introduced two international treaties that built upon the Berne Convention and its principles in terms of intellectual protection. The first is the WIPO Performances and Phonograms Treaty, which established the protection of performers, producers of phonograms and broadcasting organisations (WIPO, 1996b). More specifically, it protects performers (actors, singers, musicians, etc.), producers' phonograms (persons or legal entities that take the initiative and have the responsibility for the fixation of sounds) and broadcasting organisations' broadcast rights. The second treaty is the WIPO Copyright Treaty (WIPO, 1996a), which mentions two subjects to be protected by copyright: (a) computer programs, whatever the mode or form of their expression, and (b) compilations of data or other materials, in any form, that, because of the selection or arrangement of their contents, constitute intellectual creations.

In general terms, the objectives of the European directives stem from or are constructed in accordance with the European Commission Treaty provisions, which enable Europe to match Member States' regulations regarding free movement of goods and services (art. 45, 47(2), and 55 of the Treaty on the Functioning of the European Union; European Parliament, 2007) and, specifically, to produce the internal market (art. 95; Lang, Aigner, Scheuerle, & Stefaner, 2004). More significantly, the analysis below illustrates the European Union's attempts to address multiple issues through the directives. The European Union seeks (a) to establish standards, (b) to harmonise national copyright regimes into a European regime or a common regime, (c) to diminish national discrepancies among European Member States, (d) to settle upon or construct the necessary level of protection to foster creativity and secure investments, (e) to promote cultural diversity, and (f) to improve for consumers and business access to digital content and services across Europe.

Moreover, in the recent past, the European Commission monitors the timely and correct implementation of European copyright law, while the Court of Justice of the European Union (CJEU) has developed a substantive body of case law interpreting the provisions of the directives. This has significantly contributed to the consistent application of the copyright rules across the European countries. A brief analysis of the directives that constitute the European Union's regulatory framework for copyright and neighbouring rights follows.

DIRECTIVES

Satellite and Cable Directive

Council Directive 93/83/EEC of 27 September 1993 on the Coordination of Certain Rules Concerning Copyright and Rights Related to Copyright Applicable to Satellite Broadcasting and Cable Retransmission (European Council, 1993)

The first directive to be examined is the directive on the coordination of certain rules concerning copyright and rights related to copyright applicable to satellite broadcasting and cable retransmission. Scholars argue that there are several reasons that led to its introduction (Sandholtz, 1993; Sandholtz & Sweet, 1998). In particular: (a) the Treaty of Rome establishing the European Economic Community (articles 52(2) and 66 thereof provide for the establishment of a common market and an area without internal frontiers; European Commission, 1957); (b) measures to achieve this include the abolition of obstacles to the free movement of services and the institution of a system ensuring that competition in the common market is not distorted; (c) the European Council may adopt directives for the coordination of the provisions laid down by law, regulation or administrative action in Member States concerning the taking up and pursuit of activities as self-employed persons; (d) broadcasts transmitted across frontiers within the European Community—specifically by satellite and cable—are one of the most important ways of pursuing these European objectives; and (e) the European Council has already adopted Directive 89/552/EEC of 3 October 1989 on the coordination of certain provisions laid down by law, regulation or administrative action in Member States concerning the pursuit of television broadcasting activities.

As broadcasting and cable transmission have evolved since the 1990s, the distribution of information has increased and, consequently, copyright issues have emerged. As Evens and Donders argue, there has been a great change in the European market regarding satellite broadcasters (Evens & Donders, 2013). Moreover, broadcasters used to depend on simple revenue streams for several years until the audiovisual markets were liberalised. With such liberalisation, a dual order emerged in which public service broadcasters' funding models did not change and continued to rely on private sources (Michalis, 2008). This directive acknowledged the need to protect information transmitted through new technology.

The Satellite and Cable Directive concerns the harmonisation of copyright laws in the field of broadcasting. In addition, it aims to facilitate the licensing of copyright and related rights, and thereby to improve the cross-border provision and reception of satellite broadcasting and cable retransmission services in the European market. It has been in force since 1 January 1995 and aims to facilitate the cross-border transmission of audiovisual programs, particularly broadcasting via satellite and retransmission by cable. For satellite broadcasting, the directive establishes that the copyright-relevant act takes place in the country of origin of the broadcast. In the case of simultaneous cable retransmissions, the directive introduces the collective management of the rights. In 2002, the European Commission issued a report on the functioning of this directive. Since then, new technology and business models for content distribution have emerged. The Commission considered that it is necessary to adapt copyright rules to these new technological realities for the rules to continue to meet their objectives. The emergence of personal computers brought the necessity of protection for the associated information databases. Thus, the European Commission perceived the necessity of introducing another pillar for the European copyright regime, which is examined below.

Database Directive

Directive 96/9/EC of the European Parliament and of the Council of 11 March 1996 on the Legal Protection of Databases (European Commission, 1996)

This directive addresses the importance of the legal protection of databases (Mazziotti, 2008; Schneider, 1998; Seville, 2009). Various databases of information were created over time around the European Union, and they needed to be protected (Davison, 2003). In particular, this directive was adopted in February 1996 and created a new exclusive "sui generis" right for database producers, valid for 15 years, to protect their investment of time, money, and effort, irrespective of whether the database is in itself innovative (*non-original* databases). In the process, the directive harmonised the copyright law applicable to the framework and arrangement of the contents of databases (*original* databases; Wald, 2001).

The Internet has a profound effect on many aspects of the social, cultural, economic, and legal systems, and poses a challenge to regulation in the copyright context (Samuelson, 2000). The Internet has constituted a tool to disseminate information, and it is possible to provide online databases for information (Quah, 2000). The creation of databases also introduced the electronic information industry, which is one of the fastest-growing areas of the European economy (Casey, 1991). Self-evidently, the databases comprise an important mechanism to gather information, such as demographic, bibliographic, medical, technological, news, financial, and travel materials (Ramakrishnan & Gehrke, 2000; Revesz, 2009). It follows that databases can also host information relevant to medical treatment, education, scientific research and other fields that contribute to the growth of society. Therefore, access to such information is vital for every section of global society. Gathering different sorts of information and storing it on databases also facilitates Europe's creative output, which plays a meaningful role in terms of growth, identity, and social progress. However, for such progress to occur, copyright and related legislation do not operate in isolation. Hence, the European Commission considered that another directive should be introduced to provide harmonisation by addressing certain aspects of copyright and related rights. The analysis of this directive follows below.

Information Society (InfoSoc) Directive

Directive 2001/29/EC of the European Parliament and of the Council of 22 May 2001 on the Harmonisation of Certain Aspects of Copyright and Related Rights in the Information Society (European Commission, 2001)

Throughout the world, information and communications technologies are generating a new industrial revolution already as important and far-reaching as those of the past. It is a revolution based on information, itself the expression of human knowledge. Technological advancements now enable us to process, store, disseminate, exchange, retrieve and communicate information in whatever forms they may take (oral, written or visual), unconstrained by distance, time and volume. This revolution brings new capacities to human intelligence and constitutes a resource that shifts the ways of collaboration (Webster, 2014). Because of the immense creativity that stems from this information revolution, reasonable concerns have arisen regarding practices to improve copyright protection. The WIPO, at the December 1996 Diplomatic Conference, justified this fact where two treaties of paramount importance to copyright and related rights were signed.

The European Union already forms a substantial part of this revolution. An information society establishes a means to achieve so many of its overarching objectives (Jordana, 2002). The information society has the potential to improve European citizens' life quality, the efficiency of social and economic organisation and to reinforce cohesion in Europe (Beniger, 2009). Following this statement, the European Commission introduced its initial proposal for the InfoSoc Directive on 10 December 1997, followed by an amended proposal on 21 May 1999 and the common position on 28 September 2000. The InfoSoc Directive was finally adopted on 22 May 2001 (Dreier & Hugenholtz, 2006). Its scope was twofold: (a) to reflect technological advancements through specific regulations concerning copyright and related rights, and (b) shift into community law the principal international obligations that stem from the two WIPO treaties mentioned before. This scope of the directive illustrates that it was fundamental for the original Lisbon Strategy of 2000 (Copeland & Papadimitriou, 2012). Accordingly, the Lisbon Strategy objective was to foster economic prosperity, jobs and growth, particularly by boosting the knowledge-based economy via enhancing the quality of European Community regulation (Dieckhoff & Gallie, 2007).

The ever-growing digitisation of information has led to the information society in which more and more information is available (Rannenberg, Royer, & Deuker, 2009). Another related issue that has arisen because of the digitisation of information concerns the resale right regarding the author's benefit from an original work of art. In particular, the issue is whether and how the artists should receive royalties on their works when they are resold; this is the topic for discussion below.

Resale Right Directive

Directive 2001/84/EC of the European Parliament and of the Council of 27 September 2001 on the Resale Right for the Benefit of the Author of an Original Work of Art (European Commission, 2001a)

The European Directive 2001/84/3C constructs a framework for protection concerning authors' royalties that are generated when their products are resold. The directive was made in accordance with the provisions of the common European market of the Treaty of Rome (Garrett, 1995; Wirsching, 2005). The right that stems from this directive is usually known by its French name, *droit de suite* (Ginsburgh, 2005; Reddy, 1994; Solow, 1998), which also appears in the Berne Convention for the Protection of Literary and Artistic Works (art. 14b; Ricketson & Ginsburg, 2006).

The background context of this directive is that there was a tendency for sellers of works of art to sell them in countries without an author's permission (e.g., the United Kingdom) to avoid paying the royalty. Accordingly, this directive was conceived with three basic aims: (a) to provide creators with an adequate and standard level of protection and eliminate the distortion in the conditions for competition currently existing within the single market for contemporary art, (b) to ensure that authors of graphic and plastic works of art share in the economic success of their original works of art (i.e., Recital (3) of the examined directive), and (c) to harmonise the application of the right across the European Union. Putting such a right into operation has a crucial impact on the commitment to pay for resale. Therefore, such a right is a factor that it is possible to influence the relevant competition in the European Union (i.e., Recital (9) of the examined directive).

It is in pursuance of these aims that the directive promoted harmonisation of the substantive premises with regard to the application of the resale right and, particularly: (a) eligibility and the duration of protection, (b) the categories of works of art to which the resale right applies, (c) the scope of the acts to be covered, (d) the royalty rates applicable across defined price bands, (e) the maximum threshold for a minimum resale price attracting the right, and (e) provisions on third-country nationals entitled to receive royalties (European Commission, 2011a). Through this directive, the European Commission recognises that authors' royalties, which demonstrate compensation of property use and usually copyrighted works (Hansmann & Santilli, 2001; Turner, 2012), are crucial for the economic framework of Europe and should be protected. In conclusion, the examined directive acknowledges the entitlement to royalties on resale and the following directive addresses the issue of protection through the enforcement of intellectual property rights.

Enforcement Directive (IPRED)

Directive 2004/48/EC of the European Parliament and of the Council of 29 April 2004 on the Enforcement of Intellectual Property Rights (European Commission, 2004b)

Through the directive on the enforcement of intellectual property rights, the European Commission's aim is to secure an efficient intellectual property infrastructure that allows creators and inventors in the European Union to reap appropriate returns from welfare-enhancing innovations for European citizens. Legitimate tools, such as this directive, already exist in Europe to prevent the infringement of intellectual property rights. Through this directive, the European Commission is calling for a stronger cooperation among European Member States to protect the community from intellectual property infringements.

Regarding the subject matter and the objectives of this directive, European Member States are required to implement effective, dissuasive and proportionate remedies and penalties against those engaged in counterfeiting and piracy. In this way, the directive pursues the aim to produce a level playing field for right holders in Europe. Harbottle argues that the main objectives for this directive are twofold. The first objective is to provide greater consistency between European Member States regarding the relief available to injured rights owners; the second objective is to facilitate the fight against illicit trade (Harbottle, 2006).

Rental and Lending Directive

Directive 2006/115/EC of the European Parliament and of the Council of 12 December 2006 on Rental Right and Lending Right and on Certain Rights Related to Copyright in the Field of Intellectual Property (European Commission, 2006)

On 19 November 1992, the European Commission took a crucial step towards additional protection afforded to the holders of audio and video recordings. This directive provides authors, performers and producers with an absolute right to prevent rental of their works, or to receive an equitable reward if a transferee later authorises rental of the work (Rosenbloum, 1995).

This directive stems from the European Commission's Green Paper on Copyright and the Challenge of Technology 1998 (Commission of the European Communities, 1988; European Commission, 1995). The original proposal for a directive was released by the Commission on 5 December 1990 and was followed by a revised proposal on 29 April 1992. Scholars claim that the directive goes further than the Green Paper on Copyright and the Challenge of Technology with regard to the extension of lending rights and the proposed rental rights to authors and performers (Eechoud, 2009). To Nérisson, it was a significant European legal tool that deals with actual authors' rights and goes beyond the right to make available protected works and their content. She also claims that it is an important source for explicit justification in the applicable European copyright regime (Nérisson, 2014). In 2006, another crucial step was made for the construction of the intellectual property regime in Europe through revision of this directive. This directive supports the harmonisation of certain copyrights and neighbouring rights.

Software Directive

Council Directive 91/250/EEC of 14 May 1991 on the Legal Protection of Computer Programs (European Council, 1991)

With the publication of this directive, also called the Software Directive, it is argued that the European Commission overtook the US and Japan, two global actors with great success in the area of computer technology, in the specificity with which significant problems of legal protection for computer software are directed (Palmer & Vinje, 1992). The implementation of this directive completed a three-year process that involved intense lobbying attempts between the European Commission and the European Parliament, towards relevant policies that should be introduced in Europe (Crouch, 2000; Olsen, 2002).

The copyright protection provided from this directive applies to: (a) the expression in any form of a computer program (ideas and principles that underlie a computer program or any elements thereof are not included in this protection), (b) a computer program when it is original, in the sense that it is the author's own intellectual creation, and (c) computer programs created before 1 January 1993 (European Council, 1993).

The Green Paper on Copyright and the Challenge of Technology assessed European copyright law and elaborated on the possibility of sui generis protection. A significant portion of the Green Paper refers to the protection of computer software, particularly Chapter Five of that document. Specifically, the Green Paper proposed that copyright law protect computer software. It also described alternative approaches for several copyright issues. This directive was officially adopted on 14 May 1991.

The complexity of the issues involved is illustrated in the following example relating to the SAS Institute. Samuelson, Vinje, & Cornish claim that:

[C]ompetition and innovation in the software industry in Europe will be seriously undermined if the Court of Justice of the European Union in SAS Institute, Inc. v. World Programming Ltd. holds the copyright protection for computer programs extends to the functional behaviour of computer programs, to programming languages, and to data forms and data interface essential for achieving interoperability (Samuelson, Vinje, & Cornish, 2011).

It is necessary to explain this case further in order to understand the issues for the central argument of the book.

The dispute between SAS and World Programming Ltd. (WPL) was first heard by the High Court in July 2010 (*SAS Institute v. World Programming*, 2010). The Hon. Mr. Justice Arnold, considering that the case turned on several significant issues of interpretation of articles 1(2) and 5(3) of the Software Directive and article 2(a) of the Information Society Directive, referred a few questions to the CJEU. The case passed on to the High Court in January 2013, before being appealed to the Court of Appeal. The Court of Appeal dismissed SAS's appeal from the High Court, confirming that the outfit and the whole infrastructure of a computer program cannot be protected. By creating a software product to perform application programs written in SAS's language, WPL did not infringe SAS's copyright (Silverman, 2014).

A related topic regarding SAS's appeal is the distinction between an idea and the expression of an idea. LJ Lewison in the Court of Appeal stated in paragraph 60 that "what is critical is not the intellectual creation but the expression of the intellectual creation" (*The Hon Mr Justice Richard Arnold, 2010*), later clarifying that the functionality of a computer program establishes an idea and is therefore not protectable. Moreover, the Court of Appeal found that it was necessary to consider the policy underlying both the Software Directive and the Information Society Directive, which is identical. It would be contrary to that policy if SAS Institute could achieve copyright protection for the functionality of its program indirectly via its manual, which simply explains that functionality.

The Court of Appeal found that it was possible for WPL to be the "customer" entering the license agreement, despite being a company. Therefore, WPL was entitled to use the Learning Edition, and there was no restriction on the number of employees whom WPL might authorise to observe, study, and test the program. However, companies may unpick their competitors' programs to create their own version. Website creators are advised to consider other intellectual property rights to protect their creations, such as branding, logos, graphics or features protected by design rights. Hence, they will be able to invoke trademark, passing off, copyright or design rights to obtain some additional protection.

The directive addresses special measures in the context of copyright protection. More specifically, special protection measures will be taken against a person committing any of the following acts: any act of putting into circulation a copy of a computer program knowing, or having reason to believe, that it is a pirated copy; any possession for commercial purposes of a copy of a computer program knowing, or having reason to believe, that it is a pirated copy; any act of putting into circulation or the possession for commercial purposes of any means with the intended purpose of facilitating the unauthorised removal or circumvention of any technical device that may have been applied to protect a computer program (European Parliament & European Council, 2009).

In conclusion, the overarching objective of the directive is to harmonise European Member States' regulations concerning computer programs protection to create a legal environment that can afford a degree of security against unauthorised reproduction of such programs (Rodríguez, 2006). Thus, the directive provides additional copyright protection in the digital age and clarifies that acts regarding production, reproduction or resale of computer programs should be considered in a more efficient manner.

Term Directive

Directive 2011/77/EU of the European Parliament and of the Council of 27 September 2011 Amending Directive 2006/116/EC on the Term of Protection of Copyright and Certain Related Rights (European Commission, 2011)

The discussion and social concerns in Europe regarding the protection of copyright and certain related rights was introduced more than a decade earlier through Directive 93/98/EEC (European Council, 1993), which aimed to harmonise the term of protection of copyright and certain related rights. However, Directive 93/98/EEC has been repealed and replaced by Directive 2006/116/EC, without prejudice to the obligations of the European Member States relating to the time limits for transposition into local law of the directives, and their application (Le Galès, 1998).

In 2006, Directive 2006/116/EC was introduced to establish protection for previously unpublished works, critical and scientific publications and photographic works. The income from copyright remuneration is important for authors, performers and producers (called *creators*), as they often do not have other regular salaried income. Directive 2011/77/EC demonstrates a fully revised version of Directive 93/98/EEC; it also contains accompanying measures that provide substantial assistance to creators. The "use it or lose it" clauses that now have to be included in the contracts linking creators to their record companies grant permission for creators to claw their rights back if the record producer does not market the sound recording during the extended period. In accordance with this provision, creators will be able to either find another record producer willing to sell their work or do it themselves, something that is easily feasible via the Internet.

Orphan Works Directive

Directive 2012/28/EU of the European Parliament and of the Council of 25 October 2012 on Certain Permitted Uses of Orphan Works (European Commission, 2012)

Directive 2012/28/EU sets out common regulations on the digitisation and online display of so-called orphan works. *Orphan works* are works such as books, newspaper articles, magazine articles, and films that are still protected by copyright but whose authors or other proprietors are not known or cannot be located or contacted to obtain copyright permissions (Ringnalda, 2011). Hence, end users are not able to obtain the necessary authorisation to use such creations without the author's consent or without the risk of infringement, which can be costly and time-consuming (Vuopala, 2010). Orphan works are part of the collections held by European libraries that might remain untouched without common rules to make their digitisation and online display legally possible.

Rosati argues that the orphan works problem has become dramatic in terms of large-scale digitised projects such as the Google Books Library, also known as Google Books. Accordingly, she claims that discussion on whether Europe should deal with the orphan works issue has become intense. In 2009, the European Commission released its communication on Copyright in the Knowledge Economy that represented a follow-up to the public consultation launched via the 2008 Green Paper. Through the blueprint of the examined Directive, 2011, the European Commission clarified its intention to release a legislative proposal regarding a directive on certain permitted uses of orphan works (European Commission, 2011b). Additionally, she points out that the European Commission debated possible options to support a European-wide solution to the orphan works issue. These options comprised the adoption of a legally binding tool on the clearance and mutual recognition of orphan works, a specific exception to be added to the InfoSoc Directive (section

1.3) or guidance on cross-border mutual recognition of orphan works (European Commission, 2009). To sum up, this directive was announced from the European Commission in 2012 to offer additional support in terms of copyright licensing in Europe.

Rosati argues that this directive intends to provide a legal framework to facilitate the digitisation and dissemination of orphan works. The adoption of this directive was justified considering insufficient action at the sole level of Member States and was meant to enhance European competitiveness, while also contributing to the realisation of important actions of the Digital Agenda for Europe (Rosati, 2013). She also argues that none of these underlying objectives were fully achieved by the directive, which contains numerous notions with ambiguous meanings. Hence, Member States have been left with the difficult task of adopting implementing legislation—which carries the potential to differ greatly at the national level. To sum up, the European legislation left many gaps. The following examines the directive showing the European Commission's intention to fill them.

Collective Rights Management (CRM) Directive

Directive 2014/26/EU of the European Parliament and of the Council of 26 February 2014 on Collective Management of Copyright and Related Rights and Multi-Territorial Licensing of Rights in Musical Works for Online Use in the Internal Market (European Commission, 2014)

This directive forms a substantial part of the European Commission's Digital Agenda for Europe and the Europe 2020 flagship initiative. The directive also constitutes a set of measures whose scope is to improve the licensing framework and accessibility to digital material. The central aim of the directive is to ensure collective management organisations (CMOs) act in the best interest of the proprietors they represent. More importantly, its focal policy objectives are to modernise and better the standards of governance, financial management, and transparency of the European CMOs by ensuring proprietors are able to contribute in the decision-making procedure and receive accurate and timely royalty payments (Ficsor, 2002). Other objectives are to support a level playing area for the multi-territorial licensing of online music and to produce innovative and active cross-border licensing frameworks to encourage further support of legal online music services (Gervais, 2010). In conclusion, the directive establishes crucial protections for proprietors, comprising those who are not members of CMOs, and it also provides a framework for best practice in licensing, comprising obligations on licensees concerning data provision.

This directive provides the appropriate binding legal tool on collective management of copyright and related rights in Europe (Drexl, Nérisson, Trumpke, & Hilty, 2013). The Max Planck Institute has also supported this directive. It constitutes the European Commission's efforts to create a level playing field among collecting societies by introducing governance and transparency standards. The institute also appreciates the Commission's attempts to foster the grant of multi-territorial licences for online uses of musical works and, more specifically, the centralised grant of such licences for the repertoires or performances of multiple proprietors and collecting societies (so-called one-stop shops).

The above discussion of various directives helps in understanding the legislative terrain of copyright issues in the contemporary age of the Internet and extensive digitisation. Their significance for OAP will become evident with a discussion of the Horizon 2020 program in the following section.

THE HORIZON 2020 PROGRAM: GOVERNANCE THROUGH REGULATION

Imperative Distinction Between Regulations and Directives

The following discussion will be clearer if a distinction between regulations and directives is kept in mind. A regulation is a binding legislative act. It must be applied in its entirety across the European Union (Eberhard-Harribey, 2006). For example, when the European Union wanted to ensure that there are common safeguards on goods imported from outside Europe, the Council adopted a regulation. On the other hand, a directive is a legislative act that sets out a goal that all EU countries must achieve. However, it is up to the individual countries to devise their own laws on how to reach these goals. For instance, the European directive for consumer rights strengthens consumers' rights across Europe by eliminating hidden charges and costs on the Internet and by extending the period under which consumers can withdraw from a sales contract (Apostolache, 2015). Therefore, in the following discussion, a brief overview of the regulations comprising Horizon 2020 is given.

It should be noted that the European Commission and the European Member States are mandated by regulations that lay down application framework for the European Structural and Investment Funds (ESIF), Horizon 2020 and other programs directly managed by the Commission in the areas of research, innovation and competitiveness. Hence, Horizon 2020 forms a substantial part of the European regulations. This program introduces open access as a core element of European research policy, with long-term perspectives for information resources. Specifically, this program focuses on research outcomes and determines an example of whether the European information society can facilitate new thinking.

The Development of Open Access Pathways

A brief discussion of the development of open access and examination of some of the consequences of it being put into practice follows. Guedon argues that open access as a concept appeared as a response to the rapidly growing prices of scholarly and scientific journals. Librarians were concerned with the high prices of journals, while there was restricted access due to constrained economic means. In a gradual way, such concerns evolved are related to access issues and associated costs. Additionally, Guedon argues that open access has focused on articles because (a) scientists as readers tend to pay more attention to articles, (b) online publishing maintains the journal titles mainly for branding reasons, and (c) the very dynamics of the open access practice have also contributed to offering greater prominence to the articles as a unit.

More specifically, open access became a movement after a meeting in Budapest in December 2001, organised by the Information Program of the Open Society Institute (Chan et al., 2002). That meeting witnessed a vigorous consideration of definitions, tactics and practices; two approaches emerged from this discussion. First, existing journals find a way to transform themselves into open access publications, or open access journals are created. Second, authors or institutions "self-archive" published peer-reviewed articles or a combination that then becomes the equivalent of published, peer-reviewed articles.

The first practice amounts to a reform of the existing publication regime. It fundamentally relies on journals as its basic unit, and it simply aims to convert or create the largest possible number of open access journals. BioMed Central, a commercial operation, has played an important pioneering role in this context. More recently, the non-profit Public Library of Science (PLoS) has joined it (Gentleman et al., 2004). This practice obviously threatens the "reader pays" business plan and, therefore, immediately faces the issue of financial viability, with the result that spirited discussions have been generated, largely centred on the viability of the "author pays" model used by BioMed Central and PLoS (Hernández-Borges et al., 2006; Schroter & Tite, 2006). In other parts of the world, several research councils have begun transforming their journals into open access publications (Björk et al., 2010). In such cases, the issue of financial viability simply rests on the will of governments to support scientific publishing.

However, the concern is whether to homogenize the publication costs with research costs, given that research is largely supported by public sources. The self-archiving method appears much more complicated and subtle when approached conceptually. It both relies on journals and rests on the pre-eminence of the article as the fundamental unit. From this perspective, journals matter only to differentiate between peer-reviewed articles and non-peer-reviewed publications and to provide symbolic value. Therefore, journals contribute to the impact of individual articles by their reputation among scholars, a fact that is associated with the notion of *impact factor* (Xia, 2008; Xia & Sun, 2007).

In summary, self-archiving is a practice that has been designed by researchers and for researchers, with little interest for any other actor involved in scientific publishing. It simply aims at improving the research impact of established scientists and little else. Additionally, it is a tough-minded vision, narrowly focused on scientific communication. Supporters of this vision are essentially interested in only one thing: extracting every ounce of impact a published article may hope to claim (Antelman, 2004). The following discussion examines the Horizon 2020 program, which introduced open access to research outcomes as a means of facilitating the exchange of information and knowledge.

Open Access in Horizon 2020: Importance, Benefits, and Future Perspectives

In February 2007, the Commission in Brussels hosted a crucial conference on the future of open access in Europe. Through that meeting, the European Commission encouraged open access, while not mandating it de facto across Europe. European Regulation No 1291/2013 establishes the Horizon 2020 program, which is an attempt to support OA practice. It determines the framework for research and innovation from 2014 to 2020. Specifically, paragraph 28 of this regulation, with the title, "to grow the circulation and exploitation of knowledge" says, first, that open access to scientific publications should be secured and, second, that open access to research data resulting from publicly funded research under Horizon 2020 should be promoted, considering limitations for privacy, national security and intellectual property rights (European Parliament, 2013, para. 18).

The Guidelines on Open Access to Scientific Publications and Research Data in Horizon 2020 also emphasise open access. These guidelines review and clarify the regulations on OA covering beneficiaries in projects funded or co-funded in the context of Horizon 2020 (European Commission, 2016). These guidelines are significant, as they highlight article 29 of Horizon 2020, which sets out detailed legal requirements on open access for scientific publications.

It is claimed that this program will bring breakthroughs, discoveries and world-firsts by taking great ideas from the lab to the market (Gaspar et al., 2012). Horizon 2020 is the financial instrument implementing the Innovation Union, a Europe 2020 flagship initiative aimed at securing Europe's global competitiveness. Seen as a means to drive economic growth and create jobs, Horizon 2020 has the political backing of Europe's leaders and the members of the European Parliament. The European Parliament and the European Council agree that research is an investment in our future and so put it at the heart of Europe's blueprint for smart, sustainable and inclusive growth and jobs (Kuhlmann & Arie, 2014). By coupling research and innovation, Horizon 2020 is helping to achieve this by highlighting the concepts of excellent science, industrial leadership, and tackling societal challenges. The objective is to ensure that Europe generates world-class science, removes obstacles to innovation and offers incentives to public and private sectors to cooperate beneficially for innovation.

Through the Horizon 2020 program, the European Commission demonstrates that open access can be considered an effective response of intellectual property protection in Europe in the digital age. Arguably, the European Commission views open access not as an end in itself, but as an instrument to accommodate and improve the dissemination of information in the ERA and beyond (Breschi & Cusmano, 2004). Moreover, the European Commission recognises that there are several ways of arriving at open access, since different European countries and stakeholders are in different situations and have different necessities. Hence, it supports both main routes to open access—that is, the "green" and the "gold" roads.

Rodrigues argues that, recently, open access to publicly funded research has been attracting steady support from policymakers and funders across Europe, both at the national level and within the European Union context (Rodrigues, 2014). Another important institution for the European Commission's intention towards open access is the European Research Council (ERC). The ERC released a statement that supports open access practice (European Research Council, 2006). This statement was followed by guidelines for researchers funded by the ERC, which indicate that all peer-reviewed publications funded from ERC should be made openly accessible shortly after publication (European Research Council, 2012). The support of institutions and scholars is a significant factor in determining the terms of open access practices. OARs are one institutional mechanism relevant in this regard. Thus, the following section presents a discussion of OARs as examples of mechanisms supporting open access.

THE EUROPEAN PERSPECTIVE ON ADVOCACY OF OARS: OPEN ACCESS AND THE GROWTH OF OARS

The institutional repository is argued to be a digital-asset management framework that is growing rapidly as a key element of the current discussion about open access and the shift of the scholarly communication process (Cullen & Chawner, 2011). Several pro-open access scholars also argue that OARs constitute the most cost-effective and immediate channel to support access regarding publicly funded research outcomes (Harnad, 2005, 2012). Crow claims that an OAR constitutes a way to grow an institution's reputation by illustrating its faculty's research outcomes. Another definition is that an

OAR is an online archive of scholarly material created by the members of a defined institution. Thus, the institution also determines the content of the repository and the associated policies about gathering information (Jantz & Wilson, 2008; Johnson, 2002).

The following discussion helps me determine whether and how the directives are put into practice. In this context, an examination of selected open access initiatives is undertaken.

The Wellcome Trust Open Access Policy (October 2003)

Nowadays, the Wellcome Trust is an independent charitable foundation dedicated to improving health and influencing health policy across the globe (Larson, 2009). The Wellcome Trust supports open access to the published output of research as a crucial part of its charitable objectives and as a public benefit to be encouraged. This statement is based on its stated objectives. In particular, the Trust (a) expects authors of research papers, monographs and book chapters to maximise opportunities to make their results available for free; (b) requires electronic copies of any research papers that have been accepted for publication in a peer-reviewed journal and that are supported in whole or in part by Wellcome Trust funding to be made available through PubMed Central (PMC) and Europe PMC as soon as possible, and in any event within six months of the journal publisher's official date of final publication; (c) expects Trust-funded researchers to select publishing routes that ensure the work is available immediately on publication in its final published form; (d) provide beneficiaries with additional funding to cover open access charges to meet the Trust's requirements; (e) encourages authors and publishers to licence research papers using the Creative Commons Attribution license (CC BY) provided that such uses are fully attributed; and f) affirms the principle that it is the intrinsic merit of the work that should be considered in making funding decisions (Church, 2015).

Additionally, another aspect for the mission of the Wellcome Trust is to improve health by supporting access to information through open access and public engagement. A notable example is the Kenya Medical Research Institute Wellcome Trust Research Program (KWTRP) in Kilifi, Kenya. The Kenya Medical Research Institute (KEMRI) worked with Wellcome Trust through a collaborative multidisciplinary research program established in 1979 that focuses on the major cause of ill health in Kenya and sub-Saharan Africa. The concept of informed consent is crucial for ethical health research. However, important challenges are encountered worldwide in ensuring regulatory and practical requirements for informed consent are met (Corneli et al., 2006; Molyneux, Peshu, & Marsh, 2004). Such challenges are partly assignable to differences in the understanding of research concepts and procedures between researchers and research participants. These differences are most acute where there are large gaps between these groups in access to information resources, literacy levels and in the context where access to biomedical health care is heavily impeded (Marshall, 2008). Within this research program experience, the Wellcome Trust strengthens the informed consent process in international health research through open access practice. Hence, this will foster a richer research culture and well-informed societies.

Another significant example regarding applied open access on behalf of the Wellcome Trust is the Human Genome Project. The example of the Wellcome Trust's involvement in the Human Genome Project shows that applying or implementing open access with regard to comprehensive genomic data empowers drug discovery research in academic and commercial organisations. On 11 April 2013, the International Human Genome Consortium announced the successful completion of the Human Genome Project, more than two years ahead of schedule. This project is an effort to decode the information embedded in the human genome. Such information produced will improve the practice of medicine by providing instruments to establish the hereditary element of virtually all diseases. This will lead towards better approaches to foresee increased risk and support more effective treatment practices. These improvements in research and health care must be accessible, and this depends on participation from a broad spectrum of the population in deliberations of ethics and public policy (Collins & Mansoura, 2001). In addition, the HGP has helped us by providing information about how remarkably similar human beings are.

From a practical perspective, more than 350 biomedical advances have reached the clinical trial stage. One of the demands for the research community at the time was that the reference of the human sequence should be finished to the highest standards possible. Such accuracy for the human genome sequence will allow researchers to establish genes involved in more complex diseases, including cancer and diabetes. Dr Jane Rogers, Head of Sequencing at the Wellcome Trust, said, "We have reached the limits we set on this project, achieving tremendously high standards of quality much more quickly than we hoped (Rogers, para. 8)." It should be ensured that the risks of such research efforts are considered carefully and medical benefits that stem from these efforts are accessible by researchers to build upon them for better results in the long term (Pisani & AbouZahr, 2010). This investment shows that a change in the culture of science requires the buy-in of key research teams, and it also requires significant commitments from funders such as the Wellcome Trust.

The European Research Consortium for Informatics and Mathematics: Statement on Open Access (January 2006)

The European Research Consortium for Informatics and Mathematics (ERCIM) is an important consortium of leading research institutions from 17 European countries committed to information technology and applied mathematics. The ERCIM aims to increase cooperation with European industry and to foster collaborative work within the European research community. The consortium features different working groups. Their purpose is to create and maintain a network of ERCIM researchers in a scientific field. Each working group is open to any researcher in its scientific field. The working groups are also the focus of internal mobility within the consortium. ERCIM participates in numerous projects as a coordinator or associated partner. Several member institutes carry out the research, while ERCIM takes care of administrative tasks (Clarysse, Wright, Lockett, Van de Velde, & Vohora, 2005).

The ERCIM researchers have an interest in open access as producers and consumers of research publications and as developers of technology to enable and sustain open access. Recognising the inability of research libraries to meet the costs of sustaining their collections, and participating actively in the development of appropriate technology, ERCIM has followed the developments in open access from the Budapest Declaration (G. Craig, Gorman, & Vercseg, 2004) through the Bethesda Declaration (Suber et al., 2003) to the Berlin Declaration and events since. ERCIM member organisations have been involved in dialogue with national libraries, research funding agencies, commercial publishers, learned societies and government departments. ERCIM supports the following principles: (a) research that is funded by the public via government agencies or charities should be available freely and electronically at the point of use; (b) other research should be made equally available subject only to confidentiality required by commercial, military, security or personal medical constraints; (c) quality assurance of research publications must be continued through rigorous peer review associated with research publications, and research datasets and software should be equally openly available; and (d) open access should be provided as cost-effectively as possible and should also carry the responsibility for curation of the digital content, including cataloguing, archiving, reproducing, safekeeping and media migration (Carbonell & Stephanidis, 2002).

In the context of its practices, the most recent and accomplished program funded by ERCIM is EUREKA (Bayona-Sáez & García-Marco, 2010; Rossum & Cabo, 1995), which established cooperation between European firms and research institutes in advanced technologies. The projects associated with EUREKA subsidised the competitiveness of European enterprises via international cooperation and in building connections for innovation through open access to quality research and development outcomes (Bayona-Sáez & García-Marco, 2010; Rossum & Cabo, 1995).

In addition, ERCIM pioneered a pilot project demonstrating homogeneous access to heterogeneous technical reports, and it has experience with the technology through the Delos projects and Network of Excellence (Candela et al., 2007). It is at the leading edge of integrating appropriate open access technology with Grids via the Diligent project (Castelli, Candela, Pagano, & Simi, 2005). Individual ERCIM organisations have researched many aspects of the technology required for open access. Jeffery argues that member organisations of ERCIM that do not already have an open access policy will adopt these principles and implement them (Jeffery, 2006).

The Scientific Council of the European Research Council: Open Access Mandate (December 2007)

Scholars claim that, since the end of the 20th century, expectations about the added value and logic of the European science policy have been considered. First, the perception of added value shifted to incorporate competition. More specifically, in 2003, an expert group called for competition regarding the excellence in research to become a significant part of a new, long-term definition of the European added value (Nedeva & Stampfer, 2012). A year later, this call was answered in official European Commission documents as “the added value which comes from competition at the European level” (European Commission, 2004, p. 14). Policy attention shifted from mainly coordinating national outcomes to growing a broader European science base (Luukkonen, 2014).

Second, Europe had to recognise that its concerns regarding science went beyond applications. By the late 1990s, it was recognised that European countries were lagging behind the US and Japan, both in science and its applications (Rosenberg, 2002). These changes to policy assumptions and logics made possible the establishment of the European Research Council (ERC) in 2007, the first dedicated research funding agency to support investigator-driven research, with a focus on excellence.

The Scientific Council of ERC stresses the fundamental significance of peer-reviewed journals in securing the verification and distribution of high-quality scientific research and in guiding the appropriate allocation of research funds. Policies towards access to scientific research must guarantee the ability of the system to continue to deliver high-quality verification services. While the verification quality of the scientific publication system is not in doubt, the high prices of some journals raise significant worries concerning the ability of the system to deliver wide access and, therefore, efficient dissemination of research results, with the resulting risk of stifling further scientific progress.

These considerations lead the ERC Scientific Council to highlight the attractiveness of policies mandating the public availability of research results—in OARs—soon after publication. Nevertheless, general open access policies are not trivial to implement, because (a) the speed of "obsolescence" of knowledge varies across disciplines and (b) so does the availability of OARs. Additionally, coordination between research funders is highly desirable (Luukkonen, 2012).

Nevertheless, it is the firm intention of the ERC Scientific Council to issue specific guidelines for the mandatory deposit in OARs of research results obtained due to ERC grants, as soon as pertinent repositories become operational (Mens, 2009). To sum up, the ERC Scientific Council hopes that research funders across Europe will join forces in establishing common OA rules and in building European OARs that will help make these rules operational.

Modernisation of European Copyright Regime: The European Bureau of Library, Information and Documentation Associations and the International Federation of Library Associations and Institutions Statement

Another significant statement is the comment on behalf of the European Bureau of Library, Information and Documentation Associations [EBLIDA] (Charlton, 2014; Peterson-Sloss, 2011) and the International Federation of Library Associations and Institutions [IFLA] (IFLA, 2005) on the European Commission's communication released on 9 December 2015 (European Commission, 2015b). Accordingly, Europe anticipates broadening access to online content and modernising the European copyright regime based on a long-term perspective. Education, research and European cultural diversity are important in terms of the creative economy and the needs of Europe; thus, both should be supported by an up-to-date copyright regime that is able to track continuous technological advancements and provide cross-border access to library and online content.

Jukka Relander, president of EBLIDA, declared that:

[B]ecause libraries and archives in Europe do not have uniform exceptions and limitations available to them in their Member States, they cannot effectively share information across Europe's borders. Citizens in the 28 EU Member States have different and unequal access to information. 21st century libraries and archives need legal certainty to ensure that they can achieve their public service missions of providing free access to information to help build an innovative and inclusive society.

EBLIDA agrees with the European Commission that widening access to content across Europe is necessary and welcomes the opportunity to participate in consultations that consider exceptions to copyright rules for an innovative and inclusive society (Häggström, 2004). Aligned with this statement, Donna Scheeder, President of IFLA, also claimed that:

[W]e welcome the Commission's commitment to copyright exceptions and limitations related to knowledge, research and education being a key priority of the coming Digital Single Market. That the Commission is considering new

exceptions and limitations to permit text and data mining, remote consultation of library holdings and digital preservation demonstrates its understanding of the challenges libraries and archives face in the digital age (EBLIDA & IFLA, 2015).

CONCLUSION

At the beginning of the chapter, the background of the current European copyright regime was set up in order to show its historical development during the process of European integratio. In the second part, there was an examination of specific European directives that established the European copyright regime. Then, discussion followed about the crucial European regulation of Horizon 2020 and considerations regarding perspectives that support the operation of OARs at the European level.

In 2015, a press release by the European Commission stressed the significance of access to online content and outlined its vision to modernise European copyright regulations (European Commission, 2015a). Based on this press release, the overarching objective of the European Commission regarding intellectual protection is to modify copyright rules to fit the digital age. Additionally, this press release shows the European Commission's vision of a modern European copyright framework. This political preview can be translated into legislative proposals and policy initiatives in the future, considering all inputs from several public consultations. Overall, the European Commission wants to ensure that Europeans can access a wide legal offering of content, while ensuring that authors and other rights holders are better protected and remunerated. The key sectors of education, culture, research, and innovation will also benefit from a more modern and European framework. This statement helps me to argue that open access practice should be integrated with forthcoming European directives.

Examination of open access growth in Europe determines how crucial the role of OARs is in disseminating information and improving European citizens' assets. Moreover, such examination clarifies that the relevant regime for the governance of OARs is also important. In the European context, open access practice can demonstrate an important factor for trade, improvement of negotiations in industry and exchange of information resources that potentially lead towards development, innovation and new knowledge. Thus, gradually, collaboration among European countries emerges. Such collaboration can facilitate access to information resources via European agreements, policies, and initiatives addressed in this chapter.

The following chapter examines the relevant governance framework for OARs in Greece as a European case study. This consideration would help to argue that European countries, such as Greece, should follow and implement soft laws issued by the European Commission. Additionally, the next chapter shows the transition from the international context, reflected by the European regime, to the local context, reflected by the Greek regime. This transition will help me argue that the development of international law complements the development of domestic law. Such a transition would help to argue that OARs have the potential to become of relevance for sharing information and publishing at local and international levels.

REFERENCES

Abrahamson, P. (2005). *Welfare and families in Europe*. Ashgate.

Antelman, K. (2004). Do open-access articles have a greater research impact? *College & Research Libraries, 65*(5), 372–382. doi:10.5860/crl.65.5.372

Antezana, M. E. (2003). The European union internet copyright directive as even more than it envisions: Toward a supra-EU harmonization of copyright policy and theory. *Boston College International and Comparative Law Review, 26*, 415.

Apostolache, M. C. (2015). The relevance of the European regulations regarding the improvement of transparency and integrity in local public administration: Analysis of the implications on the legislation. *Juridical Tribune, 5*(1), 90–98.

Bayona-Sáez, C., & García-Marco, T. (2010). Assessing the effectiveness of the Eureka Program. *Research Policy, 39*(10), 1375–1386. doi:10.1016/j.respol.2010.07.007

Beniger, J. (2009). *The control revolution: Technological and economic origins of the information society*. Harvard University Press.

Björk, B.-C., Welling, P., Laakso, M., Majlender, P., Hedlund, T., & Guðnason, G. (2010). Open access to the scientific journal literature: Situation 2009. *PLoS One*, *5*(6), e11273. doi:10.1371/journal.pone.0011273 PMID:20585653

Breschi, S., & Cusmano, L. (2004). Unveiling the texture of a European research area: Emergence of oligarchic networks under EU framework programmes. *International Journal of Technology Management*, *27*(8), 747–772. doi:10.1504/IJTM.2004.004992

Bretherton, C., & Vogler, J. (1999). *The European Union as a global actor*. Psychology Press.

Button, K. J., & Pentecost, E. J. (1995). Testing for convergence of the EU regional economies. *Economic Inquiry*, *33*(4), 664–671. doi:10.1111/j.1465-7295.1995.tb01887.x

Candela, L., Castelli, D., Ferro, N., Ioannidis, Y., Koutrika, G., Meghini, C., . . . Schuldt, H. (2007). The DELOS digital library reference model. In *Foundations for Digital Libraries*. ISTI-CNR. Retrieved from http://www.delos.info/files/pdf/ReferenceModel/DELOS_DLReferenceModel_0.98.pdf

Carbonell, N., & Stephanidis, C. (2002). European Research Consortium for Informatics and Mathematics Workshop adjunct proceedings. In N. Carbonell & C. Stephanidis (Eds.), *7th ERCIM Workshop "User Interfaces for All"* (p. 210). Chantilly, France: INRIA. Retrieved from https://hal.inria.fr/inria-00101022

Casey, M. (1991). The electronic information industry in Europe: An analysis of trends and prospects in less developed economies. *Journal of Librarianship and Information Science*, *23*(1), 21–36. doi:10.1177/096100069102300103

Castelli, D., Candela, L., Pagano, P., & Simi, M. (2005). DILIGENT: A digital library infrastructure for supporting joint research. In *International Symposium on Mass Storage Systems and Technology* (pp. 56–59). Los Alamitos, CA: IEEE Computer Society. 10.1109/LGDI.2005.1612465

Castells, M. (2002). *The Internet galaxy: Reflections on the Internet, business, and society*. OUP Oxford. doi:10.1093/acprof:oso/9780199255771.001.0001

Chalmers, D., Davies, G., & Monti, G. (2010). *European Union law: Cases and materials*. Cambridge University Press. doi:10.1017/CBO9780511841408

Chan, L., Cuplinskas, D., Eisen, M., Friend, F., Genova, Y., Guédon, J.-C., . . . Velterop, J. (2002, February 14). *Budapest Open Access Initiative.* Retrieved November 10, 2016, from http://www.opensocietyfoundations.org/openaccess/read

Charlton, J. (2014). EBLIDA urges copyright reform. *Information Today, 31*(1), 14.

Church, R. (2015). *Burroughs Wellcome in the USA and the Wellcome Trust: Pharmaceutical innovation, contested organisational cultures and the triumph of philanthropy.* Carnegie Publishing.

Clarysse, B., Wright, M., Lockett, A., Van de Velde, E., & Vohora, A. (2005). Spinning out new ventures: A typology of incubation strategies from European research institutions. *Journal of Business Venturing, 20*(2), 183–216. doi:10.1016/j.jbusvent.2003.12.004

Collins, F. S., & Mansoura, M. K. (2001). The Human Genome Project. *Cancer, 91*(S1), 221–225. doi:10.1002/1097-0142(20010101)91:1+<221::AID-CNCR8>3.0.CO;2-9 PMID:11148583

Commission of the European Communities. (1988). *Green paper on copyright and the challenge of technology: copyright issues requiring immediate action.* Brussels: Commission of the European Communities.

Copeland, P., & Papadimitriou, D. (2012). *The EU's Lisbon Strategy: Evaluating success, understanding failure.* Palgrave Macmillan. doi:10.1057/9781137272164

Corneli, A. L., Bentley, M. E., Sorenson, J. R., Henderson, G. E., Horst, C., Moses, A., ... Jamieson, D. J. (2006). Using formative research to develop a context-specific approach to informed consent for clinical trials. *Journal of Empirical Research on Human Research Ethics; JERHRE, 1*(4), 45–60. doi:10.1525/jer.2006.1.4.45 PMID:19385837

Cowles, M. G., Caporaso, J. A., & Risse-Kappen, T. (2001). *Transforming Europe: Europeanization and domestic change.* Cornell University Press.

Craig, G., Gorman, M., & Vercseg, I. (2004). The Budapest declaration: Building European civil society through community development. *Community Development Journal: An International Forum, 39*(4), 423–429. doi:10.1093/cdj/bsh040

Craig, P., & de Búrca, G. (2011). *EU law: Text, cases, and materials*. OUP Oxford. doi:10.1093/he/9780199576999.001.0001

Crouch, C. (2000). *After the Euro: Shaping institutions for governance in the wake of European monetary union*. OUP Oxford. doi:10.1093/0198296398.001.0001

Cuadrado-Roura, J. R. (2001). Regional convergence in the European Union: From hypothesis to the actual trends. *The Annals of Regional Science*, *35*(3), 333–356. doi:10.1007001680100054

Cullen, R., & Chawner, B. (2011). Institutional repositories, open access, and scholarly communication: A study of conflicting paradigms. *Journal of Academic Librarianship*, *37*(6), 460–470. doi:10.1016/j.acalib.2011.07.002

Davies, N. (2014). *Europe: A history*. Random House.

Davison, M. J. (2003). *The legal protection of databases*. Cambridge University Press. doi:10.1017/CBO9780511495236

de la Porte, C., Pochet, P., & Room, B. G. (2001). Social benchmarking, policy making and new governance in the EU. *Journal of European Social Policy*, *11*(4), 291–307. doi:10.1177/095892870101100401

Dieckhoff, M., & Gallie, D. (2007). The renewed Lisbon Strategy and social exclusion policy. *Industrial Relations Journal*, *38*(6), 480–502. doi:10.1111/j.1468-2338.2007.00460.x

Dinan, D. (2010). *Ever closer union: An introduction to European integration* (4th ed.). Boulder, Colorado: Lynne Rienner. doi:10.1007/978-1-137-09963-1

Dreier, T., & Hugenholtz, P. B. (2006). *Concise European copyright law*. Kluwer Law International.

Drexl, J., Nérisson, S., Trumpke, F., & Hilty, R. M. (2013). Comments of the Max Planck Institute for Intellectual Property and Competition Law on the proposal for a directive of the European Parliament and of the Council on Collective Management of Copyright and related rights and multi-territorial licensing of rights in musical works for online uses in the internal market: COM (2012)372. *IIC—International Review of Intellectual Property and Competition Law, 44*(3), 322–350. doi:10.100740319-013-0024-7

Eberhard-Harribey, L. (2006). Corporate social responsibility as a new paradigm in the European policy: How CSR comes to legitimate the European regulation process. *Corporate Governance: The International Journal of Business in Society*, *6*(4), 358–368. doi:10.1108/14720700610689487

European Bureau of Library, Information and Documentation Associations & International Federation of Library Associations and Institutions. (2015). *Modernisation of EU copyright rules: yes, but...* Retrieved from http://www.eblida.org/news/modernisation-of-eu-copyright-rules-yes,-but.html

European Commission. (1957). *Treaty of Rome, 1206 ME/TXT § (1957).* Retrieved from http://www.ab.gov.tr/files/ardb/evt/1_avrupa_birligi/1_3_antlasmalar/1_3_1_kurucu_antlasmalar/1957_treaty_establishing_eec.pdf

European Commission. (1995). *Green paper on copyright and related rights in the information society.* Retrieved from http://europa.eu/legislation_summaries/information_society/data_protection/l24152_en.htm

European Commission. (2004a). *Europe and basic research (Communication from the Commission No. COM (2004) 9 final).* Retrieved from http://cordis.europa.eu/pub/era/docs/com2004_9_en.pdf

European Commission. (2007). *Commission staff working document report to the Council, the European Parliament and the Economic and Social Committee on the application of Directive 2001/29/EC on the harmonisation of certain aspects of copyright and related rights in the information society.* Retrieved from http://www.ipex.eu/IPEXL-WEB/dossier/document.do?code=SEC&year=2007&number=1556&extension=FIN

European Commission. (2009). *Copyright in the knowledge economy (No. 532 final).* Retrieved from http://ec.europa.eu/internal_market/copyright/docs/copyright-infso/20091019_532_en.pdf

European Commission. (2011a). *Report on the implementation and effect of the Resale Right Directive (2001/84/EC) (COM No. 878 final)* (p. 14). Brussels: European Commission. Retrieved from http://ec.europa.eu/internal_market/copyright/docs/resale/report_en.pdf

European Commission. (2011b). *Single market for intellectual property rights (No. 297 final).* Retrieved from http://www.eesc.europa.eu/?i=portal.en.int-opinions.19154

European Commission. (2013). *Fact sheet: Open access in Horizon 2020.* Retrieved from https://ec.europa.eu/programmes/horizon2020/sites/horizon2020/files/FactSheet_Open_Access.pdf

European Commission. (2014). *Directive on Collective Management of Copyright 2014/26/EU.* Retrieved from http://ec.europa.eu/internal_market/copyright/management/index_en.htm

European Commission. (2015a). *Commission takes first steps to broaden access to online context and outlines its vision to modernise EU copyright rules.* Retrieved from http://europa.eu/rapid/press-release_IP-15-6261_en.htm

European Commission. (2015b). *Towards a modern, more European copyright framework.* Retrieved from http://ec.europa.eu/newsroom/dae/document.cfm?action=display&doc_id=12526

European Commission. (2016). *Guidelines on open access to scientific publications and research data in Horizon 2020.* Retrieved from http://ec.europa.eu/research/participants/data/ref/h2020/grants_manual/hi/oa_pilot/h2020-hi-oa-pilot-guide_en.pdf

European Commission. (1996). *Directive 96/9/EC of the European Parliament and of the Council of 11 March 1996 on the legal protection of databases.* Pub. L. No. 31996L0009, OJ L 077 (1996).

European Commission. (2004b). *Directive 2004/48/EC of the European Parliament and of the Council of 29 April 2004 on the enforcement of intellectual property rights* (Text with EEA relevance). Pub. L. No. 32004L0048, OJ L 157 (2004).

European Commission. (2006). *Directive 2006/115/EC of the European Parliament and of the Council of 12 December 2006 on rental right and lending right and on certain rights related to copyright in the field of intellectual property (codified version).* Pub. L. No. 32006L0115, OJ L 376 (2006).

European Commission. (2011). *Directive 2011/77/EU of the European Parliament and of the Council of 27 September 2011 amending Directive 2006/116/EC on the term of protection of copyright and certain related rights.* Pub. L. No. 32011L0077, OJ L 265 (2011).

European Commission. (2012). *Directive 2012/28/EU of the European Parliament and of the Council of 25 October 2012 on certain permitted uses of orphan works* (Text with EEA relevance). Pub. L. No. 32012L0028, OJ L 299 (2012).

European Communities. (2001). *Directive 2001/29/EC of the European Parliament and of the Council*. Official Journal of the European Communities, L. 167, 10–19.

European Council. (1993a). *Council Directive 93/98/EEC Harmonizing the Term of Protection of Copyright and Certain Related Rights*. Retrieved from http://eur-lex.europa.eu/legal-content/EN/TXT/?uri=celex:31993L0098

European Council. (1991). *Council Directive 91/250/EEC of 14 May 1991 on the legal protection of computer programs*. Pub. L. No. 31991L0250, 122 (1993).

European Council. (1993b). *Council Directive 93/83/EEC of 27 September 1993 on the coordination of certain rules concerning copyright and rights related to copyright applicable to satellite broadcasting and cable retransmission*. Pub. L. No. 31993L0083, OJ L 248 (1993).

European Parliament. (2013). *Regulation (EU) No 1291/2013 of the European Parliament and of the Council of 11 December 2013 Establishing Horizon 2020—The Framework Programme for Research and Innovation (2014–2020) and Repealing Decision No 1982/2006/EC* (No. L 347/ 104). Retrieved from http://eur-lex.europa.eu/legal-content/EN/TXT/?qid=1445880041822&uri=CELEX:32013R1291

European Parliament & European Council. (2009). *Directive 2009/24/EEC of the European Parliament and of the Council on the Legal Protection of Computer Programs*. Retrieved from http://eur-lex.europa.eu/legal-content/EN/TXT/?uri=uriserv:mi0016

European Parliament. (2007). *Treaty on the Functioning of the European Union*. Retrieved from http://www.europarl.europa.eu/ftu/pdf/en/FTU_3.1.2.pdf

European Parliament. The Single European Act, xy0027 EYR-Lex § (1987).

European Research Council. (2006). *ERC Scientific Council statement on open access*. Retrieved from https://erc.europa.eu/sites/default/files/press_release/files/erc_scc_statement_2006_open_access_0.pdf

European Research Council. (2012). *Open access guidelines for researchers funded by the ERC*. Retrieved from https://erc.europa.eu/sites/default/files/document/file/open_access_policy_researchers_funded_ERC.pdf

Evens, T., & Donders, K. (2013). Broadcast market structures and retransmission payments: A European perspective. *Media Culture & Society*, *35*(4), 417–434. doi:10.1177/0163443713483797

Ficsor, M. (2002). *Collective management of copyright and related rights*. World Intellectual Property Organization.

Garrett, G. (1995). The politics of legal integration in the European Union. *International Organization*, *49*(01), 171–181. doi:10.1017/S0020818300001612

Gaspar, R., Aksu, B., Cuine, A., Danhof, M., Takac, M. J.-M., Linden, H. H., ... Dencker, L. (2012). Towards a European strategy for medicines research (2014–2020): The EUFEPS position paper on Horizon 2020. *European Journal of Pharmaceutical Sciences*, *47*(5), 979–987. doi:10.1016/j.ejps.2012.09.020 PMID:23046836

Gentleman, R. C., Carey, V. J., Bates, D. M., Bolstad, B., Dettling, M., Dudoit, S., ... Zhang, J. (2004). Bioconductor: Open software development for computational biology and bioinformatics. *Genome Biology*, *5*(10), R80. doi:10.1186/gb-2004-5-10-r80 PMID:15461798

Gervais, D. J. (2010). *Collective management of copyright and related rights*. Kluwer Law International.

Giannopoulou, A. (2012). Copyright enforcement measures: The role of the ISPs and the respect of the principle of proportionality. *European Journal of Law and Technology*, *3*(1). Retrieved from http://ejlt.org/article/view/122

Ginsburgh, V. (2005). The Economic consequences of droit de suite in the European Union. *Economic Analysis and Policy*, *35*(1–2), 61–71. doi:10.1016/S0313-5926(05)50004-3

Goodwin, I., & Spittle, S. (2002). The European Union and the information society: Discourse, power and policy. *New Media & Society*, *4*(2), 225–249. doi:10.1177/146144480200400206

Granieri, M., & Renda, A. (2012). *Innovation law and policy in the European Union: Towards Horizon 2020*. Springer Science & Business Media. doi:10.1007/978-88-470-1917-1

Häggström, B. M. (2004). EBLIDA's action in Europe. *LIBER Quarterly, 14*(3–4). doi:10.18352/lq.7792

Hansmann, H., & Santilli, M. (2001). Royalties for artists versus royalties for authors and composers. *Journal of Cultural Economics, 25*(4), 259–281. doi:10.1023/A:1017923625973

Harbottle, G. (2006). The implementation in England and Wales of the European Enforcement Directive. *Journal of Intellectual Property Law & Practice, 1*(11), 719–727. doi:10.1093/jiplp/jpl170

Harnad, S. (2005). The implementation of the Berlin Declaration on Open Access. *D-Lib Magazine, 11*(3). doi:10.1045/march2005-harnad

Harnad, S. (2012). Open access: A green light for archiving. *Nature, 487*(7407), 302. doi:10.1038/487302b PMID:22810686

Héritier, A. (2003). Composite democracy in Europe: The role of transparency and access to information. *Journal of European Public Policy, 10*(5), 814–833. doi:10.1080/1350176032000124104

Hernández-Borges, A. A., Cabrera-Rodríguez, R., Montesdeoca-Melián, A., Martínez-Pineda, B., Torres-Álvarez de Arcaya, M. L., & Jiménez-Sosa, A. (2006). Awareness and attitude of Spanish medical authors to open access publishing and the author-pays model. *Journal of the Medical Library Association, 94*(4), 449–451, e218.

Hix, S., & Høyland, B. (2011). *The political system of the European Union*. Palgrave Macmillan. doi:10.1007/978-0-230-34418-1

International Federation of Library Associations and Institutions. (2005). *IFLA 112–114: World guide to library, archive, and information science associations* (M. Schweizer, Ed.). München: K.G. Saur.

Jantz, R. C., & Wilson, M. C. (2008). Institutional repositories: Faculty deposits, marketing, and the reform of scholarly communication. *Journal of Academic Librarianship, 34*(3), 186–195. doi:10.1016/j.acalib.2008.03.014

Jeffery, K. G. (2006). Open Access: An introduction. *ERCIM News, 64*(3), 16-17. Retrieved from https://www.researchgate.net/profile/Keith_Jeffery/publication/228635875_Open_Access_an_introduction/links/00b7d527a52273637a000000.pdf

Johnson, R. (2002). Institutional repositories: Partnering with faculty to enhance scholarly communication. *D-Lib Magazine*, *8*(11). Retrieved from http://www.dlib.org/dlib/november02/johnson/11johnson.html

Jones, E. (2003). *The European miracle: Environments, economies and geopolitics in the history of Europe and Asia*. Cambridge University Press. doi:10.1017/CBO9780511817700

Jordana, J. (2002). *Governing telecommunications and the new information society in Europe*. Edward Elgar Publishing. doi:10.4337/9781781950463

Kohler-Koch, B., & Eising, R. (1999). *The transformation of governance in the European Union*. Psychology Press. doi:10.4324/9780203279625

Kuhlmann, S., & Arie, R. (2014). *The challenge of addressing Grand Challenges: A think piece of how innovation can be driven towards the "Grand Challenges" as defined under the prospective European Union Framework Programme Horizon 2020*. University of Twente. Retrieved from http://doc.utwente.nl/91786/1/The_challenge_of_addressing_Grand_Challenges.pdf

Lang, M., Aigner, H.-J., Scheuerle, U., & Stefaner, M. (Eds.). (2004). *CFC legislation, tax treaties and EC law*. The Hague: Kluwer Law International.

Larson, F. (2009). *An infinity of things: How Sir Henry Wellcome collected the world*. OUP Oxford.

Le Galès, P. (1998). Regulations and governance in European cities. *International Journal of Urban and Regional Research*, *22*(3), 482–506. doi:10.1111/1468-2427.00153

Lucarelli, S., & Fioramonti, L. (2009). *External perceptions of the European Union as a global actor*. Routledge.

Luukkonen, T. (2012). Conservatism and risk-taking in peer review: Emerging ERC practices. *Research Evaluation*, *21*(1), 48–60. doi:10.1093/reseval/rvs001

Luukkonen, T. (2014). The European Research Council and the European research funding landscape. *Science & Public Policy*, *41*(1), 29–43. doi:10.1093cipolct031

Majone, G., & Baake, P. (1996). *Regulating Europe*. Psychology Press. doi:10.4324/9780203439197

Manners, I., & Whitman, R. (2000). *The foreign policies of European Union Member States*. Manchester University Press.

Marriott, S. (2009). The emergence of live television talk. *Text—Interdisciplinary Journal for the Study of Discourse, 17*(2), 181–198. doi:10.1515/text.1.1997.17.2.181

Marshall, P. A. (2008). "Cultural competence" and informed consent in international health research. *Cambridge Quarterly of Healthcare Ethics, 17*(2), 206–215. doi:10.1017/S0963180108080237 PMID:18312735

Mazziotti, G. (2008). *EU digital copyright law and the end-user*. Springer Science & Business Media.

Mens, T. (2009). The ERCIM Working Group on Software Evolution: The past and the future. In *Proceedings of the Joint International and Annual ERCIM Workshops on Principles of Software Evolution (IWPSE) and Software Evolution (Evol) Workshops* (pp. 1–4). New York, NY: ACM. 10.1145/1595808.1595809

Michalis, M. (2008). Governing European communications: From unification to coordination. *Reference and Research Book News, 23*(1).

Molyneux, C. S., Peshu, N., & Marsh, K. (2004). Understanding of informed consent in a low-income setting: Three case studies from the Kenyan coast. *Social Science & Medicine, 59*(12), 2547–2559. doi:10.1016/j.socscimed.2004.03.037 PMID:15474208

Moussis, N. (2014). *Access to the European Union: Law, economics, policies* (20th ed.; Vol. 1). Beaverton, United States: Ringgold Inc.

Nedeva, M., & Stampfer, M. (2012). From "science in Europe" to "European science.". *Science, 336*(6084), 982–983. doi:10.1126cience.1216878 PMID:22628638

Nérisson, S. (2014). The rental and lending rights directive. In *EU copyright law* (pp. 149–202). Edward Elgar Publishing. doi:10.4337/9781781952436.00017

Olsen, J. P. (2002). Reforming European institutions of governance. *Journal of Common Market Studies, 40*(4), 581–602. doi:10.1111/1468-5965.00389

Palmer, A. K., & Vinje, T. C. (1992). The EC directive on the legal protection of computer software: New law governing software development. *Duke Journal of Comparative & International Law*, *2*(1), 65–87.

Peterson-Sloss, C. (2011, September). EBLIDA (European Bureau of Library, Information and Documentation Associations). *Computers in Libraries*, *31*(7), 41.

Pisani, E., & AbouZahr, C. (2010). Sharing health data: Good intentions are not enough. *Bulletin of the World Health Organization*, *88*(6), 462–466. doi:10.2471/BLT.09.074393 PMID:20539861

Quah, D. (2000). Internet cluster emergence. *European Economic Review*, *44*(4–6), 1032–1044. doi:10.1016/S0014-2921(99)00055-0

Ramakrishnan, R., & Gehrke, J. (2000). *Database management systems* (2nd ed.). Berkeley, CA: Osborne/McGraw–Hill.

Rannenberg, K., Royer, D., & Deuker, A. (2009). *The future of identity in the information society: Challenges and opportunities*. Springer Science & Business Media. doi:10.1007/978-3-642-01820-6

Reddy, M. B. (1994). The droit de suite: Why American fine artists should have a right to a resale royalty. *Loyola of Los Angeles Entertainment Law Journal*, *15*, 509.

Revesz, P. (2009). *Introduction to databases: From biological to spatio-temporal*. Springer Science & Business Media.

Ricketson, S., & Ginsburg, J. (2006). *International copyright and neighbouring rights: The Berne Convention and beyond* (2nd ed.). Oxford, UK: Oxford University Press.

Ringnalda, A. (2011). *Orphan works, mass rights clearance, and online libraries: The flaws of the draft orphan works directive and extended collective licensing as a solution (SSRN Scholarly Paper No. ID 2369974)*. Rochester, NY: Social Science Research Network. Retrieved from http://papers.ssrn.com/abstract=2369974

Rodrigues, E. (2014). *Open access to publications and research data in Horizon 2020: What are the requirements and how can institutional repositories and OpenAIRE help to meet them?* Retrieved April 4, 2016, from http://sci-gems.math.bas.bg:8080/jspui/handle/10525/2404

Rodríguez, A. A. (2006). The relationship between copyright software protection and piracy: Evidence from Europe. *European Journal of Law and Economics*, *21*(1), 29–51. doi:10.100710657-006-5670-5

Rogers, J. (2003, April 13). *DNA scientists write "book of life."* Retrieved August 27, 2019, from https://www.telegraph.co.uk/news/1427490/DNA-scientists-write-book-of-life.html

Rosati, E. (2013). The Orphan Works Directive, or throwing a stone and hiding the hand. *Journal of Intellectual Property Law & Practice*, *8*(4), 303–310. doi:10.1093/jiplp/jpt015

Rosenberg, N. (2002). Knowledge and innovation for economic development: Should universities be economic institutions? In *Knowledge for inclusive development* (pp. 35–47). Greenwood Publishing Group.

Rosenbloum, R. A. (1995). The Rental Rights Directive: A step in the right and wrong directions. *Loyola of Los Angeles Entertainment Law Journal*, *15*, 547.

Rossum, W. V., & Cabo, P. G. (1995). The contribution of research institutes in EUREKA projects. *International Journal of Technology Management*, *10*(7–8), 853–866. doi:10.1504/IJTM.1995.025662

Sabel, C. F., & Zeitlin, J. (2010). *Experimentalist governance in the European Union: Towards a new architecture*. OUP Oxford.

Samuelson, P. (2000). *Five challenges for regulating the global information society (SSRN Scholarly Paper No. ID 234743)*. Rochester, NY: Social Science Research Network. Retrieved from http://papers.ssrn.com/abstract=234743

Samuelson, P., Vinje, T. C., & Cornish, W. R. (2011). *Does copyright protection under the EU Software Directive extend to computer program behaviour, languages and interfaces? (SSRN Scholarly Paper No. ID 1974890)*. Rochester, NY: Social Science Research Network. Retrieved from http://papers.ssrn.com/abstract=1974890

Sandholtz, W. (1993). Institutions and collective action: The new telecommunications in western Europe. *World Politics*, *45*(2), 242–270. doi:10.2307/2950659

Sandholtz, W., & Sweet, A. S. (1998). *European integration and supranational governance*. Oxford University Press. doi:10.1093/0198294646.001.0001

SAS Institute v. World Programming. (2010). EWHC 1829 (Ch). Retrieved from http://www.bailii.org/ew/cases/EWHC/Ch/2010/1829.html

Schneider, M. (1998). The European Union Database Directive. *Berkeley Technology Law Journal*, *13*(1), 551–564.

Schroter, S., & Tite, L. (2006). Open access publishing and "author pays' business models: A survey of authors' knowledge and perceptions. *Journal of the Royal Society of Medicine*, *99*(3), 141–148. PMID:16508053

Seville, C. (2009). *EU intellectual property law and policy*. Edward Elgar Publishing. doi:10.4337/9781848447462

Silverman, I. (2014). SAS: Major software copyright ruling upheld. *Journal of Intellectual Property Law & Practice*, *9*(3), 179–181. doi:10.1093/jiplp/jpt264

Solow, J. L. (1998). An economic analysis of the droit de suite. *Journal of Cultural Economics*, *22*(4), 209–226. doi:10.1023/A:1007505016512

Suber, P., Brown, P. O., Cabell, D., Chakravarti, A., Cohen, B., Delamothe, T., . . . Watson, L. (2003). *Bethesda statement on open access publishing*. Retrieved from https://dash.harvard.edu/handle/1/4725199

Taylor-Gooby, P. (2004). *New risks, new welfare: The transformation of the European welfare state*. Oxford University Press. doi:10.1093/01992672 6X.001.0001

The Hon Mr Justice Richard Arnold. (2010). SAS Institute Inc v World Programming Ltd [2010] EWHC 1829 (Ch). EWHC (Ch).

Tschmuck, P. (2012). The emergence of the phonographic industry within the music industry. In *Creativity and innovation in the music industry* (pp. 9–25). Springer Berlin Heidelberg; doi:10.1007/978-3-642-28430-4_2

Tsebelis, G., & Garrett, G. (2001). The institutional foundations of intergovernmentalism and supranationalism in the European Union. *International Organization*, *55*(2), 357–390. doi:10.1162/00208180151140603

Turner, S. B. (2012). *The artist's resale royalty right: Overcoming the information problem (SSRN Scholarly Paper No. ID 2009087)*. Rochester, NY: Social Science Research Network. Retrieved from https://papers.ssrn.com/abstract=2009087

van Eechoud, M. M. M. (2009). *Harmonizing European copyright law: The challenges of better lawmaking*. Kluwer Law International.

Vuopala, A. (2010). *Assessment of the orphan works issue and costs for rights clearance (Access to information no. unit 34)*. European Commission. Retrieved from http://www.ace-film.eu/wp-content/uploads/2010/09/Copyright_anna_report-1.pdf

Wald, J. (2001). Legislating the Golden Rule: Achieving comparable protection under the European Union Database Directive. *Fordham International Law Journal*, *25*, 987.

Wallace, H., Pollack, M. A., & Young, A. R. (2015). *Policy-making in the European Union*. Oxford University Press.

Webster, F. (2014). *Theories of the information society*. Routledge. doi:10.4324/9781315867854

Whitley, R., & Kristensen, P. H. (1996). *The changing European firm: Limits to convergence*. Cengage Learning EMEA.

Wirsching, J. J. (2005). The time is now: The need for federal resale royalty legislation in light of the European Union Directive. *Southwestern University Law Review*, *35*, 431.

World Intellectual Property Organization. (1996a). *WIPO Copyright Treaty (WCT)*. Retrieved from http://www.wipo.int/wipolex/en/details.jsp?id=12740

World Intellectual Property Organization. (1996b). *WIPO Performances and Phonograms Treaty (WPPT)*. Retrieved from http://www.wipo.int/wipolex/en/details.jsp?id=12743

Xia, J. (2008). A comparison of subject and institutional repositories in self-archiving practices. *Journal of Academic Librarianship*, *34*(6), 489–495. doi:10.1016/j.acalib.2008.09.016

Xia, J., & Sun, L. (2007). Assessment of self-archiving in institutional repositories: Depositorship and full-text availability. *Serials Review*, *33*(1), 14–21. doi:10.1080/00987913.2007.10765087

Chapter 5
Examining the Governance Framework of OARs in Greece as a European Case Study

ABSTRACT

In modern times, technological development is continuous, and one of its distinctive features is open access, which has been greatly discussed in the preceding chapter. The literature reflects that open access practice is distinguished from a variety of instruments, and the most renowned is OARs. This chapter's analysis is designed to juxtapose the European copyright framework with copyright in a domestic context. Additionally, the chapter examines the status of OARs in Greece and proposes potential changes to improve its governance framework.

INTRODUCTION

Chapter four discussed the design of the copyright regime of the European Union and examined a few examples where open access policies have been put into practice. The preceding chapter also included a literature review about the governance framework of OARs in the European Union. That discussion demonstrates that there is ncreasing interest regarding the development of OARs as an additional way of disseminating information (Lynch, 2003). In

DOI: 10.4018/978-1-7998-1131-2.ch005

this chapter, the Greek open access model is analysed in comparison with the European governance framework. The analysis is designed to juxtapose the European example of copyright regime with that in a domestic context.

This chapter is divided into four parts. The first part is twofold and is also divided into two subparts. In the first subpart, the background context of how the Greek regulations system works is set, to understand in layman terms the process that should be followed for a statute to be introduced and implemented. In the second subpart, a consideration of Greek laws (constitution and specific statutes) that facilitate access to information is undertaken. An analysis of the Greek copyright regime will be undertaken to explore how information can be disseminated in the Greek context. In the context of the contemporary copyright law in Greece, it follows consideration of specific legal provisions in the Greek system that facilitate access to information. The legal instruments have been selected as examples to determine both issues of how they have introduced the concept of freedom of information and whether they make a required connection among the concepts of information and knowledge. Further, how can the connections between these concepts be strengthened through education? The starting assumption is that there is an inevitable link between information and knowledge, which helps me argue that access to information is imperative.

In the second part of the chapter, there is a discussion about the implications for the Greek Copyright Act from the latest developments in European directives that refer to additional sharing and dissemination of information. This analysis helps to assess the potential desirability and growth of open access practice in Greece. Hence, the third part of the chapter discusses the emergence of open access practice in Greece and considers: when open access was introduced and the manner of its implementation; and what were the relevant initiatives and programs that facilitated such introduction. This consideration further leads to investigate whether the Greek copyright framework should be reformed to keep pace with continuous technological growth and to define more strictly the concept of open access for the beneficial spread of information. In the last part of this chapter, surveys conducted by Greek scholars regarding the status and progress of the Greek OARs are also examined. Such examination helps to argue about long-term perspectives and future potential that can emerge for Greek OARs. The following discussion sets the appropriate theoretical background to help us understand how the Greek legislative system operates. A consideration of the Greek Constitution and Greek Law 4009/2011 is also undertaken.

THE GREEK REGULATIONS SYSTEM: A PROCEDURAL PERSPECTIVE

The purposes of the analysis of the Greek Constitution and Greek Law 4009/2011 are significant and clarify whether information access and knowledge should be connected through education. First, the constitution of a state outlines how the government of that state will work, including the division of powers, e.g., executive, state legislature and state courts (Jappelli & Pagano, 2002; Otjacques, Hitzelberger, & Feltz, 2007), and emphasises that information for research should be accessible by citizens. Additionally, state regulations should be aligned and associated with the constitution, and this provision helps me argue about Greek Law 4009/2011. This analysis supports the argument that access to information is established through the Greek Constitution. As argued in chapter three, access to information empowers people and leads to knowledge improvement; therefore, access to knowledge should happen within education. It follows that this rationale is founded in Greek Law 4009/2011

The Procedural Aspects of the Greek Legislative System

Several introductory notes regarding the Greek legislative system are required as preliminary steps for the following discussion. The Greek Government's intentions or the willingness to enact any regulation is put into practice through legislation and their related system (Ehrenberg, 2013). The Greek Government considers new policies in pursuance of the public good by the process where proposals for new regulations are introduced into the Greek Parliament. The Parliament's process is to discuss such new proposals twice a week (Dimitrakopoulos, 2001). New institutions and procedures emerge, and financial resources are addressed towards the accomplishment of associated objectives. However, recommendations and proposals for new legislation or statutes can be produced either from ministers, other government representatives or assemblymen from different political parties which do not constitute the Government at the time (Andreou, 2006; Lazarides, 2011).

The main bodies responsible for the introduction of any legislation or statutes are the Greek ministries, which are allocated responsibilities for different portfolios. For example, the Ministry of Finance, the Ministry of Justice and the Ministry of Education and Religions will all have different responsibilities. Most importantly for present purposes, there is a specific process to be followed to introduce new legislation or statutes. Initially, the minister involved with the new proposal should assign the work of creating such rules to a pro-legislation committee (PLC). This committee should draft a plan for this regulation, which is to be considered prior to discussion in Parliament. In the next stage of the legislation process, the Greek Central Committee for Legislations (GCCL) considers this plan. The GCCL falls under the General Administration for the Greek Government. The GCCL is also able to make recommendations on the proposed draft plan from the PLC before its submission to Parliament for further discussion. It is required to do so by article 75(3) of the Greek Constitution. Article 75(1) of the Greek Constitution also states that a list of justifications and objectives for this regulation should be attached with the draft plan, as well as reports associated with financial costs and potential economic impacts. Thereafter, the draft plan is referred by the President of Parliament to be considered either by the political parties, parliamentary departments or standing committees (art. 72, Greek Constitution). In case the draft plan is referred or directed to a standing committee, it should be instantly introduced for discussion in Parliament. It will be voted upon in the Parliament at this stage.

Contemporary Greek society is part of European society and, thereby, it is part of the renowned *information society* that is claimed to persist in Europe since 2000 (Beniger, 2009; Castells & Himanen, 2003). Given this fact, the European context of regulating access to information in the information age are of direct relevance and should be considered in conjunction with the Greek regulatory regimes. After the Lisbon Summit of the European Commission in 2000, the Lisbon Treaty and the directives (examined in Chapter Four) show that there is a growing interest in Europe regarding the spread of information resources towards knowledge and empowerment of European citizens' skills (Ertl, 2006; Soriano & Mulatero, 2010). It is in this context that, for the purposes of the argument in this part of the chapter, it is necessary to analyse the importance of access to information, particularly in the context of the education sector. Therefore, legal provisions that facilitate information access and exchange should be considered. As far as the Greek Copyright Act is concerned, it is founded upon this rationale and will be analysed below. The rationale is derived from article 16 of the Greek Constitution and Greek Statute/Law 4009/2001. In the following section, there is an examination of specific provisions of the Greek Constitution, i.e., art. 16(1), 16(2), and Greek Statute 4009/2011, i.e., art. 1(a), 2(a), 3(a).

Provisions That Facilitate Access to Information: Article 16 of the Greek Constitution and the Greek Statute/Law 4009/2011

Article 16 of the Greek Constitution stipulates that education is provided free in state institutions and that private universities are prohibited from existing. Psacharopoulos argues that article 16 forms an outdated law with social costs (Psacharopoulos, 2003). However, it introduces the importance of education regarding knowledge and the consequent connection or importance of its link with access to information (Rowley & Hartley, 2008; Wiley & Hilton, 2009).

Article 16 is part of the second section of the Constitution that refers to citizens' rights (individual and social rights). Most importantly, the first and second subsections are addressed to education and highlight the significance of access to information that leads to knowledge. More specifically, these subsections mention:

Article 16(1): Arts, science, research and teaching and associated information should be accessible and free. Their promotion and production should be part of priorities for the Greek State . . . (Greek Parliament, 2010)

Article 16(2): Education determines the central objective/mission for the Greek State and pursues to improve a moral, intellectual, professional and wealthy treatment for Greek citizens, a beneficial growth regarding national and religious consciousness. Additionally, education should provide instruments to Greek citizens to become free and liable . . . (Greek Parliament, 2010)

Hence, this legislation illustrates that information dissemination constitutes the overarching objective for the Greek educational curriculum and indicates that open access should be part of the educational process as well as growth. This endorsement of access to free education in the Constitution helps me argue that access to information facilitates the same aim of acquiring knowledge. And it follows that in this context, open access can be an effective instrument that facilitates access to information and knowledge. In turn, this provides further support for the book argument regarding access to information through OARs, which will be developed in the following chapter. In the present context, open access should be the tool directed towards equal opportunities for Greek citizens to empower them through access to knowledge. Therefore, open access should be the basic element of education, and it could be integrated into teaching design, which would lead to further research and innovation goals of education.

Education is a crucial instrument that can make possible access to knowledge and, in turn, the enhanced possibilities of intellectual creation. It follows that these aims can be pursued by the creation and dissemination of information; in this context, the Greek copyright regime is relevant for the preservation and development of Greek culture (Sianou-Kyrgiou, 2008). Greek Law 4009/2011 is associated with Greek Copyright Act 2121/1993 and illustrates the need for access to information to facilitate teaching methods. Therefore, it will be considered briefly below. Articles 3 and 4 of Greek Law 4009/2011 clarify that the necessity to share, exchange, and disseminate information should be attached to the Greek education curriculum. In addition, both articles highlight the significant role of universities and academia in terms of the exchange, dissemination and sharing of information towards the knowledge and empowerment of Greek citizens. Article 3 (subsection 1) mentions (Greek Government, 2011):

1. Through Higher Education Institutions (Universities, Technical Educational Institutions, Colleges and Institutes of Technology) the academic freedom is established for further research and improved methods of teaching as well as a freely exchange and dissemination of information, notions and views . . .

Article 4, subsections 1(a), 2(a), and 3(a), state:

1. The overarching objective for the Higher Education Institutions is to: (a) promote, produce and transmit knowledge through research and teaching and efficient use of information resources. Higher Education Institutions should also prepare students to become able to apply such principles and values in a professional level and help them to grow Greek arts and culture . . .

2. For education purposes, Higher Education Institutions should aim to: (a) emphasize in high level and comprehend education, aligned with arts and science requirements as well as aligned with international scientific practices . . .

3. For the fulfilment of purpose, Higher Education Institutions are organized and operate under regulations and practices to ensure compliance and protection in principles such as: (a) access to educational resources, freedom of research and improvements for teaching method . . .

The articles mentioned above illustrate the acceptance of the premise in the Greek legal system that access to information resources empowers teaching. In turn, such teaching equips Greek citizens with new knowledge assets; therefore, wide access to information should be vital for the educational infrastructure of Greece (Makridou, Araka, & Koutras, 2012). To recapitulate briefly, the above discussion of selected articles in the Greek Constitution shows that the abovementioned provision (i.e. Art. 4) is the foundation of access to information resources. Since education is the primary means of creating and disseminating knowledge, it may be argued that universities should perform a substantial role regarding the sharing, dissemination and exchange of information.

The above discussion clarifies that sharing of information is supported in the Greek Constitution, and in earlier times copyright laws performed the function of regulating such sharing. However, after the digital revolution, circumstances have changed dramatically, and dissemination of published works now occurs all the time.

Scholars argue that Gutenberg's invention of the printing press established an innovation that fundamentally changed the procedure through which knowledge can be created, exchanged, and shared (McLuhan, Gordon, Lamberti, & Scheffel-Dunand, 2011). Electronic publication and digital networking are the equivalent of the printing press in contemporary society. While wide dissemination is desirable, it is equally significant to encourage creativity and, therefore, the interests of the content makers and publishers need to be protected. The reasons to improve the balance among the interests of authors and publishers stem from the infrastructure of online publishing offered from the Internet and the academia's role in the context of electronic publishing.

The emergence of the World Wide Web (WWW) and the digital revolution have created novel situations regarding publishing and dissemination of published works. The WWW is not synonymous with the Internet but is the most important feature of the Internet (Berners-Lee, Cailliau, Groff, & Pollermann, 2010; Liaw, 2002). Scholars argue that the WWW determines a techno-social framework for individuals' interaction based on technological networks through which there is ease of information exchange (Aghaei,

Nematbakhsh, & Farsani, 2012). Thus, the notion of the techno-social system addresses a system that enhances human cognition, cooperation and communication. Therefore, it is a system to share and disseminate information (Bandura, 2001; Berkenkotter & Huckin, 2016).

In addition, the infrastructure of this system helped the emergence of Web-enhanced teaching and learning that determines a way based on which student participation has been improved as an alternative language to learn and acquire knowledge (Churchill, 2009). Another fact that shows the influence of Web technologies and the Internet is that modern librarians should also provide services as information-technology educators (Beetham & Sharpe, 2013; Oakleaf, 2009; Rader, 1997); they are required to be well educated in information technology issues, such as computer-access programs or access by other means (Becker, 2007; Luke, Woods, & Weir, 2013).

Another issue to be considered is relevant to university campuses and their infrastructure. Specifically, campuses created their own networked environment while providing their students with access to computers (Bowker, Baker, Millerand, & Ribes, 2009; Bowker et al., 2009; Crook, 2002). Consequently, the ease of exchange and sharing of information became a reality. Further, such technological advancements provoked the need to modernise university structures and facilities. The significant issue faced by academia's administrators/authorities was whether a new library could add value to the educational enterprise and reinforce campus-based learning (Lankes, 2011). In modern times, to design and construct a library involved a reconsideration of the entire educational mission, at least in part with the aim of integrating new technologies allowing online information resources to provide additional support and expand the library's traditional print holdings (Raschke, 2003; Schmidt & Cohen, 2013). In this context, access to information can be considered a crucial factor for the knowledge economies of the future and fortified if, among other things, OARs are given a fair chance of both survival and development. Therefore, the role of academia, along with OARs' function regarding access to information, is of paramount importance.

What is more, the open access movement is growing and would allow free access to information with no restrictions on reuse (Gargouri, Larivière, Gingras, Carr, & Harnad, 2012). In academia, the open access growth stems from the fact that access to research databases is limited worldwide by the high cost of subscription journals, which urge readers to pay for their content. It should be noted that scientific research used in educational literature and news is often restricted by publishers, who request authors to sign over their rights and then control what is done with the published work (Tennant, 2014). Thus, it is logical to argue that open access offers more direct access to knowledge. The information revolution has given open access the best chance it will get; therefore, the enlargement of information accessibility safeguards human rights for th future of developing and developed countries. It follows that open access should be tailored to copyright law without changing copyright standards. A good sign is that in 2014, the Greek Government introduced new legislation (Law 4305/2014) regarding open access to publicly funded research outcomes. This law works as a means towards further access to information (Dalakou, 2014), and it also provides additional support to the Greek Copyright Act, which is considered below.[1]

EXAMINATION OF GREEK COPYRIGHT ACT (NO. 2121/1993)

The literature on IP rights primarily concentrates on the copyright holder or proprietor. The same emphasis is demonstrated in the Greek copyright law. This discussion highlights the central objective for the Greek Copyright Act, which is to protect copyright owners' interests. Botti reflects this emphasis when she argues that creators' rewards and affiliated rights should be considered a priority (Grodzinsky & Bottis, 2007). Aligned with this statement, Kallinikou claims that the *creator's right* is an important element for the Greek Copyright Act. He further claims that its overarching objective is to clarify that intellectual property rights should focus on the creator's role (Kallinikou, 2007).

The first article of the Greek Copyright Act clarifies the object of copyright and its content. It says the authors shall have the right of copyright in their work, which includes, as exclusive and absolute rights, the right to exploit the work (economic right) and the right to protect their personal connection with the work (moral right). This article is based on the assumption that a work should be the outcome of an individual's intellectual creation. In addition, a work should be considered unique when it shows a minimum degree of creativity in such a way as to be distinguished from what is already known.

Under the Greek Copyright Act, there is no specific regime for copyright registration. Article 2 clarifies that rights are vested in the author of a work without having to resort to any formality. Namely, protection begins with creation, regardless of its results. Additionally, article 2 includes a list of works to be considered for protection. The list refers to works such as musical compositions, plays, choreographies, pantomimes, audio-visual works, works of visual arts (painting, sculpture, etc.), architectural works, photographs and works of applied arts (for instance, maps related to geography and topography).

Another article worthy of consideration is article 13, which addresses legal provisions about reproduction, referring to any means, such as mechanical, audio-visual, electronic or digital, used for circulation through the online channels offered from the Internet. Often the question arises as to whether the introduction of an original intellectual creation on the Internet constitutes a reproduction of the work or another way to demonstrate it publicly and share it with others (Synodinou, 2015). It is also argued that the introduction of a project directly on an Internet server is undoubtedly an act of reproduction (Alexandropoulou, 2011). Hence, new ways to exploit the related digital or electronic reproduction belong to copyright owners. In the context, one of these new ways can be determined from/through the operation of OARs that offer online reproduction.

It should be mentioned that the Greek Copyright Act has been amended ten times (i.e., amendments: Bill 2435/1993, Bill 2188/1994, Bill 2196/1994, Bill 2435/1996, Bill 2459/1997, Bill 2557/1997, Bill 2819/2000, Bill 3049/2002, Bill 3057/2002 and Bill 3316/2005), and this fact illustrates that the area of intellectual property law gradually keeps expanding. Such expansion is justified as resulting from the ongoing technological advancements that bring into existence new types of creative works that require or may require intellectual protection (Kapczynski, 2008; Rhoten & Powell, 2007). A good example of such expansion of the scope of intellectual property is provided by international agreements; this is illustrated specifically in the Australia and United States Free Trade Agreement (FTA; Fischer, 2005).

Dee argues that chapter 17 of this agreement discusses intellectual property rights and addresses substantive provisions that require changes to Australian legislation. For example, Australia is required to extend the term of copyright protection by an additional 20 years, bringing Australia into closer conformity with the United States. It is worth noting that this is in contrast with the literature on this issue, as Rimmer argues that extension of the copyright term should occur only when it is associated with the public interest (Rimmer, 2007). This claim helps me argue that copyright extension should occur only when it is a public inquiry. Apparently, the agreement requires Australia to adopt United States standards, but only when they broaden rather than narrow the scope of intellectual property protection. Hence, such adoption of United States standards could possibly override processes towards reform of Australian regulations. Therefore, it is possible to set another problematic example for the domestic intellectual property law designation.

In addition, this agreement impedes greater competition that would benefit consumers. It contains provisions to tighten up the protections afforded producers and/or performers of protected works, so users have access only at a higher expense. From the patent law perspective, relevant provisions may affect the introduction of generic drugs into the Australian market, which in turn may cause delays to reductions in drug prices in Australia (Dee, 2005; Dent, 2010). Other scholars argue that this bilateral agreement may greatly impact Australia's intellectual property framework, as it is required to pass a form of the WIPO Copyright and Performances and Phonograms Treaties to supply additional rights for intellectual protection, such as trademarks (Lim, Elms, & Low, 2012).

In the Greek Copyright Act, there are 77 articles; the discussion is focused on those of relevance to the monograph argument. According to the Greek Copyright Act, the author of an intellectual creation has an intangible right of ownership over that work, being inclusive and binding over third parties (art. 1). In addition, this right covers patrimonial rights and moral rights (art. 1(1), 3, and 4). The concept of authorship refers to the person(s) who have produced the work. Under the Greek copyright framework, a legal entity can be a copyright proprietor only as a successor in title. Another positive aspect for the Greek Copyright Act is that there is no requirement for copyright registration for a work to be protected, since it is protected as a matter of law, by the fact of its production. Therefore, original works created online are also protected since their upload. It is argued that copyright exists in every form of the original, whether written on paper, deposited on a hard disk, uploaded online or created offline (Maniotis, 2011). Such protection has been established through chapter seven of the Greek Copyright Act referring to software protection and continuous technological growth.

Indeed, continuous technological growth brings new concepts related to online creation (such as online posts, videos and photo uploads) that, under previous provisions, are also protected. Therefore, international regulations play a significant role in national and relevant policymaking processes. Given this, the Greek Copyright Act has been reformed in accordance with the European regulations, it has ratified the European directives, it follows the contemporary technological growth that brings new copyright issues associated with the new concept mentioned before, and it helps further the dissemination and protection of information. Hence, the following issue to consider is the direct bearing of European laws on Greek copyright law.

EUROPEAN REGULATIONS HAVE A DIRECT BEARING ON GREEK COPYRIGHT LAW

The European directives, as explained in the previous chapter, provide directions for national laws to incorporate certain provisions and also what should be the basic norms for their structure. The European directives are legal acts that require European Member States to achieve a specific result, but this is done without dictating the means of achieving that result. This is a direct consequence of the Treaty on the Functioning of the European Union. Specifically, article 288 of this treaty declares that "[a] directive shall be binding, as to the result to be achieved, upon each European Member State to which it is addressed, but shall leave to the national authorities the choice of form and methods" (European Commission, 2012).

Additionally, various articles in the Greek Copyright Act illustrate the interconnection between European legislation and local regulations in Member States. This means that directives introduce provisions that should be considered by the local governments of the Member States; for the purposes of the argument in this chapter, some of them are considered next:

1. Article 2(3) is added in the Greek Copyright Act in the application of Council Directive 91/250/EEC concerning the legal protection of computer programs. Specifically, this directive provides directions concerning creations that constitute computer programs and software and thus considers software as copyrightable work. However, rationales and principles that establish a component for computer software should not be considered for copyright protection under this article.
2. Article 3(1) is added in the Greek Copyright Act in the application of Council Directive 92/100/EEC regarding the rental and lending rights and certain other rights in relation to copyright. This article addresses the creator's or the author's exclusive right (a) to rent their work directly

or indirectly, partially or entirely via any means, (b) to lend their work and (c) to lend a copy of their work to the public through any sales point or by using a variety of such means.

3. Article 68(1) added in the Greek Copyright Act in the application of the Council Directive 93/98/EEC for harmonising the term of protection of copyright and certain related rights. This directive offers a framework of protection for works for which protection is expired. These additional copyright provisions show the influence of European regulation and further support provided by local regulations.
4. Article 3(3) is added in the Greek Copyright Act as an implementation of Directive 96/9/EC of the European Parliament and of the council on the legal protection of databases; it highlights the copyright owner's exclusive right to his/her database. More specifically, under this directive the copyright owner has the exclusive right (a) to provide temporary or permanent reproduction of information enclosed in the database through means either partially or as a comprehensive project; (b) to translate, modify, change, add, remove or make other relevant shifts to his/her database; and (c) to disseminate/distribute the database or its copy to the public. Such provisions are mentioned in articles 5 and 6 of Directive 96/9/EC (Davison, 2003; Lynskey, 2014; Rosler, 1995). This specific change introduced into the Greek Copyright Act illustrates how European legislation is helpful in bringing about improvement and better copyright protection that can be provided by the domestic laws of any European Member State.
5. Article 46(2) is added in the Greek Copyright Act in the application of Directive 2001/29/EC and its article 5(3) regarding the harmonisation of certain aspects of copyright and related rights in the information society. In particular, the directive refers to exceptions or limitations to the reproduction and public communication rights. The article clarifies that the right to reproduce or publicly communicate a work or creation can be acknowledged for the benefit of people with a disability. Such a right should be directly related to the disability and be of a non-commercial nature and should be limited only to the extent required by the specific disability (European Communities, 2001, p. 29). The exceptions and limitations shall only be applied in certain special cases that do not conflict with a normal exploitation of the work or other subject matter and do not unreasonably prejudice the legitimate interests of the rights holder.

It should be noted that even though the above examples relate to how the Greek legislators have responded to provisions of the international legislation in the form of European directives, all the European Member States are expected to and should incorporate these provisions for the purposes of harmonisation of copyright law (Eechoud, 2009). This statement helps me argue that cooperation between national and international regulations is significant for effective protection of copyright interests of the content creators (Fishman, 2014; Giannopoulou, 2012). In this regard, the harmonisation of law through conformity with the European directives is a crucial step in the right direction. The protection umbrella provided by the European regulations is one way of making domestic copyright protection more effective. Moreover, in the age of the Internet any infringements in the online arena should be equally subject to the law (Antezana, 2003).

The next issue to be considered is whether Greek copyright laws can provide the necessary protection for online publications and whether OARs become a mechanism to regulate online dissemination of knowledge and provide protection of authors' interests.

Karakostas argues that the Greek Copyright Act contains legal provisions concerning online creations (Hall & Graham, 2004). Since online content is original work and it is derivative work, it should be protected under the same framework of protection for copyrighted work (Karakostas, 2009). This statement introduces the issue concerning copyright protection for new works uploaded online. Therefore, the Greek Copyright Act could provide copyright protection for possible online infringements. Further, this statement can be used as a link with the potential to create a consensus among universities, associated OARs and creators of hosted content by these OARs. Such an agreement could be useful, showing that open access offers additional support in terms of sharing copyrighted creations.

THE EMERGENCE OF THE WORLD WIDE WEB AND THE BEGINNING OF OPEN ACCESS IN GREECE

Publishing, sharing, and exchanging information remained quite stable until the beginning of 2000. At the time, telecommunication infrastructure in Greece was improved significantly, with financial support provided by the European Commission for national projects.

Along with this European program and financial support, there has been a crucial development of OA in Greece during the last 15 years stemming from the immense evolution in terms of content digitisation, which is mainly funded from the European Commission and driven from the Greek university libraries. Consequently, the process of information dissemination was supported significantly. Scholars argue that the scientific and research community of Greece has always been "productive" regarding publications in all kinds of formats and types, such as articles, monographs, book chapters, and conference presentations (Georgiou & Papadatou, 2010).

Since the settlement of the Greek state, several hundred magazines and journals have been publishing and disseminating the work of Greek researchers, authors, and creators. New publications, adoption of peer-review procedures, new e-journals, online printed versions and immense digitisation of journals are some of the contemporary developments that have resulted from the electronic revolution (Kostagiolas & Banou, 2007). This development has significance in two senses. First, European financial support provides norms and incentives for collaboration. Second, the European Member States are funded to build and establish a modern infrastructure to exchange and disseminate information that aligns with technological advancements. In the discussion below, the European Union initiatives that have financially supported the Greek nation in investing in technological developments comparable to other European nations are examined. This discussion indicates that the creation of institutional OARs demonstrates a technological advancement and a significant means to disseminate information in the context of the modern technology infrastructure.

European Commission Initiatives to Assist Greece in Digital Convergence With Other Nations

On 26 October 2007, the European Commission approved an operational program for Greece for the period 2007–2013 (European Commission, 2007). The program, entitled Digital Convergence, involved Community support for Greek regions eligible under the convergence objective. The operational program falls within the framework laid out for the convergence objective and had a total budget of around 1.075 billion euros. Community assistance through the European Regional Development Fund amounts to some 860 million euros, which represents approximately 4.2% of the total European financial support invested in Greece under cohesion policy from 2007 to 2013 (Bachtler & McMaster, 2008; Molle, 2007).

The report of the National Strategic Reference Framework for the period 2007–2013 argues that Greece uses information and communication technology (ICT) to a lesser extent than the 25 other European Member States. Indeed, ICT made no significant contribution to improving the country's productivity or Greek citizens' life quality (Hahamis, Iles, & Healy, 2005; Liu, Toki, & Pange, 2014; Ntaliani, Costopoulou, Karetsos, & Molhanec, 2015). The overarching purpose of the project Digital Convergence is to contribute to the convergence of Greece with the rest of the European Member States, introducing ICT to a greater extent to Greek society. Here, introducing means an increase of the use of ICT by enterprises, streamlining procedures in the public sector and increasing utilisation of digital applications in public administration to improve citizens' life quality. Additionally, the basic scope of Digital Convergence is to emphasise the developmental directions and to particularise the strategies, means and interventions towards an effective and sustainable use and growth of ICT in Greece.

Additionally, the National Strategic Reference Framework (NSRF) for the period 2007–2013 highlights that the overarching goal of the operational program is to contribute to the digital convergence of Greece with the rest of the European Union using ICT. The program will focus on implementing a customised developmental strategy with specific emphasis on competitive Greek sectors, such as tourism, shipping, culture and sports. Program priorities include improved productivity with increased ICT use, improvement of citizens' daily life and technical assistance for ICT. NSRF's current phase is being funded by the operational program, Digital Convergence. Some of the horizontal and technical interventions carried out in this frame are related to open public data, transparency, value-added services, interoperability, multichannel distribution, and exploitation of data.

The program focuses on implementing a customised developmental strategy with specific emphasis on competitive Greek sectors, such as tourism, shipping, culture and sports. The main objectives for this program are structured according to two priorities.

Priority 1: Improved productivity using ICT. Sub-priorities include:

- Improved ICT penetration in production processes combined with the development of innovative business practices targeting small- and medium-sized enterprises (SMEs). Emphasis will be placed on using the country's corporate human capital through the development of digitised educational material and the development of platforms and applications that manage and disseminate business content (*business gateways*).

- Increased use of ICT in day-to-day company operations
- The development of ICT applications to encourage entrepreneurship among women and people with special needs

Priority 2: Improvement of citizens' daily life using ICT. Sub-priorities include:

- Equal access of citizens to ICT use and knowledge
- Increased availability of digital public services
- The elimination of digital "gaps" caused by factors such as geography, age, and gender
- Streamlining and digitisation of frequently used public services (especially the services included in the i2010 strategy) as well as services offered by local public-sector organisations
- Encouraging citizens to take part in community activities through the development of ICT applications targeting NGOs
- Promoting the cultural heritage of Greece
- Development of ICT applications and services that offer equal access for women and people with special needs

Creation of Online Databases and Digital Repositories

The first efforts of digitisation were commenced a couple of decades before. In particular, the National Documentation Center (NDC) created the first online database for printed doctoral theses, ARGO and IATROTEK were the first online databases in the 1990s, and the first digital repository was introduced from the University of Crete in 1997. Since then, there has been an ongoing effort towards modernisation with a beneficial impact that stems from the financial support of Greek academic libraries. Through their participation in European projects and collaboration with other European libraries, Greek academic libraries entered into a new era.

Open science initiatives in Greece have been funded mainly through structural funds and have been part of the country's strategy for the project Digital Convergence, the funding deriving from the financial support mentioned above. The major actors in these initiatives are the NDC, the Greek institution for the aggregation, documentation, preservation, dissemination and reuse of scientific, technological, and cultural e-content; the Hellenic Academic Libraries Link (HEAL-Link), the Greek Research and Technology Network (GRNET); and the Greek Universities Network (GUNET). Each of these institutions plays a different role in supporting open science policies.

Nevertheless, the most important effort was carried out through financial support for national projects provided by the European Commission. Such funding was addressed to the creation of new services provided by university libraries in Greece. That period saw the foundation of HEAL-Link (Hormia-Poutanen et al., 2006) and the creation of the first digital library for grey literature (Pappas & Williams, 2011), called Artemis (Abbas, Norris, & Soloway, 2002). The example of grey literature shows the significance of OARs in disseminating unpublished information of an institution, such as annual reports, technical plans, research projects, white papers and materials or research produced by institutions outside of the commercial or academic publishing channels (Rothstein & Hopewell, 2009). It can be said in conclusion that open access in Greece has developed gradually. OARs are making efforts to ensure that the institutions' grey literature is online and available prior to becoming part of published works. Chantavaridou argues that, for the time being, OARs are developing in a beneficial way and can measure up against equivalent OARs abroad (Chantavaridou, 2009).

THE STATUS AND PROGRESS OF GREEK OARS

This section argues for a potential integration or unification of Greek OARs into one system, which should have specific access regulations and should provide an environment that is user-friendly. Therefore, this overview of the status of Greek OARs begins with a presentation of their basic components in the form of tables based on research findings from a paper presented during an international conference in Athens (February 2013). In that paper, the author of this book argued about the potential attached to OARs (Koutras & Bottis, 2013), and a survey conducted in December 2015 by visiting 30 operational Greek OARs (30 out of 35 according to the Directory of OARs—OpenDOAR). This survey is a follow-up (2015) to one which was conducted earlier (2013). Since then, there was no comparable information from other studies that could be used.

The gathered information is going to be presented as follows: (a) platform used (such as Dublin Core, DSpace and so forth), (b) access to their database and (c) regulations in terms of registration. These tables clarify the most common online platform in use, whether full or restricted access is permitted, and whether end users are obligated to register or not to be able to gather information. There is also analysis and examination of online surveys conducted by the author of this book in 2013 and 2015 that focused on end users' attributes regarding the OAR of the Ionian University in Corfu, Greece (Moreleli-Cacouris, Makridou, & Asmanidis, 2007).

Repositories conform to an internationally agreed set of technical standards. It follows that they expose the metadata and bibliographic details (such as authors' names, institutional affiliation, date, titles of the article and abstract) of each item they contain in the same basic way. In other words, they are interoperable. The common protocol to which they all conform is called the Open Archives Initiative Protocol for Metadata Harvesting (OAI-PMH). The contents of all repositories are then indexed by Web search engines, such as Google and Google Scholar, producing online databases that are freely accessible. As the status of self-archiving (i.e., when authors deposit their work in repositories) steadily increases, it follows that the practice of open access will be adopted to a greater extent and it will represent an increasingly large proportion of the scholarly literature.

There are several definitions for the concept of OAR that differ in their specifics. There are scholars who argue that an OAR would host, manage, preserve and provide access to the whole research output of the institution, namely: PhD and related postgraduate theses, dissertations, reports, data sets and specific versions of the institution's staff publications (Moreleli-Cacouris, Makridou, & Asmanidis, 2007). From 2000 to 2010, OARs were developed via Greek academic libraries. After 2005, most of them were given form through the financial support of European programs and initiatives. During this period, and particularly from 2005 to 2010, the Technology and Education Sciences Institute (TEI) of Athens made the first effort to establish an OAR. However, this had poor results because of the lack of content contributions. In 2011, the Department of Library Science and Information Systems of TEI in Athens took over the leadership of the project—titled TEI of Athens Library: Growth of Digital Services—that currently operates through the Digital Plan Program financed by the European Union. In accordance with this framework, the new repository anticipates collecting and publishing online work of faculty members, student theses, dissertations and educational material; what is more, it incorporates a major collection, comprising the archives of the institute (Koulouris, Kyriaki-Manessi, Giannakopoulos, & Zervos, 2013).

Georgiou and Papadatou, notable scholars in the field concerning OARs in Greece, argue that OARs should follow specific regulations concerning access and protection. Thus, there are a variety of options regarding how users can use the database of each OAR. For example, it is the case for several repositories that registration is compulsory, while such registration is not obligatory for others. Hence, it is obvious that in the context of mutual benefits among universities and institutions that utilise OARs, a Greek common policy that could be implemented is required. Such harmonisation of practices, in terms of dissemination of information, would serve as a pillar for the effective spread of information while copyright protection is provided. Table 1 provides detailed information about the status of Greek OARs regarding content, registration and access to full content.

It is evident from the information provided in Table 1 that there is a variety of platform software used in the various Greek OARs with regard to their operation and services offered (Trohopoulos, 2009). Some researchers have reported low awareness and usage of OARs. Swan and Brown, in a 2005 study (Swan & Brown, 2005; Xia et al., 2012), examined the perceptions of open access and self-archiving in a survey of 1,296 researchers. While 49% of respondents had self-archived their papers in repositories or websites, the remainder had not. Of those who had not yet self-archived, 71% were unaware of open access and self-archiving. In another study of OARs, Smith et al. collected data from Cornell's DSpace to calculate descriptive statistics and interviewed 11 faculty members for a deeper understanding of their attitudes and behaviours (Smith et al., 2003). DSpace had 2,646 items as of October 2006, categorised into 196 collections, of which almost 30% contained no materials. Further, of 519 unique contributors, nearly 50% uploaded only a single item, reinforcing the interview finding that faculty members lacked both knowledge and motivation to use institutional repositories.

The plethora of software used by Greek OARs provides a variety of options, but it also causes difficulties in interactions between repositories and end users. A common trait concerning Greek OARs is that most of them follow the same copyright regulations regarding access. Generally, they are characterised by a specific sort of instructions and guidelines regarding full-text accessibility. The most significant conclusion from these surveys is that there is a need for uniformity in how the Greek OARs are operated and regulated.

Table 1. Greek OARs

Repository	Type of Content	Platform	Access to the Full Content		Registration Required	
			Yes	No	Yes	No
Nemertes, University of Patras (http://nemertes.lis.upatras.gr/jspui)	Digitised bachelor's and master's dissertations, doctoral theses, scientific publications	DSpace	✓			✓
Eureka (http://195.251.240.227/jspui/)	Online database of intellectual production (from scientific, academic and historical aspect) of the Technological Educational Institute of Thessaloniki	DSpace		✓	✓	
NTUA, University of Athens (http://efessos.lib.uoa.gr/greylit.nsf)	Bachelor's and master's dissertations, PhD theses and digitised material (books and magazines) from NTUA's library	DSpace		✓	✓	
Pandektis (http://pandektis.ekt.gr/pandektis)	Major digital collections of Greek history and civilisation. The collections have been developed by the Institute of Neohellenic Research, the Institute of Byzantine Research and the Institute of Greek and Roman Antiquity	Open-source software	✓			✓
Pergamos (https://pergamos.lib.uoa.gr/uoa/dl/frontend/index.html)	Historical Archive of the University of Athens, Folklore Collection, Theatrical Collection and K. A. Psachos Music Library Collection	Open-source software	✓			✓
Helios (http://helios-eie.ekt.gr/EIE)	Digitised archives of the Documentation Centre, Institute of Biology and Biotechnology, Institute of Medical Research Studies, Institute of Theoretical and Applied Chemistry, and educational events	Open-source software	✓		✓	
Anemi (http://anemi.lib.uoc.gr)	Rich collection of digitised material related to modern Greek studies	Keystone		✓	✓	
Okeanos (https://okeanos-dspace.hcmr.gr)	Hellenic Centre for Marine Research	DSpace	✓		✓	
IKEE (http://ikee.lib.auth.gr)	Digital archives of collections of scientific works	Invenio 1.2.1.17		✓	✓	
Psepheda, University of Macedonia (http://dspace.lib.uom.gr)	Digitised archives of scientific journals, publications, music data, bachelor's and master's dissertations, doctoral theses	Dublin core		✓	✓	
Psifiothiki (http://digital.lib.auth.gr)	Dissertations and scientific publications produced by members of the Aristotle University of Thessaloniki	Invenio 1.2.1.17		✓	✓	
Foss (http://repository.ellak.gr)	Reports, presentations, digital collections, conference proceedings, studies, videos and photos. The repository's organised digital environment also offers advanced navigation and search functions.	Open-source software		✓	✓	
Acropolis Educational Resources, Acropolis Museum (http://repository.acropolis-education.gr/acr_edu)	Educational resources produced by the Information and Education Department of the Acropolis Restoration Service. These resources dynamically support the representation and interpretation of the past. Teachers, students and families can explore the repository and enrich their classroom teaching and visits to the Archaeological Site and the Acropolis Museum.	Open-source software	✓			✓
Parthenon Frieze, Acropolis Museum (http://repository.parthenonfrieze.gr/frieze)	Collection of digitised material and archives regarding the artistic work of Frieze	DSpace	✓			✓

continued on the following page

Table 1. Continued

Repository	Type of Content	Platform	Access to the Full Content		Registration Required	
			Yes	No	Yes	No
Ergani (http://www.ergani-repository.gr/ergani)	Documented archival material that presents 200 years of local history, culture and entrepreneurialism in the north-eastern Aegean	DSpace		✓	✓	
National Archive of PhD Theses (https://phdtheses.ekt.gr/eadd)	A rich collection of Greek doctoral theses	Open-source software	✓			✓
Ionian University Repository (http://iup.ionio.gr)	80,000 books, 700 magazine titles, more than 3,500 audiovisual records	PHP-Nuke	✓		✓	
Public Digital Library of Serres (http://ebooks.serrelib.gr/serrelib)	Digitised material, books, collections, newspapers, etc.	Open-source software	✓			✓
Public Digital Library of Livadia (http://ebooks.liblivadia.gr/liblivadia)	Rare collections and a variety of texts of local and nationwide interest (history, literature and poetry)	Open-source software	✓			✓
Digital Library "E-Dull" (http://repository.edulll.gr/edull)	Published material and studies produced in the Operational Programme "Education and Lifelong Learning"	Open-source software	✓			✓
The Argo (http://argo.ekt.gr)	Bibliographic resources and content searching facilities for librarians, scientists, educators and students	ABEKT Z39.50 Web gate 4.0	✓			✓
E-Locus (http://elocus.lib.uoc.gr/index.tkl)	The material is organised in collections, and until now it consisted of graduate, postgraduate and doctoral dissertations issued at the University of Crete; study guides of the university departments and technical reports.	Keystone	✓			✓
Archipelago (https://code.grnet.gr/projects/archipelago/repository)	Digital collections of the Aegean University	CDS Invenio 0.99.1		✓	✓	
Pandemos (http://pandemos.panteion.gr)	Digital library of Panteion University	Fedora		✓	✓	
Anaktisis (http://anaktisis.teiwm.gr)	Digital archives, scientific journals, bachelor's and master's dissertations of Technological Educational Institute of Western Macedonia	Eprints 3.0		✓	✓	
Olympias (http://olympias.lib.uoi.gr/jspui)	Digital collections of the library of the University of Ioannina	DSpace	✓			✓
Dione (http://dione.lib.unipi.gr/xmlui)	Digital collection of undergraduate, postgraduate dissertations and doctoral theses by students and research scholars of the University of Piraeus	ELiDOC		✓	✓	
Foundation of Simitis, former Prime Minister (http://repository.costas-simitis.gr/sf-repository)	Biographical archives, photos and documentation	Open-source software		✓	✓	
Kosmopolis (http://kosmopolis.lis.upatras.gr)	Digitised journals on philosophy	Open journals system 2.1.1.0		✓	✓	

As demonstrated in chapter four, European initiatives are designed to create uniformity. Therefore, it is necessary that information be gathered conveniently, and its access should not be restrained by unjust legal rules, nor bureaucracy (Koutras & Bottis, 2013). In this way, OARs can play a significant role in supporting scholarly communication and dissemination of information.

The contemporary barriers regarding Greek OARs include a series of legal issues and indicate a need to design a modern legislative regime that regulates online data resources. Although open access infrastructure exists in Greece, the institutions and corporations preserve and protect their databases based on older regulations that are not aligned with contemporary trends and ongoing technological developments (Pinfield, 2005). However, this weakness may be addressed by using, for instance, Creative Commons licenses, which provide bargains of access and intellectual protection in accordance with the author's choice (Aliprandi, 2010). Regardless of the aforementioned drawbacks, within the contemporary Greek copyright regime, there is a widespread idea that there can be an effective co-existence between open access and copyright (Mueller-Langer & Watt, 2010; Newman & Feldman, 2011).

In conclusion, it can be said that open access practice and OARs in Greece constitute new scientific currents as far as scholarly communication is concerned (Kounoudes, Artemi, & Zervas, 2010). In contemporary times, additional access opportunities to scientific data can help in the wider dissemination of research outcomes by reducing the costs of accessing such knowledge. However, many unresolved issues remain. Thus, the possibility of partnerships among institutional repositories of Greek academic communities considers whether it is desirable to have an agreement or a form of mutual commitment regarding database protection and internal dissemination of information.

The previous discussion about the institutional outcomes towards the creation of OARs will be relevant if the academics in various universities and other higher education institutions adopt them. Therefore, it is relevant to revisit an earlier study concerning the utility of online databases by Greek academics. In the present context, its findings remain significant.

ANALYSIS OF CONDUCTED SURVEYS ABOUT GREEK OPEN ACCESS REPOSITORIES

Online Survey for Academia's Awareness Regarding Open Access: Open Access Repositories Bring Potential Towards Scholarly Communication Enhancement

An online survey conducted by Makridou et al. in 2012 illustrates whether and to what extent Greek academics are aware of OARs and the role and importance of OARs in utilising these information resources. The questionnaire was constructed on the same lines as the one conducted by the Organization for Economic Co-operation and Development (OECD) in 2007 (Tuomi, 2006). The questionnaire was addressed to the whole academic community of Greece and consisted of 13 questions. The 489 responses covered many scientific fields and academic levels from 25 of 38 universities in Greece. An analysis of relevant research findings follows.

The first questions were about personal details, respondents' affiliations with the examined university and their field of expertise. Table 2 reflects the answers to the first question, which addresses respondents' participation and their engagement or involvement with OA initiatives or projects. The overwhelming percentage of negative responses (82%) illustrates that OA practice is not well known, and Greek academics are not familiar with many OA initiatives.

The question addressed in Table 3 concerned the creation of OARs and whether the Greek respondents do or do not create OARs. Their responses present a complex picture; that is, there is great concern regarding OA practice, though the potential for greater engagement with OARs seems to be present and can be developed.

The next question presented in Table 4 referred to the Greek academics' views regarding obstacles or impediments for the creation of OARs. They considered that basic impediments for such creation consist of: (a) lack of

Table 2. Participation and engagement

Participation—Open Access Initiative or Project	Valid Percent
Yes	18%
No	82%

Table 3. Creation of OARs

Creation of OARs	Valid Percent
No, not at all	28%
Yes, to a limited extent	50%
Yes, extensively	22%

Table 4. Greek academics' views on obstacles and impediments

Discipline (Expertise)	Lack of Information About OAR Creation and Use	Lack of Time	Lack of Equipment	Lack of Interest in New Pedagogical Methods	Lack of a Model for Open Content Initiatives	Lack of Administration Support
Humanities and Arts	✓	✓	✓			✓
Social and Economic Sciences		✓	✓			✓
Business Administration and Management	✓		✓	✓	✓	✓
Natural Sciences, Mathematics, and Informatics		✓		✓		
Mechanics and Engineering				✓		✓
Earth Science, Agriculture and Veterinary	✓			✓		
Health Sciences						✓
Other				✓	✓	

interest concerning new or alternative methods for teaching and pedagogical methods, and (b) lack of administration support.

Another issue relevant to the argumentation of this book stems from the research findings regarding the next question, presented in Table 5. The question points to whether the use of an OAR is considered of paramount importance. The question addressed Greek academics' beliefs regarding potential and benefits associated with the use of OARs.

Table 5. Importance of using OARs

Discipline	Gain access to the Best Possible Resources	Promotion of Scientific Research and Publicly Open Activities	Reducing Costs for Students	Reducing Costs of Course Creation for the University	Outreach to Special-Skilled People	Becoming Independent from Publishers	Creation of More Flexible Educational Material
Humanities and Arts	Of little importance	Neutral	Neutral	Of little importance	Neutral	Neutral	Neutral
Social and Economic Sciences	Very important	Very important	Neutral	Very important	Very important	Neutral	Neutral
Business Administration and Management	Important	Neutral	Neutral	Neutral	Very important	Unimportant	Very important
Natural Sciences, Mathematics and Informatics	Important	Of little importance	Unimportant	Neutral	Unimportant	Of little important	Neutral
Mechanics and Engineering	Very important	Very important	Very important	Very important	Important	Neutral	Very important
Earth Science, Agriculture and Veterinary	Neutral	Neutral	Important	Very important	Very important	Important	Important
Health Sciences	Unimportant	Of limited importance	Of little importance	Unimportant	Of little importance	Unimportant	Neutral
Other	Important	Important	Of little importance	Neutral	Unimportant	Very important	Very important

From the above information, it can be concluded that, given the fact that many Greek academics are only partially aware of OARs and their importance in terms of publishing, sharing and information exchange, there is scope for change. These findings also help me argue that the Greek academic community has the potential to become a crucial actor in terms of information dissemination within OARs. However, efforts are required to make intellectual arguments for the value of OARs, to provide practical help in terms of constructing OARs and to train consumers (academics and present generation students) to use them effectively.

Therefore, it follows that the greater use of OARs is also fundamentally linked to how well the OARs are designed as software and whether they are user-friendly. The next section relies on a survey conducted by the author earlier, but its findings are quite relevant.

Online Surveys for the Open Access Repository of the Ionian University

Most Greek OARs operate under the DSpace software platform (Robinson, 2009). Certainly, the shape of Greek OARs is not based on a specific online platform and, thus, there are influences in relation to interoperability. Hence, one should consider whether an OAR (associated with a Greek university) using such a software platform can be useful for the academic community, whether its users are satisfied and what kind of services they receive in relation to the use of this OAR. For this purpose, an online survey was conducted to investigate the institutional repository of the Ionian University, which uses the DSpace software platform. The first (actual) survey conducted in 2013 in collaboration with the Greek research group, Information: History, Regulation, and Culture. Additionally, the second (online) survey conducted in 2015, aimed to use its research findings, as far as the issue of OARs in Greece was concerned. Both surveys aimed to demonstrate that the local academic community who were aware of the OARs were relying on them as significant research resources. The main objective for both surveys was to use this information to argue that the relevance of OARs extends to all sections of society.

The online survey was addressed to registered members of institutional repositories (such as undergraduates, postgraduates, academic staff and external academic fellows). The survey's URL was sent to registered members within an email message and consisted of three multiple-choice questions plus one question concerning the member's affiliation. 69 responses were received out of 681 registered members. Further, the primary scope of this survey included questions designed to determine registered members' level of knowledge about the digital platform of the OAR of the Ionian University, to illustrate its publicity and members' attitudes in relation to this repository, to define frequency of use by registered members and to explore registered members' levels of satisfaction with the OARs as an online information resource.

Table 6 presents the information about registered members' position within the university; it is noteworthy that there is a crucial divergence among the respondents who agreed to participate. Specifically, 76.19% of undergraduates, 14.29% of postgraduates, 4.76% of academic staff (professors, lecturers, and tutors), 3.17% of administrators, and 1.59% of external academic fellows agreed. Therefore, it seems that undergraduates were by far more interested

Table 6. Affiliations

Answers	2013	2015
Undergraduates	76.19%	70.21%
Postgraduates	14.29%	15.96%
Academic staff (professors, lecturers, tutors)	4.76%	7.45%
Administrators	3.17%	1.6%
External fellows	1.59%	5.78%

in participating in the online survey, which focused on the university's OAR. This may be a validation of the common sense understanding that younger generations are more familiar with online interactions. Though, it is also a strong reason to invest in creating efficient OARs that will be the primary research resource in the near future, if not already so.

The first question (see Table 7) concerns registered members' views regarding the popularity of the Ionian University OAR. The responses show positive outcomes in relation to the issue of popularity, with the overwhelming percentage of 85.07%, which is the total sum of the following answers: *Quite well-known*, *Well-known (adequate)*, and *Well-known (more than adequate)*.

In response to question three (see Table 8) on whether the respondents use or do not use the OAR, more than half answered *Yes, enough* and *Yes, quite enough*. However, 31.34% responded *No, not at all.*

Table 7. Popularity

Answers	2013	2015
Not well-known	14.93%	17.35%
Quite well-known	37.31%	37.76%
Well-known (adequate)	38.81%	34.69%
Well-known (more than adequate)	8.96%	10.2%

Table 8. Usage

Answers	2013	2015
No, not at all	31.34%	29.59%
Yes, enough	35.82%	31.63%
Yes, quite enough	23.88%	29.59%
Yes, very much	8.96%	9.18%

Regarding the last question (see Table 9), which indicates registered members' satisfaction with the services provided, there were no negative answers; the result indicates that the Ionian University OAR operates in a proper and effective manner for its users.

There is obviously a tendency for the respondents to be favourably inclined towards the OAR as these are the people who have chosen to participate. However, despite their satisfaction with this particular OAR, it remains the case that certain problems still exist. As part of the discussion regarding the infrastructure of Greek OARs, it should be mentioned that if an end user wants to access an OAR, he/she should devote substantial time, effort and resources to remember a series of usernames and passwords and the particular credentials for Greek OARs. Additionally, there are OARs of the same body that operate under different software, require a repetition for registration regarding the same user and sometimes separate registration process to gain access to sub-databases. For instance, the University of Athens has two repositories, NTUA and Pergamos, operating under DSpace and Open Source Software platforms, respectively. For the NTUA repository, users should remember their username and password to fully access the repository's content, material and archives, while for Pergamos, repository users can fully access its content. Similarly, there is almost the same situation regarding the museum of Acropolis, as it has two different repositories. In particular, the Acropolis Educational Resources and the Parthenon Frieze repositories, while operating under Open Source Software and DSpace, respectively require different sets of information from the user. Apart from registration details that should be recalled by users, there are avoidable overlaps. For example, information concerning the Parthenon frieze can also be gathered via the Acropolis Education Resources repository. Thus, there remains a considerable scope for improvement in the existing OARs.

Table 9. Satisfaction

Answers	2013	2015
Not satisfied	0%	0%
Satisfied (enough)	22.39%	22.45%
Satisfied (quite enough)	47.76%	46.94%
Satisfied (much)	23.88%	26.53%
Absolutely satisfied	5.97%	4.08%

The same conclusions are reached by various scholars. For example, Crow's early work suggests that institutional repositories could be contributing factors in "a new disaggregated model" of scholarly publishing, one that may help to weaken the monopolistic power of the traditional academic journal system over scholarly communication (Crow, 2002; Kenning Arlitsch & Patrick S. O'Brien, 2012). Through developing and maintaining "institutionally defined," scholarly," "cumulative and perpetual," and "open and interoperable" repositories, he argues that institutions can increase their visibility and prestige by centralising the intellectual work of their members, thus enabling researchers to find relevant materials more easily (Ghosh & Kumar Das, 2007; Maitrayee Ghosh, 2011).

Shearer identifies potential factors that need to be considered for repositories to be successful, including input activity, disciplines, advocacy activities, archiving policies, copyright policies, content type, staff support, quality control policies, software, and use (Shearer, 2003). Shearer assumes that the input activity—that is, submission of papers by researchers—would be one of the most important factors and wants to see the relationship between it and other factors.

Markland examined the effectiveness of Google in retrieving papers deposited in institutional repositories, choosing one item each from 26 UK institutional repositories, checking their availability and investigating the ease of finding them through five search strategies: (a) a search at the repository interface, (b) a Google search using a keyword or phrase from the title, (c) a Google search using the complete title, (d) a Google Scholar search using a keyword or phrase from the title, and (e) a Google Scholar search using the complete title (Markland, 2006).

Markland's study found that three of the items could not be retrieved through the repository interface. For results of searches from Google and Google Scholar using keyword phrases from titles, 17 of 26 items in repositories were retrieved from Google and 8 of 26 from Google Scholar. When using a complete title search, 25 of 26 were retrieved through Google and 17 of 26 through Google Scholar, suggesting that a simple title search via Google was the most effective means of retrieving repository items.

In a study of attitudes and behaviours, Watson interviewed 21 researchers from Cranfield University (Watson, 2007). Interviewees considered it crucial to share their work. Yet, most were not aware of the potential of OARs to provide such a framework of communication, and among those who were aware of the existence of OARs, many were not using them. Xia found researchers to be increasingly aware of open access, but only at a very basic level, with insufficient comprehension of participation in open access initiatives, suggesting that increased awareness alone may not be adequate for the faculty in terms of incentives for additional use of OARs (Xia, 2010).

Nicholas et al. investigated scientific researchers' perceptions of OARs (Nicholas, Rowlands, Watkinson, Brown, & Jamali, 2012). They examined 1,685 survey responses obtained from faculty members and students who had been registered in the Institute of Physics Publishing. They found that 63.7% of survey respondents had deposited their research outcomes in a repository and that 44.1% had specifically used OARs.

Oguz and Assefa conducted a survey in a medium-sized university to investigate its members' perceptions and attitudes concerning OARs. They observed positive perceptions among 52.9% of respondents and negative perceptions among 47.1% (Oguz & Assefa, 2014). In general, although there are some variations across disciplines and institutions (Cullen & Chawner, 2011), there appears to be a growing rate of participation on behalf of authors in creating/constructing OARs, but there is potential for further development in the future (Björk, Laakso, Welling, & Paetau, 2014).

CONCLUSION

From the above discussion, it can be concluded that it remains necessary for Greek OARs to modify and become more efficient. In addition, and more specifically, in the context of this thesis, there is also a need for them to operate under the same regulations regarding issues of gaining access to their content. Therefore, there is a need for potential copyright changes that may facilitate the integration of open access practices. However, this does not necessarily mean that we need a change of copyright standards.

Lessig advocates a new approach regarding access to copyrighted works (Lessig, 2008). He argues that copyright law has not kept up with technological growth and is, in fact, holding it back. To Lessig, the Internet-enabled world and the new online information environment have led to a new culture of creation. He is more than just an observer, as he has been engaged with new approaches to copyright protection, and he founded Creative Commons licenses, a San Francisco-based non-profit that helps many companies and end users navigate the uncharted fields between full copyright and public domain. Thus, Creative Commons licenses could be the start point to establish a beneficial connection between copyrighted works and open access or a connection with positive future perspectives in terms of sharing, while also being protected in terms of copyright (Lessig, 2005). Lessig's views about a new approach for copyright protection helps me to argue that it could be beneficial if the current framework for copyright protection in Greece followed such an approach. That is, there is a need for developing connections between Greek copyright law and open access, and any suggestion of change does not necessarily have to mean a call for a change of copyright standards.

For example, simple instructions could be provided to users to recruit them as contributors to each repository for enhancing interaction with users. In accordance with the online survey presented above, students are particularly keen on using a repository, and they are satisfied with the current services. Therefore, it is possible to say that the Ionian University's repository software is user-friendly and not characterised by restrictions, and, thus, it demonstrates a beneficial example in terms of functionality. However, it does not allow me to argue that all information repositories should adopt the same standard.

Any suggestion for the construction of one sole repository for all Greek academic institutions would face seemingly insurmountable political objections, confront non-governmental groups with interests and deal with separate disputes regarding financial support. Nevertheless, anticipating beneficial prospects towards diminishing inequalities concerning ICT and broadening possible means of communication dictate that the issue of Greek OARs and their integration should be made a priority. At the same time, it is also an existential reality that OARs are institutional responses that can exist and operate only with public financial support. The Greek Government ought to create funding sources, which should be part of the state budget, regarding educational issues on an annual basis. This is currently not a popular—or some may say even a viable—suggestion, but the point is that this is too important a matter to be left as a private-sector responsibility.

What is more, Greek authorities should also simplify integrated repository use and make it as user-friendly as possible by eliminating registration (e.g., passwords) and broaden access opportunities. Taking everything into consideration, this would be a courageous step towards knowledge for the citizenry in Greece. Thus, the integration of Greek OARs that requires interoperability to be applied/implemented consistently has the potential to bring efficient options regarding sharing, exchange and dissemination through open access. The assessment of the governance framework for OARs in Greece determines the need for integration for efficiency while establishing a beneficial balance between the competing interests of copyright owners and end users.

Access to knowledge is crucial for the flourishing of knowledge economies that form the economies of the future. Informational resources and data are major knowledge assets. These knowledge assets should be as open as efficiency and justice allow. Through directives and regulations, this occurs in Europe and determines the harmonisation of politics among Member States. In this context, the role of OARs is of paramount importance and should be part of this knowledge economy, and they should provide equal opportunities to access information resources.

European legislation and initiatives, such as directives, regulations and research projects, aim to improve European citizens' skills in furtherance of a knowledge economy based on information. Moreover, in terms of urban competitiveness of the European economy, the Greek Government, in collaboration with educational institutes such as primary schools, universities, colleges, technology educational institutes and libraries, should play a crucial role and should establish a more comprehensive role for Greek society, in terms of information dissemination. Thus, emerges the need to harmonise publishing and sharing policy.

In this chapter, it was set out to argue how the Greek regulation system operates. Specific provisions of the Greek Constitution and Greek Statute 4009/2011 considered and demonstrate how information can be distributed in Greece. Further examination of implications of the European directives for the Greek Copyright Act followed and a number of surveys conducted by Greek scholars and the author of this book for the status and progress of the Greek OARs were also considered.

The next chapter will set the background context concerning the emergence and development of the open access movement. Then, it follows the conceptual meanings of the OARs, as the literature reflects that there is no unique definition, and different scholars' perspectives will be examined. There is also discussion about the perspectives of open access advocates, which will help to describe the pros and cons associated with the operation of OARs. In the context, the actors involved in academic publishing are going to be considered. These main actors are commercial publishers and academic scholarly communities as authors and as publishers of academic journals. First, commercial publishers' responses to the open access movement as a modern practice for publishing academic works will be examined. This will be followed by a consideration of the interests of academic scholarly publishing communities. The interests of the academic scholarly community contradict those of commercial publishers and possibly the knowledge pursuit is going to be abandoned. Relevant subscription fees for journals determine the basic barrier that prevents the dissemination of scientific information. To conclude, the basis for a "profitable" agreement among the interests of authors, publishers, and users of online published works can arise only when these interests are satisfied. Such discussion follows in the next chapter.

REFERENCES

Abbas, J., Norris, C., & Soloway, E. (2002). Middle school children's use of the ARTEMIS digital library. *Proceedings of the 2Nd ACM/IEEE-CS Joint Conference on Digital Libraries*, 98–105. 10.1145/544220.544239

Aghaei, S., Nematbakhsh, M. A., & Farsani, H. K. (2012). Evolution of the World Wide Web: From Web 1.0 to Web 4.0. *International Journal of Web & Semantic Technology*, *3*(1), 1–10. doi:10.5121/ijwest.2012.3101

Alexandropoulou, E. (2011). Personal financial data: Regulatory framework of their e-processing focusing on the function of interbanking information systems in Greece and France. In *An Information Law for the 21st Century* (pp. 237–252). Retrieved from https://papers.ssrn.com/abstract=2621496

Aliprandi, S. (2010). *Creative Commons: A user guide*. Italy: lulu.com.

Andreou, G. (2006). EU cohesion policy in Greece: Patterns of governance and Europeanization. *South European Society & Politics*, *11*(2), 241–259. doi:10.1080/13608740600645865

Antezana, M. E. (2003). The European Union Internet Copyright Directive as even more than it envisions: Toward a supra-EU harmonization of copyright policy and theory. *Boston College International and Comparative Law Review*, *26*, 415.

Arlitsch, K., & O'Brien, P. S. (2012). Invisible institutional repositories: Addressing the low indexing ratios of IRs in Google Scholar. *Library Hi Tech*, *30*(1), 60–81. doi:10.1108/07378831211213210

Bachtler, J., & McMaster, I. (2008). EU cohesion policy and the role of the regions: Investigating the influence of structural funds in the new Member States. *Environment and Planning. C, Government & Policy*, *26*(2), 398–427. doi:10.1068/c0662

Bandura, A. (2001). Social cognitive theory of mass communication. *Media Psychology*, *3*(3), 265–299. doi:10.1207/S1532785XMEP0303_03

Becker, J. D. (2007). Digital equity in education: A multilevel examination of differences in and relationships between computer access, computer use and state-level technology policies. *Education Policy Analysis Archives*, *15*(0), 3. doi:10.14507/epaa.v15n3.2007

Beetham, H., & Sharpe, R. (2013). *Rethinking pedagogy for a digital age: Designing for 21st century learning*. Routledge.

Beniger, J. (2009). *The control revolution: Technological and economic origins of the information society*. Harvard University Press.

Berkenkotter, C., & Huckin, T. N. (2016). *Genre knowledge in disciplinary communication: Cognition/culture/power*. Routledge. doi:10.4324/9781315538747

Berners-Lee, T., Cailliau, R., Groff, J., & Pollermann, B. (2010). World-Wide Web: The information universe. *Internet Research*, *20*(4), 461–471. doi:10.1108/10662241011059471

Björk, B.-C., Laakso, M., Welling, P., & Paetau, P. (2014). Anatomy of green open access. *Journal of the Association for Information Science and Technology*, *65*(2), 237–250. doi:10.1002/asi.22963

Bowker, G. C., Baker, K., Millerand, F., & Ribes, D. (2009). Toward information infrastructure studies: Ways of knowing in a networked environment. In J. Hunsinger, L. Klastrup, & M. Allen (Eds.), *International Handbook of Internet Research* (pp. 97–117). doi:10.1007/978-1-4020-9789-8_5

Castells, M., & Himanen, P. (2003). *The information society and the welfare state: The Finnish model.* Oxford University Press.

Chantavaridou, E. (2009). Open access and institutional repositories in Greece: Progress so far. OCLC *Systems & Services. International Digital Library Perspectives*, *25*(1), 47–59. doi:10.1108/10650750910931922

Churchill, D. (2009). Educational applications of Web 2.0: Using blogs to support teaching and learning. *British Journal of Educational Technology, 40*(1), 179–183. doi:10.1111/j.1467-8535.2008.00865.x

Crook, C. (2002). The campus experience of networked learning. In C. Steeples & C. Jones (Eds.), *Networked Learning: Perspectives and Issues* (pp. 293–308)., doi:10.1007/978-1-4471-0181-9_17

Crow, R. (2002). The case for institutional repositories: A SPARC position paper. *Research on Institutional Repositories: Articles and Presentations.* Retrieved from http://digitalcommons.bepress.com/repository-research/27

Cullen, R., & Chawner, B. (2011). Institutional repositories, open access, and scholarly communication: A study of conflicting paradigms. *Journal of Academic Librarianship, 37*(6), 460–470. doi:10.1016/j.acalib.2011.07.002

Dalakou, V. (2014). *The institutional framework of open access to publicly funded research efforts.* Retrieved from http://helios-eie.ekt.gr/EIE/handle/10442/14433

Davison, M. J. (2003). *The legal protection of databases.* Cambridge University Press. doi:10.1017/CBO9780511495236

Dee, P. (2005). *The Australia–US Free Trade Agreement: An assessment.* Retrieved from https://openresearch-repository.anu.edu.au/handle/1885/43027

Dent, C. M. (2010). Free trade agreements in the Asia-Pacific a decade on: Evaluating the past, looking to the future. *International Relations of the Asia-Pacific, 10*(2), 201–245. doi:10.1093/irap/lcp022

Dimitrakopoulos, D. G. (2001). Incrementalism and path dependence: European integration and institutional change in national parliaments. *Journal of Common Market Studies, 39*(3), 405–422. doi:10.1111/1468-5965.00296

Ehrenberg, V. (2013). The Greek state (Routledge Library Editions). *Political Science (Wellington, N.Z.), 23.*

Ertl, H. (2006). European Union policies in education and training: The Lisbon agenda as a turning point? *Comparative Education, 42*(1), 5–27. doi:10.1080/03050060500515652

European Commission. (2007). *Operational programme "Digital convergence"*. Retrieved January 17, 2017, from Regional Policy website: http://ec.europa.eu/regional_policy/en/atlas/programmes/2007-2013/greece/operational-programme-digital-convergence

European Commission. (2012). *Consolidated version of the Treaty on the Functioning of the European Union* (Official Journal of the European Union No. C 326/ 47; p. 344). Retrieved from http://eur-lex.europa.eu/legal-content/EN/TXT/HTML/?uri=CELEX:12012E/TXT&from=EN

European Communities. (2001). *Directive 2001/29/EC of the European Parliament and of the Council*. Official Journal of the European Communities, L. 167, 10–19.

Fischer, R. (2005). *The expansion of intellectual property rights by international agreement: A case study comparing Chile and Australia's bilateral FTA negotiations with the U.S. Bepress Legal Series*. Retrieved from http://law.bepress.com/expresso/eps/549

Fishman, S. (2014). *The copyright handbook: What every writer needs to know*. Nolo.

Gargouri, Y., Larivière, V., Gingras, Y., Carr, L., & Harnad, S. (2012). *Green and gold open access percentages and growth, by discipline*. Retrieved from http://arxiv.org/abs/1206.3664

Georgiou, P., & Papadatou, F. (2010). Open access in Greece. In *Open access in southern European countries* (pp. 39–62). Academic Press. Retrieved from http://www.researchgate.net/post/Open_Access_in_Southern_European_Countries

Ghosh, M. (2011). Advocacy for open access: A selected review of the literature and resource list. *Library Hi Tech News*, *28*(2), 19–23. doi:10.1108/07419051111135245

Ghosh, S. B., & Kumar Das, A. (2007). Open access and institutional repositories—A developing country perspective: A case study of India. *IFLA Journal*, *33*(3), 229–250. doi:10.1177/0340035207083304

Giannopoulou, A. (2012). Copyright enforcement measures: The role of the ISPs and the respect of the principle of proportionality. *European Journal of Law and Technology*, *3*(1). Retrieved from http://ejlt.org/article/view/122

Greek Government. (2011). Structure, validation of studies and internationalization of higher education institutions., Pub. L. No. 195. *Greek Government Newspaper, 48.*

Greek Parliament. (2010). *Greek Constitution.* Retrieved from http://www.hellenicparliament.gr/UserFiles/8c3e9046-78fb-48f4-bd82-bbba28ca1ef5/SYNTAGMA.pdf

Grodzinsky, F. S., & Bottis, M. C. (2007). Private use as fair use: Is it fair? *SIGCAS Comput. Soc.*, *37*(2), 11–24. doi:10.1145/1327325.1327326

Hahamis, P., Iles, J., & Healy, M. (2005). E-government in Greece: Bridging the gap between need and reality. *Electronic Journal of E-Government*, *3*(4), 185–192.

Hall, H., & Graham, D. (2004). Creation and recreation: Motivating collaboration to generate knowledge capital in online communities. *International Journal of Information Management*, *24*(3), 235–246. doi:10.1016/j.ijinfomgt.2004.02.004

Hormia-Poutanen, K., Xenidou-Dervou, C., Kupryte, R., Stange, K., Kuznetsov, A. V., & Woodward, H. M. (2006). Consortia in Europe: Describing the various solutions through four country examples. *Library Trends*, *54*(3), 359–381. doi:10.1353/lib.2006.0026

Jappelli, T., & Pagano, M. (2002). Information sharing, lending and defaults: Cross-country evidence. *Journal of Banking & Finance*, *26*(10), 2017–2045. doi:10.1016/S0378-4266(01)00185-6

Kallinikou, D. (2007). *Regulations for intellectual property and relevant rights in Greece*. Athens: Sakkoulas.

Kapczynski, A. (2008). *The access to knowledge mobilization and the new politics of intellectual property* (SSRN Scholarly Paper No. ID 1323525). Retrieved from Social Science Research Network website: https://papers.ssrn.com/abstract=1323525

Karakostas, I. (2009). *Common law and Internet* (3rd ed.). Athens: Sakkoulas.

Kostagiolas, P., & Banou, C. (2007). *Managing expectations for open access in Greece: Perceptions from the publishers and academic libraries* (L. Chan & B. Martens, Eds.). Retrieved from http://eprints.rclis.org/10041/

Koulouris, A., Kyriaki-Manessi, D., Giannakopoulos, G., & Zervos, S. (2013). Institutional repository policies: Best practices for encouraging self-archiving. *Procedia: Social and Behavioral Sciences*, *73*, 769–776. doi:10.1016/j.sbspro.2013.02.117

Kounoudes, A. D., Artemi, P., & Zervas, M. (2010). Ktisis: Building an open access institutional and cultural repository. In M. Ioannides, D. Fellner, A. Georgopoulos, & D. G. Hadjimitsis (Eds.), *Digital Heritage* (pp. 504–512). doi:10.1007/978-3-642-16873-4_41

Koutras, N., & Bottis, M. (2013). Institutional repositories of open access: A paradigm of innovation and changing in educational politics. *Procedia: Social and Behavioral Sciences*, *106*, 1499–1504. doi:10.1016/j.sbspro.2013.12.169

Lankes, R. D. (2011). *The atlas of new librarianship (Har/Chrt edition)*. Cambridge, MA: MIT Press. doi:10.7551/mitpress/8755.001.0001

Lazarides, T. (2011). Corporate governance legal and regulatory framework's effectiveness in Greece: A response. *Journal of Financial Regulation and Compliance*, *19*(3), 244–253. doi:10.1108/13581981111147874

Lessig, L. (2005). *Free culture: The nature and future of creativity*. New York: Penguin Books.

Lessig, L. (2008). *Remix: Making art and commerce thrive in the hybrid economy*. The Penguin Press. doi:10.5040/9781849662505

Liaw, S.-S. (2002). An Internet survey for perceptions of computers and the World Wide Web: Relationship, prediction, and difference. *Computers in Human Behavior*, *18*(1), 17–35. doi:10.1016/S0747-5632(01)00032-2

Lim, C. L., Elms, D. K., & Low, P. (2012). *The trans-Pacific partnership: A quest for a twenty-first century trade agreement*. Cambridge University Press. doi:10.1017/CBO9781139236775

Liu, X., Toki, E. I., & Pange, J. (2014). The use of ICT in preschool education in Greece and China: A comparative study. *Procedia: Social and Behavioral Sciences*, *112*, 1167–1176. doi:10.1016/j.sbspro.2014.01.1281

Luke, A., Woods, A., & Weir, K. (2013). *Curriculum, syllabus design, and equity: A primer and model*. Routledge.

Lynch, C. A. (2003). Institutional repositories: Essential infrastructure for scholarship in the digital age. *Portal (Baltimore, Md.)*, *3*(2), 327–336. doi:10.1353/pla.2003.0039

Lynskey, O. (2014). Deconsructing data protection: The "added-value" of a right to data protection in the EU legal order. *The International and Comparative Law Quarterly*, *63*(3), 569–597. doi:10.1017/S0020589314000244

Makridou, E., Araka, I., & Koutras, N. (2012). Open educational resources and freedom of teaching in college education in Greece: Rivals or fellows? In *Proceedings of the 5th International Conference of Information Law and Ethics (ICIL)* (pp. 605–628). Athens: NB Production.

Maniotis, D. (2011). *Cyber law in Greece*. Kluwer Law International.

Markland, M. (2006). Institutional repositories in the UK: What can the Google user find there? *Journal of Librarianship and Information Science*, *38*(4), 221–228. doi:10.1177/0961000606070587

McLuhan, M., Gordon, W. T., Lamberti, E., & Scheffel-Dunand, D. (2011). *The Gutenberg galaxy: The making of typographic man*. University of Toronto Press.

Molle, W. (2007). *European cohesion policy*. Routledge. doi:10.4324/9780203945278

Moreleli-Cacouris, M., Makridou, E., & Asmanidis, Y. (2007). Institutional repositories: A proposal for a national policy based upon a Greek case. Presented at the *16th Hellenic Academic Libraries Conference*, Piraeus, Greece.

Mueller-Langer, F., & Watt, R. (2010). *Copyright and open access for academic works* (SSRN Scholarly Paper No. ID 1647586). Retrieved from Social Science Research Network website: https://papers.ssrn.com/abstract=1647586

Newman, J. C., & Feldman, R. (2011). Copyright and open access at the bedside. *The New England Journal of Medicine*, *365*(26), 2447–2449. doi:10.1056/NEJMp1110652

Nicholas, D., Rowlands, I., Watkinson, A., Brown, D., & Jamali, H. R. (2012). Digital repositories ten years on: What do scientific researchers think of them and how do they use them? *Learned Publishing*, *25*(3), 195–206. doi:10.1087/20120306

Ntaliani, M., Costopoulou, C., Karetsos, S., & Molhanec, M. (2015). Citizen e-empowerment in Greek and Czech municipalities. In S. K. Katsikas & A. B. Sideridis (Eds.), *E-Democracy—Citizen Rights in the World of the New Computing Paradigms* (pp. 124–133). doi:10.1007/978-3-319-27164-4_9

Oakleaf, M. (2009). The information literacy instruction assessment cycle: A guide for increasing student learning and improving librarian instructional skills. *The Journal of Documentation*, *65*(4), 539–560. doi:10.1108/00220410910970249

Oguz, F., & Assefa, S. (2014). Faculty members' perceptions towards institutional repository at a medium-sized university: Application of a binary logistic regression model. *Library Review*, *63*(3), 189–202. doi:10.1108/LR-07-2013-0088

Otjacques, B., Hitzelberger, P., & Feltz, F. (2007). Interoperability of e-government information systems: Issues of identification and data sharing. *Journal of Management Information Systems*, *23*(4), 29–51. doi:10.2753/MIS0742-1222230403

Pappas, C., & Williams, I. (2011). Grey literature: Its emerging importance. *Journal of Hospital Librarianship*, *11*(3), 228–234. doi:10.1080/15323269.2011.587100

Pinfield, S. (2005). A mandate to self archive? The role of open access institutional repositories. *Serials: The Journal for the Serials Community*, *18*(1), 30–34. doi:10.1629/1830

Psacharopoulos, G. (2003). The social cost of an outdated law: Article 16 of the Greek Constitution. *European Journal of Law and Economics*, *16*(2), 123–137. doi:10.1023/A:1024117632649

Rader, H. B. (1997). Educating students for the Information Age: The role of the librarian. *RSR. Reference Services Review*, *25*(2), 47–52. doi:10.1108/00907329710306661

Raschke, C. A. (2003). *The digital revolution and the coming of the postmodern university*. Routledge. doi:10.4324/9780203451243

Rhoten, D., & Powell, W. W. (2007). The frontiers of intellectual property: Expanded protection versus new models of open science. *Annual Review of Law and Social Science*, *3*(1), 345–373. doi:10.1146/annurev.lawsocsci.3.081806.112900

Rimmer, M. (2007). *Digital copyright and the consumer revolution: Hands off my iPod*. Edward Elgar Publishing. doi:10.4337/9781847207142

Robinson, M. (2009). Promoting the visibility of educational research through an institutional repository. *Serials Review*, *35*(3), 133–137. doi:10.1080/00987913.2009.10765230

Rosler, D. B. (1995). The European Union's proposed directive for the legal protection of databases: A new threat to the free flow of information. *High Technology Law Journal*, *10*(1), 105–146.

Rothstein, H. R., & Hopewell, S. (2009). Grey literature. In H. Cooper, L. V. Hedges, & J. C. Valentine (Eds.), *The handbook of research synthesis and meta-analysis* (2nd ed.; pp. 103–125). New York, NY: Russell Sage Foundation.

Rowley, J., & Hartley, R. J. (2008). *Organizing knowledge: An introduction to managing access to information*. Ashgate Publishing, Ltd.

Schmidt, E., & Cohen, J. (2013). The new digital age: Reshaping the future of people, nations and business. Hachette UK.

Shearer, K. (2003). *Institutional repositories: Towards the identification of critical success factors*. Retrieved from http://prism.ucalgary.ca//handle/1880/43357

Sianou-Kyrgiou, E. (2008). Social class and access to higher education in Greece: Supportive preparation lessons and success in national exams. *International Studies in Sociology of Education*, *18*(3–4), 173–183. doi:10.1080/09620210802492757

Smith, M., Barton, M., Branschofsky, M., McClellan, G., Walker, J. H., Bass, M., ... Tansley, R. (2003). DSpace: An open source dynamic digital repository. *D-Lib Magazine*, *9*(1). doi:10.1045/january2003-smith

Soriano, F. H., & Mulatero, F. (2010). Knowledge policy in the EU: From the Lisbon Strategy to Europe 2020. *Journal of the Knowledge Economy*, *1*(4), 289–302. doi:10.100713132-010-0020-9

Swan, A., & Brown, S. (2005). *Open access self-archiving: An author study*. Retrieved September 11, 2015, from http://eprints.soton.ac.uk/260999/

Synodinou, T.-E. (2015). Intermediaries' liability for online copyright infringement in the EU: Evolutions and confusions. *Computer Law & Security Review*, *31*(1), 57–67. doi:10.1016/j.clsr.2014.11.010

Tennant, J. (2014). Top scientific publisher chooses not to advance open access. *The Conversation*. Retrieved December 14, 2014, from http://theconversation.com/top-scientific-publisher-chooses-not-to-advance-open-access-31248

Trohopoulos, I. (2009). Harvesting metadata of Greek institutional repositories in the context of EuropeanaLocal. *Workshop on Harvesting Metadata: Practices and Challenges. Presented at the 13th European Conference on Digital Libraries, Greece*. Retrieved from http://users.teiath.gr/akoul/pubs/ecdl2009.pdf

Tuomi, I. (2006). *Open educational resources: What they are and why do they matter*. Retrieved from http://citeseerx.ist.psu.edu/viewdoc/download?doi=10.1.1.693.9373&rep=rep1&type=pdf

van Eechoud, M. M. M. (2009). *Harmonizing European copyright law: The challenges of better lawmaking*. Kluwer Law International.

Watson, S. (2007, November). *Authors' attitudes to, and awareness and use of, a university institutional repository*. Retrieved January 23, 2017, from https://dspace.lib.cranfield.ac.uk/handle/1826/2017

Wiley, D., & Hilton, J. (2009). Openness, dynamic specialization, and the disaggregated future of higher education. *The International Review of Research in Open and Distributed Learning*, *10*(5). doi:10.19173/irrodl.v10i5.768

Xia, J. (2010). A longitudinal study of scholars attitudes and behaviors toward open-access journal publishing. *Journal of the American Society for Information Science and Technology*, *61*(3), 615–624. doi:10.1002/asi.21283

Xia, J., Gilchrist, S. B., Smith, N. X. P., Kingery, J. A., Radecki, J. R., Wilhelm, M. L., . . . Mahn, A. J. (2012). *A review of open access self-archiving mandate policies*. doi:10.13016/M2H12D

ENDNOTE

1 For the purposes of this section, the term *Greek Copyright Act* refers to Greek Law No. 2121/1993, which was amended by Law No. 2435/1996 (art. 3 and 10), Law No. 2557/1997 (art. 8), Law No. 2819/2000 (art. 7), Law No. 3057/2002 (art. 81) and Law No. 3207/2003 (art. 10, par. 33).

Chapter 6
The Evolving Role of Commercial Publishers and the Future of Online Access Repositories

ABSTRACT

Since the modes of publishing content have changed in the digital age, OA practice could be an effective response towards the challenges generated by the ongoing technological advancements. It could respond to the competing concerns of copyright protection and equitable access to information, simultaneously. This final chapter analyzes the interconnections between commercial publisher and author interests and argues that OARs could be considered as an instrument towards common benefits. In the context of continuous technological growth, OA could also be seen as an alternative instrument for the protection of intellectual property to facilitate modern or digital publishing and benefit publisher and intellectual creator, as well. Traditionally, commercial publishers are gatekeepers of the standards of merit of academic works even though they get almost all of the profits. However, while they rely on academics' expertise to remain commercially viable, they do not pay for this expertise, appropriately. In contemporary days it is feasible for authors to not rely on commercial publishers. It is, therefore, in the interests of commercial publishers that academics keep publishing with them. As gatekeepers of standards of merit, they can benefit the academic world and remain viable themselves. This claim will be substantiated with examples of relevant licensing forms and other initiatives of OA.

DOI: 10.4018/978-1-7998-1131-2.ch006

INTRODUCTION

The preceding chapters established that primarily for digital publishing OA is one of the distinctive manifestations of technological developments (Laakso et al., 2011). Therefore, the fundamental question for this book is whether the previous regulatory framework for the ownership of intellectual property rights is adequate to deal with the current situation and whether it can adequately regulate issues arising out of OA.

Initially, there was a short discussion about the history of copyright before OA, and the background context for addressing this issue was set. This historical account helps explain the significance of OARs. As explained in preceding chapters, the OA phenomenon considered as a tool for social justice and social cohesion that could enhance copyright regimes and make access to information more widely available. Hence, OARs in the digital age could be seen as a contemporary response for sharing and dissemination of information resources. Nowadays, the end users of knowledge should have the widest possible access to knowledge. An examination of the governance framework of OARs in the European Union and in Greece examined the examples of OARs that could enhance the dissemination and spread of information. In this chapter, the issue of OA is analysed from the perspective of the producers of knowledge: authors, publishers and, more specifically, commercial publishing firms.

The most desirable regulatory regime for OARs is the "just" green agreement. It has three components, sequentially explaining what just access is, what green OA is (also known as self-archiving) and the agreement involving the interests of all three stakeholders (authors, publishers, and users). This argument addresses the issues that authors, publishers, and users all benefit by appropriate regulation of access. On the one hand, authors can adopt online publishing, but they cannot effectively enforce their IPRs. On the other hand, publishers can claim IPRs in the traditional form, but it would be almost impossible to enforce them in the context of online publishing. Therefore, authors and publishers both need to respond to these changes. If publishers do not join the online revolution, potentially they become irrelevant from a commercial perspective. If they become part of such a revolution, they should not be obliged to disregard their commercial interests in IPRs. However, to pursue their commercial interests, it is evident that they would need to modify their business models. So too do authors need the commercial publishers, at least in the academic world. This is for a few reasons, including that in academic scholarship, it is desirable to publish through commercial and reputable publishers. In such cases, IPRs are usually given to the publishers. Hence, even though the authors possess a few more choices since the arrival of digital and online publishing, they still need publishers. In other words, there is always an inevitable link between academic authors and commercial publishers.

Therefore, in this chapter, the first part discusses the contemporary developments in publishing practices, including Creative Commons and OARs. The second part undertakes an analysis of the implications of these technological changes for commercial publishing. The third part discusses the response of publishers to OA practice with the example of soft regulation introduced by the Open Access Scholarly Publishers Association (OASPA). In this part, there is also an analysis of the practices of the Emerald publishing house to examine how OA has been practised. In the last part, a critique of the contemporary regulations and practices will yield a model for the future regulation of OARs.

TRENDS OF PUBLISHING

Online Publishing: Conceptualisation of Open Access Repositories

Continuous technological growth is one of the defining features of present times, and it gives rise to new situations regarding ways in which information is produced, shared, and published. This technological evolution brings new circumstances, such as online platforms and the creation of databases for both social media and academia (Burgess & Green, 2013). Because of the rapid growth of the Internet, our modes and needs for distributing information and communicating have shifted dramatically. Therefore, digital archives and online creations, such as a post on a social network (e.g., Facebook and LinkedIn), create a new phenomenon that may require regulation.

Technological developments in publishing and disseminating have led to increasing concern about uncertain applications of IPRs. In copyright law, it is argued that its relationship with technology is symbiotic (Depoorter, 2009). Thus, current copyright regimes should keep up with rapid technological developments with legal provisions to offer online protection. Otherwise, it is inevitable that legal uncertainty emerges. Another equally important issue is that the current copyright regime is beset by practical difficulties regarding the intellectual protection of online data. This is because the ongoing technological evolution bombards the framework of copyright laws (Feenberg & Feenberg, 2012; Larsson, 2011). For these reasons, there is an urgent need to enhance copyright regimes to offer better intellectual protection responsive to the necessities of the digital age (Palfrey, Gasser, Simun, & Barnes, 2009).

OA, as a concept, and OARs as the relevant mechanism, can be one example of a response to the shifting needs of authors and readers (Frosio, 2017). Therefore, relevant conceptual analysis of OA and OARs is imperative to frame the background of the discussion about OAP, also known as self-archiving, which addresses depositing articles in OARs (Koulouris, Kyriaki-Manessi, Giannakopoulos, & Zervos, 2013). In this part, a brief analysis of the literature on OA sets the context for arguing that OARs are a suitable mechanism for OA. Thus, a brief overview of the concept of OAP and OARs follows below.

There is no agreement about the definition of the concept of OA. But, three initiatives lead to statements of support of OA and have played a fundamental role in creating a relevant discourse. From a chronological perspective, the first initiative concerning OA took place in Budapest 2002, namely the Budapest Open Access Initiative (BOAI). Its origins stem from the Open Society Institute, which invited a group of people working in this area to a discussion in Budapest in December 2001 (Stone, 2010). That group discussed a variety of strategies to achieve OA and agreed on two main strategies: self-archiving and journals publishing. In early 2002, the group agreed on a statement that was circulated to a wider group of individuals, before its release on 14 February 2002. It is examined below.

According to the statement of BOAI, OA means that there is free access online to literature that scholars give to the world without expectation of payment. In other words, free availability of such literature on the public Internet, permitting any users to read, download, copy, distribute, print, search or link to the full texts of these articles, crawl them for indexing, pass them as data to software or use them for any other lawful purpose, without financial, legal or technical barriers other than those inseparable from gaining access to the Internet itself. The only impediment on reproduction and distribution, and the only role for copyright in this domain, should be to give authors control over the integrity of their work and the right to be properly acknowledged and cited (Budapest Open Access Initiative [2002], 2012).

More than a year later, on June 2003, another initiative to give additional support for OA emerged during a meeting on OAP in the US, namely the Bethesda Statement on OAP (BSOAP). At the headquarters of the Howard Hughes Medical Institute in Chevy Chase, Maryland, a document was released that was meant to stimulate discussion within the biomedical research community on how to proceed, as rapidly as possible, to the widely held goal of providing OA to the primary scientific literature. The overarching goal was to agree on the crucial steps that relevant parties could take to promote the rapid and efficient transition to OAP. In this way, the BSOAP rationale builds upon the BOAI and enriches the definition of OA.

It is relevant to examine the BSOAP in the context of the argumentation of this book. Its structure is twofold; it states: (a) The author(s) and copyright holder(s) grant(s) to all users a free, irrevocable, worldwide, perpetual right of access to, and a license to copy, use, distribute, transmit, and display the work publicly and to make and distribute derivative works, in any digital medium for any responsible purpose, subject to proper attribution of authorship, as well as the right to make small numbers of printed copies for their personal use. (b) A complete version of the work and all supplemental materials, including a copy of the permission as stated above, in a suitable standard electronic format is deposited immediately upon initial publication in at least one online repository that is supported by an academic institution, scholarly society, government agency or other well-established organisation that seeks to enable OA, unrestricted distribution, interoperability and long-term archiving (Suber et al., 2003).

A few months after the BSOAP initiative, in October 2003, another initiative arose from a meeting organised in Berlin. The Max Planck Society and the European Cultural Heritage Online project co-organised this meeting that brought together international experts with the aim of producing a new Web-based research environment using OA as a tool for making scientific knowledge and cultural heritage accessible worldwide. Consequently, leading international research, scientific and cultural institutions issued and signed the Berlin Declaration on Open Access to Knowledge (BDOAK) in the Sciences and Humanities. This document outlines concrete steps to promote the Internet as a medium for disseminating global knowledge.

The BDOAK builds upon the BOAI, just as the BSOAP statement did earlier; it calls for the results of research produced by authors to be made widely available on the Internet, without expectation of payment. It also calls for granting of permissions necessary for users to use and reuse results in a way that accelerates the pace of scholarship and research. It should be noted that nearly 300 research institutions, libraries, archives, museums, funding agencies and governments from around the world have signed the BDOAK statement. The geographic and disciplinary diversity of the support for the Berlin Declaration is illustrated by the signatories, which range from the leaders of the Max Plank Society to the Chinese Academy of Sciences, to Academia Europaea. Most recently, both Harvard University and the International Federation of Library Associations added their names to the roster of signatories ("Berlin Declaration on Open Access to Knowledge in the Sciences and Humanities," 2012).

These initiatives constitute the policy statements for OA and identify the requirements it must meet. They set the theoretical background for OA content and objectives. However, in the relevant literature, there is presently an argument as to whether another definition for OA should be considered. One of the participants in the BSOAP, Peter Suber, widely considered the de facto leader of the worldwide OA movement, contributes to this discussion for OA by providing his conceptual approach. Specifically, he "filters" the definitions of BOAI, BSOAI, and BDOAK for OA, and has titled it the BBB definition. It is worth mentioning that this definition removes the issue of permission and price impediments (Suber, 2012).

It is useful at this point to chart the conceptual development in these definitions of OA. The first one posited that OA means free access with no extra cost. The second one described further the main strategies that should be applied for publishing through OA. The third one responded to the technological evolution that created the Internet. It is the third definition that further the argument of the book about the utility of OARs. This definition is associated with the Internet, which comprises the digital environment, online databases and information resources that can be hosted from OARs. Most importantly, this definition sets the background of discussion concerning online publishing through OARs.

With this conceptualisation of OA, the next issue is about the potential ways to apply OA and is pursued in the following section.

Applications of Open Access Publishing

Apparently, there is nearly an unlimited range of options for research scholars to distribute their work and research outcomes using OA. These extend from setting up a personal Weblog (blog), to depositing an article in an OAR, to including it in a peer-reviewed OA journal or book (Brown, 2007). Puplett and Madjarevic argue that OAP grows the probability that academic research will be a top Google search hit for policymakers, journalists and NGOs who use the Internet to gather information towards the updating of their publishing policies (Puplett & Madjarevic, 2011).

OAP characterises the basic contemporary trend of publishing (Bjork, 2009; Björk & Solomon, 2012; Davis, Lewenstein, Simon, Booth, & Connolly, 2008). Many definitions exist for OAP and the associated advantages that characterise the level of access provided from the variety of options for OAP, e.g., green, gold and gratis or libre OA, which are considered in the next subsection (Dulong De Rosnay M., 2012; Jeffrey Silva, 2008; Sha Li Zhang, 2007). The literature reflects that OAP can be considered an efficient practice for publishing, and it lends additional support to the argumentation in this book (Herb, 2010). One of the advantages that stem from OAP concerns publication fees, as many OA journals do not charge such fees. For instance, many OA journals published by Australian universities have no additional publication fees to gain access. Given this, OAP as a practice seems to have gradually gained ground in the publishing industry and has become more attractive to academic institutions.

It is also important to recognise that someone's work includes several versions to be published online. It follows that the issue of post-printing should be considered in the context of advantages offered from OAP. The version that is sent to a journal or conference for review is called the submitted version or pre-print, whereas the accepted version or post-print is the final peer-reviewed version of the work sent to the publisher. Hence, this is the best version to be made freely accessible to affiliated or associated scholars through institution-based or university-based OARs, as such an option is offered based on the agreement between universities and commercial publishers (e.g., journal's subscription). Indeed, in contemporary times, most universities have relied on commercial publishers to publish their journals and other scholarly works (Frank, 2013). The issue of post-printing became part of the discussion for OAP because of the operation of OARs and their role in the examined agreement. In other words, OARs determine the tool to provide online access, and this perspective helps me argue that depositing in OARs is imperative for the scholarly communication and sharing of scientific information. Moreover, the idea that publicly funded research should be freely available to all manifests increasingly as the norm whereby the outcomes of these funding programs should be available free to the public.

In addition, there are advantages if the OAP authors' works become widely available. More people can be informed, educated, and consequently improve their qualifications and knowledge. From the author's perspective, it is more desirable to publish within OA, as it helps to spread personal views or research to a wider audience (Coonin, 2011). Thus, the readership or the audience is increased (Davis, 2011). Ultimately, an increased number of readers can convert into an increased number of citations for the author.

However, there are difficulties regarding access opportunities for researchers in developing countries, and this should be considered (Christian, 2008; North, 2007). The lack of access to subscription-based journals is a commonly cited problem for researchers in developing countries (Cockerill & Knols, 2008; Lewis, 2012). This lack of accessibility helps me argue that OARs can offer access opportunities to scientists in such countries to participate in the international research community and scientifically contribute to knowledge, with some OA journals even offering discounted or waived publication fees for papers from low-income countries. Additional incidental advantages include page limits not being so restricted for online journals and the possibility and relative ease of publishing further information. In addition, online journals provide more efficient alerting and search engine services, which obviate the need to scan journal content pages, while reference linking via Digital Object Identifiers (DOIs) leads to exploration and knowledge acquisition (Park, Zo, Ciganek, & Lim, 2011). Thus, it is reasonable to conclude that these are all good reasons for individuals and institutions to adopt OAP.

In the following section, two possibilities to put OA into practice are examined: (a) OARs and (b) Creative Commons.

Open Access Repositories

OARs are one of the means by which the OA movement is put into practice (Aguillo, Ortega, Fernández, & Utrilla, 2010; Harnad et al., 2004). Scholars argue that a repository constitutes space reserved for permanent or intermediate storage of content (Reitz, 2004; Vlieghe et al., 2006; Way, 2010). A digital repository is where digital content is stored and can be retrieved for later use (Armbruster & Romary, 2009; Cramer & Kott, 2010). There are various definitions of OARs. For example, OARs can be defined as online databases that make the full text of items they contain directly available without access limitations and extra costs (Creaser et al., 2010). Another definition of OARs is a collection of digital files or digital data produced and retained to support free access to information in an online format as a tool towards facilitating research and scholarship (Berquist, 2015). Similarly, Pinfield argues that an OAR is an online database on the Internet that provides free and instant access to the full text of its contents without any access restrictions (Pinfield et al., 2014). Thus, OA exists where there is free, immediate and unrestricted availability of content.

OARs may be institutionally based, enhancing the visibility and impact of the institution, or they may contain subject-based collections, as with the national subject repository of EconStor in Germany. Institutional repositories usually constitute digital compilations of the outputs produced from a university or a research centre, or another type of institution such as a university library (Cullen & Chawner, 2011).

Commercial publishers mainly use the gold OA option to share information that does not involve OARs. This option requires fees to be covered by authors to publish their works when they want their work to be accessed freely by end users. Even when publishers offer the green OA option (permission to authors to deposit their work in a university-based or institution-based repository), copyrights do not remain with the authors. It is argued that public institutions make genuine free access available, but commercial publishers do not act as such (Buchanan, 2014; Jaeger & Bertot, 2010). The commercial publishers provide the "label" or "brand" through their publishing models (Aaker & Biel, 2013). At the moment, OARs lack such labelling, and so individual academics still prefer to publish and spread their scientific work with the commercial publishers.

The literature also indicates that there are negative aspects of OARs that should be considered. One is related to their presence on the Web. Since OARs are an important instrument to access scholarly knowledge and gather scientific information online, their online presence is imperative; such presence should be indexed in two well-known search tools: Google and Google Scholar. The case of Latin American repositories and their low ratio of online visibility indicates a lack of correspondence between repository archives and data produced by the search engines mentioned above (Orduña-Malea & López-Cózar, 2015).

Scholars also argue about another drawback of OARs: that of the variable quality of deposited archives and insecurity over their long-term viability. A 2012 study illustrates that scholars are concerned about the potential for confusion caused by different versions of the same archive being disseminated. Given this, scholars would feel that OARs add to increasing fragmentation in the literature (Nicholas, Rowlands, Watkinson, Brown, & Jamali, 2012).

Despite these drawbacks, other works help me to argue that OARs determine the future of information dissemination. Fuchs and Sandoval argue about the future of academia (Fuchs & Sandoval, 2013). They claim that the publishing world should take non-commercial, non-profit OA seriously, as it constitutes a tool to foster public service and a commons perspective. This statement helps me to argue that OARs can establish such an academic publishing model to make scientific knowledge a common good. In addition, practice and associated strategies of OA (e.g., green, gold, gratis, and libre OA) should be further considered. A brief discussion of these levels of OA follows below.

Green, Gold, Gratis, and Libre Open Access: Different Levels of Access

Suber's definition of OA, titled the Budapest–Bethesda–Berlin (BBB) definition, which was examined in the first section of this chapter and "filters" the definitions of BOAI, BSOAI, and BDOAK for OA and removes the issue of permission and price impediments, is quite inclusive and helps us understand that there are various types of OAP. From this perspective, four categories of OAP have been recognised by the literature: green, gold, gratis, and libre. The OAP options rely on the delivery instrument of the articles. The distinction in such delivery instruments of OA research outputs relates to the qualifiers, green and gold, indicating whether the work is available as OA within a repository (green) or a journal (gold).

The first differentiation between green and gold OA was proposed more than a decade ago (Gargouri, Larivière, Gingras, Carr, & Harnad, 2012). It should be noted that OASPA argues:

Gold open access refers to implementing the free and open dissemination of original scholarship by publishers, as opposed to green open access, in which free and open dissemination is achieved by archiving and making freely available copies of scholarly publications that may or may not have been previously published (Open Access Scholarly Publishers Association, 2016).

Other conditions applied concerning access limitations, such as price and permission for reuse, are specified from the terms gratis and libre. The distinction has been made by Suber, who borrowed these terms from software language. In contrast to the gold or green distinction, which answers the question about how content is delivered, the gratis and libre distinction answers the question about how open the content is. A gratis OA publication is free of price barriers; the publication is openly available, free of charge. The business models for achieving these results are various, including the most common system whereby publishers charge the author a fee to "free" the work. A publication is considered libre if price barriers are removed and at least some permissions barriers are also relaxed. Therefore, in the libre OA scenario, the content is also free of some copyright restrictions.

Green or Gold?

The issue of adopting either green or gold OA is a matter of intense debate throughout scholarly communities around the world. Scholars argue about what is imperative for green OA to be mandated by research funders and institutions so that the self-archiving of published, peer-reviewed journal articles (e.g., green OA) can lead towards full OA (Harnad, 2005).

Another notable scholar in the field of OA, Stevan Harnad, argues about the important differentiation between OA options that should be considered (Harnad, 2010). It follows that the most frequent misunderstanding about OA is that when there is a discussion about OA, it seems that gold OA is solely addressed. He also claims that the fastest way to share information through OA is the green OA or self-archiving, for two significant reasons: (a) providing green OA is entirely in the interests of the providers of the research itself—the global research community—and (b) green OA can be mandated, whereas gold OA is in commercial publishers' interests. The green OA should be the core, fundamental component of policies adapted by institutions as well as funders, worldwide. Therefore, it could be a sustainable instrument to attain universal OA when green OA is institutionally mandated and to extend knowledge assets further.

In addition, another study focused on extending current knowledge about green OA (Laakso & Björk, 2012). Typically, green OA copies become available after considerable time delays, partly caused by publisher-imposed embargo periods and partly by author tendencies to archive manuscripts only periodically (Harnad & Brody, 2004). Although green OA copies should ideally be archived in OARs, many are stored on home pages and similar locations, with no assurance of long-term maintenance. The technical foundation for green OA uploading is becoming increasingly sophisticated, largely due to the rapid increase in the number of OARs (Björk, Laakso, Welling, & Paetau, 2014).

Other scholars argue that each pathway of OA corresponds to a phase in the movement towards OA. In other words, the mere fact of self-archiving is not enough, as providing some "branding" or "labelling" ability to OARs is needed. In the following section, there is discussion about a potential collaboration between institutions that host OARs and publishers to balance relevant and competing interests. The OA policies applied by a publisher are analyzed below.

Implementation of Open Access: The Case Study of Emerald Publishing Group

Emerald's objective is to secure the widest possible distribution of research and future innovation in scholarly communication. Most importantly, it is argued that through the OA approach, Emerald seeks to respond to the needs of researchers in the disciplines served. In a recent interview, Tony Roche, the Publishing Director of Emerald, argues that Emerald's approach to OA and its efforts to work closely with academia serve to balance the requirements and rights of authors, funders and policymakers with the sustainability and growth of titles.

The key features that constitute Emerald's OA policy and associated options of either green or gold access that they offer are as follows. In terms of archiving, Emerald is fully RoMEO green across all its journal titles. In accordance with RoMEO policy, authors can archive pre-print, post-print or publisher PDFs. Based on Emerald's OA policy, the author's right to voluntarily self-archive their works without payment or embargo is also provided. However, the Emerald group recently (10 July 2015) announced the launch of its green OA trial, Zero Embargo, applicable to all mandated articles submitted to the company's library and information science (LIS) journals and selected information and knowledge management journals. This shift allows authors to deposit the post-print version of the article into their respective OAR immediately upon official publication (Poynder, 2013). Therefore, I suggest that this action could be considered a checkpoint or initial point on behalf of the publishers to disseminate additional information with informal cooperation with OARs.

Further, Emerald's OA policy shows that if an author has adequate financial resources to meet an article processing charge (APC), Emerald can publish his/her article via the gold OA option under a CC BY license. This last element of Emerald's OA policy illustrates the importance of OARs. In cases where authors are commissioned to make their work available as OA work but have no financial resources to cover an APC, it is possible for them to deposit the accepted manuscript of their article into a subject or institutional repository and the author's funder's research catalogue, subject to embargo periods. This part of Emerald's OA policy shows that self-archiving, also known as green OA, can be an alternative option for OAP. Particularly, this example illustrates that commercial publishers have started adopting the use of OARs as part of their OA policy concerning accepted manuscripts.

While commercial publishers are intent on charging the authors, another mechanism of providing wider access to knowledge is the system of storage known as Creative Commons, discussed next.

Creative Commons

Creative Commons is a non-profit organisation in the US devoted to expanding the range of creative works available for others to build upon legally and to share. The organisation has released several copyright licenses that establish the renowned Creative Commons licensing system that can be applied with no extra cost (Fitzgerald, 2007). In addition, this licensing regime allows creators to communicate which rights they reserve and which rights they waive for the benefit of the recipients or other creators (Aliprandi, 2010). Creative Commons licensing provides authors and creators of copyright works with an option for free, downloadable licenses that can easily be attached to their works (Alecu, 2012). The Creative Commons licensing system has played a significant role in terms of production and dissemination of creative works. Its rapid development established a set of legal instruments to facilitate the open licensing of copyrighted works, which also determines one of the most important instances regarding production and dissemination of culture (Zuiderwijk & Janssen, 2014).

All Creative Commons licenses require that someone who uses another's work in any way should give him or her credit in the way he/she requests. From a practical perspective, when a Creative Commons license is applicable, it means that the work is accessible and can be viewed, copied or distributed according to the terms provided by the copyright owner and such use of the work does not infringe copyright.

Thus, the Creative Commons licensing framework provides additional support to OA in the public interest, as authors can share copyright-protected works (Dusollier, 2006). The adoption of the Creative Commons licenses on behalf of the National Library of New Zealand shows that this new licensing system can work beneficially in the public interest (Carnaby, 2008; Douglas, 2016). Specifically, the growth of Creative Commons Aotearoa licenses in New Zealand in 2006 was a means to share with local people the rationale and scope of Creative Commons licensing and how beneficial it can be to the public interest, and spreading the notion of New Zealand's intellectual and cultural property law for digital content creators. It is worth noting the associated benefits and prospects for local end users concerning access to information that the National Library of New Zealand generated after such application. The Association of Public Library Managers released a report in 2016 that shows that the Aotearoa licensing platform has become one of the main objectives for this association (Associaton of Public Library Managers, 2016). The report illustrates that this licensing platform will provide equitable access to public libraries that enhance New Zealand's communities. Further, the Aotearoa licenses will benefit the development of consistently excellent public library services.

However, the discussion below shows that copyright infringement may occur under specific circumstances, even though a Creative Commons license is applicable (Katz, 2006). There are several drawbacks to Creative Commons licensing frameworks that should be examined. For example, Lawrence Lessig, a noted scholar in this field and one of the founders of the Creative Commons licenses, is concerned about how the commercial interests are taking precedence. He considers that the Creative Commons licensing system as presently practised tends to become a permission culture—with drawbacks (Mayer-Schonberger, 2008). From a practical perspective, adopting a Creative

Commons license means that a copyright owner authorises anyone who has access to the work to use it in ways that would otherwise be prohibited by copyright law, such as copying or distributing the work.

Another drawback for Creative Commons concerns copyright protection and stems from online publishing photos attached with a Creative Commons license. For example, by applying the Creative Commons Non-Commercial license to a photo uploaded on a social network site (e.g., Facebook, LinkedIn or Instagram), whoever has access to this photo is entitled to copy, distribute, display, perform, modify and use it for any purpose other than a commercial purpose. Only when permission is granted by the author of the photo for commercial purposes can it be used accordingly. Given this, someone who has already downloaded the photo is able to modify and use it for commercial purposes, yet this does not comply with terms and conditions of the Creative Commons license. Nevertheless, this scenario helps me argue that it can happen.

Another drawback concerning the Creative Commons licensing system is the increasing variety of Creative Commons licenses that are being created. This profusion may provoke user confusion. This profusion of licenses occurs as licensors struggle to determine what may be the best-suited license for their needs, while at the same time the licensees fail to understand the obligations and rights attached to a copyrighted work. What is more, Creative Commons licenses cannot be revoked. According to the fine print on the Creative Commons website, Creative Commons licenses are irrevocable once they have been applied to a work. That means that authors should be certain about their willingness to publicly provide OA to their work.

The discussion above shows that the Creative Commons licensing system, while offering a variety of advantages (e.g., ease of access and the capacity to accommodate educational use of creative works), comes with potential drawbacks. In comparison, OARs might be better suited in terms of ensuring copyright protection and reducing these drawbacks through their operational framework.

The example of the UK higher education institutions' practices in implementing OA policies through associated OARs shows that their governance and regulatory regime address important issues that can remedy the drawbacks of Creative Commons. Picarra explains that the areas of the OA policy applied in the examined institutions refer to whether or not the policy is to be mandatory and whether the policy stipulates how OA should be provided (through an OAR or by publication in OA journals); where repository-based

OA is concerned, OA policy concerns in which repository (or repositories) items may be deposited, the length of permitted embargoes, whether there are to be sanctions in the case of non-compliance and whether there are to be any particular requirements regarding licensing, including whether authors should retain certain rights over their work (Picarra, 2015). In practice, this means retaining the right to make the work OA by depositing it in an OAR. The OA policy that characterises the OARs in the UK higher education institutions helps me argue that the regulatory framework implemented in OARs can be more efficient and adequate compared with the licensing framework provided by Creative Commons.

This is because of the existence of regulations about reuse that secure owners' copyrights. For example, various university-based OARs have already applied OA mandates for sharing the scientific information (articles, reports, dissertations, theses, research papers, etc.) they host. In this case, a scholar deposits his or her work in a university-based OAR while retaining copyright. In the previous chapter, there was a discussion about the example of how the Ionian University organises its OAR. Those who deposit their works in that OAR retain copyright over the work; in that way, the protection provided by the OAR is in line with article 3(3) of the Greek Copyright Act. This helps us to argue that there is scope for further refining the balance between providing wider access and protecting the interests of authors and publishers.

OARs can play a crucial role as the connecting link among these actors towards broadening information access in the public interest. Given this, another option for OARs can be through a "just" green agreement. Here, the term *just* refers to fairness and stems from the main exceptions to copyright infringement in Australia under the general heading of fair dealing in the Australian Copyright Act. Green refers to green OA where works are deposited in an institution-based or university-based OAR, and agreement refers to the fact that in any OAR there would be more than two actors involved of whom all agree to the terms of use. For example, an agreement between the university research centres, university libraries or authors and these institutions, or between publishers and authors or OARs, all involve more than two actors.

OARs are conceptually desirable, but the issue is that it is mostly the universities and other public institutions that use them. In this, they come up against the dominance of the commercial publishers and the prestige still attached to conventional publishing. Commercial publishers have migrated online but have created various avenues to protect their revenue streams. It follows consideration of the tensions in scientific and other academic scholarship pursuing not-for-profit publishing and relying on commercial publishers.

THE NEW TECHNOLOGICAL ENVIRONMENT: IMPLICATIONS FOR PUBLISHING

Academic Scholarly Publishing: Non-Profit Ventures

The concept of academic scholarly publishing refers to a means of communication and broad dissemination of knowledge. Academic publishing is a non-profit activity that is increasingly being carried out with a reliance on commercial publishers. In contemporary times, such publishing has introduced a complex set of interests that need to be protected; that is, author autonomy, author copyrights and publisher profit margins. In the literature (Harley, Acord, Earl-Novell, Lawrence, & King, 2010; Sompel, Payette, Erickson, Lagoze, & Warner, 2004; Xia, 2010), it is reflected that the following actors are involved in the academic scholarly publishing process: (a) research scholars and authors (university libraries, colleges, university research offices or departments, and research centres that mainly cover expenses associated with required journal subscription fees) and (b) publishers. For scholars and authors, the issue of visibility is imperative and constitutes their non-profit interest, which is to share their views and research outcomes. The move to commercial publishers is partly explainable as stemming from the academic institutions' need to ensure that the publishing standard is acceptable and that these works are disseminated as widely as possible. Therefore, academic institutions have moved towards using commercial publishers.

Thus, information published online modifies the environment of academic scholarly publishing; therefore, it is critical for the universities to develop the full range of their resources towards a better service to public interest (Bauer, Jensen, Bentley, & Kyvik, 2011; Ginns, Kitay, & Prosser, 2010; Griffiths & Brophy, 2005). Leitner argues that research scholars and students determine a university's most important resources and their relations and organisational routines; their most important output is knowledge (Leitner, 2004). It is also argued that such resources can be interpreted as intellectual capital (Alexander Serenko, Nick Bontis, Lorne Booker, Khaled Sadeddin,

& Timothy Hardie, 2010). Hence, a revised engagement with publishing determined by technological advancements could lead universities to realise the potential impact of their academic curriculums and to improve the reputation of their research institutions and relevant scientific outcomes (López, 2010; Shapley, Sheehan, Maloney, & Caranikas-Walker, 2010; Vreeburg Izzo, Yurick, Nagaraja, & Novak, 2010). Given this, evidently, there is a need to reshape universities' role in the context of academic scholarly publishing by improving their resources in a broader sense.

The practice in the recent past has been for higher education institutions to hand over the publishing of their in-house journals to commercial publishers. Therefore, it is the commercial publishers who are now the target of the argument that OARs are desirable. There are arguments for and against the responsibilities of commercial publishers, briefly examined in the discussion below. The discussion begins with a brief overview of commercial publishers' aim to generate high returns while abandoning the pursuit of knowledge. There are plausible reasons why academic scholarly publishing requires the contribution of commercial publishers. Therefore, the real issue is how to strike a balance between competing interests so that maximum access to knowledge can be created while preserving commercial interests.

Commercial Publishers Aim for High Returns While the Pursuit of Knowledge Has Been Abandoned

Commercial publishers are in the business of making a profit. They are not expected to pursue the aims of education or the wider dissemination of knowledge. Their business model is focused on profits, which distinguishes such business models (Teece, 2010). Their primary responsibility, as for-profit corporations, is connected with financial performance (Levinthal & Wu, 2010). In other words, they operate on a for-profit basis, and their major incentive is to maintain or increase profit margins (Van Noorden, 2013). Hence, their directors are legally required to act in the interests of the corporation rather than those of customers or the broader academic world (Taylor, 2012). It is this imperative that partially explains the gradual increase in the prices of academic commercial publications over time.

There are a variety of reasons for price increases (McGuigan & Russell, 2008). In a letter addressed to librarians posted on Elsevier's website, the steady price increases are justified on the basis of an increase in articles per issue, the increase of electronic use and the increased associated expenses with sustaining their digital infrastructure (Elsevier, 2016). However, on Elsevier's website, one of its position statements paradoxically claims that Elsevier publishing house is committed to making their written submissions and evidence open and transparent for everyone to read (Elsevier, 2017). Woll argues that for-profit publishing constitutes a substantial way to develop a business (Woll, 2010). That said, it is also the case that these publishers gain by their association with academic publishing. Commercial publishers stand to gain by engaging in academic publishing at various levels.

Commercial publishers benefit by the fact that the works published by academic authors differ in many respects from those created by other writers. For example, even though research scholars and authors through the elaboration of their work provide scientific information, they do not anticipate being paid by the commercial publishers. What is more, research scholars' and authors' engagement include editing and drafting; as a result, the work is delivered almost ready to be published. Publishers gain further "profits" as they are relieved from such work. This kind of collaboration between authors and publishers in academic publishing is unique and benefits the publishers (Miller & Harris, 2004; Nyquist, 2010).

The academic scholarly publishing industry includes production, review, packaging and distribution of information in multiple formats for use mainly by academic and scientific consumers (Van Orsdel & Born, 2009). A notable trend in recent times is that of commercial publishers now handling such publishing. The academic scholarly community discovered that partnerships with commercial publishers of high reputation are desirable, since it absolves the academic institutions of the associated expenses and administrative issues associated with the publishing process.

However, in taking charge of many scientific publications previously controlled by the non-profit academic scholarly community, the commercial publishers are pursuing a different set of values (Gendron, 2015; Larivière, Haustein, & Mongeon, 2015; Shinn & Lamy, 2006). Edwards and Shulenburger claim that "[t]he commercial publishers, which recognized the relative inelasticity of both supply and demand, acquired top-quality journals, and then dramatically raised prices, expecting that they would lose relatively little of the market" (Edwards & Shulenburger, 2010). In fact, such expectations were realised. Commercial publishers entered the market to increase their business profits; at the same time, academia has become reliant on them.

Publishers maintain a high profit margin, while academic libraries function under increasing financial duress (Abel, 2002). It is also argued that university libraries cannot cover the subscription prices for scholarly journals (de Camargo, 2014). Given this, university libraries confront a crisis that has continued for many years, revealing a commercial publishing framework that, as a business model for publishing, does not support sharing scientific information. Therefore, the issue is how best to balance the interests of various stakeholders; this discussion follows below.

Academic Scholarly Publishing Requires the Contribution of Commercial Publishers

It is evident that the collaboration between universities and publishers can be problematic, since research scholars and authors increasingly cannot publish without access to the journals controlled by for-profit publishers. As mentioned before, the academic community "offers" publishing control to publishers, as nowadays they are the gatekeepers to scholarly and scientific information. Hence, it is not practical for research scholars and authors to deny publishing under a publisher's terms. Although commercial publishers cover publishing costs, they do not give the rights of reproduction or dissemination to authors. Hence, sharing of information requires a closer collaboration between academics and commercial publishers.

Publishers may be interested in engaging with OARs because they need the business of academic publishing, they have a CSR and the moral basis of IP rights has always been sharing at an optimum level. Yet the literature indicates that publishers are not that interested in engaging with OARs to publish (Graf et al., 2007). However, if their profits could be safeguarded, it would be an incentive and generate interest in the adoption of OARs as part of their publishing policies. One such option could be self-archiving. Self-archiving, also known as green OA, refers to depositing in institution-based or university-based OARs. Such OARs can play the role of intermediator for publishing; thus, OARs could be considered as a tool to enhance collaboration and agreements between publishers and academia.

Arguments for CSR are usually similarly aligned with the rationale that it is in a business's long-term self-interest to be socially responsible (Di Giuli & Kostovetsky, 2014; Epstein & Buhovac, 2014; Moon, 2014). This statement helps us argue that if publishing businesses are to enjoy a healthy climate in which to function in the future, they should consider ensuring their long-term viability through relevant actions (A. B. Carroll & Shabana, 2010). Commercial publishers should act as such, as the future of science and publishing is attached to OA. Recently in 2016, the European Competitiveness Council, during a two-day meeting in Brussels, issued a communication based on which the new objective for Europe is to provide full OA to scientific papers by 2020 (European Commission, 2016).

The example of the OAR of the University of Trento in Italy shows the potential that stems from the active role of its research office for the university-based OAR, which has been operating since 2008. Based on its OA mandate policy, those who deposit their work in the university's OAR (students, academics and research scholars) retain copyright. This work includes research papers, unpublished work, doctoral theses and postgraduate dissertations. Pre-print versions of scientific works approved for publication can also be included, though with an embargo of 12 months. That means that 12 months after official publication in the journal, the OAR can share the work. Such construction helps me argue that incentives are offered to local academia to spread its scientific outcomes and research, and affiliated authors/scholars who deposit their work in this OAR can share it with no extra cost. This example, in conjunction with the examined communication above, shows the importance of OARs' functions concerning publishing and sharing of information and helps me to argue that publishers should reconsider modifying their publishing models.

Concentrating on the potential financial impact on academic journals, there are several possible ways in which the function of OARs influences commercial publishers' primary objective of profit (Ghosh & Kumar Das, 2007). Free access to the final written version of a submitted article could provoke a reduction in demand for subscribed access (Chan, 2004). In other words, if the option to avoid extra expenses is available, it is a great incentive for those interested in freely accessing desired articles. Such option is offered by OARs, as an OA mechanism fulfils and establishes further dissemination of information.

According to the outcomes of an empirical study conducted during the undersigned author's Erasmus research visit in Italy (November 2016 to April 2017), OARs could bring together universities to serve the public interest. This is illustrated from three Italian university consortia (CASPUR,[1] CINECA,[2] and CILEA[3]) that have worked, since 2008, on the project titled PLEIADI. [4] This project aims to build a national platform that offers centralised OA to the scholarly literature archived in Italian university-based repositories (such as dissertations, research papers and theses). These consortia initiated the merging process on 1 September 2012 by the Italian Ministry of Education, University and Research. Considering the European recommendation of 2012, the Italian Government introduced OA practice after a year, with a new Regulation (112/2013) on OA to publicly fund research findings (European Commission, 2012, p. 17). Such influence from the European Commission's actions was examined in a previous chapter, as Greece introduced such regulations in 2014. This process shows a very significant change, because it allows these three consortia under their mutual objective—to support research and technological innovation in Italy—to finally work together and share their experience to improve/ameliorate the needs of the national academic framework.

The OAR of the University of Trento, examined earlier, shows the important contribution of a university-based OAR. According to its OA policy for depositing research, authors retain copyrights while their work is freely available to readers (M. W. Carroll, 2013). This example helps us argue that universities that host OARs can boost/generate discussion along these lines, especially regarding the role of OARs towards new norms of publishing and sharing of information in the public interest.

CONCLUSION

Commercial Publishers and Open Access Publishers

In conclusion, there are a few reasons why commercial publishers could be expected to adopt the philosophy and practice of OAP and participate in the creation of OARS. It is understandable that the commercial publishers need to make a profit, though as responsible actors, they are equally required to pursue CSR.

Profits, Ideas, and Intellectual Property Rights

Commercial publishers' business models are designed to maximise profits; therefore, it is in their interest to keep increasing their capacity to secure publishing rights for the greatest number of books and at the lowest possible cost. This indicates the necessity of a crucial transition in publisher practices in the digital age and introduces a hope for the future of the e-book industry (Herther, 2005; House, 2013; Shelburne, 2009). Yet, another reason why commercial publishers should adapt to the changing world is that they face real competition from self-publishers. An obvious advantage of online publishing is the one associated with self-publishing (Greco, 2013). In the traditional modes of publishing associated with the earlier age of printing, self-publishing was not a viable option. However, with the digital technology advances and the associated online revolution, authors currently have incentives and the potential to gain profits by entering the world of authorship (Beecroft, 2010; Koppel & Schler, 2004; Perianes-Rodríguez, Olmeda-Gómez, & Moya-Anegón, 2010). Therefore, self-interest also suggests that commercial publishers should move in the direction of greater OA to their publications.

Of course, a stronger argument for such a move can be made on moral grounds, in that OA is more beneficial for everyone. Willinksy argues that the beneficial aspect of online publishing constitutes an improvement for publishing towards information dissemination. He claims that "[E]lectronic journals offer readers a particular ease of access. They can readily work across different journals, find exactly where certain ideas are being discussed, or move readily from citation to source" (Willinsky, 2003). Thus, OA determines a factor that could greatly influence publishing practices, especially in the context of online publishing that characterises modern times.

In the third chapter, it was established that the technical know-how of printing and the rise of commercial publishers played a crucial role in the past concerning information dissemination, which empowered end users and improved their knowledge assets. This same imperative exists in the digital age and helps me to argue that the role of commercial publishers should be to become more active in creating OA.

It is appropriate here to briefly recapitulate the central tension between the freedom to engage in ideas and knowledge and the desire to encourage investment in creativity that lies at the heart of IP. The original impetus for IPRs reflects that the object of IP laws is ideas (Bently & Sherman, 2014). By nature, ideas are free (Husserl, 2012). They are more naturally free than individuals or persons, since they can be publicly released with no restrictions. Ang argues that ideas are restricted by regulations that are enforced by persons to enhance their use (Ang, 2013). Following this statement, IPRs demonstrate the framework for the potection of ideas (David & Halbert, 2015;

Granstrand & Holgersson, 2015; Manhart & Thalmann, 2015). That is, IPRs provide ownership rights to individuals while excluding others from the use of these ideas (Thumm, 2013). Peter Menell argues that IP constitutes the product of original thought, which is generally characterised as non-physical property (Menell, 2011). Thus, many thinkers accept that copyright protection encourages creation (Bubela, FitzGerald, & Gold, 2012). A significant example that illustrates this can be observed in the biopharmaceutical industry (Bhardwaj et al., 2011). Drug research and growth leads to the discovery of tomorrow's new life-changing and life-saving medicines. Biopharmaceutical IP protection proides the incentives that spur relevant research and growth (Glasgow, 2002).

However, it is also true that IPRs have to change in step with technology, and in the present context the technology of publishing. There are also proponents who argue that IPRs are always changing, and technological evolution has enhanced the need for change (Dutfield, 2009). For example, such instances of change can be observed in relation to digitised products. IP protection in such products is complex, for several reasons: (a) the nature of these products is ambiguous, (b) error-free and cheap digital copying separates content and medium economically, (c) the Internet's high monitoring potential and (d) network effects of some information products (Mueller, 2003). Therefore, it is to be expected that the commercial publishers will adapt their practices. A brief sketch of how the commercial publishers have collaborated to adopt OA follows.

The International Perspectives: Further Advocacy on OARs

The Confederation of Open Access Repositories

The Confederation of Open Access Repositories (COAR) is an international association with over 100 members and partners from around the world representing diverse perspectives of libraries, universities, research institutions, government funders and others. The COAR brings together the repository community and major repository networks in order to build capacity, align policies and practices, and act as a global voice for the repository community.

In addition, a major strategic priority for COAR is to align repository networks in order to create a seamless global repository network and demonstrate that repositories offer a viable solution for open access. In 2014,

COAR lunched a major initiative to further aligning practices globally, making their collections more valuable as it enables new services to be built on top of their aggregated contents. The activities target three levels of engagement: (a) strategic, (b) technical and semantic interoperability, and (c) services.

It should be mentioned that over 1600 individuals and organizations from 52 countries around the world signed the COAR's statement (released since 20 May 2015). The statement denounces Elsevier's recently introduced policy that impedes sharing and open access to information (Bolick, 2017). Particularly, this statement urges Elsevier to reconsider its publishing policy that does not advance sharing. In fact, the COAR statement goes as far as to declare that Elsevier's policy imposes unacceptably long embargo periods of up to 48 months.

COAR has also issued a joint statement with UNESCO about open access, which was recently published (9 May 2016). The statement focuses on policymakers and highlights the need for further implementation of OA around the world (Friesike et al., 2016). This statement shows the benefits and importance that stem from networking between global actors who support open access in a more official manner. Scholars claim that open access becomes more widespread thus OARs play an increasingly crucial role in the ecosystem, acting as the foundation for a distributed, globally networked infrastructure for scholarly communication (McCutcheon, Nixon, & De Castro, 2014). Hence, OARs are gaining ground in international discussions as a means of scholarly communication. In turn, such instances indicate that international players can establish efficient networks for the transmission and further dissemination of scholarly information.

The Emergence of First Collaboration Among Publishers: The Open Access Scholarly Publishers Association

Although OAP first emerged as a new publishing model that was regarded as experimental, today it is a mainstream approach for disseminating scientific developments or other original works. In an otherwise highly competitive publishing market, OAPs find it useful to be open and frank about their business models, experiences and plans. Specifically, groups of OAPs initiated discussions on the potential of creating a more formal partnership that would support OA as an emerging model for publishing. They recognised the value of bringing the community together to develop appropriate business models, tools and standards to support OA journals.

These discussions brought upon initiatives that led to the formation of OASPA. OASPA is a trade association established in 2008 to represent the interests of OA journals and book publishers worldwide in all scientific, technical and scholarly disciplines. Its mission is to disseminate knowledge by sharing information, setting standards, and aiding, educating and promoting innovation. The OASPA blog is designed to serve as a critical forum for communicating crucial issues in relation to OAPs, and it frequently presents posts from guest authors. Willinsky claims there have also been significant shifts in relation to modern publishing practices from 2004 onwards. He argues that:

[T]he major corporate publishers of academic journals . . . had to blink in the midst of all the attention being paid to "free" journals and access to knowledge . . . In May 2004, Reed Elsevier, the largest of them . . . changed its policies on its authors' rights (Willinsky, 2006, p. 4).

The examined association indicates that the scholarly publishing industry is subject to a great shift because of continuous technological growth. This technological growth urged a transition of the publishing industry from printed abstracting services to online databases (Oppenheim, 2008). In addition, such growth introduced a major issue into the academic and research community in terms of scholarly communication (Rocco & Hatcher, 2011; Yiotis, 2005). As was demonstrated in Chapter Two, copyright issues emerged from this technological growth. Thus, the main requirments for copyright protection for innovation to continue should also employ moral views (Sweet & Eterovic Maggio, 2015). In this context, the relationship between authors and publishers is crucial for innovations to continue/resume and was considered in this chapter. Therefore, mutual respect between them is required, which in turn forms a moral basis for copyright protection (Austin & Seitanidi, 2012). Merges' ideas show that IPRs have a future, as they are one way of creating mutual respect between authors and publishers (Merges, 2011).

Another issue to be considered is the ethical terminology utilised in contemporary international conventions. The negotiators at the Uruguay round of the GATT found it appropriate to formulate some of the TRIPS Agreement's vital provisions concerning its ethical perspective. Article 7 of the GATT refers to "the mutual advantage of producers and users of technological knowledge and in a manner conducive to social and economic welfare" to ameliorate the "balance of rights and obligations." The words "mutual advantage" and "balance of rights and obligations" shows the importance of the moral perspective that nowadays should be enclosed/attached to the discussion about IP protection.

One of the functions of academic publishing is for reputed publishers to help maintain academic standards, as they act as the gatekeepers of what is published. However, in the digital age when anyone can publish, the problem is that there is very little, if any, agreement on the standards, and there are difficulties in finding ways to enforce such standards.

There have been efforts in this regard, as illustrated by the existence of a great body of bibliographical resources regarding publication ethics (Sismondo & Doucet, 2010; Wallace & Siersema, 2015). Many organisations are also engaged in creating and implementing relevant guidelines relating to the enforcement of these standards. One such multinational organisation is the Committee on Publication Ethics (COPE), which plays a fundamental role in regulating the relations between authors and publishers. It also endeavours to define best practices in the ethics of scholarly publishing and to assist authors, editorial board members, owners of journals and publishers to achieve this. COPE released a code of conduct in 2004 that determines a response to continuous technological evolution and new ways to share and exchange information based on ethical standards for publishing.

The earlier discussion in this chapter demonstrated that cooperation between publishers and institutions that host OARs and implement OA policy is required. Both parties (publishers and institutions) should collaborate to improve the governance framework of OARs and broaden access opportunities to balance competing interests. Therefore, these parties should generate such regulations and embrace social responsibility as part of their potential cooperation. Thus, the issue of CSR emerges and is considered next.

Corporate Social Responsibility as the Basis for Adoption of Open Access Repositories

Based on a global CSR study by Cone Communications, citizens have a desire to address social issues and consider companies as partners in progress. Most importantly, a key finding shows that 91% expect companies to accomplish more than a profit, thus responsibly addressing social issues. Hence, a cooperation between commercial publishing companies and institutions should be characterised as such. Therefore, CSR can work as additional support on OARs' governance framework to broaden access opportunities.

Therefore, a significant reason why commercial publisher could be expected to participate in OARs is that it would be compatible with their CSRs. The concept of CSR has continued to grow in importance (Matten & Moon, 2008). It has been the subject of considerable discussion, theory building, and research (Deng, Kang, & Low, 2013; Flammer, 2013; Khan, Muttakin, & Siddiqui, 2013). Despite the continuous deliberations regarding its conceptualisation, CSR has developed in academic communities worldwide (Babor & Robaina, 2012; Cho, Lee, & Pfeiffer Jr., 2013). The notion that business corporations, such as commercial publishers, have some responsibilities to society beyond making profits for shareholders has been discussed at length (Crane, Matten, & Spence, 2013; Erhemjamts, Li, & Venkateswaran, 2013).

CSR has also become a research priority in public relations, having been considered one of the key aspects of that field for decades (Lindgreen & Swaen, 2010). Several studies have shown the importance of the Internet and of corporate websites as public relations tools and the growing relevance of corporate websites for communicating approaches to corporate responsibility. CSR can provide an appropriate framework for efficient and broader consensus between publishers and institutions (such as research institutes, research centres, university libraries, university research offices and collective management organisations [CMOs]). Therefore, the operation of OARs could establish a means with the potential for beneficial collaboration between publishers and institutions.

Companies engage in CSR activities because they consider that competitive advantage arises from them (Cheng, Ioannou, & Serafeim, 2014). It is argued that resource-based perspectives are useful to recognise the reasoning about companies' engagement in CSR activities. From a resource-based perspective, CSR provides internal or external benefits, or both. Investments in socially responsible activities may have internal benefits by helping a company develop new resources and capabilities related to know-how and corporate culture.

It is generally agreed that companies need to manage relationships with their stakeholders, but the way in which they choose to do so varies substantially. Thus, when publishing companies want to communicate with stakeholders about their CSR initiatives (for the purposes of the argument of the monograph, stakeholders means either institutions or universities that host OARs), they need to involve them in a two-way communication process, defined as an ongoing iterative sense-giving and sense-making process as part of good governance for an OARs regime.

Based on empirical illustrations and prior research, it is argued that managers need to move from informing and responding to "involving" stakeholders in CSR communication. Thus, a "just" green agreement between publihers and stakeholders interested in disseminating scientific information (e.g., research institutes, research centres, university libraries, university research offices and collective managements orgaisations). In addition, there are scholars who argue that managers need to expand the role of stakeholders in CSR communication processes if they want to improve their efforts to build legitimacy, a positive reputation and lasting stakeholder relationships (Aguinis & Glavas, 2012).

Finally, it is worth reminding ourselves that our needs for distributing information and communicating research outcomes have shifted dramatically due to constant technological growth and the rapid expansion of the Internet. As it has been illustrated, one of the distinctive responses to technological developments is the concept of OA. Specifically, in the context of digital publishing, OARs provide the possibility of adequately responding to the needs of all the stakeholders in academic publishing. As argued above, an appropriate standard of OA can be a "just" green agreement. In other words, a standard of the OA practice that could be used as an alternative business model.

The discussion in this monograph commenced by posing five sub-questions to substantiate the argument that OARs could be considered as a mechanism that provides balance among authors, publishers, and users of published works interests. In the first chapter, the development of the right to property and how the justifications moved from ownership of land and material things to ownership of ideas was traced. This was the origin of the rights of IP and copyright. The availability of legal protection for creative efforts is the central issue that has informed the discussion in this monograph. Copyright protection was originally designed to facilitate creativity but also to enhance the dissemination of knowledge, especially after the invention of the printing press, and has served us well until recently. However, things changed with the arrival of the digital revolution and the phenomenon of the Internet. Digital and online publishing has created new possibilities for authors and end users to publish online with relative ease. At the same time, the protection of intellectual endeavours is made difficult if not impossible. In response to this central issue, it could be argued that the widest OA to knowledge is in the best interests of a fair or just global society.

In the following chapter, the progress of argumentation constructed with the support of various theorists that a just society requires the widest possible access to knowledge by all sections of humanity. Therefore, the phenomenon of OA to knowledge and how it has given rise to OAP was examined. However, the ease of publishing online has also created the difficulty of enforcing the copyright interests of the creators or publishers. There is a necessity to balance interests of authors, publishers and users of published works; to determine what would be a suitable regulatory model, in the following two chapters the international regime of the European Union and compared it with the regulatory regime of Greece were considered. In the context of this information, in the final chapter, there was a discussion about the possibility of commercial publishers joining the OA movement. Such discussion helped us argue that the commercial publishers and public institutions (such as university libraries) have the potential to collaborate towards the creation of OARs. These OARs should be regulated in a systematic manner, as a means of creating a just society that makes knowledge accessible for the widest sections of the globe.

REFERENCES

Aaker, D. A., & Biel, A. (2013). *Brand equity & advertising: advertising's role in building strong brands*. Psychology Press. doi:10.4324/9781315799537

Abel, R. E. (2002). *Scholarly publishing: Books, journals, publishers, and libraries in the twentieth century*. John Wiley & Sons, Inc.

Aguillo, I., Ortega, J., Fernández, M., & Utrilla, A. (2010). Indicators for a webometric ranking of open access repositories. *Scientometrics*, *82*(3), 477–486. doi:10.100711192-010-0183-y

Aguinis, H., & Glavas, A. (2012). What we know and don't know about corporate social responsibility: A review and research agenda. *Journal of Management*, *38*(4), 932–968. doi:10.1177/0149206311436079

Alecu, F. (2012). Information technology trends, creative commons licenses. *Oeconomics of Knowledge, 4*(5).

Aliprandi, S. (2010). *Creative Commons: A user guide*. lulu.com.

Ang, S. (2013). *The moral dimensions of intellectual property rights*. Edward Elgar Publishing. doi:10.4337/9781782546689

Armbruster, C., & Romary, L. (2009). *Comparing repository types: Challenges and barriers for subject-based repositories, research repositories, national repository systems and institutional repositories in serving scholarly communication (SSRN Scholarly Paper No. ID 1506905)*. Rochester, NY: Social Science Research Network. Retrieved from https://papers.ssrn.com/abstract=1506905

Associaton of Public Library Managers. (2016). *Submission to the Ministry of Business, Innovation & Employment*. Retrieved from http://www.mbie.govt.nz/info-services/business/intellectual-property/copyright/marrakesh-treaty/submissions/18-Public%20Libraries%20of%20New%20Zealand.pdf

Austin, J. E., & Seitanidi, M. M. (2012). Collaborative value creation: A review of partnering between nonprofits and businesses. Part 2: Partnership processes and outcomes. *Nonprofit and Voluntary Sector Quarterly*, *41*(6), 929–968. doi:10.1177/0899764012454685

Babor, T. F., & Robaina, K. (2012). Public health, academic medicine, and the alcohol industry's corporate social responsibility activities. *American Journal of Public Health*, *103*(2), 206–214. doi:10.2105/AJPH.2012.300847 PMID:23237151

Bauer, M. W., Jensen, P., Bentley, P., & Kyvik, S. (2011). Academic staff and public communication: A survey of popular science publishing across 13 countries. *Public Understanding of Science (Bristol, England)*, *20*(1), 48–63. doi:10.1177/0963662510384461

Beecroft, A. (2010). *Authorship and cultural identity in early Greece and China: Patterns of literary circulation*. Cambridge University Press. doi:10.1017/CBO9780511676154

Bently, L., & Sherman, B. (2014). *Intellectual property law*. Oxford University Press. doi:10.1093/he/9780199645558.001.0001

Berlin Declaration on Open Access to Knowledge in the Sciences and Humanities. (2012). JLIS.It. *Italian Journal of Library and Information Science*, *3*(2).

Berquist, T. H. (2015). Open-access institutional repositories: An evolving process? *AJR. American Journal of Roentgenology*, *205*(3), 467–468. doi:10.2214/AJR.15.15234 PMID:26295632

Bhardwaj, A., Scaria, V., Raghava, G. P. S., Lynn, A. M., Chandra, N., Banerjee, S., ... Brahmachari, S. K. (2011). Open source drug discovery–A new paradigm of collaborative research in tuberculosis drug development. *Tuberculosis (Edinburgh, Scotland)*, *91*(5), 479–486. doi:10.1016/j.tube.2011.06.004 PMID:21782516

Bjork, B.-C. (2009). Scientific journal publishing: Yearly volume and open access availability. *Information Research: An International Electronic Journal, 14*(1). Retrieved from https://eric.ed.gov/?id=EJ837278

Björk, B.-C., Laakso, M., Welling, P., & Paetau, P. (2014). Anatomy of green open access. *Journal of the Association for Information Science and Technology*, *65*(2), 237–250. doi:10.1002/asi.22963

Björk, B.-C., & Solomon, D. (2012). Open access versus subscription journals: A comparison of scientific impact. *BMC Medicine*, *10*(1), 73. doi:10.1186/1741-7015-10-73 PMID:22805105

Bolick, J. (2017). *Exploiting Elsevier's Creative Commons license requirement to subvert embargo*. Retrieved from https://kuscholarworks.ku.edu/handle/1808/24107

Brown, L. G., Griffiths, R., Rascoff, M., & Guthrie, K. (2007). University publishing in a digital age. *The Journal of Electronic Publishing: JEP*, *10*(3). doi:10.3998/3336451.0010.301

Bubela, T., FitzGerald, G. A., & Gold, E. R. (2012). Recalibrating intellectual property rights to enhance translational research collaborations. *Science Translational Medicine*, *4*(122), 122cm3. doi:10.1126citranslmed.3003490 PMID:22357536

Buchanan, J. M. (2014). *Public finance in democratic process: Fiscal institutions and individual choice*. UNC Press Books.

Budapest Open Access Initiative. (2002). *Italian Journal of Library and Information Science*, *3*(2). http://dx.doi.org.simsrad.net.ocs.mq.edu.au/10.4403/jlis.it-8629

Burgess, J., & Green, J. (2013). *YouTube: Online video and participatory culture*. John Wiley & Sons.

Carnaby, P. (2008). Creating a digital New Zealand: New Zealand's Digital Content Strategy, opportunities and challenges for the education and research sectors. *Proceedings of the IATUL Conferences*. Retrieved from http://docs.lib.purdue.edu/iatul/2008/papers/1

Carroll, A. B., & Shabana, K. M. (2010). The business case for corporate social responsibility: A review of concepts, research and practice. *International Journal of Management Reviews*, *12*(1), 85–105. doi:10.1111/j.1468-2370.2009.00275.x

Carroll, M. W. (2013). Creative Commons and the openness of open access. *The New England Journal of Medicine*, *368*(9), 789–791. doi:10.1056/NEJMp1300040 PMID:23445090

Chan, L. (2004). Supporting and enhancing scholarship in the digital age: The role of open access institutional repository. *Canadian Journal of Communication*, *29*(3). doi:10.22230/cjc.2004v29n3a1455

Cheng, B., Ioannou, I., & Serafeim, G. (2014). Corporate social responsibility and access to finance. *Strategic Management Journal*, *35*(1), 1–23. doi:10.1002mj.2131

Cho, S. Y., Lee, C., & Pfeiffer, R. J. Jr. (2013). Corporate social responsibility performance and information asymmetry. *Journal of Accounting and Public Policy*, *32*(1), 71–83. doi:10.1016/j.jaccpubpol.2012.10.005

Christian, G. E. (2008). *Open access initiative and the developing world (SSRN Scholarly Paper No. ID 1304665)*. Rochester, NY: Social Science Research Network. Retrieved from https://papers.ssrn.com/abstract=1304665

Cockerill, M. J., & Knols, B. G. J. (2008). Open access to research for the developing world. *Issues in Science and Technology*, *24*(2), 65–69.

Coonin, B. (2011). Open access publishing in business research: The authors' perspective. *Journal of Business & Finance Librarianship*, *16*(3), 193–212. doi:10.1080/08963568.2011.581606

Cramer, T., & Kott, K. (2010). Designing and implementing second generation digital preservation services: A scalable model for the Stanford Digital Repository. *D-Lib Magazine*, *16*(9/10). doi:10.1045eptember2010-cramer

Crane, A., Matten, D., & Spence, L. J. (2013). *Corporate social responsibility in a global context (SSRN Scholarly Paper No. ID 2322817)*. Rochester, NY: Social Science Research Network. Retrieved from https://papers.ssrn.com/abstract=2322817

Creaser, C., Fry, J., Greenwood, H., Oppenheim, C., Probets, S., Spezi, V., & White, S. (2010). Authors' awareness and attitudes toward open access repositories. *New Review of Academic Librarianship, 16*(sup1), 145–161. doi:10.1080/13614533.2010.518851

Cullen, R., & Chawner, B. (2011). Institutional repositories, open access, and scholarly communication: A study of conflicting paradigms. *Journal of Academic Librarianship, 37*(6), 460–470. doi:10.1016/j.acalib.2011.07.002

David, M., & Halbert, D. (2015). Owning the world of ideas: Intellectual property and global network capitalism. *Sage (Atlanta, Ga.)*.

Davis, P. M. (2011). Open access, readership, citations: A randomized controlled trial of scientific journal publishing. *The FASEB Journal, 25*(7), 2129–2134. doi:10.1096/fj.11-183988 PMID:21450907

Davis, P. M., Lewenstein, B. V., Simon, D. H., Booth, J. G., & Connolly, M. J. L. (2008). Open access publishing, article downloads, and citations: Randomised controlled trial. *BMJ (Clinical Research Ed.), 337*(jul31 1), a568. doi:10.1136/bmj.a568 PMID:18669565

de Camargo, K. R. Jr. (2014). Big publishing and the economics of competition. *American Journal of Public Health, 104*(1), 8–10. doi:10.2105/AJPH.2013.301719 PMID:24228678

De Martin, J. C. (2012). *The digital public domain: Foundations for an open culture*. Retrieved March 23, 2017, from http://porto.polito.it/2504638/

Deng, X., Kang, J., & Low, B. S. (2013). Corporate social responsibility and stakeholder value maximization: Evidence from mergers. *Journal of Financial Economics, 110*(1), 87–109. doi:10.1016/j.jfineco.2013.04.014

Depoorter, B. (2009). Technology and Uncertainty: The Shaping Effect on Copyright Law. *University of Pennsylvania Law Review, 157*(6), 1831.

Di Giuli, A., & Kostovetsky, L. (2014). Are red or blue companies more likely to go green? Politics and corporate social responsibility. *Journal of Financial Economics, 111*(1), 158–180. doi:10.1016/j.jfineco.2013.10.002

Douglas, J. (2016). Developing Kia Tene/Off the Cuff–A resource for field educators in social work in Aotearoa New Zealand. *Aotearoa New Zealand Social Work*, *23*(4), 34–44. doi:10.11157/anzswj-vol23iss4id148

Dusollier, S. (2006). The master's tools v. the master's house: Creative commons v. copyright. (Print symposium: Contract options for individual artists). *The Columbia Journal of Law & the Arts*, *29*(3), 271–293.

Dutfield, G. (2009). *Intellectual property rights and the life science industries: Past, present and future*. World Scientific. doi:10.1142/6917

Edwards, R., & Shulenburger, D. (2010). The high cost of scholarly journals (and what to do about it). *Change: The Magazine of Higher Learning*, *35*(6), 10–19. doi:10.1080/00091380309604123

Elsevier. (2016). *Pricing*. Retrieved March 31, 2017, from https://www.elsevier.com/about/company-information/policies/pricing

Elsevier. (2017). *Position statements*. Retrieved April 16, 2017, from https://www.elsevier.com/about/open-science/position-statements

Epstein, M. J., & Buhovac, A. R. (2014). *Making sustainability work: Best practices in managing and measuring corporate social, environmental, and economic impacts*. Berrett-Koehler Publishers.

Erhemjamts, O., Li, Q., & Venkateswaran, A. (2013). Corporate social responsibility and its impact on firms' investment policy, organizational structure, and performance. *Journal of Business Ethics*, *118*(2), 395–412. doi:10.100710551-012-1594-x

European Commission. (2012, July 17). *Commission Recommendation of 17 July 2012 on access to and preservation of scientific information*. Retrieved from http://eur-lex.europa.eu/legal-content/EN/TXT/PDF/?uri=CELEX:32012H0417&rid=1

European Commission. (2016). *Open innovation, open science, open to the world—A vision for Europe (No. Unit A1)*. Brussels: Directorate-General for Research and Innovation. Retrieved from http://cache.media.education.gouv.fr/file/2016/45/1/Openinnovationbook_592451.pdf

Feenberg, A. (2012). *Questioning technology*. Routledge. doi:10.4324/9780203022313

Fitzgerald, B. (2007). *Open content licensing (OCL) for open educational resources*. Retrieved from http://www.oecd.org/edu/ceri/38645489.pdf

Flammer, C. (2013). Corporate social responsibility and shareholder reaction: The environmental awareness of investors. *Academy of Management Journal*, *56*(3), 758–781. doi:10.5465/amj.2011.0744

Frank, M. (2013). Open but not free—Publishing in the 21st century. *The New England Journal of Medicine*, *368*(9), 787–789. doi:10.1056/NEJMp1211259 PMID:23445089

Friesike, S., Widenmayer, B., Gassmann, O., & Schildhauer, T. (2015). Opening science: Towards an agenda of open science in academia and industry. *The Journal of Technology Transfer*, *40*(4), 581–601. doi:10.100710961-014-9375-6

Frosio, G. F. (2017). *Resisting the resistance: Resisting copyright and promoting alternatives (SSRN Scholarly Paper No. ID 2908966)*. Rochester, NY: Social Science Research Network. Retrieved from https://papers.ssrn.com/abstract=2908966

Fuchs, C., & Sandoval, M. (2013). The diamond model of open access publishing: Why policy makers, scholars, universities, libraries, labour unions and the publishing world need to take non-commercial, non-profit open access serious. *TripleC*, *11*(2), 428–443. doi:10.31269/triplec.v11i2.502

Gargouri, Y., Larivière, V., Gingras, Y., Carr, L., & Harnad, S. (2012). *Green and gold open access percentages and growth, by discipline*. Retrieved from http://arxiv.org/abs/1206.3664

Gendron, Y. (2015). Accounting academia and the threat of the paying-off mentality. *Critical Perspectives on Accounting*, *26*, 168–176. doi:10.1016/j.cpa.2013.06.004

Ghosh, S. B., & Kumar Das, A. (2007). Open access and institutional repositories—A developing country perspective: A case study of India. *IFLA Journal*, *33*(3), 229–250. doi:10.1177/0340035207083304

Ginns, P., Kitay, J., & Prosser, M. (2010). Transfer of academic staff learning in a research-intensive university. *Teaching in Higher Education*, *15*(3), 235–246. doi:10.1080/13562511003740783

Glasgow, L. J. (2002). Stretching the limits of intellectual property rights: Has the pharmaceutical industry gone too far? *IDEA the Journal of Law and Technology*, *41*, 227.

Graf, C., Wager, E., Bowman, A., Fiack, S., Scott-Lichter, D., & Robinson, A. (2007). Best practice guidelines on publication ethics: A publisher's perspective. *International Journal of Clinical Practice*, *61*, 1–26. doi:10.1111/j.1742-1241.2006.01230.x PMID:17206953

Granstrand, O., & Holgersson, M. (2015). Intellectual property. In *The Wiley Blackwell Encyclopedia of Consumption and Consumer Studies*. John Wiley & Sons, Ltd. doi:10.1002/9781118989463.wbeccs151

Greco, A. N. (2013). *The book publishing industry*. Routledge. doi:10.4324/9780203834565

Griffiths, J. R., & Brophy, P. (2005). *Student searching behavior and the web: Use of academic resources and Google-ProQuest*. Academic Press.

Harley, D., Acord, S. K., Earl-Novell, S., Lawrence, S., & King, C. J. (2010). Assessing the future landscape of scholarly communication: An exploration of faculty values and needs in seven disciplines. *Center for Studies in Higher Education*. Retrieved from http://escholarship.org/uc/item/15x7385g

Harnad, S. (2005). *Fast-forward on the green road to open access: The case against mixing up green and gold*. Retrieved from http://arxiv.org/abs/cs/0503021

Harnad, S. (2010). *Gold open access publishing must not be allowed to retard the progress of green open access self-archiving*. Retrieved from http://eprints.soton.ac.uk/271818/1/logospaper.pdf

Harnad, S., & Brody, T. (2004). Comparing the impact of open access (OA) vs. non-OA articles in the same journals. *D-Lib Magazine*, *10*(6). Retrieved from https://eprints.soton.ac.uk/260207/

Harnad, S., Brody, T., Vallières, F., Carr, L., Hitchcock, S., Gingras, Y., ... Hilf, E. R. (2004). The access/impact problem and the green and gold roads to open access. *Serials Review*, *30*(4), 310–314. doi:10.1080/00987913.2004.10764930

Herb, U. (2010). Sociological implications of scientific publishing: Open access, science, society, democracy and the digital divide. *First Monday*, *15*(2). doi:10.5210/fm.v15i2.2599

Herther, N. K. (2005). The e-book industry today: A bumpy road becomes an evolutionary path to market maturity. *The Electronic Library*, *23*(1), 45–53. doi:10.1108/02640470510582727

House, E. (2013). Challenges facing the UK book industry. *Publishing Research Quarterly*, *29*(3), 211–219. doi:10.100712109-013-9320-9

Husserl, E. (2012). *Ideas: General introduction to pure phenomenology*. Routledge. doi:10.4324/9780203120330

Jaeger, P. T., & Bertot, J. C. (2010). Transparency and technological change: Ensuring equal and sustained public access to government information. *Government Information Quarterly*, *27*(4), 371–376. doi:10.1016/j.giq.2010.05.003

Katz, Z. (2006). Pitfalls of open licensing: An analysis of creative commons licensing. *IDEA: The Intellectual Property Law Review*, *46*, 391.

Khan, A., Muttakin, M. B., & Siddiqui, J. (2013). Corporate governance and corporate social responsibility disclosures: Evidence from an emerging economy. *Journal of Business Ethics*, *114*(2), 207–223. doi:10.100710551-012-1336-0

Koppel, M., & Schler, J. (2004). Authorship verification as a one-class classification problem. In *Proceedings of the Twenty-first International Conference on Machine Learning* (p. 62). New York, NY: ACM. 10.1145/1015330.1015448

Koulouris, A., Kyriaki-Manessi, D., Giannakopoulos, G., & Zervos, S. (2013). Institutional repository policies: Best practices for encouraging self-archiving. *Procedia: Social and Behavioral Sciences*, *73*, 769–776. doi:10.1016/j.sbspro.2013.02.117

Laakso, M., & Björk, B.-C. (2012). Anatomy of open access publishing: A study of longitudinal development and internal structure. *BMC Medicine*, *10*(1), 124. doi:10.1186/1741-7015-10-124 PMID:23088823

Laakso, M., Welling, P., Bukvova, H., Nyman, L., Björk, B.-C., & Hedlund, T. (2011). The development of open access journal publishing from 1993 to 2009. *PLoS One*, *6*(6), e20961. doi:10.1371/journal.pone.0020961 PMID:21695139

Larivière, V., Haustein, S., & Mongeon, P. (2015). The oligopoly of academic publishers in the digital era. *PLoS One*, *10*(6), e0127502. doi:10.1371/journal.pone.0127502 PMID:26061978

Larsson, S. (2011). *Metaphors and norms—Understanding copyright law in a digital society*. Stefan Larsson.

Leitner, K.-H. (2004). Intellectual capital reporting for universities: Conceptual background and application for Austrian universities. *Research Evaluation, 13*(2), 129–140. doi:10.3152/147154404781776464

Levinthal, D. A., & Wu, B. (2010). Opportunity costs and non-scale free capabilities: Profit maximization, corporate scope, and profit margins. *Strategic Management Journal, 31*(7), 780–801. doi:10.1002mj.845

Lewis, D. W. (2012). The inevitability of open access. *College & Research Libraries, 73*(5), 493–506. doi:10.5860/crl-299

Lindgreen, A., & Swaen, V. (2010). Corporate social responsibility. *International Journal of Management Reviews, 12*(1), 1–7. doi:10.1111/j.1468-2370.2009.00277.x

López, O. S. (2010). The digital learning classroom: Improving English language learners' academic success in mathematics and reading using interactive whiteboard technology. *Computers & Education, 54*(4), 901–915. doi:10.1016/j.compedu.2009.09.019

Manhart, M., & Thalmann, S. (2015). Protecting organizational knowledge: A structured literature review. *Journal of Knowledge Management, 19*(2), 190–211. doi:10.1108/JKM-05-2014-0198

Matten, D., & Moon, J. (2008). "Implicit" and "Explicit" CSR: A conceptual framework for a comparative understanding of corporate social responsibility. *Academy of Management Review, 33*(2), 404–424. doi:10.5465/amr.2008.31193458

Mayer-Schonberger, V. (2008). Demystifying Lessig. *Wisconsin Law Review, 2008*, 713–746.

McCutcheon, V., Nixon, W., & De Castro, P. (2014). *Repository profile: University of Glasgow-"Enlighten" IR & research system. Confederation of Open Access Repositories*. Retrieved from http://eprints.gla.ac.uk/98412/1/98412.pdf

McGuigan, G., & Russell, R. (2008). The Business of academic publishing: A strategic analysis of the academic journal publishing industry and its impact on the future of scholarly publishing, *Electronic Journal of Academic and Special Librarianship, 9*(3). Retrieved from http://southernlibrarianship.icaap.org/content/v09n03/mcguigan_g01.html

Menell, P. S. (2011). Governance of intellectual resources and disintegration of intellectual property in the digital age. *Berkeley Technology Law Journal, 26*(4), 1523–1559.

Merges, R. P. (2011). *Justifying intellectual property*. Harvard University Press. doi:10.4159/harvard.9780674061125

Miller, C., & Harris, J. (2004). Scholarly journal publication: Conflicting agendas for scholars, publishers, and institutions. *Journal of Scholarly Publishing, 35*(2), 73–91. doi:10.3138/jsp.35.2.73

Moon, J. (2014). *Corporate social responsibility: A very short introduction*. OUP Oxford.

Mueller, R. A. E. (2003). The evolution of intellectual property rights for digital information products-impact on agroindustry. In *Proceedings of the EFITA Conference, Debrecen, Hungary* (pp. 331–338). Retrieved from http://www.agric-econ.uni-kiel.de/Abteilungen/II/PDFs/efita03.pdf

Nicholas, D., Rowlands, I., Watkinson, A., Brown, D., & Jamali, H. R. (2012). Digital repositories ten years on: What do scientific researchers think of them and how do they use them? *Learned Publishing, 25*(3), 195–206. doi:10.1087/20120306

North, D. C. (2007). *Limited access orders in the developing world: A new approach to the problems of development*. World Bank Publications. doi:10.1596/1813-9450-4359

Nyquist, C. (2010). An academic librarian's response to the "ITHAKA faculty survey 2009: Key strategic insights for libraries, publishers, and societies." *Journal of Interlibrary Loan. Document Delivery & Electronic Reserve, 20*(4), 275–280. doi:10.1080/1072303X.2010.508419

Open Access Scholarly Publishers Association. (2016). Retrieved January 12, 2016, from http://oaspa.org/

Oppenheim, C. (2008). Electronic scholarly publishing and open access. *Journal of Information Science, 34*(4), 577–590. doi:10.1177/0165551508092268

Orduña-Malea, E., & López-Cózar, E. D. (2015). The dark side of open access in Google and Google Scholar: The case of Latin-American repositories. *Scientometrics*, *102*(1), 829–846. doi:10.100711192-014-1369-5

Palfrey, J., Gasser, U., Simun, M., & Barnes, R. F. (2009). Youth, creativity, and copyright in the digital age. *International Journal of Learning and Media*, *1*(2), 79–97. doi:10.1162/ijlm.2009.0022

Park, S., Zo, H., Ciganek, A. P., & Lim, G. G. (2011). Examining success factors in the adoption of digital object identifier systems. *Electronic Commerce Research and Applications*, *10*(6), 626–636. doi:10.1016/j.elerap.2011.05.004

Perianes-Rodríguez, A., Olmeda-Gómez, C., & Moya-Anegón, F. (2010). Detecting, identifying and visualizing research groups in co-authorship networks. *Scientometrics*, *82*(2), 307–319. doi:10.100711192-009-0040-z

Picarra, M. (2015). Open Access policy effectiveness: A briefing paper for UK Higher Education Institutions. *Zenodo*, *6*. doi:10.5281/zenodo.44325

Pinfield, S., Salter, J., Bath, P. A., Hubbard, B., Millington, P., Anders, J. H. S., & Hussain, A. (2014). Open-access repositories worldwide, 2005–2012: Past growth, current characteristics, and future possibilities. *Journal of the Association for Information Science and Technology*, *65*(12), 2404–2421. doi:10.1002/asi.23131

Poynder, R. (2013, June 17). *Open and shut? Open access: Emerald's green starts to fade?* Retrieved January 25, 2016, from http://poynder.blogspot.com.au/2013/06/open-access-emeralds-green-starts-to.html

Puplett, D., & Madjarevic, N. (2011, October 28). *By championing open access publishing, the academic community can bring us closer to making research available to all.* Retrieved April 15, 2017, from http://blogs.lse.ac.uk/impactofsocialsciences/2011/10/28/championing-open-access/

Reitz, J. M. (2004). *Dictionary for library and information science*. Libraries Unlimited.

Rocco, T. S., & Hatcher, T. G. (2011). *The handbook of scholarly writing and publishing*. John Wiley & Sons.

Serenko, A., Bontis, N., Booker, L., Sadeddin, K., & Hardie, T. (2010). A scientometric analysis of knowledge management and intellectual capital academic literature (1994–2008). *Journal of Knowledge Management*, *14*(1), 3–23. doi:10.1108/13673271011015534

Sha, L. Z. (2007). The flavors of open access. *OCLC Systems & Services: International Digital Library Perspectives*, *23*(3), 229–234. doi:10.1108/10650750710776332

Shapley, K. S., Sheehan, D., Maloney, C., & Caranikas-Walker, F. (2010). Evaluating the implementation fidelity of technology immersion and its relationship with student achievement. *The Journal of Technology, Learning, and Assessment*, *9*(4). Retrieved from https://ejournals.bc.edu/ojs/index.php/jtla/article/view/1609

Shelburne, W. A. (2009). E-book usage in an academic library: User attitudes and behaviors. *Library Collections, Acquisitions & Technical Services*, *33*(2–3), 59–72. doi:10.1016/j.lcats.2009.04.002

Shinn, T., & Lamy, E. (2006). Paths of commercial knowledge: Forms and consequences of university–enterprise synergy in scientist-sponsored firms. *Research Policy*, *35*(10), 1465–1476. doi:10.1016/j.respol.2006.09.024

Silva, J. (2008). Open access: No one's sure of definitions in this new territory. *RCR Wireless News*, *27*(33), 12.

Sismondo, S., & Doucet, M. (2010). Publication ethics and the ghost management of medical publication. *Bioethics*, *24*(6), 273–283. doi:10.1111/j.1467-8519.2008.01702.x PMID:19222451

Sompel, H. d., Payette, S., Erickson, J., Lagoze, C., & Warner, S. (2004, September). *Rethinking scholarly communication: Building the system that scholars deserve.* Retrieved March 29, 2017, from http://dspace.library.uu.nl/handle/1874/3165

Stone, D. (2010). Private philanthropy or policy transfer? The transnational norms of the Open Society Institute. *Policy and Politics*, *38*(2), 269–287. doi:10.1332/030557309X458416

Suber, P. (2012). Ensuring open access for publicly funded research. *BMJ (Clinical Research Ed.)*, *345*(aug08 1), e5184. doi:10.1136/bmj.e5184 PMID:22875953

Suber, P., Brown, P. O., Cabell, D., Chakravarti, A., Cohen, B., Delamothe, T., . . . Watson, L. (2003). *Bethesda statement on open access publishing*. Retrieved from https://dash.harvard.edu/handle/1/4725199

Sweet, C. M., & Eterovic Maggio, D. S. (2015). Do stronger intellectual property rights increase innovation? *World Development*, *66*, 665–677. doi:10.1016/j.worlddev.2014.08.025

Taylor, M. (2012, March 26). *Visibility is currency in academia but it is scarcity in publishing: the push for open access shows that academic publishers can't serve two masters*. Retrieved April 16, 2017, from http://blogs.lse.ac.uk/impactofsocialsciences/

Teece, D. J. (2010). Business models, business strategy and innovation. *Long Range Planning*, *43*(2–3), 172–194. doi:10.1016/j.lrp.2009.07.003

Thumm, N. (2013). *Intellectual property rights: National systems and harmonisation in Europe*. Springer Science & Business Media.

Van Noorden, R. (2013). The true cost of science publishing. *NATNews*, *495*(7442), 426–429. PMID:23538808

Van Orsdel, L. C., & Born, K. (2009). Reality bites: Periodicals price survey 2009. *Library Journal*, *134*(7), 36–40.

Vlieghe, D., Sandelin, A., & Bleser, D. (2006). A new generation of JASPAR, the open-access repository for transcription factor binding site profiles. *Nucleic Acids Research*, *34*(suppl. 1), D95–D97. doi:10.1093/nar/gkj115 PMID:16381983

Vreeburg Izzo, M., Yurick, A., Nagaraja, H. N., & Novak, J. A. (2010). Effects of a 21st-century curriculum on students' information technology and transition skills. *Career Development for Exceptional Individuals*, *33*(2), 95–105. doi:10.1177/0885728810369348

Wallace, M., & Siersema, P. (2015). Ethics in publication. *Endoscopy*, *47*(07), 575–578. doi:10.1055-0034-1392435 PMID:26099116

Way, D. (2010). The open access availability of library and information science literature. *College & Research Libraries*, *71*(4), 302–309. doi:10.5860/crl-38r1

Willinsky, J. (2003). The nine flavours of open access scholarly publishing. *Journal of Postgraduate Medicine*, *49*(3), 263. PMID:14597793

Woll, T. (2010). *Publishing for profit: Successful bottom-line management for book publishers*. Chicago Review Press.

Xia, J. (2010). A longitudinal study of scholars attitudes and behaviors toward open-access journal publishing. *Journal of the American Society for Information Science and Technology*, *61*(3), 615–624. doi:10.1002/asi.21283

Yiotis, K. (2005). The open access initiative: A new paradigm for scholarly communications. *Information Technology and Libraries*, *24*(4), 157–162. doi:10.6017/ital.v24i4.3378

Zuiderwijk, A., & Janssen, M. (2014). Open data policies, their implementation and impact: A framework for comparison. *Government Information Quarterly*, *31*(1), 17–29. doi:10.1016/j.giq.2013.04.003

ENDNOTES

1 Acronym for *Consorzio Interuniversitario per le Applicazioni di Supercalcolo per Università e Ricerca.*

2 Acronym for *Consorzio Interuniversitario del Nord Est Italiano per il Calcolo Automatico.*

3 Acronym for *Consorzio Interuniversitario Lombardo per l'Elaborazione Automatica.*

4 Acronym for *Portale per la Letteratura Scientifica Elettronica Italiana su Archivi Aperti e Depositi Istituzionali.*

Compilation of References

Aaker, D. A., & Biel, A. (2013). *Brand equity & advertising: advertising's role in building strong brands*. Psychology Press. doi:10.4324/9781315799537

Abbas, J., Norris, C., & Soloway, E. (2002). Middle school children's use of the ARTEMIS digital library. *Proceedings of the 2Nd ACM/IEEE-CS Joint Conference on Digital Libraries*, 98–105. 10.1145/544220.544239

Abbott, F. (2002). *The Doha Declaration on the TRIPS Agreement and Public Health: Lighting a Dark Corner at the WTO*. Rochester, NY: Social Science Research Network. Retrieved from http://papers.ssrn.com/abstract=1493725

Abel, R. E. (2002). *Scholarly publishing: Books, journals, publishers, and libraries in the twentieth century*. John Wiley & Sons, Inc.

Abrahamson, P. (2005). *Welfare and families in Europe*. Ashgate.

Abrizah, A., A, N., & K, K. (2017). Global visibility of Asian universities' Open Access institutional repositories. *Malaysian Journal of Library and Information Science*, *15*(3), 53–73.

Aghaei, S., Nematbakhsh, M. A., & Farsani, H. K. (2012). Evolution of the World Wide Web: From Web 1.0 to Web 4.0. *International Journal of Web & Semantic Technology*, *3*(1), 1–10. doi:10.5121/ijwest.2012.3101

Aguillo, I., Ortega, J., Fernández, M., & Utrilla, A. (2010). Indicators for a webometric ranking of open access repositories. *Scientometrics*, *82*(3), 477–486. doi:10.100711192-010-0183-y

Aguinis, H., & Glavas, A. (2012). What we know and don't know about corporate social responsibility: A review and research agenda. *Journal of Management*, *38*(4), 932–968. doi:10.1177/0149206311436079

Agyeman, J. (2003). *Just sustainabilities: Development in an unequal world*. MIT Press.

Alecu, F. (2012). Information technology trends, creative commons licenses. *Oeconomics of Knowledge*, *4*(5).

Alexandropoulou, E. (2011). Personal financial data: Regulatory framework of their e-processing focusing on the function of interbanking information systems in Greece and France. In *An Information Law for the 21st Century* (pp. 237–252). Retrieved from https://papers.ssrn.com/abstract=2621496

Ali Feki, M., Kawsar, F., Boussard, M., & Trappeniers, L. (2013). The Internet of Things. *The Next Technological Revolution.*, *26*(February), 24–25. doi:10.1109/MC.2013.63

Aliprandi, S. (2010). *Creative Commons: A user guide.* Italy: lulu.com.

Aliprandi, S. (2010). *Creative Commons: A user guide.* lulu.com.

Alonso, J. (n.d.). *Improving access to government through better use of the web.* Retrieved from http://www.epractice.eu

Andersen, I.-E., & Jæger, B. (1999). Scenario workshops and consensus conferences: Towards more democratic decision-making. *Science & Public Policy*, *26*(5), 331–340. doi:10.3152/147154399781782301

Andreou, G. (2006). EU cohesion policy in Greece: Patterns of governance and Europeanization. *South European Society & Politics*, *11*(2), 241–259. doi:10.1080/13608740600645865

Ang, S. (2013). *The moral dimensions of intellectual property rights.* Edward Elgar Publishing. doi:10.4337/9781782546689

Antelman, K. (2004). Do open-access articles have a greater research impact? *College & Research Libraries*, *65*(5), 372–382. doi:10.5860/crl.65.5.372

Antezana, M. E. (2003). The European union internet copyright directive as even more than it envisions: Toward a supra-EU harmonization of copyright policy and theory. *Boston College International and Comparative Law Review*, *26*, 415.

Antezana, M. E. (2003). The European Union Internet Copyright Directive as even more than it envisions: Toward a supra-EU harmonization of copyright policy and theory. *Boston College International and Comparative Law Review*, *26*, 415.

Apostolache, M. C. (2015). The relevance of the European regulations regarding the improvement of transparency and integrity in local public administration: Analysis of the implications on the legislation. *Juridical Tribune*, *5*(1), 90–98.

Archibugi, D., & Filippetti, A. (2010). The globalisation of intellectual property rights: Four learned lessons and four theses. *Global Policy*, *1*(2), 137–149. doi:10.1111/j.1758-5899.2010.00019.x

Arezzo, E. (2007). Struggling around the natural divide: The protection of tangible and intangible indigenous property. *Cardozo Arts & Entertainment Law Journal*, *25*, 367.

Aristotle. (2004). *Politics.* Digireads.com Publishing.

Arlitsch, K., & O'Brien, P. S. (2012). Invisible institutional repositories: Addressing the low indexing ratios of IRs in Google Scholar. *Library Hi Tech*, *30*(1), 60–81. doi:10.1108/07378831211213210

Armbruster, C., & Romary, L. (2009). *Comparing repository types: Challenges and barriers for subject-based repositories, research repositories, national repository systems and institutional repositories in serving scholarly communication (SSRN Scholarly Paper No. ID 1506905)*. Rochester, NY: Social Science Research Network. Retrieved from https://papers.ssrn.com/abstract=1506905

Ash, C. (2000). Social-Self-Interest. *Annals of Public and Cooperative Economics*, *71*(2), 261–284. doi:10.1111/1467-8292.00142

Associaton of Public Library Managers. (2016). *Submission to the Ministry of Business, Innovation & Employment*. Retrieved from http://www.mbie.govt.nz/info-services/business/intellectual-property/copyright/marrakesh-treaty/submissions/18-Public%20Libraries%20of%20New%20Zealand.pdf

Atkinson, B., & Fitzgerald, B. (2014). Access and networking. In *A Short History of Copyright*. Retrieved from http://link.springer.com

Atkinson, B., & Fitzgerald, B. (2014). *A Short History of Copyright: The Genie of Information*. Springer Science & Business Media. doi:10.1007/978-3-319-02075-4

Atkinson, B., & Fitzgerald, B. (2014). The nineteenth century: Liberty and literary property. In *A short history of copyright* (pp. 37–43). Springer International Publishing. doi:10.1007/978-3-319-02075-4_5

Aurore, N., Caruso, J., & Archambault, E. (2013). *Open data access policies and strategies in the European research area and beyond*. Retrieved from http://www.science-metrix.com

Austin, J. E., & Seitanidi, M. M. (2012). Collaborative value creation: A review of partnering between nonprofits and businesses. Part 2: Partnership processes and outcomes. *Nonprofit and Voluntary Sector Quarterly*, *41*(6), 929–968. doi:10.1177/0899764012454685

Australian Law Reform Commission. (2014). *Copyright and the Digital Economy (Copyright and the Digital Economy No. 122)*. Retrieved from http://www.alrc.gov.au/publications/copyright-report-122

Ayris, P. (2007, August 9). Embedding Open Access into the European Landscape – the Contribution of LIBER. *LIBER Quarterly*, *17*(2). doi:10.18352/lq.7876

Babor, T. F., & Robaina, K. (2012). Public health, academic medicine, and the alcohol industry's corporate social responsibility activities. *American Journal of Public Health*, *103*(2), 206–214. doi:10.2105/AJPH.2012.300847 PMID:23237151

Babovic, S., & Wasan, K. M. (2011). Impact of the trade-related aspects of intellectual property rights (TRIPS) agreement on India as a supplier of generic antiretrovirals. *Journal of Pharmaceutical Sciences*, *100*(3), 816–821. doi:10.1002/jps.22326 PMID:20740678

Bachtler, J., & McMaster, I. (2008). EU cohesion policy and the role of the regions: Investigating the influence of structural funds in the new Member States. *Environment and Planning. C, Government & Policy*, *26*(2), 398–427. doi:10.1068/c0662

Bacon, F. (2008). *Francis Bacon: The major works* (B. Vickers, Ed.). New York: Oxford University Press.

Bacon, F. (2013). *Complete works of Francis Bacon*. Minerva Classics.

Bailey, C. W. Jr. (2007). Open access and libraries. *Collection Management, 32*(3–4), 351–383. doi:10.1300/J105v32n03_07

Balganesh, S. (2013). Copyright Infringement Markets Essay. *Columbia Law Review, 113*(8), 2277–2332.

Ball, S. J. (2013). *Foucault and Education: Disciplines and Knowledge*. Routledge. doi:10.4324/9780203092781

Bandura, A. (2001). Social cognitive theory of mass communication. *Media Psychology, 3*(3), 265–299. doi:10.1207/S1532785XMEP0303_03

Barker, N. (1992). *Aldus Manutius and the development of Greek script & type in the fifteenth century*. Fordham Univ Press.

Barron, A. (2006). Copyright. *Theory, Culture & Society, 23*(2–3), 278–282. doi:10.1177/026327640602300237

Bauer, M. W., Jensen, P., Bentley, P., & Kyvik, S. (2011). Academic staff and public communication: A survey of popular science publishing across 13 countries. *Public Understanding of Science (Bristol, England), 20*(1), 48–63. doi:10.1177/0963662510384461

Baynes, K. (2015). *Habermas*. Routledge. doi:10.4324/9781315696423

Bayona-Sáez, C., & García-Marco, T. (2010). Assessing the effectiveness of the Eureka Program. *Research Policy, 39*(10), 1375–1386. doi:10.1016/j.respol.2010.07.007

Bean, J. (1989). *From lord to patron: Lordship in late medieval England*. Manchester University Press.

Becker, J. D. (2007). Digital equity in education: A multilevel examination of differences in and relationships between computer access, computer use and state-level technology policies. *Education Policy Analysis Archives, 15*(0), 3. doi:10.14507/epaa.v15n3.2007

Beecroft, A. (2010). *Authorship and cultural identity in early Greece and China: Patterns of literary circulation*. Cambridge University Press. doi:10.1017/CBO9780511676154

Beetham, H., & Sharpe, R. (2013). *Rethinking pedagogy for a digital age: Designing for 21st century learning*. Routledge.

Beinin, J. (2001). *Workers and peasants in the modern Middle East*. Cambridge University Press. doi:10.1017/CBO9780511612800

Beniger, J. (2009). *The control revolution: Technological and economic origins of the information society*. Harvard University Press.

Bently, L., Suthersanen, U., & Torremans, P. (Eds.). (2010). Global copyright: Three hundred years since the Statute of Anne, from 1709 to cyberspace (1st ed.). Cheltenham, UK: Edward Elgar Pub.

Bently, L., & Sherman, B. (2014). *Intellectual property law*. Oxford University Press. doi:10.1093/he/9780199645558.001.0001

Bergstrom, C. (2007). Eigenfactor: Measuring the value and prestige of scholarly journals. *College & Research Libraries News*, *68*(5), 314–316. doi:10.5860/crln.68.5.7804

Berkenkotter, C., & Huckin, T. N. (2016). *Genre knowledge in disciplinary communication: Cognition/culture/power*. Routledge. doi:10.4324/9781315538747

Berlin Declaration on Open Access to Knowledge in the Sciences and Humanities. (2012). JLIS. It. *Italian Journal of Library and Information Science*, *3*(2).

Berners-Lee, T., Cailliau, R., Groff, J., & Pollermann, B. (2010). World-Wide Web: The information universe. *Internet Research*, *20*(4), 461–471. doi:10.1108/10662241011059471

Berquist, T. H. (2015). Open-access institutional repositories: An evolving process? *AJR. American Journal of Roentgenology*, *205*(3), 467–468. doi:10.2214/AJR.15.15234 PMID:26295632

Besson, S., & Martí, J. L. (2006). *Deliberative democracy and its discontents*. Ashgate Publishing, Ltd.

Bhardwaj, A., Scaria, V., Raghava, G. P. S., Lynn, A. M., Chandra, N., Banerjee, S., ... Brahmachari, S. K. (2011). Open source drug discovery–A new paradigm of collaborative research in tuberculosis drug development. *Tuberculosis (Edinburgh, Scotland)*, *91*(5), 479–486. doi:10.1016/j.tube.2011.06.004 PMID:21782516

Bhat, M. H. (2010). Open Access Repositories. *RE:view*, 356.

Biagioli, M., & Galison, P. (2014). *Scientific authorship: Credit and intellectual property in science*. Routledge. doi:10.4324/9780203954270

Billieux, J., & Van der Linden, M. (2012). Problematic use of the Internet and self-regulation: A review of the initial studies. *The Open Addiction Journal*, *5*(1), 24–29. doi:10.2174/1874941001205010024

Birkland, T. A. (2014). *An introduction to the policy process: Theories, concepts and models of public policy making*. Routledge. doi:10.4324/9781315706399

Birn, R. (2005). Book censorship in eighteenth-century: France and Rousseau's response. In *History of Ideas; Travel Writing; History of the Book; Enlightenment and Antiquity*. Academic Press.

Bishop, P., & Davis, G. (2002). Mapping public participation in policy choices. *Australian Journal of Public Administration*, *61*(1), 14–29. doi:10.1111/1467-8500.00255

Bjork, B.-C. (2009). Scientific journal publishing: Yearly volume and open access availability. *Information Research: An International Electronic Journal, 14*(1). Retrieved from https://eric.ed.gov/?id=EJ837278

Björk, B.-C., Laakso, M., Welling, P., & Paetau, P. (2014). Anatomy of green open access. *Journal of the Association for Information Science and Technology*, *65*(2), 237–250. doi:10.1002/asi.22963

Björk, B.-C., & Solomon, D. (2012). Open access versus subscription journals: A comparison of scientific impact. *BMC Medicine*, *10*(1), 73. doi:10.1186/1741-7015-10-73 PMID:22805105

Björk, B.-C., Welling, P., Laakso, M., Majlender, P., Hedlund, T., & Guðnason, G. (2010). Open access to the scientific journal literature: Situation 2009. *PLoS One*, *5*(6), e11273. doi:10.1371/journal.pone.0011273 PMID:20585653

Black, J. (2015). *The power of knowledge: How information and technology made the modern world*. New Haven, CT: Yale University Press.

Blakeney, M. (2012). *Intellectual property enforcement: A commentary on the Anti-Counterfeiting Trade Agreement (ACTA)*. Edward Elgar Publishing. doi:10.4337/9781781006009

Bloom, A. D. (1991). *The Republic of Plato*. Basic Books.

Bloom, T., Ganley, E., & Winker, M. (2014). Data access for the open access literature: PLoS's data policy. *PLoS Biology*, *12*(2), e1001797. doi:10.1371/journal.pbio.1001797

Boeder, P. (2005). Habermas' heritage: The future of the public sphere in the network society. *First Monday*, *10*(9). doi:10.5210/fm.v10i9.1280

Bold, C. (2011). *The Oxford history of popular print culture*. Oxford University Press. doi:10.1093/acprof:osobl/9780199234066.001.0001

Bolick, J. (2017). *Exploiting Elsevier's Creative Commons license requirement to subvert embargo*. Retrieved from https://kuscholarworks.ku.edu/handle/1808/24107

Bottomley, S. (2014). *The British patent system during the Industrial Revolution 1700–1852: From privilege to property*. Cambridge, UK: Cambridge University Press.

Boucher, D., & Kelly, P. (Eds.). (2003). *The social contract from Hobbes to Rawls*. Routledge. doi:10.4324/9780203392928

Bouchoux, D. E. (2012). *Intellectual property: The law of trademarks, copyrights, patents, and trade secrets*. Cengage Learning.

Boudreau, K. J. (2007). *Does opening a platform stimulate innovation? The effect on systemic and modular innovations (SSRN Scholarly Paper No. ID 913402)*. Rochester, NY: Social Science Research Network. Retrieved from http://papers.ssrn.com/abstract=913402

Bovaird, T., Löffler, E., & Loeffler, E. (2004). *Public Management and Governance*. Routledge. doi:10.4324/9780203884096

Bowker, R. (2012). *Copyright: Its history and its law*. Retrieved from http://www.gutenberg.org/ebooks/39502#download

Bowker, G. C., Baker, K., Millerand, F., & Ribes, D. (2009). Toward information infrastructure studies: Ways of knowing in a networked environment. In J. Hunsinger, L. Klastrup, & M. Allen (Eds.), *International Handbook of Internet Research* (pp. 97–117). doi:10.1007/978-1-4020-9789-8_5

Boyd, D., & Crawford, K. (2012). Critical questions for big data. *Information Communication and Society*, *15*(5), 662–679. doi:10.1080/1369118X.2012.678878

Boyle, J. (2003). The second enclosure movement and the construction of the public domain. *Law and Contemporary Problems*, *66*(1/2), 33–74.

Bradford, L. (2015). *Inventing patents: A story of legal and technical transfer*. Rochester, NY: Social Science Research Network. Retrieved from http://papers.ssrn.com/abstract=2566162

Brady, E. (2010). Aristotle, Adam Smith and the Virtue of Propriety. *Journal of Scottish Philosophy*, *8*(1), 79–89. doi:10.3366/E1479665109000529

Brants, K. (2005). Guest editor's introduction: The Internet and the public sphere. *Political Communication*, *22*(2), 143–146. doi:10.1080/10584600590933133

Breakey, H. (2012). Property concepts. *Internet encyclopedia of philosophy*. Retrieved from http://www.iep.utm.edu/prop-con/

Breschi, S., & Cusmano, L. (2004). Unveiling the texture of a European research area: Emergence of oligarchic networks under EU framework programmes. *International Journal of Technology Management*, *27*(8), 747–772. doi:10.1504/IJTM.2004.004992

Bretherton, C., & Vogler, J. (1999). *The European Union as a global actor*. Psychology Press.

Briggs, A., & Burke, P. (2010). Social history of the media: From Gutenberg to the Internet. *Polity*.

Brown, J. (2010). *What is participatory democracy? It means you get involved*. Retrieved January 14, 2016, from http://www.glasgowdailytimes.com/opinion/what-is-participatory-democracy-it-means-you-get-involved/article_d0e062df-de30-502e-94bd-7cfdf00a5130.html

Brown, E. (1974). The tyranny of a construct: Feudalism and historians of medieval Europe. *The American Historical Review*, *79*(4), 1063–1088. doi:10.2307/1869563

Brown, L. G., Griffiths, R., Rascoff, M., & Guthrie, K. (2007). University publishing in a digital age. *The Journal of Electronic Publishing: JEP*, *10*(3). doi:10.3998/3336451.0010.301

Brunschwig, J. (2003). *A guide to Greek thought: Major figures and trends*. Harvard University Press.

Bubela, T., FitzGerald, G. A., & Gold, E. R. (2012). Recalibrating intellectual property rights to enhance translational research collaborations. *Science Translational Medicine*, *4*(122), 122cm3. doi:10.1126citranslmed.3003490 PMID:22357536

Buchanan, G., & Masoodian, M. (2008). Digital Libraries: Universal and Ubiquitous Access to Information. In *11th International Conference on Asian Digital Libraries, ICADL 2008, Bali, Indonesia, December 2-5, 2008, Proceedings*. Springer Science & Business Media. 10.1007/978-3-540-89533-6

Buchanan, J. M. (2014). *Public finance in democratic process: Fiscal institutions and individual choice*. UNC Press Books.

Budapest Open Access Initiative. (2002). *Italian Journal of Library and Information Science*, *3*(2). http://dx.doi.org.simsrad.net.ocs.mq.edu.au/10.4403/jlis.it-8629

Burgess, J., & Green, J. (2013). *YouTube: Online video and participatory culture*. John Wiley & Sons.

Buringh, E., & Van Zanden, J. L. (2009). Charting the "rise of the West": Manuscripts and Printed books in Europe, a long-term perspective from the sixth through eighteenth centuries. *The Journal of Economic History*, *69*(02), 409–445. doi:10.1017/S0022050709000837

Burk, D. L., & Cohen, J. E. (2007). *Fair use infrastructure for copyright management systems (SSRN Scholarly Paper No. ID 1007079)*. Rochester, NY: Social Science Research Network. Retrieved from https://papers.ssrn.com/abstract=1007079

Busch, H.-C. S. (2008). Personal respect, private property, and market economy: What critical theory can learn from Hegel. *Ethical Theory and Moral Practice*, *11*(5), 573–586. doi:10.100710677-008-9118-6

Button, K. J., & Pentecost, E. J. (1995). Testing for convergence of the EU regional economies. *Economic Inquiry*, *33*(4), 664–671. doi:10.1111/j.1465-7295.1995.tb01887.x

Cabannes, Y. (2004). Participatory budgeting: A significant contribution to participatory democracy. *Environment and Urbanization*, *16*(1), 27–46. doi:10.1630/095624704323026133

Cairney, P. (2012). *Understanding public policy: theories and issues*. New York: Palgrave Macmillan. doi:10.1007/978-0-230-35699-3

Calhoun, C. J. (1992). *Habermas and the public sphere*. MIT Press.

Calkins, M. J., & Werhane, P. H. (1998). Adam Smith, Aristotle, and the virtues of commerce. *The Journal of Value Inquiry*, *32*(1), 43–60. doi:10.1023/A:1004273132568

Calland, R., & Bentley, K. A. (2013). *The impact and effectiveness of transparency and accountability initiatives: Freedom of information (SSRN Scholarly Paper No. ID 2305479)*. Rochester, NY: Social Science Research Network. Retrieved from http://papers.ssrn.com/abstract=2305479

Cammaerts, B. (2011). The hegemonic copyright-regime vs. the sharing copyright users of music? *Media Culture & Society*, *33*(3), 491–502. doi:10.1177/0163443711398764

Candela, L., Castelli, D., Ferro, N., Ioannidis, Y., Koutrika, G., Meghini, C., . . . Schuldt, H. (2007). The DELOS digital library reference model. In *Foundations for Digital Libraries*. ISTI-CNR. Retrieved from http://www.delos.info/files/pdf/ReferenceModel/DELOS_DLReferenceModel_0.98.pdf

Canning, J. (2014). *A history of medieval political thought: 300–1450*. Routledge. doi:10.4324/9781315020617

Cantwell, J., & Santangelo, G. D. (2001). Capitalism, profits and innovation in the new techno-economic paradigm. In P. D. D. C. Mueller & P. D. U. Cantner (Eds.), *Capitalism and democracy in the 21st century* (pp. 137–163). Physica-Verlag HD. doi:10.1007/978-3-662-11287-8_8

Carbonell, N., & Stephanidis, C. (2002). European Research Consortium for Informatics and Mathematics Workshop adjunct proceedings. In N. Carbonell & C. Stephanidis (Eds.), *7th ERCIM Workshop "User Interfaces for All"* (p. 210). Chantilly, France: INRIA. Retrieved from https://hal.inria.fr/inria-00101022

Carlaw, K., Oxley, L., Walker, P., Thorns, D., & Nuth, M. (2006). Beyond the hype: Intellectual property and the knowledge society/knowledge economy. *Journal of Economic Surveys*, *20*(4), 633–690. doi:10.1111/j.1467-6419.2006.00262.x

Carnaby, P. (2008). Creating a digital New Zealand: New Zealand's Digital Content Strategy, opportunities and challenges for the education and research sectors. *Proceedings of the IATUL Conferences*. Retrieved from http://docs.lib.purdue.edu/iatul/2008/papers/1

Carroll, A. B., & Shabana, K. M. (2010). The business case for corporate social responsibility: A review of concepts, research and practice. *International Journal of Management Reviews*, *12*(1), 85–105. doi:10.1111/j.1468-2370.2009.00275.x

Carroll, M. W. (2006). The movement for open access on law. *Lewis & Clark Law Review*, *10*, 741.

Carroll, M. W. (2013). Creative Commons and the openness of open access. *The New England Journal of Medicine*, *368*(9), 789–791. doi:10.1056/NEJMp1300040 PMID:23445090

Casey, M. (1991). The electronic information industry in Europe: An analysis of trends and prospects in less developed economies. *Journal of Librarianship and Information Science*, *23*(1), 21–36. doi:10.1177/096100069102300103

Caso, R., & Giovanella, F. (Eds.). (2014). *Balancing Copyright Law in the Digital Age: Comparative Perspectives* (2015 edition). Springer.

Castelli, D., Candela, L., Pagano, P., & Simi, M. (2005). DILIGENT: A digital library infrastructure for supporting joint research. In *International Symposium on Mass Storage Systems and Technology* (pp. 56–59). Los Alamitos, CA: IEEE Computer Society. 10.1109/LGDI.2005.1612465

Castells, M. (2002). *The Internet galaxy: Reflections on the Internet, business, and society*. OUP Oxford. doi:10.1093/acprof:oso/9780199255771.001.0001

Castells, M., & Himanen, P. (2003). *The information society and the welfare state: The Finnish model.* Oxford University Press.

Castillo, A. (2009). *GRIN-banned books: Censorship in eighteenth-century England.* Retrieved from http://www.grin.com/en/e-book/156569/banned-books-censorship-in-eighteenth-century-england

Chalmers, D., Davies, G., & Monti, G. (2010). *European Union law: Cases and materials.* Cambridge University Press. doi:10.1017/CBO9780511841408

Chambers, S. (2009). Rhetoric and the public sphere: Has deliberative democracy abandoned mass democracy? *Political Theory, 37*(3), 323–350. doi:10.1177/0090591709332336

Chan, L., Cuplinskas, D., Eisen, M., Friend, F., Genova, Y., Guédon, J.-C., . . . Velterop, J. (2002, February 14). *Budapest Open Access Initiative.* Retrieved November 10, 2016, from http://www.opensocietyfoundations.org/openaccess/read

Chan, L. (2004). Supporting and Enhancing Scholarship in the Digital Age: The Role of Open Access Institutional Repository. *Canadian Journal of Communication, 29*(3). doi:10.22230/cjc.2004v29n3a1455

Chantavaridou, E. (2009). Open access and institutional repositories in Greece: Progress so far. *OCLC Systems & Services, 25*(1), 47–59. doi:10.1108/10650750910931922

Charlton, J. (2014). EBLIDA urges copyright reform. *Information Today, 31*(1), 14.

Chartier, R. (1994). *The order of books: Readers, authors, and libraries in Europe between the fourteenth and eighteenth centuries.* Stanford University Press.

Cheng, B., Ioannou, I., & Serafeim, G. (2014). Corporate social responsibility and access to finance. *Strategic Management Journal, 35*(1), 1–23. doi:10.1002mj.2131

Chesal, R. (2012). *Loosen up copyright law, says Dutch government.* Retrieved December 13, 2016, from https://www.rnw.org/archive/loosen-copyright-law-says-dutch-government

Chitty, A. (2013). Recognition and property in Hegel and the early Marx. *Ethical Theory and Moral Practice, 16*(4), 685–697. doi:10.100710677-013-9408-5

Cho, S. Y., Lee, C., & Pfeiffer, R. J. Jr. (2013). Corporate social responsibility performance and information asymmetry. *Journal of Accounting and Public Policy, 32*(1), 71–83. doi:10.1016/j.jaccpubpol.2012.10.005

Christian, G. E. (2008). *Open access initiative and the developing world (SSRN Scholarly Paper No. ID 1304665).* Rochester, NY: Social Science Research Network. Retrieved from https://papers.ssrn.com/abstract=1304665

Churchill, D. (2009). Educational applications of Web 2.0: Using blogs to support teaching and learning. *British Journal of Educational Technology, 40*(1), 179–183. doi:10.1111/j.1467-8535.2008.00865.x

Church, R. (2015). *Burroughs Wellcome in the USA and the Wellcome Trust: Pharmaceutical innovation, contested organisational cultures and the triumph of philanthropy*. Carnegie Publishing.

Clarysse, B., Wright, M., Lockett, A., Van de Velde, E., & Vohora, A. (2005). Spinning out new ventures: A typology of incubation strategies from European research institutions. *Journal of Business Venturing*, *20*(2), 183–216. doi:10.1016/j.jbusvent.2003.12.004

Clobridge, C., & Clobridge, A. (2014). All About Open Access Repositories: The Other Side of Open Access. *Online Searcher*, *38*(5), 38–41.

Cockerill, M. J., & Knols, B. G. J. (2008). Open access to research for the developing world. *Issues in Science and Technology*, *24*(2), 65–69.

Cohen, J. L., & Arato, A. (1994). *Civil society and political theory*. MIT Press.

Collins, F. S., & Mansoura, M. K. (2001). The Human Genome Project. *Cancer*, *91*(S1), 221–225. doi:10.1002/1097-0142(20010101)91:1+<221::AID-CNCR8>3.0.CO;2-9 PMID:11148583

Commission of the European Communities. (1988). *Green paper on copyright and the challenge of technology: copyright issues requiring immediate action*. Brussels: Commission of the European Communities.

Commission of the European Communities. (2005). *Communication from the Commission to the Council, the European Parliament, the European Economic and Social Committee and the Committee of the Regions: "i2010—A European Information Society for Growth and Employment."* SEC (2005) 717.

Coonin, B. (2011). Open access publishing in business research: The authors' perspective. *Journal of Business & Finance Librarianship*, *16*(3), 193–212. doi:10.1080/08963568.2011.581606

Copeland, P., & Papadimitriou, D. (2012). *The EU's Lisbon Strategy: Evaluating success, understanding failure*. Palgrave Macmillan. doi:10.1057/9781137272164

Corlett, J. A. (2005). *Interpreting Plato's dialogues* (Vol. 47). Parmenides Pub.

Corneli, A. L., Bentley, M. E., Sorenson, J. R., Henderson, G. E., Horst, C., Moses, A., ... Jamieson, D. J. (2006). Using formative research to develop a context-specific approach to informed consent for clinical trials. *Journal of Empirical Research on Human Research Ethics; JERHRE*, *1*(4), 45–60. doi:10.1525/jer.2006.1.4.45 PMID:19385837

Corrado, E. M. (2005). The Importance of Open Access, Open Source, and Open Standards for Libraries. *Issues in Science and Technology Librarianship*, (42). Retrieved from http://www.istl.org/05-spring/article2.html

Correa, C. (2000). *Intellectual property rights, the WTO and developing countries: The TRIPS Agreement and policy options*. Zed Books.

Correa, C. (2007). *Trade related aspects of intellectual property rights: A commentary on the TRIPS Agreement*. Oxford University Press. doi:10.1093/law/9780199271283.001.0001

Costas, B. R. (2012). *Print culture and peripheries in early modern Europe: A contribution to the history of printing and the book trade in small European and Spanish cities*. BRILL.

Cowles, M. G., Caporaso, J. A., & Risse-Kappen, T. (2001). *Transforming Europe: Europeanization and domestic change*. Cornell University Press.

Craig, G., Gorman, M., & Vercseg, I. (2004). The Budapest declaration: Building European civil society through community development. *Community Development Journal: An International Forum*, *39*(4), 423–429. doi:10.1093/cdj/bsh040

Craig, P., & de Búrca, G. (2011). *EU law: Text, cases, and materials*. OUP Oxford. doi:10.1093/he/9780199576999.001.0001

Cramer, T., & Kott, K. (2010). Designing and implementing second generation digital preservation services: A scalable model for the Stanford Digital Repository. *D-Lib Magazine*, *16*(9/10). doi:10.1045eptember2010-cramer

Cramond, S. (2011). *Explainer: Open access vs traditional academic journal publishers*. Retrieved June 2, 2017, from http://theconversation.com/explainer-open-access-vs-traditional-academic-journal-publishers-2511

Crane, A., Matten, D., & Spence, L. J. (2013). *Corporate social responsibility in a global context (SSRN Scholarly Paper No. ID 2322817)*. Rochester, NY: Social Science Research Network. Retrieved from https://papers.ssrn.com/abstract=2322817

Crawford, W. (2012). *Open access: What you need to know now*. American Library Association.

Creaser, C., Fry, J., Greenwood, H., Oppenheim, C., Probets, S., Spezi, V., & White, S. (2010). Authors' Awareness and Attitudes Toward Open Access Repositories. *New Review of Academic Librarianship, 16*(sup1), 145–161. doi:10.1080/13614533.2010.518851

Crombie, I. M. (2012). *An examination of Plato's doctrines, Volume 2: Plato on knowledge and reality*. Routledge.

Crook, C. (2002). The campus experience of networked learning. In C. Steeples & C. Jones (Eds.), *Networked Learning: Perspectives and Issues* (pp. 293–308)., doi:10.1007/978-1-4471-0181-9_17

Cropanzano, R., Byrne, Z. S., Bobocel, D. R., & Rupp, D. E. (2001). Self-enhancement biases, laboratory experiments, George Wilhelm Friedrich Hegel, and the increasingly crowded world of organizational justice. *Journal of Vocational Behavior*, *58*(2), 260–272. doi:10.1006/jvbe.2001.1798

Crossley, N., & Roberts, J. M. (2004). *After Habermas: New perspectives on the public sphere*. Sociological Review Monograph. Retrieved from https://philpapers.org/rec/HABAHN

Crouch, C. (2000). *After the Euro: Shaping institutions for governance in the wake of European monetary union*. OUP Oxford. doi:10.1093/0198296398.001.0001

Crow, R. (2002). The case for institutional repositories: A SPARC position paper. *Research on Institutional Repositories: Articles and Presentations*. Retrieved from http://digitalcommons.bepress.com/repository-research/27

Cuadrado-Roura, J. R. (2001). Regional convergence in the European Union: From hypothesis to the actual trends. *The Annals of Regional Science*, *35*(3), 333–356. doi:10.1007001680100054

Cullen, R., & Chawner, B. (2011). Institutional repositories, open access, and scholarly communication: A study of conflicting paradigms. *Journal of Academic Librarianship*, *37*(6), 460–470. doi:10.1016/j.acalib.2011.07.002

Curran, J., & Seaton, J. (2009). *Power without responsibility: Press, broadcasting and the Internet in Britain*. Routledge. doi:10.4324/9780203871409

Curzon, V. (1989). Non-discrimination and the rise of "material" reciprocity. *World Economy*, *12*(4), 481–500. doi:10.1111/j.1467-9701.1989.tb00473.x

Dahlberg, L. (2005). The Habermasian public sphere: Taking difference seriously? *Theory and Society*, *34*(2), 111–136. doi:10.100711186-005-0155-z

Dahlgren, P. (2005). The Internet, public spheres, and political communication: Dispersion and deliberation. *Political Communication*, *22*(2), 147–162. doi:10.1080/10584600590933160

Dalakou, V. (2014). *The institutional framework of open access to publicly funded research efforts*. Retrieved from http://helios-eie.ekt.gr/EIE/handle/10442/14433

Darling-Hammond, L. (1995). *Inequality and access to knowledge*. Retrieved from http://eric.ed.gov/?id=ED382721

David, M., & Halbert, D. (2015). Owning the world of ideas: Intellectual property and global network capitalism. *Sage (Atlanta, Ga.)*.

David, P. A., & Foray, D. (2002). An introduction to the economy of the knowledge society. *International Social Science Journal*, *54*(171), 9–23. doi:10.1111/1468-2451.00355

Davies, N. (2014). *Europe: A history*. Random House.

Davis-Floyd, R., & Sargent, C. (1996). The social production of authoritative knowledge in pregnancy and childbirth. *Medical Anthropology Quarterly*, *10*(2), 111–120. doi:10.1525/maq.1996.10.2.02a00010 PMID:8744079

Davison, M. J. (2003). *The legal protection of databases*. Cambridge University Press. doi:10.1017/CBO9780511495236

Davis, P. M. (2011). Open access, readership, citations: A randomized controlled trial of scientific journal publishing. *The FASEB Journal*, *25*(7), 2129–2134. doi:10.1096/fj.11-183988 PMID:21450907

Davis, P. M., Lewenstein, B. V., Simon, D. H., Booth, J. G., & Connolly, M. J. L. (2008). Open access publishing, article downloads, and citations: Randomised controlled trial. *BMJ (Clinical Research Ed.)*, *337*(jul31 1), a568. doi:10.1136/bmj.a568 PMID:18669565

de Camargo, K. R. Jr. (2014). Big publishing and the economics of competition. *American Journal of Public Health*, *104*(1), 8–10. doi:10.2105/AJPH.2013.301719 PMID:24228678

De Dreu, C., & Nauta, A. (2009). Self-interest and other-orientation in organizational behavior: Implications for job performance, prosocial behavior, and personal initiative. *The Journal of Applied Psychology*, *94*(4), 913–926. doi:10.1037/a0014494 PMID:19594234

de la Porte, C., Pochet, P., & Room, B. G. (2001). Social benchmarking, policy making and new governance in the EU. *Journal of European Social Policy*, *11*(4), 291–307. doi:10.1177/095892870101100401

De Martin, J. C. (2012). *The digital public domain: Foundations for an open culture*. Retrieved March 23, 2017, from http://porto.polito.it/2504638/

Deazley, R. (2008). *Commentary on the Statute of Anne 1710*. Retrieved from www.copyrighthistory.org

Deazley, R. (2004). *On the origin of the right to copy: Charting the movement of copyright law in eighteenth century Britain*. Portland, OR: Hart Publishing.

Deazley, R. (2006). *Rethinking copyright: History, theory, language*. Edward Elgar Publishing. doi:10.4337/9781847201621

Dee, P. (2005). *The Australia–US Free Trade Agreement: An assessment*. Retrieved from https://openresearch-repository.anu.edu.au/handle/1885/43027

Deere, C. (2009). *The implementation game: the TRIPS Agreement and the global politics of intellectual property reform in developing countries*. Oxford, UK: Oxford University Press.

Demaio, A., Dorch, B., & Herch, F. (2012). *Open access: Everyone has the right to knowledge*. Retrieved December 14, 2014, from The Conversation website: http://theconversation.com/open-access-everyone-has-the-right-to-knowledge-10342

den Bossche, P. V. (2008). *The law and policy of the World Trade Organization: Text, cases and materials*. Cambridge University Press. doi:10.1017/CBO9780511818394

Deng, X., Kang, J., & Low, B. S. (2013). Corporate social responsibility and stakeholder value maximization: Evidence from mergers. *Journal of Financial Economics*, *110*(1), 87–109. doi:10.1016/j.jfineco.2013.04.014

Dent, C. M. (2010). Free trade agreements in the Asia-Pacific a decade on: Evaluating the past, looking to the future. *International Relations of the Asia-Pacific*, *10*(2), 201–245. doi:10.1093/irap/lcp022

Depoorter, B. (2009). Technology and Uncertainty: The Shaping Effect on Copyright Law. *University of Pennsylvania Law Review*, *157*(6), 1831.

Di Giuli, A., & Kostovetsky, L. (2014). Are red or blue companies more likely to go green? Politics and corporate social responsibility. *Journal of Financial Economics*, *111*(1), 158–180. doi:10.1016/j.jfineco.2013.10.002

Di Vita, G. (2013). The TRIPS Agreement and technological innovation. *Journal of Policy Modeling*, *35*(6), 964–977. doi:10.1016/j.jpolmod.2013.02.001

Dieckhoff, M., & Gallie, D. (2007). The renewed Lisbon Strategy and social exclusion policy. *Industrial Relations Journal*, *38*(6), 480–502. doi:10.1111/j.1468-2338.2007.00460.x

Dimitrakopoulos, D. G. (2001). Incrementalism and path dependence: European integration and institutional change in national parliaments. *Journal of Common Market Studies*, *39*(3), 405–422. doi:10.1111/1468-5965.00296

Dinan, D. (2010). *Ever closer union: An introduction to European integration* (4th ed.). Boulder, Colorado: Lynne Rienner. doi:10.1007/978-1-137-09963-1

Dinwoodie, G. (2007). *Copyright lawmaking authority: An (inter)nationalist perspective on the treaty clause*. Rochester, NY: Social Science Research Network. Retrieved from http://papers.ssrn.com/abstract=1001268

Dobusch, L., & Schüßler, E. (2014). Copyright reform and business model innovation: Regulatory propaganda at German music industry conferences. *Technological Forecasting and Social Change*, *83*, 24–39. doi:10.1016/j.techfore.2013.01.009

Dols, M. (1977). *The Black Death in the Middle East*. Princeton, NJ: Princepton Legacy Library Press.

Douglas, J. (2016). Developing Kia Tene/Off the Cuff–A resource for field educators in social work in Aotearoa New Zealand. *Aotearoa New Zealand Social Work*, *23*(4), 34–44. doi:10.11157/anzswj-vol23iss4id148

Downes, S. (2007). *Places to Go*. Sakai: Innovate.

Drahos, P., & Braithwaite, J. (2002). *Information feudalism: Who owns the knowledge economy?* Earthscan.

Dreier, T., & Hugenholtz, P. B. (2006). *Concise European copyright law*. Kluwer Law International.

Drexl, J., Nérisson, S., Trumpke, F., & Hilty, R. M. (2013). Comments of the Max Planck Institute for Intellectual Property and Competition Law on the proposal for a directive of the European Parliament and of the Council on Collective Management of Copyright and related rights and multi-territorial licensing of rights in musical works for online uses in the internal market: COM (2012)372. *IIC—International Review of Intellectual Property and Competition Law, 44*(3), 322–350. doi:10.100740319-013-0024-7

Dryzek, J. S. (2005). Deliberative democracy in divided societies alternatives to Agonism and Analgesia. *Political Theory, 33*(2), 218–242. doi:10.1177/0090591704268372

Dunn, W. (2003). *Public policy analysis: An introduction* (3rd ed.). Prentice Hall.

Durham, A. L. (2013). *Patent law essentials: A concise guide* (4th ed.). Santa Barbara, CA: Praeger.

Dusollier, S. (2006). The master's tools v. the master's house: Creative commons v. copyright. (Print symposium: Contract options for individual artists). *The Columbia Journal of Law & the Arts, 29*(3), 271–293.

Dutfield, G. (2009). *Intellectual property rights and the life science industries: Past, present and future*. World Scientific. doi:10.1142/6917

Dwyer, C., Hiltz, S. R., & Passerini, K. (2007). Trust and privacy concern within social networking sites: A comparison of Facebook and MySpace. In *Proceedings of the Thirteenth Americas Conference on Information Systems* (pp. 339–351). Retrieved from https://aisel.aisnet.org/amcis2007/339/

Eberhard-Harribey, L. (2006). Corporate social responsibility as a new paradigm in the European policy: How CSR comes to legitimate the European regulation process. *Corporate Governance: The International Journal of Business in Society, 6*(4), 358–368. doi:10.1108/14720700610689487

Ebrahim, N. A. (2017). *Improving research visibility part 4: Open access repositories*. doi:10.6084/m9.figshare.5010749.v1

Ederington, J. (2001). International coordination of trade and domestic policies. *The American Economic Review, 91*(5), 1580–1593. doi:10.1257/aer.91.5.1580

Edwards, R., & Shulenburger, D. (2010). The high cost of scholarly journals (and what to do about it). *Change: The Magazine of Higher Learning, 35*(6), 10–19. doi:10.1080/00091380309604123

Eeckhout, J., & Jovanovic, B. (2002). Knowledge spillovers and inequality. *The American Economic Review, 92*(5), 1290–1307. doi:10.1257/000282802762024511

Ehrenberg, V. (2013). The Greek state (Routledge Library Editions). *Political Science (Wellington, N.Z.), 23*.

Eisenstein, E. (2005). *The printing revolution in early modern Europe*. Cambridge University Press. doi:10.1017/CBO9780511819230

Ekman, J., & Amnå, E. (2012). Political participation and civic engagement: Towards a new typology. *Human Affairs, 22*(3), 283–300. doi:10.247813374-012-0024-1

Elden, P. S., & Crampton, D. J. W. (2012). *Space, knowledge and power: Foucault and geography*. Ashgate Publishing, Ltd.

Elias, S., & Stim, R. (2004). *Patent, copyright & trademark* (7th ed.). Nolo.

Elliott, K., & Bayard, T. (1994). *Reciprocity and retaliation in U.S. trade policy*. Peterson Institute for International Economics. Retrieved from https://ideas.repec.org/b/iie/ppress/78.html

Elsevier. (2016). *Pricing*. Retrieved March 31, 2017, from https://www.elsevier.com/about/company-information/policies/pricing

Elsevier. (2017). *Position statements*. Retrieved April 16, 2017, from https://www.elsevier.com/about/open-science/position-statements

Eltantawy, N., & Wiest, J. B. (2011). The Arab Spring: Social media in the Egyptian revolution: Reconsidering resource mobilization theory. *International Journal of Communication*, *5*(0), 18.

Epstein, M. J., & Buhovac, A. R. (2014). *Making sustainability work: Best practices in managing and measuring corporate social, environmental, and economic impacts*. Berrett-Koehler Publishers.

Epstein, R. (2004). *Liberty versus property? Cracks in the foundations of copyright law*. Rochester, NY: Social Science Research Network. Retrieved from http://papers.ssrn.com/abstract=529943 doi:10.2139srn.529943

Epstein, S. (1991). *Wage labor and guilds in medieval Europe*. UNC Press Books.

Erhemjamts, O., Li, Q., & Venkateswaran, A. (2013). Corporate social responsibility and its impact on firms' investment policy, organizational structure, and performance. *Journal of Business Ethics*, *118*(2), 395–412. doi:10.100710551-012-1594-x

Eriksen, E. O., & Weigard, J. (2004). *Understanding Habermas: Communicating action and deliberative democracy*. London: Bloomsbury Academic.

Eriksen, E. O., & Weigard, J. (2004). *Understanding Habermas: Communicating Action and Deliberative Democracy*. London: Bloomsbury Academic.

Ertl, H. (2006). European Union policies in education and training: The Lisbon agenda as a turning point? *Comparative Education*, *42*(1), 5–27. doi:10.1080/03050060500515652

European Bureau of Library, Information and Documentation Associations & International Federation of Library Associations and Institutions. (2015). *Modernisation of EU copyright rules: yes, but. . .* Retrieved from http://www.eblida.org/news/modernisation-of-eu-copyright-rules-yes,-but.html

European Commission. (1957). *Treaty of Rome, 1206 ME/TXT § (1957)*. Retrieved from http://www.ab.gov.tr/files/ardb/evt/1_avrupa_birligi/1_3_antlasmalar/1_3_1_kurucu_antlasmalar/1957_treaty_establishing_eec.pdf

European Commission. (1995). *Green paper on copyright and related rights in the information society*. Retrieved from http://europa.eu/legislation_summaries/information_society/data_protection/l24152_en.htm

European Commission. (1996). *Directive 96/9/EC of the European Parliament and of the Council of 11 March 1996 on the legal protection of databases*. Pub. L. No. 31996L0009, OJ L 077 (1996).

European Commission. (2004a). *Europe and basic research (Communication from the Commission No. COM (2004) 9 final).* Retrieved from http://cordis.europa.eu/pub/era/docs/com2004_9_en.pdf

European Commission. (2004b). *Directive 2004/48/EC of the European Parliament and of the Council of 29 April 2004 on the enforcement of intellectual property rights* (Text with EEA relevance). Pub. L. No. 32004L0048, OJ L 157 (2004).

European Commission. (2006). *Directive 2006/115/EC of the European Parliament and of the Council of 12 December 2006 on rental right and lending right and on certain rights related to copyright in the field of intellectual property (codified version).* Pub. L. No. 32006L0115, OJ L 376 (2006).

European Commission. (2007). *Commission staff working document report to the Council, the European Parliament and the Economic and Social Committee on the application of Directive 2001/29/EC on the harmonisation of certain aspects of copyright and related rights in the information society.* Retrieved from http://www.ipex.eu/IPEXL-WEB/dossier/document.do?code=SEC&year=2007&number=1556&extension=FIN

European Commission. (2007). *Operational programme "Digital convergence".* Retrieved January 17, 2017, from Regional Policy website: http://ec.europa.eu/regional_policy/en/atlas/programmes/2007-2013/greece/operational-programme-digital-convergence

European Commission. (2009). *Copyright in the knowledge economy (No. 532 final).* Retrieved from http://ec.europa.eu/internal_market/copyright/docs/copyright-infso/20091019_532_en.pdf

European Commission. (2011). *Directive 2011/77/EU of the European Parliament and of the Council of 27 September 2011 amending Directive 2006/116/EC on the term of protection of copyright and certain related rights.* Pub. L. No. 32011L0077, OJ L 265 (2011).

European Commission. (2011a). *Report on the implementation and effect of the Resale Right Directive (2001/84/EC) (COM No. 878 final)* (p. 14). Brussels: European Commission. Retrieved from http://ec.europa.eu/internal_market/copyright/docs/resale/report_en.pdf

European Commission. (2011b). *Single market for intellectual property rights (No. 297 final).* Retrieved from http://www.eesc.europa.eu/?i=portal.en.int-opinions.19154

European Commission. (2012). Commission Recommendation of 17 July 2012 on Access to and Preservations of Scientific Information. *Official Journal of the European Communities*, (L 167), 39–43. Retrieved from http://eur-lex.europa.eu/legal-content/EN/TXT/PDF/?uri=CELEX:32012H0417&rid=1

European Commission. (2012). *Consolidated version of the Treaty on the Functioning of the European Union* (Official Journal of the European Union No. C 326/ 47; p. 344). Retrieved from http://eur-lex.europa.eu/legal-content/EN/TXT/HTML/?uri=CELEX:12012E/TXT&from=EN

European Commission. (2012). *Directive 2012/28/EU of the European Parliament and of the Council of 25 October 2012 on certain permitted uses of orphan works* (Text with EEA relevance). Pub. L. No. 32012L0028, OJ L 299 (2012).

European Commission. (2012, July 17). *Commission Recommendation of 17 July 2012 on access to and preservation of scientific information*. Retrieved from http://eur-lex.europa.eu/legal-content/EN/TXT/PDF/?uri=CELEX:32012H0417&rid=1

European Commission. (2013). *Fact sheet: Open access in Horizon 2020*. Retrieved from https://ec.europa.eu/programmes/horizon2020/sites/horizon2020/files/FactSheet_Open_Access.pdf

European Commission. (2014). *Directive on Collective Management of Copyright 2014/26/EU*. Retrieved from http://ec.europa.eu/internal_market/copyright/management/index_en.htm

European Commission. (2015). *Towards a Modern, More European Copyright Framework*. Retrieved from http://ec.europa.eu/newsroom/dae/document.cfm?action=display&doc_id=12526

European Commission. (2015a). *Commission takes first steps to broaden access to online context and outlines its vision to modernise EU copyright rules*. Retrieved from http://europa.eu/rapid/press-release_IP-15-6261_en.htm

European Commission. (2015b). *Towards a modern, more European copyright framework*. Retrieved from http://ec.europa.eu/newsroom/dae/document.cfm?action=display&doc_id=12526

European Commission. (2016). *Guidelines on open access to scientific publications and research data in Horizon 2020*. Retrieved from http://ec.europa.eu/research/participants/data/ref/h2020/grants_manual/hi/oa_pilot/h2020-hi-oa-pilot-guide_en.pdf

European Commission. (2016). *Open innovation, open science, open to the world—A vision for Europe (No. Unit A1)*. Brussels: Directorate-General for Research and Innovation. Retrieved from http://cache.media.education.gouv.fr/file/2016/45/1/Openinnovationbook_592451.pdf

European Communities. (2001). *Directive 2001/29/EC of the European Parliament and of the Council*. Official Journal of the European Communities, L. 167, 10–19.

European Council. (1991). *Council Directive 91/250/EEC of 14 May 1991 on the legal protection of computer programs*. Pub. L. No. 31991L0250, 122 (1993).

European Council. (1993a). *Council Directive 93/98/EEC Harmonizing the Term of Protection of Copyright and Certain Related Rights*. Retrieved from http://eur-lex.europa.eu/legal-content/EN/TXT/?uri=celex:31993L0098

European Council. (1993b). *Council Directive 93/83/EEC of 27 September 1993 on the coordination of certain rules concerning copyright and rights related to copyright applicable to satellite broadcasting and cable retransmission*. Pub. L. No. 31993L0083, OJ L 248 (1993).

European Council. (2000). Employment, economic reform and social cohesion: A strategic goal for the next decade. In *Lisbon European Council 23 and 24 March 2000: Presidency conclusions*. Retrieved from http://www.europarl.europa.eu/summits/lis1_en.htm

European Parliament & European Council. (2009). *Directive 2009/24/EEC of the European Parliament and of the Council on the Legal Protection of Computer Programs*. Retrieved from http://eur-lex.europa.eu/legal-content/EN/TXT/?uri=uriserv:mi0016

European Parliament. (2007). *Treaty on the Functioning of the European Union*. Retrieved from http://www.europarl.europa.eu/ftu/pdf/en/FTU_3.1.2.pdf

European Parliament. (2013). *Regulation (EU) No 1291/2013 of the European Parliament and of the Council of 11 December 2013 Establishing Horizon 2020—The Framework Programme for Research and Innovation (2014–2020) and Repealing Decision No 1982/2006/EC* (No. L 347/ 104). Retrieved from http://eur-lex.europa.eu/legal-content/EN/TXT/?qid=1445880041822&uri=CELEX:32013R1291

European Parliament. The Single European Act, xy0027 EYR-Lex § (1987).

European Research Council. (2006). *ERC Scientific Council statement on open access*. Retrieved from https://erc.europa.eu/sites/default/files/press_release/files/erc_scc_statement_2006_open_access_0.pdf

European Research Council. (2006). *ERC Scientific Council Statement on Open Access*. Retrieved from https://erc.europa.eu/sites/default/files/press_release/files/erc_scc_statement_2006_open_access_0.pdf

European Research Council. (2012). *Open access guidelines for researchers funded by the ERC*. Retrieved from https://erc.europa.eu/sites/default/files/document/file/open_access_policy_researchers_funded_ERC.pdf

Evans, S. J. (2011). *Public policy issues research trends*. New York: Nova Science Publishers, Inc.

Evens, T., & Donders, K. (2013). Broadcast market structures and retransmission payments: A European perspective. *Media Culture & Society*, *35*(4), 417–434. doi:10.1177/0163443713483797

Everton, M. (2005). "The would-be-author and the real bookseller": Thomas Paine and eighteenth-century printing ethics. *Early American Literature*, *40*(1), 79–110. doi:10.1353/eal.2005.0018

Fairclough, J. (2002). *Rethinking construction innovation and research—A review of the government's R&D policies and practices*. DTI Press.

Febvre, L., & Martin, H.-J. (1997). *The coming of the book: The impact of printing 1450–1800*. Verso.

Feenberg, A. (2012). *Questioning technology*. Routledge. doi:10.4324/9780203022313

Fehr, E., & Gächter, S. (2000). Fairness and Retaliation: The Economics of Reciprocity. *The Journal of Economic Perspectives*, *14*(3), 159–181. doi:10.1257/jep.14.3.159

Feinberg, J. (2014). *Rights, justice, and the bounds of liberty: Essays in social philosophy*. Princeton University Press.

Felice, W. F. (1996). *Taking suffering seriously: The importance of collective human rights*. SUNY Press.

Fennell, L. (2010). *Commons, anticommons, semicommons*. Rochester, NY: Social Science Research Network. Retrieved from http://papers.ssrn.com/abstract=1348267

Ficsor, M. (2002). *Collective management of copyright and related rights*. World Intellectual Property Organization.

Finch, J. (2012). *Accessibility, sustainability, excellence: How to expand access to research publications.* Report of the Working Group on Expanding Access to Published Research Findings. Retrieved from http://www.researchinfonet.org

Finch, J. (2013). Accessibility, sustainability, excellence: The UK approach to open access. *Information Services & Use, 33*(1), 11–18. doi:10.3233/ISU-130687

Fischer, R. (2005). *The expansion of intellectual property rights by international agreement: A case study comparing Chile and Australia's bilateral FTA negotiations with the U.S. Bepress Legal Series*. Retrieved from http://law.bepress.com/expresso/eps/549

Fischer, F. (2003). *Reframing public policy: Discursive politics and deliberative practices*. Oxford: Oxford University Press. doi:10.1093/019924264X.001.0001

Fishman, S. (2014). *The copyright handbook: What every writer needs to know*. Nolo.

Fitzgerald, B. (2005). *The Creative Commons model of open content licensing*. Retrieved from http://eprints.qut.edu.au

Fitzgerald, B. (2007). *Open content licensing (OCL) for open educational resources*. Retrieved from http://www.oecd.org

Fitzgerald, B. (2007). *Open content licensing (OCL) for open educational resources*. Retrieved from http://www.oecd.org/edu/ceri/38645489.pdf

Fitzgerald, B. F. (2006). *Open Access to Knowledge (OAK) law project report no. 1: Creating a legal framework for copyright management of open access within the Australian academic and research sector*. Retrieved from http://eprints.qut.edu.au/6099/

Fitzgerald, B. F., Coates, J. M., & Lewis, S. M. (2007). *Open content licensing: Cultivating the Creative Commons*. Sydney University Press. Retrieved from http://eprints.qut.edu.au

Flammer, C. (2013). Corporate social responsibility and shareholder reaction: The environmental awareness of investors. *Academy of Management Journal, 56*(3), 758–781. doi:10.5465/amj.2011.0744

Flyvbjerg, B. (1998). *Habermas and Foucault: Thinkers for civil society? (SSRN Scholarly Paper No. ID 2237923)*. Rochester, NY: Social Science Research Network. Retrieved from http://papers.ssrn.com/abstract=2237923

Forgeng, J. L., & Singman, J. L. (1999). *Daily life in medieval Europe*. Greenwood Publishing Group.

Forman, G., & Pufall, P. B. (2013). *Constructivism in the Computer Age*. First. doi:10.4324/9780203771242

Foucault, M. (1980). Two lectures. In C. Gordon (Ed.), *Power/knowledge: Selected interviews and other writings, 1972–1977* (1st American ed.; pp. 78–108). New York: Vintage.

Foucault, M. (1995). *Discipline & punish: The birth of the prison* (2nd ed.). (A. Sheridan, Trans.). New York: Vintage Books.

Foucault, M. (2012). *The archaeology of knowledge*. Knopf Doubleday Publishing Group.

Frank, M. (2013). Open but not free—Publishing in the 21st century. *The New England Journal of Medicine, 368*(9), 787–789. doi:10.1056/NEJMp1211259 PMID:23445089

Freeman, S. R. (2003). *The Cambridge companion to Rawls*. Cambridge University Press.

Friesike, S., Widenmayer, B., Gassmann, O., & Schildhauer, T. (2015). Opening science: Towards an agenda of open science in academia and industry. *The Journal of Technology Transfer, 40*(4), 581–601. doi:10.100710961-014-9375-6

Frosio, G. F. (2017). *Resisting the resistance: Resisting copyright and promoting alternatives (SSRN Scholarly Paper No. ID 2908966)*. Rochester, NY: Social Science Research Network. Retrieved from https://papers.ssrn.com/abstract=2908966

Fuchs, C., & Sandoval, M. (2013). The diamond model of open access publishing: Why policy makers, scholars, universities, libraries, labour unions and the publishing world need to take non-commercial, non-profit open access serious. *TripleC, 11*(2), 428–443. doi:10.31269/triplec.v11i2.502

Furlong, S. R., & Kerwin, C. M. (2005). Interest group participation in rule making: A decade of change. *Journal of Public Administration: Research and Theory, 15*(3), 353–370. doi:10.1093/jopart/mui022

Fyfe, A. (2006). Information revolution: William Chambers, the publishing pioneer. *Endeavour, 30*(4), 120–125. doi:10.1016/j.endeavour.2006.11.001 PMID:17112590

Gangopadhyay, K., & Mondal, D. (2012). Does stronger protection of intellectual property stimulate innovation? *Economics Letters, 116*(1), 80–82. doi:10.1016/j.econlet.2012.01.006

Gargouri, Y., Larivière, V., Gingras, Y., Carr, L., & Harnad, S. (2012). *Green and gold open access percentages and growth, by discipline*. Retrieved from http://arxiv.org/abs/1206.3664

Garrett, G. (1995). The politics of legal integration in the European Union. *International Organization, 49*(01), 171–181. doi:10.1017/S0020818300001612

Gaspar, R., Aksu, B., Cuine, A., Danhof, M., Takac, M. J.-M., Linden, H. H., ... Dencker, L. (2012). Towards a European strategy for medicines research (2014–2020): The EUFEPS position paper on Horizon 2020. *European Journal of Pharmaceutical Sciences, 47*(5), 979–987. doi:10.1016/j.ejps.2012.09.020 PMID:23046836

Gaventa, J., & Cornwall, A. (2013). Power and knowledge. In *The SAGE handbook of action research: participative inquiry and practice* (pp. 172–189). SAGE.

Geiger, C. (2012). *Criminal enforcement of intellectual property: A handbook of contemporary research*. Edward Elgar Publishing. doi:10.4337/9781781005149

Geller, P. (2000). Copyright history and the future: What's culture got to do with it. *Journal of the Copyright Society of the U.S.A., 47*, 209.

Gendron, Y. (2015). Accounting academia and the threat of the paying-off mentality. *Critical Perspectives on Accounting, 26*, 168–176. doi:10.1016/j.cpa.2013.06.004

Gentleman, R. C., Carey, V. J., Bates, D. M., Bolstad, B., Dettling, M., Dudoit, S., ... Zhang, J. (2004). Bioconductor: Open software development for computational biology and bioinformatics. *Genome Biology, 5*(10), R80. doi:10.1186/gb-2004-5-10-r80 PMID:15461798

Georgiou, P., & Papadatou, F. (2010). Open access in Greece. In *Open access in southern European countries* (pp. 39–62). Academic Press. Retrieved from http://www.researchgate.net/post/Open_Access_in_Southern_European_Countries

Georgiou, P., & Papadatou, F. (2010). Open Access in Greece. *Open Access in Southern European Countries*, 39–62. Retrieved from http://www.researchgate.net/post/Open_Access_in_Southern_European_Countries

Ghosh, M. (2011). Advocacy for open access: A selected review of the literature and resource list. *Library Hi Tech News, 28*(2), 19–23. doi:10.1108/07419051111135245

Ghosh, S. B., & Kumar Das, A. (2007). Open Access and Institutional Repositories — A Developing Country Perspective: A case study of India. *IFLA Journal, 33*(3), 229–250. doi:10.1177/0340035207083304

Giannopoulou, A. (2012). Copyright enforcement measures: The role of the ISPs and the respect of the principle of proportionality. *European Journal of Law and Technology, 3*(1). Retrieved from http://ejlt.org/article/view/122

Gillespie, V., & Powell, S. (2014). *A companion to the early printed book in Britain, 1476–1558*. Boydell & Brewer Ltd.

Gill, M. L., & Pellegrin, P. (2009). *A companion to ancient philosophy*. John Wiley & Sons.

Gimmler, A. (2001). Deliberative democracy, the public sphere and the Internet. *Philosophy and Social Criticism, 27*(4), 21–39. doi:10.1177/019145370102700402

Ginns, P., Kitay, J., & Prosser, M. (2010). Transfer of academic staff learning in a research-intensive university. *Teaching in Higher Education, 15*(3), 235–246. doi:10.1080/13562511003740783

Ginsburg, J. C., & Ricketson, S. (2006). Inducers and Authorisers: A Comparison of the US Supreme Court's Grokster Decision and the Australian Federal Court's Kazaa Ruling. *Media & Arts Law Review, 11*(1). Retrieved from https://papers.ssrn.com/abstract=888928

Ginsburgh, V. (2005). The Economic consequences of droit de suite in the European Union. *Economic Analysis and Policy, 35*(1–2), 61–71. doi:10.1016/S0313-5926(05)50004-3

Ginsburg, J. C. (2000). *International copyright: From a "bundle" of national copyright laws to a supranational code? (SSRN Scholarly Paper No. ID 222508)*. Rochester, NY: Social Science Research Network. Retrieved from http://papers.ssrn.com/abstract=222508

Ginsburg, J. C. (2004). The right to claim authorship in U.S. copyright and trademarks law. *Houston Law Review*, *41*, 263.

Ginsburg, J. C. (2009). The U.S. experience with mandatory copyright formalities: A love/hate relationship. *Columbia Journal of Law and the Arts*, *33*, 311.

Gintis, H. (2005). *Moral sentiments and material interests: The foundations of cooperation in economic life*. MIT Press. doi:10.7551/mitpress/4771.001.0001

Givoni, M. (2006). Development and impact of the modern high-speed train: A Review. *Transport Reviews*, *26*(5), 593–611. doi:10.1080/01441640600589319

Glasgow, L. J. (2002). Stretching the limits of intellectual property rights: Has the pharmaceutical industry gone too far? *IDEA the Journal of Law and Technology*, *41*, 227.

Glöckner, A., & Betsch, T. (2008). *Modeling option and strategy choices with connectionist networks: Towards an integrative model of automatic and deliberate decision making (SSRN Scholarly Paper No. ID 1090866)*. Rochester, NY: Social Science Research Network. Retrieved from https://papers.ssrn.com/abstract=1090866

Goff, N. (2011). Direct-response bookselling: How it died, why it is alive again, and why it will become even more important in the future. *Publishing Research Quarterly*, *27*(3), 259–267. doi:10.100712109-011-9219-2

Goldberg, L., Johnson, J., Eber, H., Hogan, R., Ashton, M. C., Cloninger, C. R., & Gough, H. G. (2006). The international personality item pool and the future of public-domain personality measures. *Journal of Research in Personality*, *40*(1), 84–96. doi:10.1016/j.jrp.2005.08.007

Goldin, I., & Reinert, K. (2012). *Globalization for development: Meeting new challenges*. Oxford University Press.

Goldstein, J., Rivers, D., & Tomz, M. (2007). Institutions in international relations: Understanding the effects of the GATT and the WTO on world trade. *International Organization*, *61*(01), 37–67. doi:10.1017/S0020818307070014

Goodwin, I., & Spittle, S. (2002). The European Union and the information society: Discourse, power and policy. *New Media & Society*, *4*(2), 225–249. doi:10.1177/146144480200400206

Gordon, M., & Raciborski, N. (2007). *US7310729 B2*. Retrieved from http://www.google.com/patents/US7310729

Grabow, S., Hilliker, M., & Moskal, J. (2006). *Comprehensive planning and citizen participation*. University of Wisconsin: Extension Service.

Graf, C., Wager, E., Bowman, A., Fiack, S., Scott-Lichter, D., & Robinson, A. (2007). Best practice guidelines on publication ethics: A publisher's perspective. *International Journal of Clinical Practice*, *61*, 1–26. doi:10.1111/j.1742-1241.2006.01230.x PMID:17206953

Granieri, M., & Renda, A. (2012). *Innovation law and policy in the European Union: Towards Horizon 2020*. Springer Science & Business Media. doi:10.1007/978-88-470-1917-1

Granstrand, O., & Holgersson, M. (2015). Intellectual property. In *The Wiley Blackwell Encyclopedia of Consumption and Consumer Studies*. John Wiley & Sons, Ltd. doi:10.1002/9781118989463.wbeccs151

Greco, A. N. (2013). *The book publishing industry*. Routledge. doi:10.4324/9780203834565

Greek Government. (2011). Structure, validation of studies and internationalization of higher education institutions., Pub. L. No. 195. *Greek Government Newspaper, 48*.

Greek Parliament. (2010). *Greek Constitution*. Retrieved from http://www.hellenicparliament.gr/UserFiles/8c3e9046-78fb-48f4-bd82-bbba28ca1ef5/SYNTAGMA.pdf

Gresser, E. (2013). *U.S. share of world intellectual property revenue—39 percent*. Retrieved April 16, 2015, from http://www.progressive-economy.org/trade_facts/u-s-share-of-world-intellectual-property-revenue-39-percent/

Griffiths, J. R., & Brophy, P. (2005). *Student searching behavior and the web: Use of academic resources and Google-ProQuest*. Academic Press.

Grodzinsky, F. S., & Bottis, M. C. (2007). Private use as fair use: Is it fair? *SIGCAS Comput. Soc.*, *37*(2), 11–24. doi:10.1145/1327325.1327326

Grossman, G., & Horn, H. (1987). *Infant-industry protection reconsidered: The case of informational barriers to entry* (Working Paper No. 2159). National Bureau of Economic Research. Retrieved from http://www.nber.org/papers/w2159

Grüttemeier, H., & Mahon, B. (2003). Open access to scientific and technical information: State of the art and future trends. In *ICSTI/INIST/INSERM Seminar, 23–24 January 2003, Paris, France*. IOS Press.

Guastello, S. J. (2013). *Chaos, catastrophe, and human affairs: Applications of nonlinear dynamics to work, organizations, and social evolution*. Psychology Press. doi:10.4324/9780203773895

Gubbi, J., Buyya, R., Marusic, S., & Palaniswami, M. (2013). Internet of Things (IoT): A vision, architectural elements, and future directions. *Future Generation Computer Systems*, *29*(7), 1645–1660. doi:10.1016/j.future.2013.01.010

Gutting, G. (1989). *Michel Foucault's archaeology of scientific reason: Science and the history of reason*. Cambridge University Press. doi:10.1017/CBO9781139172141

Gutting, G. (2005). *The Cambridge companion to Foucault*. Cambridge University Press. doi:10.1017/CCOL0521840821

Gutu, G. (2014). Interpretative dimensions on object of public property. *Contemporary Legal Institutions*, *6*(1), 163–167.

Habermas, J. (2015). *Between Facts and Norms: Contributions to a Discourse Theory of Law and Democracy*. John Wiley & Sons.

Habermas, J. (2015). *The theory of communicative action: Reason and the rationalization of society* (1st ed., Vol. 1). Polity.

Habermas, J., & Rehg, W. (2001). Constitutional democracy: A paradoxical union of contradictory principles? *Political Theory*, *29*(6), 766–781. doi:10.1177/0090591701029006002

Häggström, B. M. (2004). EBLIDA's action in Europe. *LIBER Quarterly*, *14*(3–4). doi:10.18352/lq.7792

Hahamis, P., Iles, J., & Healy, M. (2005). E-government in Greece: Bridging the gap between need and reality. *Electronic Journal of E-Government*, *3*(4), 185–192.

Hall, H., & Graham, D. (2004). Creation and recreation: Motivating collaboration to generate knowledge capital in online communities. *International Journal of Information Management*, *24*(3), 235–246. doi:10.1016/j.ijinfomgt.2004.02.004

Hampton, K. N., Livio, O., & Sessions Goulet, L. (2010). The Social Life of Wireless Urban Spaces: Internet Use, Social Networks, and the Public Realm. *Journal of Communication*, *60*(4), 701–722. doi:10.1111/j.1460-2466.2010.01510.x

Hansmann, H., & Santilli, M. (2001). Royalties for artists versus royalties for authors and composers. *Journal of Cultural Economics*, *25*(4), 259–281. doi:10.1023/A:1017923625973

Harbottle, G. (2006). The implementation in England and Wales of the European Enforcement Directive. *Journal of Intellectual Property Law & Practice*, *1*(11), 719–727. doi:10.1093/jiplp/jpl170

Harley, D., Acord, S. K., Earl-Novell, S., Lawrence, S., & King, C. J. (2010). Assessing the future landscape of scholarly communication: An exploration of faculty values and needs in seven disciplines. *Center for Studies in Higher Education*. Retrieved from http://escholarship.org/uc/item/15x7385g

Harnad, S. (2005). *Fast-forward on the green road to open access: The case against mixing up green and gold*. Retrieved from http://arxiv.org/abs/cs/0503021

Harnad, S. (2010). *Gold open access publishing must not be allowed to retard the progress of green open access self-archiving*. Retrieved from http://eprints.soton.ac.uk/271818/1/logospaper.pdf

Harnad, D. (2005). The implementation of the Berlin Declaration on Open Access. *D-Lib Magazine*, *11*(3). doi:10.1045/march2005-harnad

Harnad, S. (2007). The green road to open access: A leveraged transition. In *The Culture of Periodicals from the Perspective of the Electronic Age* (pp. 99–105). L'Harmattan. Retrieved from https://eprints.soton.ac.uk/263309/

Harnad, S. (2012). Open access: A green light for archiving. *Nature, 487*(7407), 302. doi:10.1038/487302b PMID:22810686

Harnad, S., & Brody, T. (2004). Comparing the impact of open access (OA) vs. non-OA articles in the same journals. *D-Lib Magazine, 10*(6). Retrieved from https://eprints.soton.ac.uk/260207/

Harnad, S., Brody, T., Vallières, F., Carr, L., Hitchcock, S., Gingras, Y., ... Hilf, E. R. (2004). The access/impact problem and the green and gold roads to open access. *Serials Review, 30*(4), 310–314. doi:10.1080/00987913.2004.10764930

Harris, D. (2004). TRIPS' Rebound: An historical analysis of how the TRIPS Agreement can ricochet back against the United States. *Northwestern Journal of International Law & Business, 25*(1), 99–164.

Harrison, B. H., & Matthew, H. C. G. (2004). The Oxford dictionary of national biography: In association with the British Academy: From the earliest times to the year 2000 (British Academy, Ed.). Oxford, UK: Oxford University Press.

Harrison, S., & Sullivan, P. H. Sr. (2000). Profiting from intellectual capital: Learning from leading companies. *Journal of Intellectual Capital, 1*(1), 33–46. doi:10.1108/14691930010324124

Hartzog, N. (2003). Gaining Momentum: A Review of Recent Developments Surrounding the Expansion of the Copyright Misuse Doctrine and Analylsis of the Doctrine in Its Current Form. *Michigan Telecommunications and Technology Law Review, 10*, 373–406.

Haug, K., Salek, R. M., Conesa, P., Hastings, J., de Matos, P., Rijnbeek, M., ... Steinbeck, C. (2013). MetaboLights—An open-access general-purpose repository for metabolomics studies and associated meta-data. *Nucleic Acids Research, 41*(D1), D781–D786. doi:10.1093/nar/gks1004 PMID:23109552

Head, K. (1994). Infant industry protection in the steel rail industry. *Journal of International Economics, 37*(3–4), 141–165. doi:10.1016/0022-1996(94)90043-4

Hegel, G. W. F. (1991). Hegel: Elements of the philosophy of right (A. W. Wood, Ed.; H. B. Nisbet, Trans.). Cambridge, UK: Cambridge University Press.

Hegel, G. W. F. (2015). *The philosophy of right* (A. White, Trans.). Hackett Publishing.

Hendriks, C. M. (2006). Integrated deliberation: Reconciling civil society's dual role in deliberative democracy. *Political Studies, 54*(3), 486–508. doi:10.1111/j.1467-9248.2006.00612.x

Henry, C., & Stiglitz, J. (2010). Intellectual property, dissemination of innovation and sustainable development. *Global Policy, 1*(3), 237–251. doi:10.1111/j.1758-5899.2010.00048.x

Herb, U. (2010). Sociological implications of scientific publishing: Open access, science, society, democracy and the digital divide. *First Monday*, *15*(2). doi:10.5210/fm.v15i2.2599

Héritier, A. (2003). Composite democracy in Europe: The role of transparency and access to information. *Journal of European Public Policy*, *10*(5), 814–833. doi:10.1080/1350176032000124104

Hernández-Borges, A. A., Cabrera-Rodríguez, R., Montesdeoca-Melián, A., Martínez-Pineda, B., Torres-Álvarez de Arcaya, M. L., & Jiménez-Sosa, A. (2006). Awareness and attitude of Spanish medical authors to open access publishing and the author-pays model. *Journal of the Medical Library Association, 94*(4), 449–451, e218.

Herther, N. K. (2005). The e-book industry today: A bumpy road becomes an evolutionary path to market maturity. *The Electronic Library*, *23*(1), 45–53. doi:10.1108/02640470510582727

Hesmondhalgh, D. (2005). Media and cultural policy as public policy: The case of the British Labour government. *International Journal of Cultural Policy*, *11*(1), 95–109. doi:10.1080/10286630500067861

Hesse, C. (2002). The rise of intellectual property, 700 B.C.–A.D. 2000: An idea in the balance. *Daedalus*, *131*(2), 26–45.

Hillier, J. (2003). Agonizing over consensus: Why Habermasian ideals cannot be 'real.'. *Planning Theory*, *2*(1), 37–59. doi:10.1177/1473095203002001005

Hill, M., & Varone, F. (2014). *The public policy process*. Routledge. doi:10.4324/9781315832937

Hix, S., & Høyland, B. (2011). *The political system of the European Union*. Palgrave Macmillan. doi:10.1007/978-0-230-34418-1

Hoekman, B., & Kostecki, M. (2009). *The political economy of the world trading system*. Oxford University Press.

Hohfeld, W. N. (1913). Some fundamental legal conceptions as applied in judicial reasoning. *The Yale Law Journal*. Retrieved from http://archive.org/details/jstor-785533

Hohfeld, W. N. (2008). Fundamental legal conceptions. *Nottingham Law Journal, 17*, 39.

Hollingsworth, J. R., & Boyer, R. (1997). *Contemporary capitalism: The embeddedness of institutions*. Cambridge University Press. doi:10.1017/CBO9781139174701

Honneth, A. (2010). *The pathologies of individual freedom: Hegel's social theory*. Princeton University Press.

Hopkins, J. (2011). The role of learned societies in knowledge exchange and dissemination: The case of the Regional Studies Association, 1965–2005. *History of Education*, *40*(2), 255–271. doi:10.1080/0046760X.2010.518161

Hoppe, H.-H. (2004, October 11). *The ethics and economics of private property.* Retrieved April 10, 2015, from http://mises.org/library/ethics-and-economics-private-property

Hormia-Poutanen, K., Xenidou-Dervou, C., Kupryte, R., Stange, K., Kuznetsov, A. V., & Woodward, H. M. (2006). Consortia in Europe: Describing the various solutions through four country examples. *Library Trends*, *54*(3), 359–381. doi:10.1353/lib.2006.0026

Houle, J. R. (1991). Digital audio sampling, copyright law and the American music industry: Piracy or just a bad rap. *Loyola Law Review*, *37*, 879.

House, E. (2013). Challenges facing the UK book industry. *Publishing Research Quarterly*, *29*(3), 211–219. doi:10.100712109-013-9320-9

Hua, J. (2014). Reconstruction of copyright limitations and exceptions in the digital network age: Importation of legal flexibility and certainty. *International Journal of Technology Policy and Law*, *1*(4), 363. doi:10.1504/IJTPL.2014.061637

Hugenholtz, P. B., & Okediji, R. L. (2009). *Contours of an International Instrument on Limitations and Exceptions: Global Intellectual Property and Developing Countr.* doi:10.1093/acprof:oso/9780195342109.003.0020

Hugenholtz, P. B., & Senftleben, M. (2012). *Fair use in Europe: In search of flexibilities (SSRN Scholarly Paper No. ID 2013239).* Rochester, NY: Social Science Research Network. Retrieved from https://papers.ssrn.com/abstract=2013239

Hughes, J. (2009). *A short history of intellectual property in relation to copyright.* Rochester, NY: Social Science Research Network. Retrieved from http://papers.ssrn.com/abstract=1432860

Hughes, J. M. (2006). *To the Maginot Line*. Harvard University Press.

Husserl, E. (2012). *Ideas: General introduction to pure phenomenology*. Routledge. doi:10.4324/9780203120330

Idris, K. (2003). *Intellectual property: A power tool for economic growth.* WIPO.

International Federation of Library Associations and Institutions. (2005). *IFLA 112–114: World guide to library, archive, and information science associations* (M. Schweizer, Ed.). München: K.G. Saur.

Jackson, J. (2000). *The jurisprudence of GATT and the WTO: Insights on treaty law and economic relations*. Cambridge University Press.

Jaeger, P. T., & Bertot, J. C. (2010). Transparency and technological change: Ensuring equal and sustained public access to government information. *Government Information Quarterly*, *27*(4), 371–376. doi:10.1016/j.giq.2010.05.003

Jantz, R. C., & Wilson, M. C. (2008). Institutional repositories: Faculty deposits, marketing, and the reform of scholarly communication. *Journal of Academic Librarianship*, *34*(3), 186–195. doi:10.1016/j.acalib.2008.03.014

Jappelli, T., & Pagano, M. (2002). Information sharing, lending and defaults: Cross-country evidence. *Journal of Banking & Finance*, *26*(10), 2017–2045. doi:10.1016/S0378-4266(01)00185-6

Jeffery, K. G. (2006). Open Access: An introduction. *ERCIM News, 64*(3), 16-17. Retrieved from https://www.researchgate.net/profile/Keith_Jeffery/publication/228635875_Open_Access_an_introduction/links/00b7d527a52273637a000000.pdf

Johns, A. (2010). *Piracy: The intellectual property wars from Gutenberg to Gates*. University of Chicago Press.

Johnson, D. R. (2007). Reflections on the bundle of rights. *Vermont Law Review*, *32*, 247.

Johnson, P. (2006). *Habermas: Rescuing the public sphere*. Routledge. doi:10.4324/9780203020166

Johnson, R. (2002). Institutional repositories: Partnering with faculty to enhance scholarly communication. *D-Lib Magazine*, *8*(11). Retrieved from http://www.dlib.org/dlib/november02/johnson/11johnson.html

Jones, E. (2003). *The European miracle: Environments, economies and geopolitics in the history of Europe and Asia*. Cambridge University Press. doi:10.1017/CBO9780511817700

Jordana, J. (2002). *Governing telecommunications and the new information society in Europe*. Edward Elgar Publishing. doi:10.4337/9781781950463

Jordan, B. (2014). Technology and social interaction: Notes on the achievement of authoritative knowledge in complex settings. *Talent Development and Excellence*, *6*(1), 95–132.

Journal, A. (2002). *Abstracting Knowledge Formation: A Report on Academia and Publishing (Part Three: The University and Global Restructuring: The Scholars Meet the Market)* (Critical Essay). Retrieved from https://books.apple.com/fr/book/abstracting-knowledge-formation-report-on-academia/id526086447

Kahan, D. M., & Braman, D. (2005). *Cultural cognition and public policy (SSRN Scholarly Paper)*. Rochester, NY: Social Science Research Network. Retrieved from http://papers.ssrn.com/abstract=746508

Kahn, C. H. (1998). *Plato and the Socratic dialogue: The philosophical use of a literary form*. Cambridge University Press.

Kaizer, H. (2010). *Plato and Frankfurt: Two theories of the relations between love and living well* (Honors thesis). Retrieved from http://digitalcommons.bucknell.edu/honors_theses/76

Kallinikou, D. (2007). *Regulations for intellectual property and relevant rights in Greece*. Athens: Sakkoulas.

Kameas, A., Bellis, S., Mavrommati, I., Delaney, K., Colley, M., & Pounds-Cornish, A. (2003). An architecture that treats everyday objects as communicating tangible components. In *Proceedings of the First IEEE International Conference on Pervasive Computing and Communications, 2003. [PerCom 2003]* (pp. 115–122). IEEE. 10.1109/PERCOM.2003.1192733

Kapczynski, A. (2008). *The access to knowledge mobilization and the new politics of intellectual property* (SSRN Scholarly Paper No. ID 1323525). Retrieved from Social Science Research Network website: https://papers.ssrn.com/abstract=1323525

Karaesony, G. (2013). HUNOR: The Collaboration of Hungarian Open Access Repositories. *Procedia: Social and Behavioral Sciences*, *73*, 57–61. doi:10.1016/j.sbspro.2013.02.019

Karakostas, I. (2009). *Common law and Internet* (3rd ed.). Athens: Sakkoulas.

Karjala, D. (2002). Distinguishing patent and copyright subject matter. *Connecticut Law Review*, *35*, 439.

Karolides, N., Bald, M., & Sova, D. (2011). *120 banned books: Censorship histories of world literature* (2nd ed.). New York, NY: Checkmark Books.

Katz, Z. (2006). Pitfalls of open licensing: An analysis of creative commons licensing. *IDEA: The Intellectual Property Law Review*, *46*, 391.

Kellner, D. (2014). Habermas, the Public Sphere, and Democracy. In D. Boros & J. M. Glass (Eds.), *Re-Imagining Public Space* (pp. 19–43)., doi:10.1057/9781137373311_2

Kennett, P. (2004). *A handbook of comparative social policy*. Edward Elgar Publishing.

Khan, A., Muttakin, M. B., & Siddiqui, J. (2013). Corporate governance and corporate social responsibility disclosures: Evidence from an emerging economy. *Journal of Business Ethics*, *114*(2), 207–223. doi:10.100710551-012-1336-0

Kieser, A. (1989). Organizational, institutional, and societal evolution: Medieval craft guilds and the genesis of formal organizations. *Administrative Science Quarterly*, *34*(4), 540–564. doi:10.2307/2393566

Klein, D. (2009). *The strategic management of intellectual capital*. Routledge. doi:10.4324/9780080517926

Klein, J. T. (2008). Evaluation of interdisciplinary and transdisciplinary research: A literature review. *American Journal of Preventive Medicine*, *35*(2supplement), S116–S123. doi:10.1016/j.amepre.2008.05.010 PMID:18619391

Knill, C., & Lehmkuhl, D. (2002). Private actors and the state: Internationalization and changing patterns of governance. *Governance: An International Journal of Policy, Administration and Institutions*, *15*(1), 41–63. doi:10.1111/1468-0491.00179

Knowles, D. (1983). Hegel on property and personality. *The Philosophical Quarterly*, *33*(130), 45–62. doi:10.2307/2219203

Kochin, M. S. (2002). *Gender and rhetoric in Plato's political thought*. Cambridge University Press.

Kohler-Koch, B., & Eising, R. (1999). *The transformation of governance in the European Union*. Psychology Press. doi:10.4324/9780203279625

Koppel, M., & Schler, J. (2004). Authorship verification as a one-class classification problem. In *Proceedings of the Twenty-first International Conference on Machine Learning* (p. 62). New York, NY: ACM. 10.1145/1015330.1015448

Kostagiolas, P., & Banou, C. (2007). *Managing expectations for open access in Greece: Perceptions from the publishers and academic libraries* (L. Chan & B. Martens, Eds.). Retrieved from http://eprints.rclis.org/10041/

Kostylo, J. (2008). *Commentary on Johannes of Speyer's Venetian monopoly* (1469). Retrieved April 17, 2015, from http://www.copyrighthistory.org/

Kostylo, J. (2010). *From gunpowder to print: The common origins of copyright and patent.* Retrieved from http://books.openedition.org/obp/1062

Kostylo, J. (2012). Sinking and shrinking city: Cosmopolitanism, historical memory and social change in Venice. In *Post-cosmopolitan Cities: Explorations of Urban Coexistence* (pp. 170–193). Berghahn Books.

Koulouris, A., Kyriaki-Manessi, D., Giannakopoulos, G., & Zervos, S. (2013). Institutional repository policies: Best practices for encouraging self-archiving. *Procedia: Social and Behavioral Sciences*, *73*, 769–776. doi:10.1016/j.sbspro.2013.02.117

Kounoudes, A. D., Artemi, P., & Zervas, M. (2010). Ktisis: Building an open access institutional and cultural repository. In M. Ioannides, D. Fellner, A. Georgopoulos, & D. G. Hadjimitsis (Eds.), *Digital Heritage* (pp. 504–512). doi:10.1007/978-3-642-16873-4_41

Koutras, N. (2016). History of copyright, growth and conceptual analysis: Copyright protection and the emergence of open access. *Intellectual Property Quarterly*, (2), 135-150.

Koutras, N. (2018). The copyright law framework and its interaction with open access repositories in Europe. *Publishing Research Quarterly Journal*, *34*(1), 32-53.

Koutras, N. (2016). Open access as a means for social justice in the context of cultural diversity in Europe. *Seattle Journal for Social Justice*, *15*(1). Retrieved from http://digitalcommons.law.seattleu.edu/sjsj/vol15/iss1/10

Koutras, N., & Bottis, M. (2013). Institutional repositories of open access: A paradigm of innovation and changing in educational politics. *Procedia: Social and Behavioral Sciences*, *106*, 1499–1504. doi:10.1016/j.sbspro.2013.12.169

Kraut, R., & Skultety, S. (2005). *Aristotle's Politics: Critical essays.* Rowman & Littlefield.

Kretschmer, M. (2000). Intellectual property in music: A historical analysis of rhetoric and institutional practices. *Studies in Cultures, Organizations and Societies*, *6*(2), 197–223. doi:10.1080/10245280008523547

Kretschmer, M., Bently, L., & Deazley, R. (2010). The history of copyright history: Notes from an emerging discipline. In *Privilege and property: Essays on the history of copyright* (pp. 1–20). Cambridge: Open Book Publishers. Retrieved from http://www.openbookpublishers.com/reader/26

Kuhlmann, S., & Arie, R. (2014). *The challenge of addressing Grand Challenges: A think piece of how innovation can be driven towards the "Grand Challenges" as defined under the prospective European Union Framework Programme Horizon 2020*. University of Twente. Retrieved from http://doc.utwente.nl/91786/1/The_challenge_of_addressing_Grand_Challenges.pdf

Kujansivu, P., & Lonnqvist, A. (2007). How do investments in intellectual capital create profits? *International Journal of Learning and Intellectual Capital*, *4*(3), 256–275. doi:10.1504/IJLIC.2007.015610

Kumar Roy, B., Chandra Biswas, S., & Parthasarathi, M. (2016). Status of Open Access Institutional Digital Repositories in Agricultural Sciences: A Case Study of Asia. *Library Philosophy and Practice (e-Journal), 1329*. Retrieved from http://digitalcommons.unl.edu/cgi/viewcontent.cgi?article=3615&context=libphilprac

Kumar, N. (2003). Intellectual property rights, technology and economic development: Experiences of Asian countries. *Economic and Political Weekly*, *38*(3), 209–226.

Kur, A. (2011). *Intellectual property rights in a fair world trade system: Proposals for reform of TRIPS*. Edward Elgar Publishing. doi:10.4337/9781849809580

Laakso, M. (2014). Green open access policies of scholarly journal publishers: A study of what, when, and where self-archiving is allowed. *Scientometrics*, *99*(2), 475–494. doi:10.100711192-013-1205-3

Laakso, M., & Björk, B.-C. (2012). Anatomy of open access publishing: A study of longitudinal development and internal structure. *BMC Medicine*, *10*(1), 124. doi:10.1186/1741-7015-10-124 PMID:23088823

Laakso, M., Welling, P., Bukvova, H., Nyman, L., Björk, B.-C., & Hedlund, T. (2011). The development of open access journal publishing from 1993 to 2009. *PLoS One*, *6*(6), e20961. doi:10.1371/journal.pone.0020961 PMID:21695139

Landes, D. (2003). *The unbound Prometheus: Technological change and industrial development in western Europe from 1750 to the present*. Cambridge University Press. doi:10.1017/CBO9780511819957

Landes, W. M., & Posner, R. A. (2009). *The economic structure of intellectual property law*. Harvard University Press.

Landry, R., Amara, N., & Lamari, M. (2002). Does social capital determine innovation? To what extent? *Technological Forecasting and Social Change*, *69*(7), 681–701. doi:10.1016/S0040-1625(01)00170-6

Lane, D., Pumain, D., Leeuw, S. E. d., & West, G. (2009). *Complexity perspectives in innovation and social change*. Springer Science & Business Media. doi:10.1007/978-1-4020-9663-1

Lang, M., Aigner, H.-J., Scheuerle, U., & Stefaner, M. (Eds.). (2004). *CFC legislation, tax treaties and EC law*. The Hague: Kluwer Law International.

Lankes, R. D. (2011). *The atlas of new librarianship (Har/Chrt edition)*. Cambridge, MA: MIT Press. doi:10.7551/mitpress/8755.001.0001

Larivière, V., Haustein, S., & Mongeon, P. (2015). The oligopoly of academic publishers in the digital era. *PLoS One*, *10*(6), e0127502. doi:10.1371/journal.pone.0127502 PMID:26061978

Larson, F. (2009). *An infinity of things: How Sir Henry Wellcome collected the world*. OUP Oxford.

Larsson, S. (2011). *Metaphors and norms—Understanding copyright law in a digital society*. Stefan Larsson.

Lazarides, T. (2011). Corporate governance legal and regulatory framework's effectiveness in Greece: A response. *Journal of Financial Regulation and Compliance*, *19*(3), 244–253. doi:10.1108/13581981111147874

Le Galès, P. (1998). Regulations and governance in European cities. *International Journal of Urban and Regional Research*, *22*(3), 482–506. doi:10.1111/1468-2427.00153

Leaffer, M. (2010). *Understanding copyright law*. LexisNexis.

Lee, D. (2004). Understanding the WTO dispute settlement process. In *Trade Politics*. Psychology Press. doi:10.4324/NOE0415310178.ch8

Lee, E. (2007). *Freedom of the press 2.0*. Rochester, NY: Social Science Research Network. doi:10.2139srn.1008877

Lee, J. (2000). Knowledge management: The intellectual revolution. *IIE Solutions*, *32*(10), 34–34.

Leitner, K.-H. (2004). Intellectual capital reporting for universities: Conceptual background and application for Austrian universities. *Research Evaluation*, *13*(2), 129–140. doi:10.3152/147154404781776464

Lemley, M. A. (2004). Property, intellectual property, and free riding. *Texas Law Review*, *83*, 1031.

Lepitak, S. (2013). 90% of Online content to be held behind paywalls in three years media company survey suggests. *The Drum*. Retrieved from http://www.thedrum.com

Leslie Chan et al. (2002). *Budapest Open Access Initiative*. Retrieved from http://www.opensocietyfoundations.org

Lessig, L. (2005). *Free culture: The nature and future of creativity*. Penguin Books.

Lessig, L. (2008). *Remix: Making art and commerce thrive in the hybrid economy*. The Penguin Press. doi:10.5040/9781849662505

Levine, H., & Zahradnik, A. G. (2012). Online media, market orientation, and financial performance in nonprofits. *Journal of Nonprofit & Public Sector Marketing*, *24*(1), 26–42. doi:10.1080/10495142.2012.652908

Levinthal, D. A., & Wu, B. (2010). Opportunity costs and non-scale free capabilities: Profit maximization, corporate scope, and profit margins. *Strategic Management Journal, 31*(7), 780–801. doi:10.1002mj.845

Lewis, D. W. (2012). The inevitability of open access. *College & Research Libraries, 73*(5), 493–506. doi:10.5860/crl-299

Lewis, D., Rodgers, D., & Woolcock, M. (2008). The fiction of development: Literary representation as a source of authoritative knowledge. *The Journal of Development Studies, 44*(2), 198–216. doi:10.1080/00220380701789828

Leyshon, A., Webb, P., French, S., Thrift, N., & Crewe, L. (2005). On the reproduction of the musical economy after the Internet. *Media Culture & Society, 27*(2), 177–209. doi:10.1177/0163443705050468

Liaw, S.-S. (2002). An Internet survey for perceptions of computers and the World Wide Web: Relationship, prediction, and difference. *Computers in Human Behavior, 18*(1), 17–35. doi:10.1016/S0747-5632(01)00032-2

Lim, C. L., Elms, D. K., & Low, P. (2012). *The trans-Pacific partnership: A quest for a twenty-first century trade agreement*. Cambridge University Press. doi:10.1017/CBO9781139236775

Lindgreen, A., & Swaen, V. (2010). Corporate social responsibility. *International Journal of Management Reviews, 12*(1), 1–7. doi:10.1111/j.1468-2370.2009.00277.x

Liu, J. P. (2000). Owning digital copies: Copyright law and the incidents of copy ownership. *William and Mary Law Review, 42*, 1245.

Liu, Q., Safavi-Naini, R., & Sheppard, N. P. (2003). Digital rights management for content distribution. In *Proceedings of the Australasian Information Security Workshop Conference on ACSW Frontiers 2003, 21* (pp. 49–58). Darlinghurst, Australia: Australian Computer Society, Inc. Retrieved from http://dl.acm.org/citation.cfm?id=827987.827994

Liu, X., Toki, E. I., & Pange, J. (2014). The use of ICT in preschool education in Greece and China: A comparative study. *Procedia: Social and Behavioral Sciences, 112*, 1167–1176. doi:10.1016/j.sbspro.2014.01.1281

Locke, J. (2013). *Two treatises of government*. CreateSpace Independent Publishing Platform.

Locke, J. (2016). *Second treatise of government and a letter concerning toleration*. Oxford University Press.

Long, C. (2004). Information costs in patent and copyright. *Virginia Law Review, 90*(2), 465–549. doi:10.2307/3202440

López, O. S. (2010). The digital learning classroom: Improving English language learners' academic success in mathematics and reading using interactive whiteboard technology. *Computers & Education, 54*(4), 901–915. doi:10.1016/j.compedu.2009.09.019

Lor, P. J. (2019). *International and Comparative Librarianship: Concepts and Methods for Global Studies*. Walter de Gruyter GmbH & Co KG. doi:10.1515/9783110267990

Lucarelli, S., & Fioramonti, L. (2009). *External perceptions of the European Union as a global actor*. Routledge.

Lucassen, J., Moor, T. D., & van Zanden, J. L. (2008). *The return of the guilds*. Cambridge University Press.

Luke, A., Woods, A., & Weir, K. (2013). *Curriculum, syllabus design, and equity: A primer and model*. Routledge.

Luukkonen, T. (2012). Conservatism and risk-taking in peer review: Emerging ERC practices. *Research Evaluation, 21*(1), 48–60. doi:10.1093/reseval/rvs001

Luukkonen, T. (2014). The European Research Council and the European research funding landscape. *Science & Public Policy, 41*(1), 29–43. doi:10.1093cipolct031

Lynch, C. A. (2003). Institutional repositories: Essential infrastructure for scholarship in the digital age. *Portal (Baltimore, Md.), 3*(2), 327–336. doi:10.1353/pla.2003.0039

Lynch, C. A., & Lippincott, J. K. (2005). Institutional Repository Deployment in the United States as of Early 2005. *D-Lib Magazine, 11*(09). doi:10.1045eptember2005-lynch

Lynskey, O. (2014). Deconsructing data protection: The "added-value" of a right to data protection in the EU legal order. *The International and Comparative Law Quarterly, 63*(3), 569–597. doi:10.1017/S0020589314000244

Lyon, D. (2013). *The electronic eye: The rise of surveillance society—Computers and social control in context*. John Wiley & Sons.

Maassen, P., & Stensaker, B. (2011). The knowledge triangle, European higher education policy logics and policy implications. *Higher Education, 61*(6), 757–769. doi:10.100710734-010-9360-4

MacLeod, C. (2002). *Inventing the Industrial Revolution: The English patent system, 1660–1800*. Cambridge University Press.

Madison, M. J. (2005). *Law as design: Objects, concepts and digital things*. Rochester, NY: Social Science Research Network. Retrieved from http://papers.ssrn.com/abstract=709121

Maitland, I. (2002). The human face of self-interest. *Journal of Business Ethics, 38*(1–2), 3–17. doi:10.1023/A:1015716928549

Majone, G., & Baake, P. (1996). *Regulating Europe*. Psychology Press. doi:10.4324/9780203439197

Makridou, E., Araka, I., & Koutras, N. (2012). Open educational resources and freedom of teaching in college education in Greece: Rivals or fellows? In *Proceedings of the 5th International Conference of Information Law and Ethics (ICIL)* (pp. 605–628). Athens: NB Production.

Makridou, E., Araka, I., & Koutras, N. (2012). Open educational resources and freedom of teaching in college education in Greece: Rivals or fellows? In *Proceedings of the 5th International Conference of Information Law and Ethics* (p. 605). NB Production.

Mamtora, J., Yang, T., & Singh, D. (2015). Open access repositories in the Asia–Oceania region: Experiences and guidelines from three academic institutions. *IFLA Journal, 41*(2), 162–176. doi:10.1177/0340035215582219

Manhart, M., & Thalmann, S. (2015). Protecting organizational knowledge: A structured literature review. *Journal of Knowledge Management, 19*(2), 190–211. doi:10.1108/JKM-05-2014-0198

Maniotis, D. (2011). *Cyber law in Greece*. Kluwer Law International.

Manners, I., & Whitman, R. (2000). *The foreign policies of European Union Member States*. Manchester University Press.

Mann, T. (Ed.). (2015). *Australian Law Dictionary* (2nd ed.). Oxford University Press.

Mansfield, H. (2008). *Why is political philosophy important?* Retrieved October 25, 2015, from http://bigthink.com/videos/why-is-political-philosophy-important

Mansfield, H. C. (2014). *A student's guide to political philosophy*. Open Road Media.

Margerum, R. D. (2002). Collaborative planning building consensus and building a distinct model for practice. *Journal of Planning Education and Research, 21*(3), 237–253. doi:10.1177/0739456X0202100302

Markland, M. (2006). Institutional repositories in the UK: What can the Google user find there? *Journal of Librarianship and Information Science, 38*(4), 221–228. doi:10.1177/0961000606070587

Marriott, S. (2009). The emergence of live television talk. *Text—Interdisciplinary Journal for the Study of Discourse, 17*(2), 181–198. doi:10.1515/text.1.1997.17.2.181

Marshall, L., & Frith, S. (2013). *Music and Copyright*. Second. doi:10.4324/9780203036105

Marshall, P. A. (2008). "Cultural competence" and informed consent in international health research. *Cambridge Quarterly of Healthcare Ethics, 17*(2), 206–215. doi:10.1017/S0963180108080237 PMID:18312735

Martin, H.-J. (1995). *The history and power of writing*. University of Chicago Press.

Maskus, K. (2000). *Intellectual property rights in the global economy*. Peterson Institute.

Maskus, K. E., & Reichman, J. H. (2005). *International public goods and transfer of technology under a globalized intellectual property regime*. Cambridge University Press. doi:10.1017/CBO9780511494529

Mathelier, A., Zhao, X., Zhang, A. W., Parcy, F., Worsley-Hunt, R., Arenillas, D. J., ... Wasserman, W. W. (2014). JASPAR 2014: An extensively expanded and updated open-access database of transcription factor binding profiles. *Nucleic Acids Research*, *42*(D1), D142–D147. doi:10.1093/nar/gkt997 PMID:24194598

Matten, D., & Moon, J. (2008). "Implicit" and "Explicit" CSR: A conceptual framework for a comparative understanding of corporate social responsibility. *Academy of Management Review*, *33*(2), 404–424. doi:10.5465/amr.2008.31193458

Matthews, D. (2005). *TRIPS flexibilities and access to medicines in developing countries: The problem with technical assistance and free trade agreements*. Retrieved from http://qmro.qmul.ac.uk/jspui/handle/123456789/183

Matthews, D. (2006). *From the August 30, 2003 WTO decision to the December 6, 2005 agreement on an amendment to TRIPS: Improving access to medicines in developing countries?* Retrieved from http://qmro.qmul.ac.uk/jspui/handle/123456789/2124

Matthews, D. (2003). *Globalising intellectual property rights: The TRIPS Agreement*. Routledge.

Matthews, D. (2004). WTO decision on implementation of paragraph 6 of the Doha Declaration on the TRIPS Agreement and public health: A solution to the access to essential medicines problem? *Journal of International Economic Law*, *7*(1), 73–107. doi:10.1093/jiel/7.1.73

May, C. (2013). *The global political economy of intellectual property rights: The new enclosures?* Routledge. doi:10.4324/9781315011233

Mayer, L. (2004). *Worlds made flesh: Chronicle histories and medieval manuscript culture*. Routledge. doi:10.4324/9780203500880

Mayer-Schonberger, V. (2008). Demystifying Lessig. *Wisconsin Law Review*, *2008*, 713–746.

Mayhew, R. (1997). *Aristotle's criticism of Plato's Republic*. Rowman & Littlefield Publishers.

Mazziotti, G. (2008). *EU digital copyright law and the end-user*. Springer Science & Business Media.

McCalman, P. (2005). Who enjoys "TRIPs" abroad? An empirical analysis of intellectual property rights in the Uruguay Round. *The Canadian Journal of Economics. Revue Canadienne d'Economique*, *38*(2), 574–603. doi:10.1111/j.0008-4085.2005.00293.x

McCourt, T., & Burkart, P. (2003). When Creators, Corporations and Consumers Collide: Napster and the Development of On-line Music Distribution. *Media Culture & Society*, *25*(3), 333–350. doi:10.1177/0163443703025003003

McCutcheon, V., Nixon, W., & De Castro, P. (2014). *Repository profile: University of Glasgow-"Enlighten" IR & research system. Confederation of Open Access Repositories*. Retrieved from http://eprints.gla.ac.uk/98412/1/98412.pdf

McGuigan, G., & Russell, R. (2008). The Business of academic publishing: A strategic analysis of the academic journal publishing industry and its impact on the future of scholarly publishing, *Electronic Journal of Academic and Special Librarianship, 9*(3). Retrieved from http://southernlibrarianship.icaap.org/content/v09n03/mcguigan_g01.html

McLuhan, M., Gordon, W. T., Lamberti, E., & Scheffel-Dunand, D. (2011). *The Gutenberg galaxy: The making of typographic man*. University of Toronto Press.

Mendieta, E. (2002). *The adventures of transcendental philosophy: Karl-Otto Apel's semiotics and discourse ethics*. Rowman & Littlefield.

Menell, P. S. (2007a). *Intellectual property and the property rights movement*. Rochester, NY: Social Science Research Network. Retrieved from http://papers.ssrn.com/abstract=1000061

Menell, P. S. (2007b). *The property rights movement's embrace of intellectual property: True love or doomed relationship? (SSRN Scholarly Paper No. ID 965083)*. Rochester, NY: Social Science Research Network. Retrieved from http://papers.ssrn.com/abstract=965083

Menell, P. S. (2011). Governance of intellectual resources and disintegration of intellectual property in the digital age. *Berkeley Technology Law Journal, 26*(4), 1523–1559.

Mens, T. (2009). The ERCIM Working Group on Software Evolution: The past and the future. In *Proceedings of the Joint International and Annual ERCIM Workshops on Principles of Software Evolution (IWPSE) and Software Evolution (Evol) Workshops* (pp. 1–4). New York, NY: ACM. 10.1145/1595808.1595809

Merges, R. P. (2011). *Justifying intellectual property*. Harvard University Press. doi:10.4159/harvard.9780674061125

Merriden, T. (2001). *Irresistible forces: The business legacy of Napster and the growth of the underground Internet* (1st ed.). Capstone.

Merrill, T. W., & Smith, H. E. (2011). *Making Coasean property more Coasean*. Rochester, NY: Social Science Research Network. Retrieved from http://papers.ssrn.com/abstract=1758846 doi:10.1086/661946

Mgbeoji, I. (2012). Justifying intellectual property. *Osgoode Hall Law Journal, 50*, 291–1071.

Michalis, M. (2008). Governing European communications: From unification to coordination. *Reference and Research Book News, 23*(1).

Miller, C., & Harris, J. (2004). Scholarly journal publication: Conflicting agendas for scholars, publishers, and institutions. *Journal of Scholarly Publishing, 35*(2), 73–91. doi:10.3138/jsp.35.2.73

Milward, A., & Saul, B. (2013). The economic development of continental *Europe* 1780–1870. Routledge.

Molle, W. (2007). *European cohesion policy*. Routledge. doi:10.4324/9780203945278

Molteni, L., & Ordanini, A. (2003). Consumption patterns, digital technology and music downloading. *Long Range Planning*, *36*(4), 389–406. doi:10.1016/S0024-6301(03)00073-6

Molyneux, C. S., Peshu, N., & Marsh, K. (2004). Understanding of informed consent in a low-income setting: Three case studies from the Kenyan coast. *Social Science & Medicine*, *59*(12), 2547–2559. doi:10.1016/j.socscimed.2004.03.037 PMID:15474208

Monahan, J., & Walker, W. (2014). *Social science in law* (8th ed.). Foundation Press.

Moon, J. (2014). *Corporate social responsibility: A very short introduction*. OUP Oxford.

Moreleli-Cacouris, M., Makridou, E., & Asmanidis, Y. (2007). Institutional repositories: A proposal for a national policy based upon a Greek case. Presented at the *16th Hellenic Academic Libraries Conference*, Piraeus, Greece.

Morris, S., & Shin, H. S. (2002). Social value of public information. *The American Economic Review*, *92*(5), 1521–1534. doi:10.1257/000282802762024610

Mossoff, A. (2006). Rethinking the development of patents: An intellectual history, 1550–1800. *The Hastings Law Journal*, *52*, 1255.

Moussis, N. (2014). *Access to the European Union: Law, economics, policies* (20th ed.; Vol. 1). Beaverton, United States: Ringgold Inc.

Mueller, R. A. E. (2003). The evolution of intellectual property rights for digital information products-impact on agroindustry. In *Proceedings of the EFITA Conference, Debrecen, Hungary* (pp. 331–338). Retrieved from http://www.agric-econ.uni-kiel.de/Abteilungen/II/PDFs/efita03.pdf

Mueller-Langer, F., & Watt, R. (2010). *Copyright and open access for academic works* (SSRN Scholarly Paper No. ID 1647586). Retrieved from Social Science Research Network website: https://papers.ssrn.com/abstract=1647586

Mueller, P. (2006). Exploring the knowledge filter: How entrepreneurship and university–industry relationships drive economic growth. *Research Policy*, *35*(10), 1499–1508. doi:10.1016/j.respol.2006.09.023

Müller, B. (2003). Censorship and cultural regulation: Mapping the territory. *Critical Studies*, *22*(1), 1–31.

Mun, S.-H. (2008). *Culture-related aspects of intellectual property rights: A cross-cultural analysis of copyright*. ProQuest.

Mutz, D. C. (2006). *Hearing the other side: Deliberative versus participatory democracy*. Cambridge University Press. doi:10.1017/CBO9780511617201

Nachbar, T. (2005). Monopoly, mercantilism, and the politics of regulation. *Virginia Law Review*, *91*(6), 1313–1379.

Narlikar, A., Daunton, M., & Stern, R. M. (2012). *The Oxford handbook on the World Trade Organization*. Oxford University Press.

Nedeva, M., & Stampfer, M. (2012). From "science in Europe" to "European science.". *Science*, *336*(6084), 982–983. doi:10.1126cience.1216878 PMID:22628638

Nérisson, S. (2014). The rental and lending rights directive. In *EU copyright law* (pp. 149–202). Edward Elgar Publishing. doi:10.4337/9781781952436.00017

Newman, J. C., & Feldman, R. (2011). Copyright and open access at the bedside. *The New England Journal of Medicine*, *365*(26), 2447–2449. doi:10.1056/NEJMp1110652

Nicholas, D., Rowlands, I., Watkinson, A., Brown, D., & Jamali, H. R. (2012). Digital repositories ten years on: What do scientific researchers think of them and how do they use them? *Learned Publishing*, *25*(3), 195–206. doi:10.1087/20120306

Nicolaidis, K., & Shaffer, G. (2005). Transnational mutual recognition regimes: Governance without global government. *Law and Contemporary Problems*, *68*(3/4), 263–317.

Nissenbaum, H. (2011). A Contextual Approach to Privacy Online. *Daedalus*, *140*(4), 32–48. doi:10.1162/DAED_a_00113

Nolan, L. (2011). *Primary and secondary qualities: The historical and ongoing debate*. Oxford University Press. doi:10.1093/acprof:oso/9780199556151.001.0001

Nolan, M. E. (2005). Search for original expression: Fan fiction and the fair use defense. *Southern Illinois University Law Journal. Southern Illinois University at Carbondale. School of Law*, *30*, 533.

North, D. C. (2007). *Limited access orders in the developing world: A new approach to the problems of development*. World Bank Publications. doi:10.1596/1813-9450-4359

Ntaliani, M., Costopoulou, C., Karetsos, S., & Molhanec, M. (2015). Citizen e-empowerment in Greek and Czech municipalities. In S. K. Katsikas & A. B. Sideridis (Eds.), *E-Democracy—Citizen Rights in the World of the New Computing Paradigms* (pp. 124–133). doi:10.1007/978-3-319-27164-4_9

Nyquist, C. (2002). Teaching Wesley Hohfeld's theory of legal relations. *Journal of Legal Education*, *52*(1/2), 238–257.

Nyquist, C. (2010). An academic librarian's response to the "ITHAKA faculty survey 2009: Key strategic insights for libraries, publishers, and societies." *Journal of Interlibrary Loan. Document Delivery & Electronic Reserve*, *20*(4), 275–280. doi:10.1080/1072303X.2010.508419

O'Brien, A., & Bosc, M. (Eds.). (2009). *House of Commons procedure and practice* (2nd ed.). Ottawa, Canada: Yvon Blais.

O'Faircheallaigh, C. (2010). Public participation and environmental impact assessment: Purposes, implications, and lessons for public policy making. *Environmental Impact Assessment Review*, *30*(1), 19–27. doi:10.1016/j.eiar.2009.05.001

Oakleaf, M. (2009). The information literacy instruction assessment cycle: A guide for increasing student learning and improving librarian instructional skills. *The Journal of Documentation*, *65*(4), 539–560. doi:10.1108/00220410910970249

Oakley, F. (1999). *Politics and eternity: Studies in the history of medieval and early modern political thought*. BRILL.

Oguz, F., & Assefa, S. (2014). Faculty members' perceptions towards institutional repository at a medium-sized university: Application of a binary logistic regression model. *Library Review*, *63*(3), 189–202. doi:10.1108/LR-07-2013-0088

Okediji, R. L. (Ed.). (2017). *Copyright Law in an Age of Limitations and Exceptions*. Cambridge, UK: Cambridge University Press. doi:10.1017/9781316450901

Olsen, J. P. (2002). Reforming European institutions of governance. *Journal of Common Market Studies*, *40*(4), 581–602. doi:10.1111/1468-5965.00389

Open Access Scholarly Publishers Association. (2016). Retrieved January 12, 2016, from http://oaspa.org/

Oppenheim, C. (2008). Electronic scholarly publishing and open access. *Journal of Information Science*, *34*(4), 577–590. doi:10.1177/0165551508092268

Orduña-Malea, E., & López-Cózar, E. D. (2015). The dark side of open access in Google and Google Scholar: The case of Latin-American repositories. *Scientometrics*, *102*(1), 829–846. doi:10.100711192-014-1369-5

Organisation for Economic Co-operation and Development. (2001). *The new economy: Beyond the hype. Paris: Organisation for Economic Co-operation and Development*. Retrieved from http://www.oecd-ilibrary.org/content/book/9789264033856-en

Ostrom, E., & Hess, C. (2007). *Private and common property rights (SSRN Scholarly Paper No. ID 1936062)*. Rochester, NY: Social Science Research Network. Retrieved from http://papers.ssrn.com/abstract=1936062

Otjacques, B., Hitzelberger, P., & Feltz, F. (2007). Interoperability of e-government information systems: Issues of identification and data sharing. *Journal of Management Information Systems*, *23*(4), 29–51. doi:10.2753/MIS0742-1222230403

Palfrey, J., Gasser, U., Simun, M., & Barnes, R. F. (2009). Youth, creativity, and copyright in the digital age. *International Journal of Learning and Media*, *1*(2), 79–97. doi:10.1162/ijlm.2009.0022

Palmer, A. K., & Vinje, T. C. (1992). The EC directive on the legal protection of computer software: New law governing software development. *Duke Journal of Comparative & International Law*, *2*(1), 65–87.

Papadopoulou, M. D. (2010). *Copyright limitations and exceptions in an e-education environment.* Retrieved from http://go.galegroup.com.simsrad.net.ocs.mq.edu.au/ps/i.do?ty=as&v=2.1&u=macquarie&it=DIourl&s=RELEVANCE&p=LT&qt=SN~2042-115X~~TI~%22Copyright%20limitations%20and%20exceptions%22~~VO~1~~IU~2&lm=DA~120100000&sw=w

Pappas, C., & Williams, I. (2011). Grey literature: Its emerging importance. *Journal of Hospital Librarianship, 11*(3), 228–234. doi:10.1080/15323269.2011.587100

Parel, A., & Flanagan, T. (2006). *Theories of property: Aristotle to the present.* Wilfrid Laurier Univ. Press.

Park, S., Zo, H., Ciganek, A. P., & Lim, G. G. (2011). Examining success factors in the adoption of digital object identifier systems. *Electronic Commerce Research and Applications, 10*(6), 626–636. doi:10.1016/j.elerap.2011.05.004

Pasley, J. (2002). *The tyranny of printers: Newspaper politics in the early American republic.* University of Virginia Press.

Pateman, C. (2012). Participatory democracy revisited. *Perspectives on Politics, 10*(01), 7–19. doi:10.1017/S1537592711004877

Patterson, R. (2000). Understanding the copyright clause. *Journal of the Copyright Society of the U.S.A., 47*, 365.

Perianes-Rodríguez, A., Olmeda-Gómez, C., & Moya-Anegón, F. (2010). Detecting, identifying and visualizing research groups in co-authorship networks. *Scientometrics, 82*(2), 307–319. doi:10.100711192-009-0040-z

Peterson-Sloss, C. (2011, September). EBLIDA (European Bureau of Library, Information and Documentation Associations). *Computers in Libraries, 31*(7), 41.

Pettegree, A. (2010). *The book in the Renaissance.* New Haven, CT: Yale University Press.

Picarra, M. (2015). Open Access policy effectiveness: A briefing paper for UK Higher Education Institutions. *Zenodo, 6.* doi:10.5281/zenodo.44325

Pinfield, S. (2005). A mandate to self archive? The role of open access institutional repositories. *Serials: The Journal for the Serials Community, 18*(1), 30–34. doi:10.1629/1830

Pinfield, S., Salter, J., Bath, P. A., Hubbard, B., Millington, P., Anders, J. H. S., & Hussain, A. (2014). Open-access repositories worldwide, 2005–2012: Past growth, current characteristics, and future possibilities. *Journal of the Association for Information Science and Technology, 65*(12), 2404–2421. doi:10.1002/asi.23131

Pisani, E., & AbouZahr, C. (2010). Sharing health data: Good intentions are not enough. *Bulletin of the World Health Organization, 88*(6), 462–466. doi:10.2471/BLT.09.074393 PMID:20539861

Pottage, A., & Sherman, B. (2010). *Figures of invention: A history of modern patent law. Oxford, England.* New York: Oxford University Press. doi:10.1093/acprof:osobl/9780199595631.001.0001

Poynder, R. (2013, June 17). *Open and shut? Open access: Emerald's green starts to fade?* Retrieved January 25, 2016, from http://poynder.blogspot.com.au/2013/06/open-access-emeralds-green-starts-to.html

Press, G. A. (1988). Rethinking Plato and Platonism [Review]. *Journal of the History of Philosophy, 26*(2), 311–312. doi:10.1353/hph.1988.0024

Press, G. A., & Press, G. A. G. A. (1996). Methods of interpreting Plato and his dialogues [Review]. *Journal of the History of Philosophy, 34*(1), 135–136. doi:10.1353/hph.1996.0005

Priyanto, I. (2015). *Readiness of Indonesian academic libraries for open access and open access repositories implementation: A study on Indonesian open access repositories*. Retrieved from https://digital.library.unt.edu/ark:/67531/metadc804888/

Psacharopoulos, G. (2003). The social cost of an outdated law: Article 16 of the Greek Constitution. *European Journal of Law and Economics, 16*(2), 123–137. doi:10.1023/A:1024117632649

Pugatch, M. P. (2004). *The international political economy of intellectual property rights*. Edward Elgar Publishing. doi:10.4337/9781845420741

Pugatch, M. P. (2006). *The intellectual property debate: Perspectives from law, economics and political economy*. Edward Elgar Publishing. doi:10.4337/9781847201782

Puplett, D., & Madjarevic, N. (2011, October 28). *By championing open access publishing, the academic community can bring us closer to making research available to all*. Retrieved April 15, 2017, from http://blogs.lse.ac.uk/impactofsocialsciences/2011/10/28/championing-open-access/

Putterman, E. (2010). *Rousseau, law and the sovereignty of the people*. Cambridge University Press. doi:10.1017/CBO9780511776861

Puybaret, E. (2008). *Universal declaration of human rights*. United Nations Publications.

Quah, D. (2000). Internet cluster emergence. *European Economic Review, 44*(4–6), 1032–1044. doi:10.1016/S0014-2921(99)00055-0

Rader, H. B. (1997). Educating students for the Information Age: The role of the librarian. *RSR. Reference Services Review, 25*(2), 47–52. doi:10.1108/00907329710306661

Radin, M. J. (1993). *Reinterpreting property*. University of Chicago Press.

Ramakrishnan, R., & Gehrke, J. (2000). *Database management systems* (2nd ed.). Berkeley, CA: Osborne/McGraw–Hill.

Rannenberg, K., Royer, D., & Deuker, A. (2009). *The future of identity in the information society: Challenges and opportunities*. Springer Science & Business Media. doi:10.1007/978-3-642-01820-6

Raoult, D., Aboudharam, G., Crubézy, E., Larrouy, G., Ludes, B., & Drancourt, M. (2000). Molecular identification by "suicide PCR" of Yersinia pestis as the agent of medieval Black Death. *Proceedings of the National Academy of Sciences of the United States of America*, *97*(23), 12800–12803. doi:10.1073/pnas.220225197 PMID:11058154

Raschke, C. A. (2003). *The digital revolution and the coming of the postmodern university*. Routledge. doi:10.4324/9780203451243

Rawls, J. (2001). *Justice as fairness: A restatement (E. Kelly* (M. Cambridge, Ed.). London: Belknap Press.

Rawls, J. (2009). *A theory of justice*. Harvard University Press.

Rawls, J. (2009). *A Theory of Justice*. Harvard University Press.

Reddy, M. B. (1994). The droit de suite: Why American fine artists should have a right to a resale royalty. *Loyola of Los Angeles Entertainment Law Journal*, *15*, 509.

Reed, C. (2011). *Gutenberg in Shanghai: Chinese print capitalism, 1876–1937*. UBC Press.

Reitz, J. M. (2004). *Dictionary for library and information science*. Libraries Unlimited.

Repko, A. F. (2008). Interdisciplinary research: Process and theory. *Sage (Atlanta, Ga.)*.

Resnik, D. (2003). A pluralistic account of intellectual property. *Journal of Business Ethics*, *46*(4), 319–335. doi:10.1023/A:1025631902384

Revesz, P. (2009). *Introduction to databases: From biological to spatio-temporal*. Springer Science & Business Media.

Rhoten, D., & Powell, W. W. (2007). The frontiers of intellectual property: Expanded protection versus new models of open science. *Annual Review of Law and Social Science*, *3*(1), 345–373. doi:10.1146/annurev.lawsocsci.3.081806.112900

Riahi-Belkaoui, A. (2003). Intellectual capital and firm performance of US multinational firms: A study of the resource-based and stakeholder views. *Journal of Intellectual Capital*, *4*(2), 215–226. doi:10.1108/14691930310472839

Rich, A. (2010). *A dictionary of Roman and Greek antiquities*. Nabu Press.

Richards, D., & Martin, S. (2002). *Governance and public policy in the United Kingdom*. Oxford University Press.

Richardson, J., & Wolski, M. (2012). The importance of Repositories in Supporting the Learning Lifecycle. *ICERI 2012*, 2602–2608. Retrieved from https://research-repository.griffith.edu.au/bitstream/handle/10072/48263/80937_1.pdf;sequence=1

Richardson, G. (2004). Guilds, laws, and markets for manufactured merchandise in late-medieval England. *Explorations in Economic History*, *41*(1), 1–25. doi:10.1016/S0014-4983(03)00045-7

Ricketson, S., & Ginsburg, J. (2006). *International copyright and neighbouring rights: The Berne Convention and beyond* (2nd ed.). Oxford, UK: Oxford University Press.

Ricketson, S., & Ginsburg, J. (2006). *International Copyright and Neighbouring Rights: The Berne Convention and Beyond Two volume set* (2nd ed.). Oxford, UK: Oxford University Press.

Riegel, N. (2011). *Beauty, to Kalon, and its relation to the good in the works of Plato*. University of Toronto. Retrieved from http://www.synergiescanada.org/theses/otu/29848

Rimmer, M. (2007). *Digital copyright and the consumer revolution: Hands off my iPod*. Edward Elgar Publishing. doi:10.4337/9781847207142

Ringnalda, A. (2011). *Orphan works, mass rights clearance, and online libraries: The flaws of the draft orphan works directive and extended collective licensing as a solution (SSRN Scholarly Paper No. ID 2369974)*. Rochester, NY: Social Science Research Network. Retrieved from http://papers.ssrn.com/abstract=2369974

Ritter, C. (2005). *Refusal to deal and essential facilities: Does intellectual property require special deference compared to tangible property?* Rochester, NY: Social Science Research Network. Retrieved from http://papers.ssrn.com/abstract=726683

Roberts, A. (2010). A Great and Revolutionary Law? The First Four Years of India's Right to Information Act. *Public Administration Review*, *70*(6), 925–933. doi:10.1111/j.1540-6210.2010.02224.x

Robinson, M. (2009). Promoting the visibility of educational research through an institutional repository. *Serials Review*, *35*(3), 133–137. doi:10.1080/00987913.2009.10765230

Rocco, T. S., & Hatcher, T. G. (2011). *The handbook of scholarly writing and publishing*. John Wiley & Sons.

Rocha, H. O., & Ghoshal, S. (2006). Beyond self-interest revisited. *Journal of Management Studies*, *43*(3), 585–619. doi:10.1111/j.1467-6486.2006.00603.x

Rodrigues, E. (2014). *Open access to publications and research data in Horizon 2020: What are the requirements and how can institutional repositories and OpenAIRE help to meet them?* Retrieved April 4, 2016, from http://sci-gems.math.bas.bg:8080/jspui/handle/10525/2404

Rodríguez, A. A. (2006). The relationship between copyright software protection and piracy: Evidence from Europe. *European Journal of Law and Economics*, *21*(1), 29–51. doi:10.100710657-006-5670-5

Rogers, J. (2003, April 13). *DNA scientists write "book of life."* Retrieved August 27, 2019, from https://www.telegraph.co.uk/news/1427490/DNA-scientists-write-book-of-life.html

Romer, P. (2002). When should we use intellectual property rights? *The American Economic Review*, *92*(2), 213–216. doi:10.1257/000282802320189276

Rosati, E. (2013). The Orphan Works Directive, or throwing a stone and hiding the hand. *Journal of Intellectual Property Law & Practice*, *8*(4), 303–310. doi:10.1093/jiplp/jpt015

Rose, M. (1995). *Authors and owners: The invention of copyright*. Harvard University Press.

Rose, M. (2009). Public sphere and the emergence of copyright: Areopagitica, the Stationers' Company, and the Statute of Anne. *Tulane Journal of Technology and Intellectual Property*, *12*, 123.

Rose, M. (2010). The public sphere and the emergence of copyright: Areopagitica, the Stationers' Company, and the Statute of Anne. In *Privilege and Property: Essays on the History of Copyright* (pp. 67–88). Cambridge, UK: Open Book Publishers. doi:10.2307/j.ctt5vjt9v.7

Rosenberg, N. (2002). Knowledge and innovation for economic development: Should universities be economic institutions? In *Knowledge for inclusive development* (pp. 35–47). Greenwood Publishing Group.

Rosenbloum, R. A. (1995). The Rental Rights Directive: A step in the right and wrong directions. *Loyola of Los Angeles Entertainment Law Journal*, *15*, 547.

Rosen, S. (2005). *Plato's Republic: A study*. Yale University Press.

Rosler, D. B. (1995). The European Union's proposed directive for the legal protection of databases: A new threat to the free flow of information. *High Technology Law Journal*, *10*(1), 105–146.

Rosset, V., Filippin, C., & Westphall, C. (2005). A DRM architecture to distribute and protect digital contents using digital licenses. *Advanced industrial conference on telecommunications: service assurance with partial and intermittent resources conference*, 422–427. 10.1109/AICT.2005.5

Rossum, W. V., & Cabo, P. G. (1995). The contribution of research institutes in EUREKA projects. *International Journal of Technology Management*, *10*(7–8), 853–866. doi:10.1504/IJTM.1995.025662

Rothbard, M. N. (2009). *Aristotle on private property and money*. Retrieved October 3, 2014, from http://mises.org/daily/3902/Aristotle-on-Private-Property-and-Money

Rothstein, H. R., & Hopewell, S. (2009). Grey literature. In H. Cooper, L. V. Hedges, & J. C. Valentine (Eds.), *The handbook of research synthesis and meta-analysis* (2nd ed.; pp. 103–125). New York, NY: Russell Sage Foundation.

Rouse, J. (2005). Power/knowledge. In *The Cambridge companion to Foucault* (p. 95). Cambridge University Press. doi:10.1017/CCOL0521840821.005

Rouse, R., & Rouse, M. (2000). *Manuscripts and their makers: Commercial book producers in medieval Paris, 1200–1500*. Harvey Miller Press.

Rousseau, J.-J. (2012). *Rousseau: The Basic Political Writings: Discourse on the Sciences and the Arts, Discourse on the Origin of Inequality, Discourse on Political Economy, On the Social Contract, The State of War*. Hackett Publishing.

Rowe, G., & Frewer, L. J. (2000). Public participation methods: A framework for evaluation. *Science, Technology & Human Values*, *25*(1), 3–29. doi:10.1177/016224390002500101

Rowley, J., & Hartley, R. J. (2008). *Organizing knowledge: An introduction to managing access to information*. Ashgate Publishing, Ltd.

Roy, B., Biswas, S. C., & Mukhopadhyay, P. (2012). Open Access Repositories in Asia: From SAARC to Asian Tigers. *Library Philosophy and Practice (e-Journal)*. Retrieved from http://digitalcommons.unl.edu/libphilprac/808

Sabel, C. F., & Zeitlin, J. (2010). *Experimentalist governance in the European Union: Towards a new architecture*. OUP Oxford.

Sabha, A., Sumaira, J., & Amin, I. (2013). *Status of Open access Repositories: A Global perspective*. Academic Press.

Sakaky, T., Okazaki, M., & Matsuo, Y. (2010). Earthquake shakes Twitter users: Real-time event detection by social sensors. *Proceedings of the 19th International Conference on World Wide Web*, 851–860. http://doi.acm.org/10.1145/1772690.1772777

Salter, M. (1987). Justifying private property rights: A message from Hegel's jurisprudential writings. *Legal Studies*, *7*(3), 245–262. doi:10.1111/j.1748-121X.1987.tb00365.x

Samuelson, P. (2000). *Five challenges for regulating the global information society (SSRN Scholarly Paper No. ID 234743)*. Rochester, NY: Social Science Research Network. Retrieved from http://papers.ssrn.com/abstract=234743

Samuelson, P., Vinje, T. C., & Cornish, W. R. (2011). *Does copyright protection under the EU Software Directive extend to computer program behaviour, languages and interfaces? (SSRN Scholarly Paper No. ID 1974890)*. Rochester, NY: Social Science Research Network. Retrieved from http://papers.ssrn.com/abstract=1974890

Sandholtz, W. (1993). Institutions and collective action: The new telecommunications in western Europe. *World Politics*, *45*(2), 242–270. doi:10.2307/2950659

Sandholtz, W., & Sweet, A. S. (1998). *European integration and supranational governance*. Oxford University Press. doi:10.1093/0198294646.001.0001

SAS Institute v. World Programming. (2010). EWHC 1829 (Ch). Retrieved from http://www.bailii.org/ew/cases/EWHC/Ch/2010/1829.html

Schmidt, E., & Cohen, J. (2013). The new digital age: Reshaping the future of people, nations and business. Hachette UK.

Schneider, M. (1998). The European Union Database Directive. *Berkeley Technology Law Journal*, *13*(1), 551–564.

Schroeder, J. L. (2005). Unnatural rights: Hegel and intellectual property. *University of Miami Law Review*, *60*, 453.

Schroter, S., & Tite, L. (2006). Open access publishing and "author pays' business models: A survey of authors' knowledge and perceptions. *Journal of the Royal Society of Medicine*, *99*(3), 141–148. PMID:16508053

Sell, S., & Prakash, A. (2004). Using ideas strategically: The contest between business and NGO networks in intellectual property rights. *International Studies Quarterly*, *48*(1), 143–175. doi:10.1111/j.0020-8833.2004.00295.x

Sen, A. (2000). Social justice and the distribution of income. In *Handbook of income distribution* (Vol. 1, pp. 59–85). Elsevier. doi:10.1016/S1574-0056(00)80004-4

Sennett, R. (2008). *The craftsman*. Yale University Press.

Senseney, J. (2011). *The art of building in the classical world: Vision, craftsmanship, and linear perspective in Greek and Roman architecture*. Cambridge University Press. doi:10.1017/CBO9780511976711

Serenko, A., Bontis, N., Booker, L., Sadeddin, K., & Hardie, T. (2010). A scientometric analysis of knowledge management and intellectual capital academic literature (1994–2008). *Journal of Knowledge Management*, *14*(1), 3–23. doi:10.1108/13673271011015534

Seville, C. (2009). *EU intellectual property law and policy*. Edward Elgar Publishing. doi:10.4337/9781848447462

Shafaeddin, M. (2000). *What did Frederick list actually say? Some clarifications on the infant industry argument* (UNCTAD Discussion Paper No. 149). United Nations Conference on Trade and Development. Retrieved from https://ideas.repec.org/p/unc/dispap/149.html

Sha, L. Z. (2007). The flavors of open access. *OCLC Systems & Services: International Digital Library Perspectives*, *23*(3), 229–234. doi:10.1108/10650750710776332

Shan, C., Gong, S., & McOwan, P. W. (2009). Facial expression recognition based on local binary patterns: A comprehensive study. *Image and Vision Computing*, *27*(6), 803–816. doi:10.1016/j.imavis.2008.08.005

Shao, K. (2011). Monopoly or reward: The origin of copyright and authorship in England, France and China and a new criticism of intellectual property. *Hong Kong Law Journal*, *41*, 731.

Shapley, K. S., Sheehan, D., Maloney, C., & Caranikas-Walker, F. (2010). Evaluating the implementation fidelity of technology immersion and its relationship with student achievement. *The Journal of Technology, Learning, and Assessment*, *9*(4). Retrieved from https://ejournals.bc.edu/ojs/index.php/jtla/article/view/1609

Shearer, K. (2003). *Institutional repositories: Towards the identification of critical success factors*. Retrieved from http://prism.ucalgary.ca//handle/1880/43357

Shelburne, W. A. (2009). E-book usage in an academic library: User attitudes and behaviors. *Library Collections, Acquisitions & Technical Services*, *33*(2–3), 59–72. doi:10.1016/j.lcats.2009.04.002

Shen, X. (2005). A dilemma for developing countries in intellectual property strategy? Lessons from a case study of software piracy and Microsoft in China. *Science & Public Policy*, *32*(3), 187–198. doi:10.3152/147154305781779533

Shinn, T., & Lamy, E. (2006). Paths of commercial knowledge: Forms and consequences of university–enterprise synergy in scientist-sponsored firms. *Research Policy*, *35*(10), 1465–1476. doi:10.1016/j.respol.2006.09.024

Sianou-Kyrgiou, E. (2008). Social class and access to higher education in Greece: Supportive preparation lessons and success in national exams. *International Studies in Sociology of Education*, *18*(3–4), 173–183. doi:10.1080/09620210802492757

Sider, S. (2007). *Handbook to life in Renaissance Europe*. Oxford University Press.

Silva, J. (2008). Open access: No one's sure of definitions in this new territory. *RCR Wireless News*, *27*(33), 12.

Silver, C. (2003). *Critical essays dealing with the philosophy of Plato on the good life—The Platonic philosophy on the good life*. Retrieved April 9, 2015, from http://ancienthistory.about.com/library/bl/uc_bakaoukas4b2.htm

Silverman, I. (2014). SAS: Major software copyright ruling upheld. *Journal of Intellectual Property Law & Practice*, *9*(3), 179–181. doi:10.1093/jiplp/jpt264

Sismondo, S., & Doucet, M. (2010). Publication ethics and the ghost management of medical publication. *Bioethics*, *24*(6), 273–283. doi:10.1111/j.1467-8519.2008.01702.x PMID:19222451

Slauter, W. (2013). Upright piracy: Understanding the lack of copyright for journalism in eighteenth-century Britain. *Book History*, *16*(1), 34–61. doi:10.1353/bh.2013.0011

Smith, H. E. (2011). Property is not just a bundle of rights. *Econ Journal Watch*, *8*(3), 279–291.

Smith, M., Barton, M., Branschofsky, M., McClellan, G., Walker, J. H., Bass, M., ... Tansley, R. (2003). DSpace: An open source dynamic digital repository. *D-Lib Magazine*, *9*(1). doi:10.1045/january2003-smith

Smith, W. (2010). *A concise dictionary of Greek and Roman antiquities*. London: Nabu Press.

Solow, J. L. (1998). An economic analysis of the droit de suite. *Journal of Cultural Economics*, *22*(4), 209–226. doi:10.1023/A:1007505016512

Sompel, H. d., Payette, S., Erickson, J., Lagoze, C., & Warner, S. (2004, September). *Rethinking scholarly communication: Building the system that scholars deserve*. Retrieved March 29, 2017, from http://dspace.library.uu.nl/handle/1874/3165

Soriano, F. H., & Mulatero, F. (2010). Knowledge policy in the EU: From the Lisbon Strategy to Europe 2020. *Journal of the Knowledge Economy*, *1*(4), 289–302. doi:10.100713132-010-0020-9

Spiegel, H. W. (1991). *The growth of economic thought*. Duke University Press.

Springer. (2004). *Open choice: Your research. Your choice.* Retrieved from http://www.springer.com

Stein, B. (1985). Politics, peasants and the deconstruction of feudalism in medieval India. *The Journal of Peasant Studies*, *12*(2–3), 54–86. doi:10.1080/03066158508438265

Stepanova, E. (2011). *The role of information communication technologies in the "Arab Spring"* (Eurasia Policy Memo No. 159; p. 6). Retrieved from http://www.ponarseurasia.com/sites/default/files/policy-memos-pdf/pepm_159.pdf

Stone, D. (2010). Private philanthropy or policy transfer? The transnational norms of the Open Society Institute. *Policy and Politics*, *38*(2), 269–287. doi:10.1332/030557309X458416

Stott, C., & Drury, J. (2004). The importance of social structure and social interaction in stereotype consensus and content: Is the whole greater than the sum of its parts? *European Journal of Social Psychology*, *34*(1), 11–23. doi:10.1002/ejsp.183

Stromquist, N. P. (2002). *Education in a globalized world: The connectivity of economic power, technology, and knowledge*. Rowman & Littlefield Publishers.

Suber, P. (2002). *Bethesda statement on open access publishing*. Retrieved from http://dash.harvard.edu

Suber, P. (2003). Not Napster for science. *SPARC, 66*. Retrieved from https://dash.harvard.edu/handle/1/4455490

Suber, P. (2007). *Gratis and libre open access*. Retrieved from http://dash.harvard.edu/handle/1/4322580

Suber, P., Brown, P. O., Cabell, D., Chakravarti, A., Cohen, B., Delamothe, T., . . . Watson, L. (2003). *Bethesda statement on open access publishing*. Retrieved from https://dash.harvard.edu/handle/1/4725199

Suber, P. (2012). Ensuring open access for publicly funded research. *BMJ (Clinical Research Ed.)*, *345*(aug08 1), e5184. doi:10.1136/bmj.e5184 PMID:22875953

Suber, P. (2012). *Open access*. MIT Press. doi:10.7551/mitpress/9286.001.0001

Suhr, C. (2012). Publishing for the masses: Early modern English witchcraft pamphlets. *Neuphilologische Mitteilungen*, *113*(1), 118–121.

Swan, A., & Brown, S. (2005). *Open access self-archiving: An author study*. Retrieved September 11, 2015, from http://eprints.soton.ac.uk/260999/

Sweet, C. M., & Eterovic Maggio, D. S. (2015). Do stronger intellectual property rights increase innovation? *World Development*, *66*, 665–677. doi:10.1016/j.worlddev.2014.08.025

Synodinou, T.-E. (2015). Intermediaries' liability for online copyright infringement in the EU: Evolutions and confusions. *Computer Law & Security Review*, *31*(1), 57–67. doi:10.1016/j.clsr.2014.11.010

Tan, L.-H., Abrizah, A., & Noorhidawati, A. (2013). Availability and visibility of open access digital repositories in ASEAN countries. *Information Development*, *29*(3), 274–285. doi:10.1177/0266666912466754

Taylor, M. (2012, March 26). *Visibility is currency in academia but it is scarcity in publishing: the push for open access shows that academic publishers can't serve two masters*. Retrieved April 16, 2017, from http://blogs.lse.ac.uk/impactofsocialsciences/

Taylor-Gooby, P. (2004). *New risks, new welfare: The transformation of the European welfare state*. Oxford University Press. doi:10.1093/019926726X.001.0001

Taylor, M. (2000). Communities in the lead: Power, organisational capacity and social capital. *Urban Studies (Edinburgh, Scotland)*, *37*(5–6), 1019–1035. doi:10.1080/00420980050011217

Teece, D. J. (2010). Business models, business strategy and innovation. *Long Range Planning*, *43*(2–3), 172–194. doi:10.1016/j.lrp.2009.07.003

Tennant, J. (2014). Top scientific publisher chooses not to advance open access. *The Conversation*. Retrieved December 14, 2014, from http://theconversation.com/top-scientific-publisher-chooses-not-to-advance-open-access-31248

Tennant, J. (2014). Top scientific publisher chooses not to advance open access. *The Conversation*. Retrieved from http://theconversation.com

Tenopir, C., King, D. W., Edwards, S., & Wu, L. (2009). Electronic journals and changes in scholarly article seeking and reading patterns. *Aslib Proceedings*, *61*(1), 5–32. doi:10.1108/00012530910932267

Thadeusz, F. (2010). *No copyright law: The real reason for Germany's industrial expansion?* Retrieved August 30, 2016, from http://www.spiegel.de/international/zeitgeist/no-copyright-law-the-real-reason-for-germany-s-industrial-expansion-a-710976.html

Thatcher, S. G. (2008). China's copyright dilemma. *Learned Publishing*, *21*(4), 278–284. doi:10.1087/095315108X356707

The Hon Mr Justice Richard Arnold. (2010). SAS Institute Inc v World Programming Ltd [2010] EWHC 1829 (Ch). EWHC (Ch).

Thumm, N. (2013). *Intellectual property rights: National systems and harmonisation in Europe*. Springer Science & Business Media.

Townley, B. (1993). Foucault, power/knowledge, and its relevance for human resource management. *Academy of Management Review*, *18*(3), 518–545. doi:10.5465/amr.1993.9309035149

Trohopoulos, I. (2009). Harvesting metadata of Greek institutional repositories in the context of EuropeanaLocal. *Workshop on Harvesting Metadata: Practices and Challenges. Presented at the 13th European Conference on Digital Libraries, Greece*. Retrieved from http://users.teiath.gr/akoul/pubs/ecdl2009.pdf

Trust, W. (2004). *Costs and business models in scientific research publishing: A report commissioned by the Wellcome Trust*. Retrieved from https://wellcome.ac.uk/sites/default/files/wtd003184_0.pdf

Tschmuck, P. (2012). The emergence of the phonographic industry within the music industry. In *Creativity and innovation in the music industry* (pp. 9–25). Springer Berlin Heidelberg; doi:10.1007/978-3-642-28430-4_2

Tsebelis, G., & Garrett, G. (2001). The institutional foundations of intergovernmentalism and supranationalism in the European Union. *International Organization*, *55*(2), 357–390. doi:10.1162/002081801511140603

Tuomi, I. (2006). *Open educational resources: What they are and why do they matter*. Retrieved from http://citeseerx.ist.psu.edu/viewdoc/download?doi=10.1.1.693.9373&rep=rep1&type=pdf

Turner, F. (2010). *From counterculture to cyberculture: Stewart Brand, the Whole Earth Network, and the rise of digital utopianism*. University of Chicago Press.

Turner, S. B. (2012). *The artist's resale royalty right: Overcoming the information problem (SSRN Scholarly Paper No. ID 2009087)*. Rochester, NY: Social Science Research Network. Retrieved from https://papers.ssrn.com/abstract=2009087

United Nations. (1966). *International Covenant on Civil and Political Rights*. Retrieved from http://www.ohchr.org/Documents/ProfessionalInterest/ccpr.pdf

United Nations. (2006). *Social justice in an open world: The role of the united nations*. Retrieved from http://www.un.org/esa/socdev/documents/ifsd/SocialJustice.pdf

van Eechoud, M. M. M. (2009). *Harmonizing European copyright law: The challenges of better lawmaking*. Kluwer Law International.

Van Noorden, R. (2013). Open access: The true cost of science publishing. *NATNews*, *495*(7442), 426. doi:10.1038/495426a PMID:23538808

Van Noorden, R. (2013). The true cost of science publishing. *NATNews*, *495*(7442), 426–429. PMID:23538808

Van Orsdel, L. C., & Born, K. (2009). Reality bites: Periodicals price survey 2009. *Library Journal*, *134*(7), 36–40.

van Staveren, I. (2013). *The values of economics: An Aristotelian perspective*. Routledge. doi:10.4324/9780203122396

Vierkant, P. (2013). 2012 Census of Open Access Repositories in Germany: Turning Perceived Knowledge Into Sound Understanding. *D-Lib Magazine*, *19*(11/12). doi:10.1045/november2013-vierkant

Vitale, D. (2006). Between deliberative and participatory democracy: A contribution on Habermas. *Philosophy and Social Criticism*, *32*(6), 739–766. doi:10.1177/0191453706064022

Vlieghe, D., Sandelin, A., & Bleser, D. (2006). A new generation of JASPAR, the open-access repository for transcription factor binding site profiles. *Nucleic Acids Research, 34*(suppl. 1), D95–D97. doi:10.1093/nar/gkj115 PMID:16381983

Vreeburg Izzo, M., Yurick, A., Nagaraja, H. N., & Novak, J. A. (2010). Effects of a 21st-century curriculum on students' information technology and transition skills. *Career Development for Exceptional Individuals, 33*(2), 95–105. doi:10.1177/0885728810369348

Vuopala, A. (2010). *Assessment of the orphan works issue and costs for rights clearance (Access to information no. unit 34)*. European Commission. Retrieved from http://www.ace-film.eu/wp-content/uploads/2010/09/Copyright_anna_report-1.pdf

Wacha, M., & Wisner, M. (2011). Measuring Value in Open Access Repositories. *The Serials Librarian, 61*(3–4), 377–388. doi:10.1080/0361526X.2011.580423

Wald, J. (2001). Legislating the Golden Rule: Achieving comparable protection under the European Union Database Directive. *Fordham International Law Journal, 25*, 987.

Wallace, H., Pollack, M. A., & Young, A. R. (2015). *Policy-making in the European Union*. Oxford University Press.

Wallace, M., & Siersema, P. (2015). Ethics in publication. *Endoscopy, 47*(07), 575–578. doi:10.1055-0034-1392435 PMID:26099116

Wallerstein, I. (2011). *The modern world—System I: Capitalist agriculture and the origins of the European world—Economy in the sixteenth century, with a new prologue*. University of California Press.

Walterscheid, E. C. (1999). Defining the patent and copyright term: Term limits and the intellectual property clause. *Journal of Intellectual Property Law, 7*, 315.

Wang, S. (2017). The cloud, online piracy and global copyright governance. *International Journal of Cultural Studies, 20*(3), 270–286. doi:10.1177/1367877916628239

Wang, S., & Zhu, J. J. H. (2003). Mapping film piracy in China. *Theory, Culture & Society, 20*(4), 97–125. doi:10.1177/02632764030204007

Watkins, D., & Burton, M. (2013). *Research Methods in law*. Routledge. doi:10.4324/9780203489352

Watson, S. (2007, November). *Authors' attitudes to, and awareness and use of, a university institutional repository*. Retrieved January 23, 2017, from https://dspace.lib.cranfield.ac.uk/handle/1826/2017

Way, D. (2010). The open access availability of library and information science literature. *College & Research Libraries, 71*(4), 302–309. doi:10.5860/crl-38r1

Weatherford, J. (2009). *The history of money*. Crown Publishing Group.

Weber, D. J. (2005). *Bárbaros: Spaniards and their savages in the Age of Enlightenment*. Yale University Press.

Webster, F. (2014). *Theories of the information society*. Routledge. doi:10.4324/9781315867854

Weitzner, D. J., Abelson, H., Berners-Lee, T., Feigenbaum, J., Hendler, J., & Sussman, G. J. (2008). Information accountability. *Communications of the ACM*, *51*(6), 82–87. doi:10.1145/1349026.1349043

Wenar, L. (2013). John Rawls. In E. N. Zalta (Ed.), *The Stanford encyclopedia of philosophy* (Winter 2013). Retrieved from http://plato.stanford.edu/archives/win2013/entries/rawls/

Whitley, R., & Kristensen, P. H. (1996). *The changing European firm: Limits to convergence*. Cengage Learning EMEA.

Wiley, D., & Hilton, J. (2009). Openness, dynamic specialization, and the disaggregated future of higher education. *The International Review of Research in Open and Distributed Learning*, *10*(5). doi:10.19173/irrodl.v10i5.768

Willinsky, J. (2003). The nine flavours of open access scholarly publishing. *Journal of Postgraduate Medicine*, *49*(3), 263. PMID:14597793

Willinsky, J. (2009). *The access principle: The case for open access to research and scholarship* (1st ed.). MIT Press.

Wirsching, J. J. (2005). The time is now: The need for federal resale royalty legislation in light of the European Union Directive. *Southwestern University Law Review*, *35*, 431.

Witcombe, C. L. C. E. (2004). *Copyright in the Renaissance: Prints and the privilegio in sixteenth-century Venice and Rome*. BRILL.

Woll, T. (2010). *Publishing for profit: Successful bottom-line management for book publishers*. Chicago Review Press.

Womack, J., Jones, D., & Roos, D. (2008). *The machine that changed the world*. Simon and Schuster.

World Intellectual Property Organization. (1996a). *WIPO Copyright Treaty (WCT)*. Retrieved from http://www.wipo.int/wipolex/en/details.jsp?id=12740

World Intellectual Property Organization. (1996b). *WIPO Performances and Phonograms Treaty (WPPT)*. Retrieved from http://www.wipo.int/wipolex/en/details.jsp?id=12743

Xia, J., Gilchrist, S. B., Smith, N. X. P., Kingery, J. A., Radecki, J. R., Wilhelm, M. L., . . . Mahn, A. J. (2012). *A review of open access self-archiving mandate policies*. doi:10.13016/M2H12D

Xia, J. (2008). A Comparison of Subject and Institutional Repositories in Self-archiving Practices. *Journal of Academic Librarianship*, *34*(6), 489–495. doi:10.1016/j.acalib.2008.09.016

Xia, J. (2010). A longitudinal study of scholars attitudes and behaviors toward open-access journal publishing. *Journal of the American Society for Information Science and Technology*, *61*(3), 615–624. doi:10.1002/asi.21283

Xia, J., & Sun, L. (2007). Assessment of self-archiving in institutional repositories: Depositorship and full-text availability. *Serials Review*, *33*(1), 14–21. doi:10.1080/00987913.2007.10765087

Yamada, S. (2012). *"Pirate" PUBLISHING: The battle over perpetual copyright in eighteenth-century Britain*. Shoji Yamada.

Yang, L., & Maskus, K. E. (2009). Intellectual property rights, technology transfer and exports in developing countries. *Journal of Development Economics*, *90*(2), 231–236. doi:10.1016/j.jdeveco.2008.11.003

Yiotis, K. (2005). The open access initiative: A new paradigm for scholarly communications. *Information Technology and Libraries*, *24*(4), 157–162. doi:10.6017/ital.v24i4.3378

Younting, Y. (2014). *What are the difficulties in the online copyright enforcement in China?* Retrieved August 30, 2016, from http://www.chinaiplawyer.com/difficulties-online-copyright-enforcement-china/

Yu, P. K. (2004). Currents and crosscurrents in the international intellectual property regime. *Loyola of Los Angeles Law Review*, *38*, 323.

Yu, P. K. (2007). *International enclosure, the regime complex, and intellectual property schizophrenia*. Rochester, NY: Social Science Research Network. Retrieved from http://papers.ssrn.com/abstract=1007054

Zhang, W., Shan, S., Chen, X., & Gao, W. (2007). Local Gabor binary patterns based on mutual information for face recognition. *International Journal of Image and Graphics*, *7*(4), 777–793. doi:10.1142/S021946780700291X

Ziegler, P. (2013). *The Black Death*. Faber & Faber.

Zoller, C. (2007). Interpreting Plato's dialogues [Review]. *Journal of the History of Philosophy*, *45*(3), 486–487. doi:10.1353/hph.2007.0073

Zuckert, C. H. (2009). *Plato's philosophers: The coherence of the dialogues* (1st ed.). Chicago: University of Chicago Press. doi:10.7208/chicago/9780226993386.001.0001

Zuiderwijk, A., & Janssen, M. (2014). Open data policies, their implementation and impact: A framework for comparison. *Government Information Quarterly*, *31*(1), 17–29. doi:10.1016/j.giq.2013.04.003

About the Author

Nikos Koutras holds a PhD in Political Science (Ionian University) and a PhD in Law (Macquarie University). He currently works as postdoctoral researcher at the Faculty of Law of the University of Antwerp in Belgium. His research interests focus on intellectual property law, copyright law, open access, open science and governance.

Index

www.ingramcontent.com/pod-product-compliance
Lightning Source LLC
LaVergne TN
LVHW081337300926
849161LV00008B/1997